HOW CHILDREN INVENTED HUMANITY

How Children Invented Humanity

The Role of Development in Human Evolution

DAVID F. BJORKLUND

OXFORD
UNIVERSITY PRESS

Oxford University Press is a department of the University of Oxford. It furthers the University's objective of excellence in research, scholarship, and education by publishing worldwide. Oxford is a registered trade mark of Oxford University Press in the UK and certain other countries.

Published in the United States of America by Oxford University Press
198 Madison Avenue, New York, NY 10016, United States of America.

© Oxford University Press 2021

All rights reserved. No part of this publication may be reproduced, stored in a retrieval system, or transmitted, in any form or by any means, without the prior permission in writing of Oxford University Press, or as expressly permitted by law, by license, or under terms agreed with the appropriate reproduction rights organization. Inquiries concerning reproduction outside the scope of the above should be sent to the Rights Department, Oxford University Press, at the address above.

You must not circulate this work in any other form
and you must impose this same condition on any acquirer.

Library of Congress Cataloging-in-Publication Data
Names: Bjorklund, David F., 1949- author.
Title: How children invented humanity : the role of development in human evolution / by David F. Bjorklund.
Description: New York, NY : Oxford University Press, [2021] | Includes bibliographical references and index.
Identifiers: LCCN 2020016683 (print) | LCCN 2020016684 (ebook) | ISBN 9780190066864 (hardback) | ISBN 9780190066888 (epub) | ISBN 9780190066895
Subjects: LCSH: Evolutionary psychology. | Human evolution. | Children—Evolution. | Developmental psychology. | Child development. | Child psychology.
Classification: LCC BF698.95 .B56 2021 (print) | LCC BF698.95 (ebook) | DDC 155.7—dc23
LC record available at https://lccn.loc.gov/2020016683
LC ebook record available at https://lccn.loc.gov/2020016684

1 3 5 7 9 8 6 4 2

Printed by Sheridan Books, Inc., United States of America

To Sage and Amelia

Contents

Preface ix
Acknowledgments xiii

1. Children, Childhood, and Development in
   Evolutionary Perspective   1
2. Changeable Children: Evolved Plasticity and Development   32
3. Adaptable Ancestors: Developmental Plasticity
   and Evolution   71
4. Embryos and Ancestors   92
5. The Adaptive Value of Immaturity (or The Benefits of Being
   Young at Heart)   123
6. Developing the Evolved Social Brain   171
7. Evolutionary Mismatches in the Development of Today's
   Children   220
8. Epilogue: How Children Invented Humanity   266

Notes   277
References   295
Author Index   345
Subject Index 365

Preface

How did humans become the psychologically amazing species that we are? How did a mute, tree-dwelling African ape that presumably lived in small social groups using limited technology evolve into a planet-dominating animal with language, civilization, art, science, and religion? There has been no lack of speculation about this question, and much ink has been spilled proposing how *Homo sapiens'* unique intelligence, sociality, and morality evolved over the last 5 to 7 million years. There is, of course, no single, simple answer to this question. A multitude of interacting factors produced the modern human mind. However, I am convinced that, regardless of whatever pressures pushed our ancestors to become the species we are today, these changes occurred over the course of development. It was changes in our individual ancestors—as they progressed from embryos through infancy, childhood, and adolescence to adulthood—that served as the grist for the mill of natural selection, eventually producing us. As the 20th century biologist Gavin de Beer wrote, "Embryos undergo development; ancestors have undergone evolution, but in their day they also were the products of development."[1]

It may be self-evident that our ancestors developed, but the idea that changes over the course of growing up contributed to evolutionary change has not always been welcome in mainstream evolutionary theory. As I discuss in Chapter 3, for decades evolutionary theorists ignored the role of development on evolution, noting that experiences of an animal over its lifetime have no effect on evolution. (No matter how many generations of mice have their tails snipped off, tails persist on infant rodents.) This makes development an *epiphenomenon*—something that is very important to the individual but of no consequence to the evolution of the species. There have always been some maverick scientists who have contended that development has, indeed, had a potent role to play in evolution while still staying within a Darwinian framework, but they were in the minority. Today, with the advent of the field of Evo Dev in biology (Chapter 4) and the prominence of developmental systems theory in developmental psychology (Chapter 1), development is no longer an outsider to evolutionary explication but, as I hope to show in this book, a major player in explaining how *Homo sapiens* came to be the species we are today.

This book can trace its genesis to three papers I published in the journal *Child Development* over the span of more than 20 years.[2] In the initial 1997 paper titled, "In Search of a Metatheory for Cognitive Development (or, Piaget Is Dead and I Don't Feel So Good Myself)," I argued that, with the demise of Piaget's theory as a guiding light for cognitive development, the field should look to developmental biology as a *metatheory*—a common set of broad, overarching assumptions and principles—to guide research and unify the field. In particular, I suggested that a better understanding of both proximal (for example, brain development) and distal (evolutionary) biological factors would greatly enhance psychologists' understanding of cognitive development. Over the next 20 years I spent the bulk of my scholarly efforts in the field of *evolutionary developmental psychology*, culminating in the publication in 2018 of "A Metatheory for Cognitive Development (or 'Piaget Is Dead' Revisited)," where I argued that evolutionary theory was well on its way to becoming a metatheory, not just for cognitive development, but for developmental psychology more broadly, and that an evolutionary perspective can help us achieve a better understanding of development. In a follow-up paper titled "How Children Invented Humanity," I turned this argument on its head, arguing that a developmental perspective can help us achieve a better understanding of evolution. In addition to giving the current book its title, many of the ideas presented in this short (four-page) paper served as the jumping-off point for what I've written here.

This book does not ignore the question of how an evolutionary perspective can help us better understand contemporary development; the fact that I view individual development intimately entwined with evolution requires that both sides of this evolution–development relationship be examined. In some respects, this book is an extension of my 2007 book, *Why Youth Is* Not *Wasted on the Young*, in which I argued that infants and children have an integrity of their own—as individuals with abilities and characteristics that have evolved to be especially suited to the environments they inhabit—and that immaturity is not a necessary evil but may play an *adaptive* role in children's lives and development (see especially Chapter 5). I also examine how some *evolutionary mismatches*—conflicts between psychological mechanisms that evolved in ancient environments and their utility in modern environments—may be especially prominent at certain times in development, as well as some suggestions about how to deal with them (Chapter 7).

I have enjoyed writing this book, which has helped me to organize my own thoughts on the relation between evolution and development and the consequences the relationship has for understanding both concepts, as well as for the implications it has for rearing and educating children. I hope it strikes a similar chord with readers.

David F. Bjorklund
Jupiter, Florida

Acknowledgments

I would like to thank my editors at Oxford University Press, Abby Gross and Katharine Pratt, as well as the rest of the Oxford team, for their support in publishing this book. I would also like to thank my former students, friends, and colleagues for their comments on earlier drafts of these chapters, including Ariel Bartolo-Kira, Charles Dukes, Karen Machluf, Alyson Myers, and Patrick Douglas Sellers II. I want to especially thank my friend and colleague Carlos Hernández Blasi for his encouragement and valuable feedback on every chapter of this book. And my special thanks goes to my wife Barbara Bjorklund for her constant love and support, as well as providing constructive comments on each chapter of this book.

1
Children, Childhood, and Development in Evolutionary Perspective

The most recent addition to the travel and family photos on my office desk is one of my granddaughter, Amelia, taken when she was 5 months old (Figure 1.1). Chubby-cheeked Amelia is strapped into her high chair and looking straight into the camera with a huge, toothless grin. I am surprised every time when Amelia's photo catches my eye and I break into a wide involuntary smile, coupled, I'm sure, by a surge of the feel-good neurotransmitter dopamine in my brain. The grandfather in me wants to believe that this is because Amelia is the most beautiful baby in the world (although I have vague recollections of having similar feelings for other babies), but the psychologist in me realizes there is more to the story—that Amelia's babyish features of fat cheeks, flat nose, rounded head that is large relative to body size, and large eyes relative to head size, coupled with a big grin and eye contact, evoke smiles and good feelings in almost all adults. These are features that the Austrian ethologist and Nobel Prize winner Konrad Lorenz long ago called *Kindchenschema*, or baby schema, that evolved to produce positive feelings from adults toward the infants who possess them, all in the quest to promote the infants' survival so they can one day have cute babies themselves.[1]

We don't stay cute forever. Our chins and foreheads protrude, the eyes stay about the same size as the head gets larger, the cheeks thin out, and our heads come to constitute a smaller percentage of our overall body size, with men showing more of these changes than women. Yet in another sense, as adults we remain "cuter," that is, more infantile, than our primate cousins, who also start off with features their parents apparently find appealing. Unlike humans, however, other primates show more drastic changes in face morphology as they age. Human and great ape (chimpanzees, bonobos, gorillas, and orangutans) babies really look quite a lot alike as infants, although the simians show much greater facial changes as they get older, as can be seen in the accompanying photographs (Figures 1.2 and 1.3). Over the course of the last 5 to 7 million years of evolution, humans, compared with our last

Figure 1.1. Amelia, the most beautiful baby in the world, who just happens to have facial characteristics that adults find adorable. These include fat cheeks, flat nose, rounded and large head relative to body size, and large eyes relative to head size. Combine them with a big grin and eye contact, and it's hard not to fall in love with her, or any baby who displays them.
Source: Photo by Heidi Tobiaz, with permission.

common ancestor with chimpanzees, have retained many infantile features, slowing some aspects of development in comparison with our ancient ape ancestors. This process is called *neoteny*, literally "holding youth," and characterizes a number of aspects of human evolution. The consequences of *Homo sapiens'* sometimes neotenous development have often stirred controversy, and it seems clear that many features of modern humans were not accelerations or additions of features of our ape ancestors but, instead, were achieved by slowing development, taking a step backward in a sense, permitting a "redo" that can produce evolutionary innovations.

Now consider the activities of three boys on the playground. Each wants to be Batman, but they agree that only one can be, so they decide Geoff will be Batman, Travis will be Robin, and Joshua will be the Joker, although they can switch later on. They pretend that the underside of the slide is the Bat

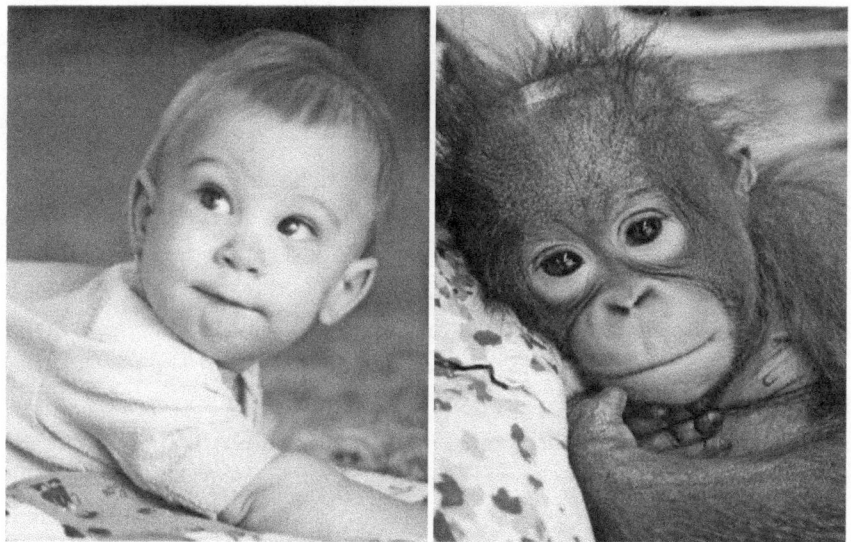

Figure 1.2. Human and great ape infants really look quite alike.
Source: Photo (left) by Barbara Bjorklund, with permission. Photo (right) by Penny Clarke. Reproduced with permission of CTQ Management Consulting trading as "Tears In The Jungle."

Figure 1.3. A chimpanzee adult and infant. Human and chimpanzee infants share many facial qualities. Although both chimps and humans become "less cute" as they age, humans retain more of the infantile facial features as they age relative to chimpanzees, a process known as *neoteny*.
Source: Naef, 1926.

Cave and that the slide itself is the Batmobile. The boys engage in a few make-believe scenarios, with the Joker threatening Batman and then capturing Robin, who is, in turn, rescued by Batman, despite the fact that the Batmobile broke down. Geoff, Travis, and Joshua stay in their roles throughout, although Travis briefly complains that, being the youngest, he almost never gets to play Batman. Jason shows up, and without missing a beat, takes on the role of the Penguin, helping the Joker battle his nemesis. And a good time was had by all.

But was that all it was, a good time? Play is, by definition, frivolous, something people choose to do without any purpose other than to play. Yet scholars who have studied play see plenty of purpose in it. The play of these boys involves planning, cooperation, emotional and cognitive control as they stay in character, and, perhaps most importantly, counterfactual thinking—behaving in ways that they know to be factually incorrect. These are all skills that children must develop to become effective adults in any society. There is one school of thought that argues that it is through play that these adult capabilities are best developed, and that play was selected for over the course of human evolution to do just that. To take things one step further, the Australian developmental psychologist Mark Nielsen has argued that it was the "invention" of pretend play by ancestral children that, among other abilities, was responsible for the modern human mind with its unsurpassed symbolic skills.[2]

Each of the examples described here involves something related to development. A baby face helps an infant bond with its parents and survive to childhood, and pretend play fosters the social and cognitive skills required to become a competent member of one's social group. These observations reflect the common-sense idea that experiences in childhood shape the adults we become, and at one level it must be true. But the other examples—retaining infantile features into adulthood, and pretend play as a cause of human intellectual abilities—demonstrate the influences of development at another level. Over the course of human evolution, changes during infancy and childhood affected not only the adults our individual foremothers and forefathers became, but also species-typical features that characterize all *Homo sapiens* today and differentiate us from our ancient ancestors.

Ontogeny and Phylogeny

Usually when we talk about *development* we are talking about the changes that each of us undergoes from conception through old age. The technical term for this type of development is *ontogeny*, and the general course of ontogeny is similar for all biologically typical members of the species. We start as infants with certain types of physical, motor, cognitive, and emotional characteristics, which year-by-year change in generally predictable ways. There is enough variation as a result of differences in genes, culture, and specific experiences to make the study of ontogeny interesting. For example, children with a certain combination of alleles (variations of a single gene, such as a gene for blue eyes and a gene for brown eyes) associated with the expression of several neurotransmitters engage in higher levels of antisocial behavior than children with other combinations, but only if they experienced severe levels of maltreatment when growing up;[3] or the thinking of children from schooled cultures is different from the thinking of children from cultures without formal education;[4] or the amount of language children hear early in life is related to their later academic achievement.[5] These and many other topics are what developmental biologists and psychologists study for a living.

The other type of development reflects changes not over lifetimes but over the history of a species. This type of development is called *phylogeny* and describes evolutionary changes over thousands and millions of years. These include the often-depicted changes in the structure of the body—from quadrupedal to bipedal locomotion, and from small to large skull and brain—and also cognitive and behavioral changes—from communicating with grunts to communicating with language, and from reading another animal's behavior to "reading its mind."

With a little imagination it's easy to see that, despite the differences in time scales, ontogeny and phylogeny must be intimately related. More specifically, each of our ancient ancestors—those who survived childhood and begat children of their own—also developed. From this perspective, evolution, or phylogeny, can be viewed as a series of successive ontogenies, and it was changes in these ontogenies over generations, brought about by genetic mutations, shifts in gene expression, or alterations in the physical or social environments, that produced adults, who in turn reproduced more of their kind who continued the developmental and evolutionary process.

Developing Humanity

The principle theme of this book is that children invented humanity. Changes in the individual development (ontogeny) of our ancestors were primarily responsible for the species and the people we have become. This book takes an *evolutionary developmental perspective*, emphasizing that *developmental plasticity*—the ability to change our physical and psychological selves early in life—is the creative force in evolution, with natural selection serving mainly as the Grim Reaper, or a filter, eliminating novel developmental outcomes that did not benefit the survival of those individuals who possessed them, while letting the more successful outcomes through. Over generations, as embryos, infants, and children continued to change, a new species was born—*Homo sapiens*—the mature members of which have created art, science, culture, and technology qualitatively different from anything that has ever existed on this planet.

Developmental plasticity was not only responsible for shaping *ancient* human bodies and minds but also continues to be important in shaping the brains, behavior, and minds of contemporary people. Some of the developmental innovations that helped shape human thought continue to do so today at the individual level. The developmental plasticity characteristic of the young of our species is altering the emotions and cognitions of people in the 21st century as they adjust to rapidly changing environments filled with gadgets such as smartphones, self-driving cars, and the Internet that our ancestors could not have imagined.

This book is about the process of *becoming*—of becoming human and of becoming mature adults. I will show how the processes of development contributed to changes in our ancestors' physical and, most importantly, psychological features, eventually resulting in the most socially and intellectually complex animal in the known universe. Yet this book is not only about ancient history but also about the present and the future. I will show how some of the same processes that influenced the species we've become continue to operate to affect the adults we develop into, sometimes to our advantage and sometimes to our disadvantage, and how taking an evolutionary perspective can help us better understand and foster development.

In the remainder of this chapter I provide a brief overview of *evolutionary developmental psychology*, the conceptual underpinning of this book. Many issues raised in this first chapter become topics of subsequent chapters. In Chapter 2, I look at the role of plasticity in shaping human thought and sociality and in affecting individual differences in how contemporary people cope with changing environments. Chapter 3 picks up where Chapter 2 left off, examining how developmental plasticity played a role in human evolution. Chapter 4 introduces the field of *evolutionary developmental biology*, or

Evo Devo, emphasizing how changes in developmental timing, particularly neoteny, led to a new species, namely us. Chapter 5 continues the emphasis on slowed development, revealing how some immature features of infants and children are adaptive in their own right and not merely things to grow out of, the sooner the better. In Chapter 6 I explore the social brain and how the confluence of increased social complexity, a large brain, and an extended pre-reproductive period led to radical changes in thinking and socializing in our ancestors, and I examine how differences in great ape and human development led to a unique form of social cognition in our species. Chapter 7 examines some evolutionary matches and mismatches with respect to the development and education of today's children, including, for example, the effects of social media on rates of mood disorders in children and adolescents and the consequences of an emphasis on academic learning during the early school years. The final short chapter provides a synthesis of the major themes of the book.

Taking an Evolutionary Perspective

I first became interested in the relation between development and evolution in graduate school while taking a class from Gilbert Gottlieb, a brilliant developmental psychologist who studied ducks for a living. (I'll have more to say about Professor Gottlieb in Chapters 2 and 3.) My research focus in graduate school and through my early career was on children's cognitive development, mainly children's use of memory strategies. However, my summer reading often included books on evolution by the likes of Richard Dawkins, Stephen Jay Gould, and E. O. Wilson. In the late 1980s the field of *evolutionary psychology* emerged as a serious discipline, and I thought I could take a break from my research on the role of knowledge base in children's memory and write a paper or two integrating my two academic loves, development and evolution. That was more than 30 years ago, and although I didn't completely abandon my research on memory development, the task of integrating ontogeny and phylogeny was more complicated and interesting than I had reckoned, and I have devoted the bulk of my scholarly attention to the topic over the past three decades.

In the following paragraphs, I provide a brief overview of mainstream evolutionary psychology, which focuses chiefly on understanding human *adult* psychology from an evolutionary perspective. In the sections to follow,

I spend a bit more time examining some of the major ideas underlying evolutionary *developmental* psychology.

Evolutionary Psychology

At its most basic, evolutionary psychology can be defined as understanding the human mind and behavior from an evolutionary perspective. As I see it, the basic tenet of evolutionary psychology is that *the human mind has been prepared by natural selection, operating over geological time, for life in a human group*. (Humans are the most social of species, and human nature cannot be understood except within a social context.) *Natural selection* was Darwin's great insight more than 150 years ago, showing that inheritable differences between members of a species were associated with survival and reproduction. Features that result in individuals surviving and reproducing tend to be passed on to future generations (or "selected for") as a result of interactions between individuals and the local environment. Features associated with early death or failure to reproduce tend not to be "selected for," and possibly "selected against," resulting in their eventual elimination. Over many generations, the gradual accumulation of changes produces new species. Although Darwin's book, *On the Origins of Species*, had little to say about *human* evolution, he did address the topic in detail in later writings, notably his 1871 book, *The Descent of Man, and Selection in Relation to Sex*, and he can be credited with being the first evolutionary psychologist when in 1859 he wrote, "In the distant future I see open fields for far more important researches. Psychology will be based on a new foundation, that of the necessary acquirement of each mental power and capacity by gradation. Light will be thrown on the origin of man and his history."[6]

There are four broad issues that evolutionary psychology focuses on: *survival*, including topics such as food preferences, predator/prey relations, and tool use; *reproduction*, including sexual attraction and choosing and keeping mates; *kin*, including nepotism and raising children; and *social relations*, including topics of reciprocity, in-group/out-group relations, status striving, and cooperation. Although evolutionary psychology does have something to say about truly modern human problems (for example, why children often find school difficult, psychopathology, and consumerism), its most important contribution is for core issues related to reproduction and survival.

Evolved Psychological Mechanisms

The founders of evolutionary psychology assumed, as had Darwin, that evolutionary changes occur gradually over millions of years (that is, sudden changes do not produce new species), that natural selection is the creative force in evolution, and that selection occurs only at the level of the individual, not the level of the group or the species. Perhaps the greatest innovation of evolutionary psychology was the assumption that what evolved were *psychological mechanisms*. That is, information-processing mechanisms (ways in which the human mind/brain encodes, categorizes, and makes decisions about things it experiences) are the "missing link" in evolutionary explication. These mechanisms were shaped by natural selection to solve recurrent adaptive problems faced by our ancestors, such as determining what is good to eat, finding and keeping a mate, and forming attachments between mothers and infants to keep babies alive.[7]

Evolutionary developmental psychologist David Geary has proposed a way of thinking about evolved psychological mechanisms that explicitly takes development into consideration. Geary proposed that what evolved is a set of hierarchically organized, self-contained information-processing mechanisms (or *modules*), each specific to a particular type of information. Geary's model is shown in Figure 1.4. There are two overarching domains in this model, social (folk psychology) and ecological, with each consisting of more specific domains (self, individual, and group for social; and biological and physical for ecological). Lower-level modules in this model are designed to process less complex information, serving as building blocks for higher-level, more complex, and flexible modules. This allows information processed at lower levels to be integrated, so that complex skills and cognitions emerge through experience.

Infants are not born with sophisticated information-processing mechanisms within any of these domains but, rather, come into the world with what Geary calls *skeletal competencies*.[8] These are often simple biases to be attentive to some information more so than others (such as the sinusoidal movement of snakes or eyespots, to be discussed later in this chapter). These skeletal competencies, or what developmental psychologist Elizabeth Spelke and her colleagues[9] refer to as *core knowledge*, get fleshed out over development through exploration, play, and social engagement. These skeletal abilities develop in the young of our species, developed in the young of our ancestors, and set the stage for the behavior of adults.

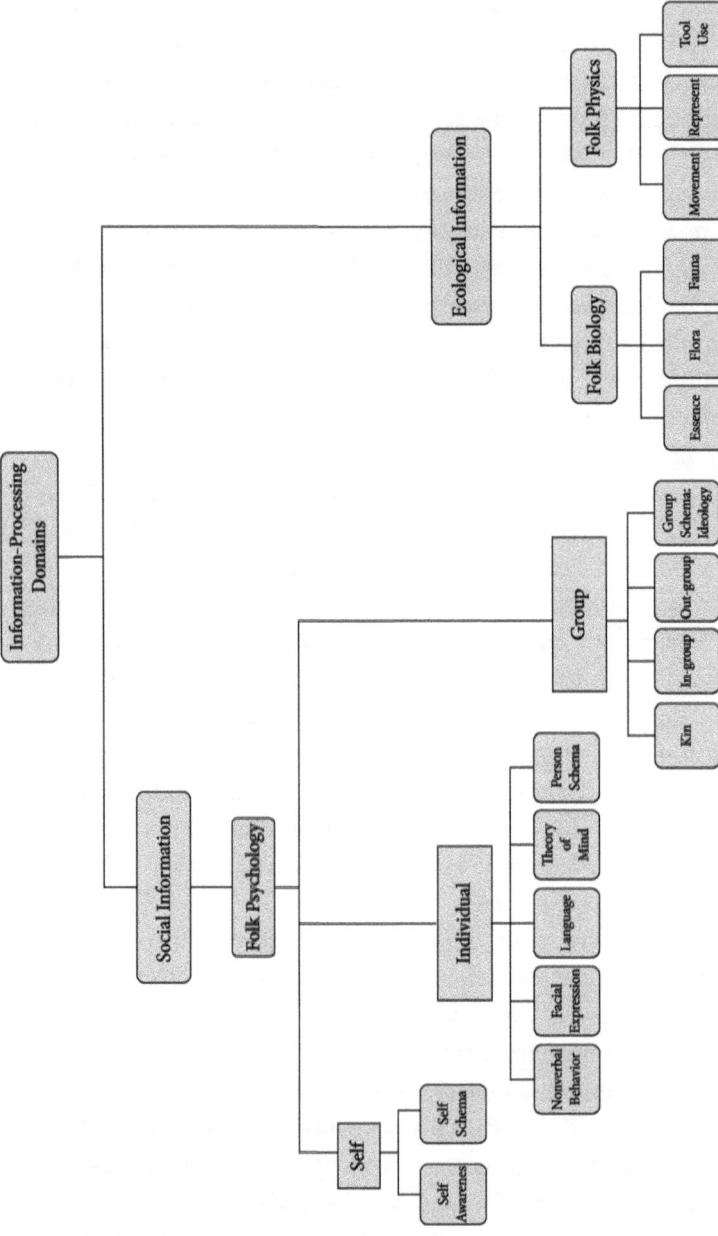

Figure 1.4. Geary proposed that the mind is hierarchically organized into domains, with lower-level modules, designed to process less complex information, serving as building blocks for higher-level, more complex, and flexible modules. Within the social domain of folk psychology, domains are further organized into those dealing with self-knowledge, dealing with individuals, and dealing with groups.
Source: Geary, 2005.

In remainder of this book, I'll be referring to psychological mechanisms evolved to solve a variety of "problems." Some of these mechanisms are expressed early in life and serve to promote caregiving of helpless infants by their parents, whereas others operate later in infancy and childhood to achieve a variety of survival-related functions. None of these should be thought of as "instincts." Rather, these are mechanisms evolved to deal with recurrent problems faced by our ancestors. Even if one accepts that humans' social and technological skills are built upon an evolved set of mechanisms, experience remains critical in the development of these skills.

Adaptations
This brings us to the concept of *adaptations*, central to evolutionary biology and psychology. According to evolutionary psychologist David Buss and his colleagues, "An adaptation may be defined as an inherited and reliably developing characteristic that came into existence as a feature of a species through natural selection because it helped to directly or indirectly facilitate reproduction during the period of its evolution."[10] Adaptations can be for some physical attribute—the opposable thumb, for example, important in making and using tools—or for behavior or cognition, for instance, feeling jealous when someone threatens an important relationship, causing one to do something to protect the relationship. An adaptation can be inferred by its reliability (it develops in all members of a species, or all members of one sex, in all "normal" environments), its efficiency (it solves a problem effectively), and its improbable usefulness.

As an example of the "improbable usefulness" of an adaptation, consider *pregnancy sickness*. This is an illness that afflicts nearly all women early in their pregnancies with symptoms of nausea, vomiting, and specific food aversions. Many readers will have experienced firsthand the often-debilitating effects of pregnancy sickness, and others may have witnessed the effects in a loved one and tried to be understanding (or maybe even gotten sick in sympathy). How can an often-debilitating illness ever be considered an adaptation? What function might pregnancy sickness play in fostering survival or reproduction? Several scholars have examined this issue and provided evidence from a variety of sources suggesting that pregnancy sickness helps women avoid ingesting harmful toxins that might interfere with the development of their growing fetus.

There are multiple sources of evidence for this interpretation, none of which alone can prove that pregnancy sickness is an adaptation, although together they strongly support the contention. First of all, pregnancy sickness occurs when the fetus is most susceptible to the effects of *teratogens*, agents that, if ingested by the mother, may transfer to the fetus via the placenta and disrupt development. Pregnancy sickness typically begins around 2 or 4 weeks and ends around 16 weeks after conception. This is a time when the fetus's major organ and physical systems are developing (though not perfected), and thus a time when harmful outside influences (that is, teratogens) will likely have their greatest impact. Once one has ten fingers and toes, for example, it's too late for a toxin to alter digit number.

Second, the foods women tend to find aversive are those that in ancient environments, and possibly still today, were likely sources of toxins, including meat (especially raw meat, a possible source of bacteria), alcohol, coffee, and strong-tasting vegetables (think Brussels sprouts and broccoli). Levels of toxins that are safe for the mother may be harmful to the fetus, thus accounting for aversions to foods that women had liked only weeks earlier. Additionally, although pregnancy sickness varies among women and is more pronounced in some cultures than others (especially in cultures that consume a lot of meat), it is universal.

The final piece of evidence supporting the claim that pregnancy sickness is an adaptation is that women with the most severe pregnancy sickness have a lower incidence of spontaneous abortions than other pregnant women. Pregnancy sickness also seems to be unique to humans, possibly attributable to the broad range of diets found among human cultures compared with other primates and mammals.[11] Given the evidence for the adaptive value of pregnancy sickness, it is somewhat ironic that the drug Thalidomide, initially developed as a sedative but later given to pregnant women in the 1960s to reduce nausea, produced deformities of the limbs, with some infants born with hands growing directly from their shoulders, or feet growing directly from their hips (Figure 1.5). The drug only had this effect when taken early in pregnancy. (This drug was never approved for use in the United States, although it was prescribed in Canada, Japan, and parts of Europe.)[12]

Although natural selection and adaptations may be the meat and potatoes of evolutionary psychology, they are not the only processes of evolution. For example, one feature of an adaptation is that it develops in all members of a species, or all members of one sex, in all species-typical environments. Such developmental reliability and universality may be necessary for adaptations, but they are not sufficient. An example I like is one used by David Buss and his colleagues, that of the belly button. The belly button is universal and

Figure 1.5. Women who took Thalidomide during the early weeks of pregnancy to eliminate nausea often had infants with deformed limbs. The nausea and food aversions characteristic of pregnancy sickness prevent women from ingesting foods that may have negative consequences for the developing fetus.
Source: Photo by Johnson et al. (2018), with permission, from *The Thalidomide Catastrophe*.

develops reliably, though it is not an adaptation but simply a *byproduct* of the umbilical cord, an important adaptation in all mammals. A more prosaic term sometimes used by evolutionary biologists and psychologists to refer to byproducts is *spandrel*, from a famous 1979 paper by biologists Stephen Jay Gould and Richard Lewontin. A spandrel is a triangular space that is formed by the intersection of two rounded arches at right angles, found in many Christian churches (see Figure 1.6). This space usually contains a sculpture or painting of biblical relevance, adding beauty to the church and giving the impression that the spandrel was an important part of the architect's design (akin to an adaptation). Yet, the space itself is a simple structural byproduct of intersecting arches, which artists make good use of. It is, in the words of Gould and Lewontin, "a secondary epiphenomenon representing a fruitful use of available parts, not a cause of the entire system."[13]

Figure 1.6. A spandrel from the Holy Trinity Church in Fulnek, Czech Republic. A spandrel is the result of two intersecting arches that artists fill with sculpture or paintings. Although they are important components of Christian churches, they are by-products, not part of the initial design of the building.
Source: Photo by Radim Scholaster, with permission.

As an example from evolutionary developmental psychology, consider the universal belief people have in magic, spirits, and fate. Things happen for a reason, often unseen reasons. Some have argued that such belief in the supernatural is an adaptation, evolved, in part, to help people make sense of their world or perhaps to prevent them from engaging in inappropriate behavior.[14] Even if other people aren't watching, God or the spirits of one's ancestors see all, preventing people from doing things that may get them in trouble if they get found out. Alternatively, and the interpretation I favor, the belief in the supernatural—that everything happens for a reason—is a spandrel—a by-product of children's developing theory of mind—understanding that people do things for reasons (although not always good ones), which is extended to situations that can't be easily attributed to people, such as the weather (blame the lightning god) or good or bad fortune (divine rewards and punishments for one's behavior). I'll have more to say about children's developing theory of mind in Chapter 6.

Evolutionary changes can also occur when a single gene or set of genes is associated with two or more features of an animal, so that selection pressure on one feature may inadvertently affect another feature. This is seen in the selection of tameness in foxes and other domesticated mammals. When foxes were selectively bred for tameness, over the course of several generations the animals also displayed changes in appearance, remaining more juvenile looking ("puppy-like") as adults.[15] I'll discuss this work in greater detail in Chapter 4.

Finally, evolutionary change can happen due to *genetic drift*, which occurs when random changes in the genetic makeup of a population increase in frequency. For example, imagine that a small population founds a new territory, and a large proportion of that population just happens to possess a rare feature, such as green eyes. So long as that population stays relatively isolated, the frequency of green eyes will increase over generations, even though green eyes provide no adaptive benefit. This type of genetic drift is called the *founder effect*. Another type of genetic drift is the *bottleneck effect*. This occurs when a population is greatly reduced in size and then rebounds, such as northern elephant seals, whose population was reduced to about 20 animals at the end of the 19th century due to human hunting and subsequently increased to over 30,000. The genetic diversity of the seals, however, was greatly reduced, not because of any adaptive advantage, but because of the small number of individuals in the surviving population.

Although natural selection is the principle mechanism of evolutionary change, it is not the only one, and we should always be mindful that not all products of evolution are adaptations.

Psychological Mechanisms Evolved in the Environment
of Evolutionary Adaptedness
As I noted earlier, evolutionary psychologists believe that psychological mechanisms evolved gradually and that it is not possible to pinpoint a precise time in a species' history when a mechanism was first present. Nonetheless, using data from different sources, including archeological (ancient artifacts), anthropological (cross-cultural studies), paleontological (old fossils), and comparative animal behavior (comparing the behavior of different animal species of varying relation to humans), we can get a general idea of when some adaptations came into being or became refined. We share some features with all primates and mammals, such as our tendencies to use aggression in certain contexts or our preference for sweet-tasting foods. Other features seem to have a much more recent origin, such as the way males and females relate, our tendency to cooperate with nonrelatives, and our ability to make and use tools. Evolutionary psychologists refer to the time and ecology when

an adaptation arose or became established in humans as the *environment of evolutionary adaptedness*. Roughly speaking, it refers to the environment to which a species is adapted.

Humans last shared a common ancestor with contemporary chimpanzees and bonobos between 5 and 7 million years ago,[16] so the environment of evolutionary adaptedness for most human-unique physical and psychological characteristics likely extends from this time period. The earliest species designated within the *Homo* label dates back about 2.5 million years ago (*Homo habilis*, or handy man, named for evidence of stone tool manufacture and use), followed in time by a series of *Homo* cousins, all living in Africa, resulting about 2.0 million years ago in *Homo erectus*, a brainier member of the *Homo* line that made more sophisticated tools than its forerunners. Fossil evidence indicates that some members of *Home erectus* left Africa about 1.8 million years ago and spread throughout Asia and Europe, while others remained in Africa (called *Homo ergaster*) and evolved into anatomically modern *Homo sapiens* as early as 300,000 years ago. Sometime between 50 and 100 thousand years ago, some of these Africans left the continent, this time colonizing the Old World and replacing, either by outcompeting or exterminating, the other *Homo* species (for example, *Homo erectus, Homo neanderthalensis*) they encountered.[17] Most scientists believe that many human-unique qualities, such as language and symbolic culture, evolved during the last hundred thousand years or so. Table 1.1 provides a brief timeline of hominin (the group consisting of modern humans, extinct human species, and all our immediate forebearers) evolution, from the time when humans last shared a common ancestor with chimpanzees (5 to 7 million years ago) to the invention of agriculture (10 thousand years ago).

How can we know what the environment of evolutionary adaptedness was like for our ancestors? We can't with any certainty, of course, but archeological evidence (for example, evidence of hearths around which people apparently shared meals; tools seemingly designed for specific purposes; artifacts including cave paintings and ornaments), fossil evidence (for example, different skull sizes for different species, suggestive of cognitive abilities; different dental structure, suggestive of diets; evidence for different rates of physical development), and the practices of modern hunter-gatherer people (who until recently seemingly lived much as early *Homo sapiens* did) together can provide a reasonably good picture of how our ancestors made a living and the conditions under which the modern human mind evolved.

Table 1.1. A brief timeline of hominin evolution

5–7 million years ago (mya)—Humans' unknown last common ancestor with chimpanzees and bonobos lives in Africa.

4–7 mya—Several short (3–4 feet tall), bipedal hominins live in Africa, including *Orrorin tugenensis*, *Sahelanthropus tchadensis*, and *Ardipithecus kadabba*. Their connection to later humans is unclear, but one of these hominins was likely the ancestor of modern people.

3.5 mya—Lucy and her kind, *Australopithecus afarensis*, live in Africa. *Australopithecus afarensis* walked upright much as humans do but had a skull the size of a chimpanzee.

2.5 mya—The first member of the *Homo* genus, *Homo habilis* (handy man), lives in eastern Africa and has a stone tool technology referred to as Olduwan.

2 mya—*Homo ergaster* (or African *Homo erectus*) lives in Africa and develops a more sophisticated stone tool kit called Acheulean.

1.8 mya—*Homo erectus* leaves Africa and populates much of Europe and Asia.

300 thousand years ago (kya) —*Archaic Homo sapiens*, having some features characteristics of both *Homo erectus* and *Homo sapiens*, live in Africa.

200–30 kya—Neanderthals (*Homo neanderthalensis*) flourish in Europe and Asia.

100–50 kya—Anatomically modern humans, *Homo sapiens*, live in African and migrate to other parts of the Old World.

30 kya—Cro-Magnon people (*Homo sapiens*) make cave paintings in Europe.

30 kya—Neanderthals go extinct.

10 kya—Agriculture, a sedentary lifestyle, and civilization begin in the Middle East.

So what's our best educated guess about the environment of evolutionary adaptedness most relevant for understanding contemporary people?[18] First, our ancestors lived as nomads in small groups ranging between 30 and 100 people and interacted with other social groups occasionally, trading goods and mates. Based partly on the size of groups in contemporary hunter-gatherer societies, anthropologist Robin Dunbar proposed that people are able to maintain stable social relations with no more than about 150 people. Beyond this, people cannot keep track of who's who and how each person relates to every other person. According to Dunbar, 150 is "the number of people you would not feel embarrassed about joining uninvited for a drink if you happened to bump into them in a bar."[19]

If modern hunter-gatherers are any indication of the lifestyles of our Stone Age ancestors, most made their living gathering fruits, nuts, vegetables, and tubers (the work of women), scavenging remains left by other predators, and hunting game in small groups (the work of men). As is the case in most of the world today, women were the primary caretakers of children; however, infants' extended period of dependency meant that mothers required help from others (*alloparents*) to care for their children. This included the child's father (humans are among only 5% of mammals in which fathers provide any care to offspring), but mainly female relatives (grandmothers, sisters, aunts), older siblings, and other unrelated women in the group. Humans became what anthropologist Sarah Hrdy calls *cooperative breeders*, with mothers receiving assistance from mainly female kin in rearing offspring.[20] Help from others to care for children actually begins at birth for humans. Unlike other primate mothers who give birth alone, human mothers across the globe give birth assisted by other women. Such assistance is needed because the head of a newborn can barely squeeze through the birth canal of its mother, necessitating that *Homo sapiens'* birth be a cooperative endeavor. I'll discuss the reasons and consequences of human babies' large heads and the brains they hold in Chapter 4.

Women likely first gave birth in their late teens or early 20s and every 3 to 5 years thereafter, nursing each offspring for 2 to 3 years. The infant mortality rate was likely about 50%, much higher than today but much lower than in chimpanzee populations. Fathers were most likely minimally involved in the care of infants and children, although they provided food and protection for their mates and offspring. Death rates during childhood and adolescence were certainly much higher than in developed societies today, with few people living past 40 years of age. However, it is probable that there were always some people who lived to old age. Some men likely had multiple "wives" (polygyny), whereas other men had no access to women at all.

This is painting the lifestyles of our ancestors with a broad brush. Cultural variation has always been a feature of human social life. Despite such diversity, some aspects of ancient human life were surely stable from generation to generation. As today, people lived in complex social webs involving cooperation and competition both within and between groups, with warfare between groups being common; men and women had distinct roles related to labor (women doing most of the gathering, men doing most of the hunting) and childrearing (mostly the work of women); and they likely never stayed in one spot too long, having a nomadic lifestyle. Such stability of lifestyles permitted the evolution of a common human nature that still influences our behavior today.

A central premise of evolutionary psychology is that human nature—psychological adaptations designed to promote survival and reproductive success—evolved in these small nomadic groups over thousands of years. Although most humans today live in very different circumstances, our brains have evolved to "expect" environments much like those that generations of our ancestors experienced. In some respects, things haven't changed much in the last 100,000 years or so, in that we remain a highly social species with complicated relations among men, women, and children. In another sense, life is substantially different from that of our foreparents, and some adaptations that evolved to deal with life in Stone Age ecologies may be irrelevant or even detrimental today. This conflict between psychological mechanisms that evolved in ancient environments and their utility in modern life is referred to as the *mismatch hypothesis*.[21] As an example, consider people's preference for sweet and fatty foods. This made great sense to our ancestors, as these sensations were cues to foods high in calories and thus good sources of nutrition. Today, with fast-food restaurants and supermarkets, these same preferences lead to overeating, obesity, high blood pressure, diabetes, and more.

The mismatch between how we evolved to interact with other people and how we do so today may be even greater than the mismatch between our ancient and modern physical environments. Rather than interact face to face with a small number of well-known individuals, in the course of a few days we interact with hundreds, often thousands, of people—sometimes in person, other times electronically—some of whom we know only in passing, if that well (such as the woman in India I spoke with this morning about my credit card account). I'll have more to say about evolutionary mismatches for today's children in Chapter 7.

Evolutionary Developmental Psychology

The "fact" of human evolution is accepted by nearly all serious scholars, and the ancient, evolved origins of human thought and feelings is increasingly being acknowledged. Nonetheless, not all embrace evolutionary psychology's view of humankind. Developmental psychologists have been among the most reluctant to jump on the evolutionary bandwagon, and this is because of evolutionary psychology's *gene's-eye view* and its implications for *genetic determinism*—the belief that all of our behaviors, thoughts, and emotions are determined by our genes. Much of this stems from Richard Dawkin's influential book *The Selfish Gene* and the proposal that it is actually genes that are competing with one another, and that plants and animals are merely vehicles for these self-replicating segments of DNA.[22] Most evolutionary psychologists chafe at the label "genetic determinist," pointing out that evolution occurs as a result of the interaction between an individual (and its genes) and the local environment. From the beginning of serious theorizing about evolution (that is, Darwin's work), evolution was never viewed as being determined solely by genes (or by other inherited mechanisms—Darwin knew nothing of genes), but by how individuals with a suite of inherited features "fit" with the local ecology. However, mainstream evolutionary psychologists have not always done a good job of making this clear, and this seemed to especially bother developmentalists, who believe that nothing in biology or psychology arises fully formed (that is, everything develops), and that evolutionary psychologists were overemphasizing the role of genes and ignoring how adaptive behaviors became expressed in adults (that is, through development).[23]

Alison Gopnik clearly points out the important role that development plays in evolutionary explanations of human nature in her book, *The Gardner and the Carpenter: What the New Science of Child Development Tells Us About the Relationship Between Parents and Children*, arguing that:

> The old "evolutionary psychology" picture was that genes were directly responsible for some particular pattern of adult behavior—a "module." However, there is more and more evidence that genes are just the first step in complex developmental sequences, cascades of interactions between organism and environment that in turn shape the adult brain. Even small changes in developmental timing can lead to big changes in who we become.[24]

In a similar vein, developmental psychologists are not fond of the concepts of *innateness* and *instincts*. Attributing some behavior as "innate" or as an "instinct" essentially stops a scientist from asking further questions about its origin: "It's innate! It merely exists and always has from the start. There's no sense in trying to figure out what might have contributed to its origins." Saying that some feature of an organism is innate implies we know more about it than we actually do. This is reflected in Patrick Bateson's analysis of the concept "instinct":

> Apart from its colloquial uses, the term instinct has at least nine scientific meanings: present at birth (or at a particular stage of development), not learned, developed before it can be used, unchanged once developed, shared

by all members of the species (or at least of the same sex and age), organized into a distinct behavioral system (such as foraging), served by a distinct neural module, adapted during evolution, and differences among individuals that are due to their possession of different genes. One does not necessarily imply another even though people often assume, without evidence, that it does.[25]

What evolutionary psychology needed was a theory of development: How do evolved, inherited information-processing mechanisms become expressed in adults? The answer is through development.

A Developmental Theory for Evolutionary Psychology
So how *do* evolved, inherited information-processing mechanisms become expressed in adults? The short answer is via the principles of *developmental systems theory*, which postulates that development is the continuous and bidirectional interaction between various components of "developmental systems"—including, but not limited to, genetic activity, structural maturation, activity emanating from structures (or function), and the environment, broadly construed.[26] *Bidirectional interaction* implies that genes, for example, do not simply "instruct" the body to build a certain structure or to influence a certain behavior, but rather, genes are sensitive to the context in which they find themselves and are influenced by other components of the developmental system. Any outcome cannot be described as being attributed to a certain percentage of nature (genes) and a certain percentage of nurture (environment, experience). Nor are genes given top billing in the interaction; nature and nurture are irreducibly entwined, making it impossible to decompose the relative contribution of each.*

---

* **Technical note**: There is no single developmental systems theory, and there is often vigorous debate among theorists about how the theory should be applied. Two broadly defined versions of the theory can be formulated: a soft and a hard version (Bjorklund & Ellis, 2014; Del Giudice & Ellis, 2016; Frankenhuis, Panchanathan, & Barrett, 2013). The soft version is essentially a theory of development, in which a developmental system comprises all the "resources" (genes, cellular structures, sensory experiences, physical parameters of the environment, and so forth) that contribute to the development of the individual organism. Development proceeds via the continuous bidirectional interaction between the organism and the environment, but the organism is the focus of natural selection, as in mainstream biology. In contrast, in the hard version of developmental systems theory, the entire organism-environment whole of replicable developmental systems is the focus of natural selection. This removes the organism as the focus of natural selection, and natural selection can only operate at the population level (see Overton, 2015; Witherington & Lickliter, 2016). The hard form of developmental systems theory is incompatible with an adaptationist perspective, and it is the soft form of developmental systems theory that evolutionary developmental psychologists advocate (see Bjorklund, 2016).

Genes are always expressed (that is, turned on or turned off) in a context. Thus, genes may provide some instructions to build the brain's visual cortex, for example, but further development of the visual cortex will depend on its function (whether and what type of visual input it gets from the eyes), which in turn will influence subsequent activation of genes associated with it, affecting further development, and so on. When all goes according to plan, an animal develops a properly functioning visual cortex connected to the eyes and can "see" and use that information effectively. However, if an animal does not get visual input, gets it too early or too late, or receives species-atypical visual input (for example, seeing only vertical lines), its visual system will not develop normally, despite the fact that it possesses perfectly normal genes associated with sight.[27] Consider, for example, research by developmental psychologist Daphne Maurer and her colleagues with infants born with cataracts over their eyes, preventing them from seeing patterned light. Infants who have their cataracts removed within the first two or three months of life developed mostly normal vision. However, infants whose cataracts are not removed until later show poorer vision, and the longer the delay in removing the cataracts, the more impaired vision tends to be. Even those infants who have their cataracts removed early and subsequently have mostly normal vision develop some problems with aspects of face processing.[28] This pattern reflects the idea of a *critical*, or *sensitive*, *period*, a time—usually early in development—when certain experiences most significantly impact brain organization and function (such as seeing). The same experience before or after the sensitive period will have little or no effect on development.

The developing organism is sensitive to its surroundings, with gene activity being modified by external events. This implies that there is substantial plasticity (that is, ability to change) during development, with experiences, broadly defined, greatly affecting the course of ontogeny. If this is so, why then are members of a species, be they humans, monkeys, or sea slugs, so similar to one another? The simple answer is that organisms inherit not only a species-typical genome (the set of genes characteristic of a species), but also a species-typical environment. For mammals, this includes a life beginning in a womb, a lactating mother following birth, and a world of sights, sounds, and physical objects. In humans this also includes a social environment of responsive people, beginning with close kin to care for them in infancy, peers to play with during childhood and to cooperate, compete, and mate with during adulthood. Thus, natural selection has produced organisms whose genes interact with their environments, providing both species-typical patterns of development on the one hand, and sufficient plasticity on the other hand to adapt to unanticipated changes in one's circumstances, accounting in large part for the diversity in thought and behavior we see for children growing up in different cultures and subcultures.

The central concept behind developmental systems theory is *epigenesis*, which describes development as a series of steps. More technically, epigenesis is defined as "an emergent process by which an organism's structure and function change from relatively undifferentiated states to increasingly specialized, differentiated forms throughout ontogeny."[29] The philosophical opposite of epigenesis is *preformationism*, which in its original framing purports that development involves simple growth. Preformationism is probably best illustrated by the proposals of 17th century scientists who noted, through the use of the newly invented microscope, that the semen of men contained tiny sperm. They inferred, correctly, that babies came from the joining of a woman's egg and one of these sperm. What they had wrong, however, was how prenatal development actually proceeded. They proposed that a fully formed human infant was housed in each microscopic sperm, and that the egg provided nourishment for the miniscule person, who grew in size over the course of 9 months (see Figure 1.7).[30] There were some scholars who believed that the small human resided in the egg ("ovists") and that the sperm provided the spark of life, a theory that is equally wrong. Such views may not be as ridiculous as they sound coming from 17th century scholars, for scientists at the time did not know there were limits to how small biological units could be, and furthermore, most accepted the Catholic Church's view that the Second Coming was near. Such a belief limited the need for too many more generations, each tucked, Russian-doll style, into the testes of a microscopic boy.

Such preformationist views persisted into the 1800s, but with increasing knowledge of prenatal development, there are no "spermists" or "ovists" today. (I do recall, however, once seeing a display by an anti-abortion group that showed a month-by-month depiction of human prenatal development with the only change being the size of the embryo/fetus from 1 to 9 months.) Modern preformationist views do not envision tiny homunculi residing in reproductive cells but, rather, propose that development is essentially determined by genes, with adult structure and function being essentially preordained (or "preformed").

The modern view of epigenesis stems from British biologist Conrad Waddington, who used the concept to describe development as the result of

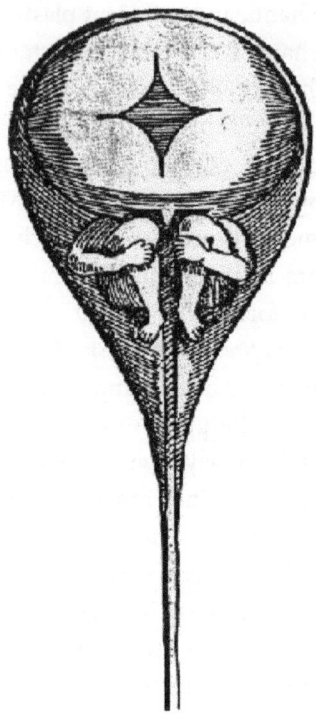

Figure 1.7. A preformationist view of human reproduction as drawn by Nicolaas Hartsoeker in 1695. Early scientists believed in *preformationism*, reflected here in the belief that a fully formed, microscopic child resided in the head of every sperm. Prenatal development begins when a sperm joins the woman's egg, with prenatal development involving only growth.

causal interactions between genes and the environment.[31] The great Swiss developmental psychologist Jean Piaget adopted Waddington's idea, stating that,

> whenever one is dealing with a structure in the psychology of intelligence, its genesis can be traced to other more elementary structures which do not constitute absolute beginnings themselves but have a prior genesis in even more elementary structures, and so on ad infinitum. I say ad infinitum, but the psychologist will stop at birth... and at this level there is, of course, the whole biological problem because the neural structures themselves have their genesis, and so it continues.[32]

More recently, Gilbert Gottlieb defined *probabilistic epigenesis* as the continuous and bidirectional interaction between all levels of the organism-environment (genes ↔ structure ↔ activity ↔ environment), which is the core concept underlying developmental systems theory. From this perspective, nothing arises fully formed but has its origins in earlier structures or functions.[33]

Adaptations of Infancy and Childhood
Clearly, it is adults who do the bulk of competing and cooperating and all the reproduction so essential to an evolutionary perspective (even if it is children who set the groundwork for adult functioning). But before the important tasks of adulthood can take place, individuals must survive gestation, infancy, childhood, and adolescence. To achieve this, natural selection must have operated to shape the behaviors, minds, and emotions of infants and children as much as, if not more so, than those of adults. It's been estimated that nearly half of all children born to our hunter-gatherer ancestors died before their fifth birthdays. This makes infancy and childhood the crucible of natural selection, and any benefits that encourage development through these stages will be favored, even if they have negative effects later on.[34]

As discussed earlier, evolutionary psychologists propose that evolved psychological mechanisms underlie behavioral and cognitive adaptations. I argued previously that most developmentalists inveigh against the idea that the mechanisms underlying adaptations can be described as instincts or are innate, as the term is conventionally understood. If adaptations are not innate, what then are they?

Evolved Probabilistic Cognitive Mechanisms. Rather than view psychological adaptations as complex innate mechanisms, they can be viewed as originating from low-level cognitive and perceptual abilities, or cognitive primitives, that develop into adaptive behavior and thought when children experience a species-typical environment. That is, adaptations are not preformed, ready to go right out of the chute, but develop. To capture this idea, my colleagues and I proposed the concept of *evolved probabilistic cognitive mechanisms*, defined as:

> information-processing mechanisms that have evolved to solve recurrent problems faced by ancestral populations; however, they are expressed in a probabilistic fashion in each individual in a generation, based on the

continuous and bidirectional interaction over time at all levels of organization, from the genetic through the cultural. These mechanisms are universal, in that they will develop in a species-typical manner when an individual experiences a species-typical environment over the course of ontogeny.[35]

Such mechanisms are similar to evolved psychological mechanisms described by mainstream evolutionary psychologists, in that they are information-processing mechanisms that underlie adaptive behavior shaped over a species' evolutionary history. Despite the claim that they are universal—that is, all typically developing members of the species possess them—the developmental outcome of an adaptation is probabilistic, in that the expression of any particular adaptation is subject to change as a result of variations in development.

As an example, consider people's fear of snakes. Many people show a decided fear of snakes, and well they should, as snakes account for more deaths to humans than any other vertebrate (except fellow humans), and they were surely as dangerous or more so to our ancestors. Adults seem especially attentive to snakes, identifying photos of snakes more quickly among photos of flowers than vice versa.[36] Infants and young children also show special attention to snakes, much as adults do, and even show distinct patterns of evoked brain potentials to photographs of snakes compared with photographs of neutral stimuli.[37] However, this greater attention to snakes among infants is not accompanied by fear, but seemingly by fascination. Yet infants and toddlers seem *prepared* to acquire a fear of snakes. This was shown in a study by developmental psychologists Judy DeLoache and Vanessa LoBue, who had 7- and 18-month-old infants watch brief videos of various animals, including snakes, while sitting on their blindfolded parents' laps. The videos were paired with a voice that uttered one of two nonsense phrases (for example, "Hat sundig pron you venzy. Fee gott laish jonkill gosterr."). Sometimes the voice was pleasant and other times fearful, and sometimes the voice was paired with a video of an exotic animal (for example, an elephant or hippopotamus) and other times a video of a snake. The researchers reported that the infants looked significantly longer at the videos of the snakes when they were paired with a fearful voice versus a pleasant voice. Type of voice made no difference in how long the infants looked at the other animals. What was it about the snakes that made this association possible? Apparently, it was snakes' unique sinusoidal movement, distinct from the movement of most vertebrates: When the experiment was repeated using still photographs rather than videos, there was no difference in looking time between the pleasant and fearful voices. In other words, it appears as if natural selection used a low-level perceptual feature, here the serpentine movement of snakes, as the basis for developing an adaptive response to a dangerous animal.[38]

As another example, consider infants' attention to faces. Faces have to be among the most important stimuli for babies, being associated as they are with people who care for them, and infants show greater attention to faces than other stimuli and can tell the difference among faces by at least 3 months of age. Yet even here, it is not necessary to posit a special "face-processing" mechanism. Babies from early on show greater attention to a set of low-level perceptual features that happen to characterize primate faces. These include top-heavy configuration (two eyes above a nose above a mouth), vertical symmetry (the right and left sides of a stimulus being similar), and eyespots, among others.[39] With increasing experience, infants are able to use other, more subtle features to tell the difference between faces. For example, whereas 3-month-olds are equally able to tell the difference between pairs of faces of monkeys, men, women, and people of different ethnic groups, as they get older and more experienced they lose the ability to makes distinctions among types of faces they do not see often (for example, monkeys, faces from ethnic groups different from their own) and become increasingly able to tell the difference among types of faces they see frequently, such as women (when their mothers are their primary caretakers) and people from their own ethnic group.[40] It's not hard to see that it is adaptive to be good at telling the difference between types of faces that one sees frequently (one's own race), although it's less important to be able to make such fine distinctions among faces one sees less often (those of other races). But such an adaptation is not inevitable and will not develop if children experience a species-*atypical* environment, such as frequently seeing monkey faces or human faces from a different ethnic group.[41]

Deferred, Ontogenetic, and Conditional Adaptations. When we think of adaptations, we usually think of behaviors, cognitions, or emotions that help us deal with recurrent problems our adult ancestors faced. In some cases, these same adaptations would be useful throughout life, and we could expect to see their origins in childhood. For example, the social-cognitive processes involved in learning to cooperate and compete with peers are useful during childhood, and in many cases they may serve to prepare children for similar interactions during adulthood. These are called *deferred adaptations*, and they were selected, at least in part, for their role in preparing children for adulthood. Social play may be an adaptation that serves this role, in that through play children learn to maneuver social hierarchies, to understand the perspectives of social others, and to negotiate, compete, and cooperate with others. These are all skills vital to competent functioning in adulthood in any society, although the specifics of how these things are done varies among cultures, requiring plasticity rather than the acquisition of a set of hard-and-fast roles and rules.

Some sex differences in play styles may be good candidates for deferred adaptations. Across cultures, boys' play is more vigorous (greater interest in rough-and-tumble play than girls, especially play fighting) and less intimate (girls know more about their play partners than do boys). The social play of boys is more likely to involve themes of dominance (for example, superheroes, cops and robbers), whereas the social play of girls is more likely to involve domestic themes (playing house or school). These differences are not inevitable but seem to be built on cognitive dispositions that are shaped by experience. Nonetheless, they are found universally and seem to prepare boys and girls for the roles they would have played as adults in traditional cultures.[42] I'll have more to say about the importance of play in development and evolution in Chapter 5.

In contrast to deferred adaptations are ontogenetic adaptations. *Ontogenetic adaptations* adapt infants and children to their immediate environment and not necessarily to a future one.[43] They promote survival at a specific time in life and disappear when they are no longer needed. Consider, for example, the placenta and umbilical cord in mammals or the yolk sack in birds. These serve vital purposes before birth (or hatching), but their functions cease, never to be resurrected again, once the animal is born and other mechanisms begin to operate. Some neonatal reflexes in humans fit the bill as ontogenetic adaptions, including the sucking and rooting reflexes (infants turning their heads in the direction of a stroke on their cheek), both valuable in nursing. The reflex-like facial expressions newborn infants make to adults who make faces at them (not always the same faces that adults are showing them, as it turns out) may serve to establish or maintain social attention between infant and parent at a time when infants cannot purposely control their own behavior.[44] Such *neonatal imitation* disappears around 2 months of age as infants gain increasing (intentional) control of their actions. And preschool children's often extreme tendency to overestimate their talents and attributes may serve to enhance their self-efficacy at a time when children are rarely proficient at any complicated behavior, thus causing them to persist in their endeavors and eventually improve their skills. Although we typically think that the "purpose" of youth is to prepare children for adulthood, we should not lose track that many aspects of infancy and childhood serve mostly to adapt the young to the niche of childhood rather than to prepare them for the future.

Finally, *conditional adaptations* can be viewed as special types of deferred adaptations that are sensitive to the local environment and direct aspects of development to an anticipated future. Pediatrician W. Thomas Boyce and evolutionary developmental psychologist Bruce Ellis defined conditional adaptations as "evolved mechanisms that detect and respond to specific features of childhood environments and entrain developmental pathways that reliably matched those features during a species' natural selective history."[45] Conditional adaptations, or contingent life strategies, use the plasticity of children to alter aspects of their behavior, cognition, or emotions in anticipation of future environments. For example, over the past decade, researchers have proposed that children during the preschool years are sensitive to differences in the harshness (for instance, abundant resources vs. poverty) and predictability (for example, stable domicile vs. frequent moves) of their immediate surroundings and adjust their development accordingly, anticipating what their adult life might be like. Children growing up in harsh and unpredictable environments tend to develop an opportunistic lifestyle, engaging in risky behavior, becoming sexually active early, and investing relatively little in their relationships. In contrast, children growing up in supportive and predictable environments tend to develop a more futuristic orientation, being relatively risk prone, and investing more in their relationships. I'll have much more to say about conditional adaptations in Chapter 2.[46]

Mastering Human Social Complexities Requires an Extended Childhood

Humans, more than any other mammal, take a long time to reach adulthood. As I mentioned earlier, it is likely that ancestral women had their first child in their late teens or early 20s, and this is a long time to wait to reproduce, given the probability of death before ever reaching adulthood. In biology, when there are great costs to a feature (such as prolonging immaturity), there are usually great benefits, otherwise the feature would have been eliminated by natural selection. What is the great benefit humans gain from growing up slowly? There is no single answer to this, although many contemporary scholars believe that humans became the cognitively sophisticated species we are because of social pressures (the *social brain hypothesis*). Having to cooperate and compete with fellow humans in relatively large social groups promoted the evolution of a big brain. However, it takes a long time to acquire the social skills necessary to survive and succeed in any human group, and this required an extended juvenile period to achieve both brain growth and to learn the ways of a particular human culture.[47] From this perspective, childhood is not an inconvenient life stage that we need to get through quickly so we can begin the important tasks of adulthood. Rather, childhood has a purpose unto itself, and rushing children through childhood is a fool's errand.[48]

Childhood evolved in very different circumstances than what most children experience today. Our forechildren lived in small groups of hunter-gatherers. Similar to their parents, they probably knew nearly every person they came in contact with. There was no formal schooling, and infants and young children were cared for by a network of related kin, mostly women. Once weaned, children spent most of their time in mixed-age play groups. If there were enough children, boys and girls likely segregated themselves into separate groups, although in most cases the play groups included both boys and girls. Ancestral children surely played much as modern children do, engaging in rough-and-tumble play (mostly boys) and make-believe, or dramatic, play. Often their play mimicked adult roles, such as pretending to cook, caring for infants, hunting, or fighting. There was little direct instruction from adults. Children learned the physical and social skills necessary to survive and thrive in their culture by observing adults and through play with other children. A number of evolutionary theorists, including Peter Gray and Melvin Konner, argue that hunter-gatherer childhoods are the models upon which we should judge the practices we use in raising our children today.[49]

Evolution and Development Matter

Homo sapiens are undeniably cultural animals. Humans have developed complex societies, and now with the ability to communicate rapidly among people across the globe and across generations, cultural change far outstrips biological change. However, explaining humanity as merely the product of culture misses the point. We are biological creatures, with culture evolving along with biology over millennia. Understanding our biological evolution provides an enhanced understanding of what it means to be human and can provide insights into people's adjustment (and maladjustment) to cultural change.

All evolutionarily influenced characteristics of adults develop, and this requires examining not only the functioning of these characteristics in adults, but also their development and their ancient origins. Evolutionary developmental psychologists are concerned with how an understanding of our species' evolution can help us better understand current development, and how to better rear successful and emotionally healthy adults. This is one of the themes of this book. The second theme turns the relation between evolution and development on its head: How can an understanding of human development help us better understand human evolution? To anticipate, the short answer is that children invented humanity, and that human evolution can be seen as modifications in the ontogeny of our ancestors, setting the stage for and leading the way to species innovation.

2
Changeable Children
Evolved Plasticity and Development

Sex in people, and mammals in general, is relatively straightforward. Embryos that inherit two X chromosomes (one from Mom and one from Dad) get a set of genes with instructions for developing a female body, and embryos that inherit an X chromosome (from Mom) and a Y chromosome (from Dad) receive a different set of genes with instructions for developing a male body. (It's actually more complicated than that, with hormones affecting how prenatal tissue develops into reproductive organs, and "experiences," such as substances mothers ingest, influencing sexual orientation.) Thus, identical twins, who share the same womb at the same time and have the same genes, must be the same sex. Other animals do sex differently, however. For some reptiles, including crocodiles, alligators, and some turtles, sex is determined by the temperature at which eggs are incubated.[1] For some, warmer temperatures produce male animals and cooler temperatures produce female animals, whereas this is reversed for others. For Galapagos turtles, for example, hotter temperatures result in females and cooler temperatures result in males. (A mnemonic for remembering this, told to me by a Galapagos Islands tour guide, is "Hot chicks and cool dudes." See Figure 2.1.) Perhaps even more extraordinary, some fish will change their sex from female to male or vice versa, depending on the sex distribution of the social group.[2] Not enough males in the group? High-ranking females will become male, and they may revert to their female status if new males enter the group. Thus, genetically identical animals can be different sexes based on the ambient temperature during early development or the number of male and female fish that swim around together. From a mammal's perspective, these are mind-blowing examples of sexual plasticity—the ability to change one's sex as a result of experience. (As an aside, global climate change is threatening the survival of many sea turtle populations, primarily because warmer temperatures increase the likelihood of producing single-sex generations.

Figure 2.1. A Galapagos turtle: Is it a boy or is it a girl? It all depends on the temperature at which the eggs were incubated—"hot chicks and cool dudes."
Source: Photo by Barbara Bjorklund, with permission.

Some turtles are showing an ability to adapt to the change, but extinction of many species is predicted.[3])

Genes, of course, are involved in sex determination in these examples. Genes must have evolved to be sensitive to environmental variation during a species' natural-selective history to produce these effects, though they do not directly *cause* these animals to become male or female, nor does temperature or composition of the social group; different genes become activated depending on specific environmental conditions, yielding adaptive outcomes. The activation of specific genes may determine the sex of these animals, but it is variation in the environment, not in the genome, that is responsible for initiating genetic expression. Yet plasticity is not unlimited. If Galapagos turtles laid their eggs in moist versus dry sand of the same temperature, the result would be a clutch of unisex baby turtles. Evolution has constrained the possible ways genes and early experience can produce adaptive outcomes, depending on a species' natural history.

Behavioral Plasticity in Development

Mammals and birds do not display this level of morphological plasticity, but mammals and birds often do display substantial *behavioral* plasticity, modifying their course of development in response to early environmental events or experiences.

The Role of Early Experience in "Instinctive" Behavior

Some of my favorite examples of behavioral plasticity come from experiments with precocial birds –such as ducks, geese, and bobwhite quail that can locomote shortly after hatching. In some duck species, for example, a duckling can walk almost immediately after cracking out of its egg, and it will follow the first quacking, moving object it sees, usually its mother. In some neighborhoods of south Florida where I live it is common to see a mother duck waddling across a street, followed by a line of ducklings. The ducklings stay close to Mom, increasing their chances of survival. The Austrian ethologist Konrad Lorenz described this phenomenon as *imprinting* and showed that hatchlings could become imprinted to any moving object (even Lorenz himself) shortly after breaking out of their shell. Lorenz viewed this as instinctive behavior, acquired "without prior experience."[4]

Subsequent research demonstrated that, hours after hatching, ducklings are able to distinguish between the maternal calls of their own species (for example, mallard) and that of another species (for example, wood duck) and will approach the call of their own species.[5] I witnessed this demonstration once in the laboratory of developmental psychobiologist Gilbert Gottlieb. A 15-hour-old mallard duckling was placed in a circular tub (see Figure 2.2). A speaker on one side of the tub played the maternal call of a mallard duck, and another speaker, on the opposite side of the tub, played the maternal call of a wood duck. I could not tell the difference between the two calls, but the duckling could. It waddled toward the speaker emanating the call of its own kind.

At first blush, this would seem to support Lorenz's idea that imprinting, here, auditory imprinting, is instinctive—no experience necessary. But were these ducklings truly without relevant experience? In the wild, ducklings hear their own mothers quacking after they hatch, and in fact, mothers begin quacking while sitting on the nest a few days before hatching, so the

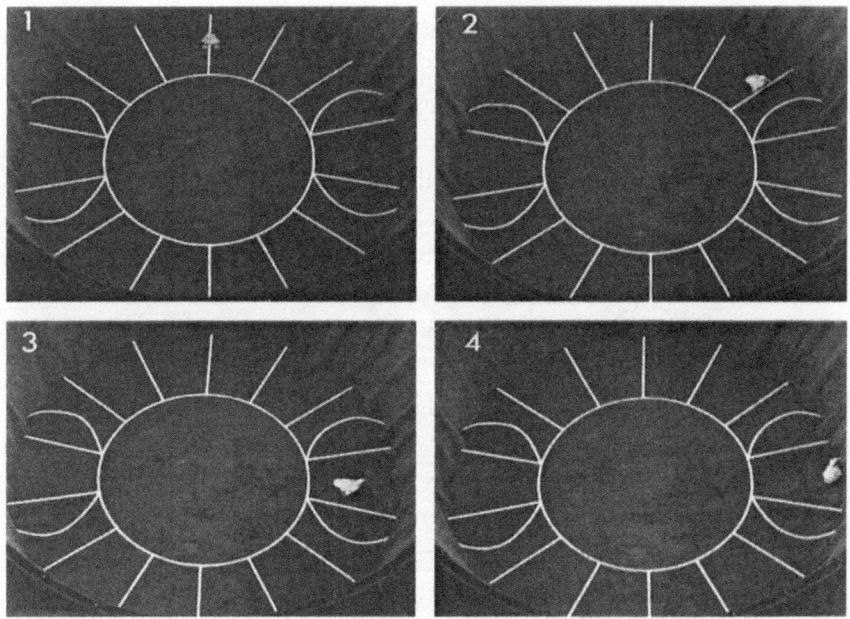

Figure 2.2. A duckling is placed in a circular tub and hears the maternal call of its own species from a speaker on one side of the tub and of another species from a speaker on the opposite side. Ducklings quickly made their way to the area broadcasting the maternal call of their own species.
Source: Gottlieb, 1975, p. 393.

ducklings typically hear their mothers' calls both before and after exiting the egg. Yet, ducklings removed from their mothers days before hatching, and thus deprived of hearing their mothers' quacks, still approach their species' call. However, these birds still heard the peeps of their brood mates (ducklings begin peeping a few days before hatching) as well as their own peeps. To eliminate this source of experience Gottlieb developed a surgical procedure that involved removing the top of the egg shell, making a small incision in the neck of the duck embryo, and coating the vocal cords of the developing duckling with glue before it begins to peep, silencing the duckling. (The effect wears off several days after hatching.) Now when an egg is placed in an incubator alone, the bird inside hears neither its mother's call, nor the peeps of its brood mates, nor its own vocalizations. Under these conditions, when tested after hatching, the devocalized ducklings generally fail to approach their own species' call and will even sometimes approach the call of a chicken!

So some experience does seem to be needed to show auditory imprinting in precocial birds. Gottlieb noted similarities in the acoustic properties of the maternal quack and the ducklings' peeps. Apparently, some auditory experience is necessary for these ducklings to show "instinctive" behavior, meaning that the behavior was not instinctive after all, at least not as the word is usually understood. Genes are, of course, involved, and must have evolved to be sensitive to auditory cues at certain times in early development to promote attachment behavior between ducklings and their mothers. Rather than being "built into" the genes, species-typical experiences (presumably all ducklings in the wild would hear both their own peeps and their mothers' quacks prior to hatching), timed with neural development, affect gene expression, resulting in adaptive species-typical behavior. Organisms do not need genes to dictate all aspects of development. In fact, this would be an impossible task. Adult humans have approximately 86 billion neurons (infants more), with possibly 10 trillion synapses, but only about 20,000 genes. There are simply not enough genes to "instruct" each neuron where to locate and what connections to make. Brains get hooked up by the coordination of gene expression, neuronal development, and experience.

What has this to do with plasticity? Given the important role that experience has in establishing species-typical behavior, animals that receive species *atypical* experience may develop in a species-*atypical* way, assuming they have the behavioral and neural plasticity to do so. This is shown by a number of studies in precocial birds in which ducks or bobwhite quail, while still in the egg, are given extra stimulation, deprived of stimulation, or receive species-atypical stimulation (for instance, exposure to visual patterns before hatching), and the effects on subsequent development examined. For example, developmental psychobiologist Robert Lickliter tested bobwhite quail for auditory imprinting in a procedure similar to that used by Gottlieb with ducks described earlier. For some quail chicks, he cut a hole in the egg near the head and exposed them to light 2 to 3 days before hatching. Other chicks served as controls, having their eggs opened but receiving no premature visual experience. In a series of experiments, a few days after hatching, the chicks were placed in a tub and played the maternal call of a quail from one speaker and that of a chicken from another. The results of these experiments are shown in Figure 2.3.[6]

As you can see, more than 90% of the quail chicks in the control condition (no premature visual stimulation) approached the bobwhite quail maternal call. In contrast, most of the chicks who received the premature visual

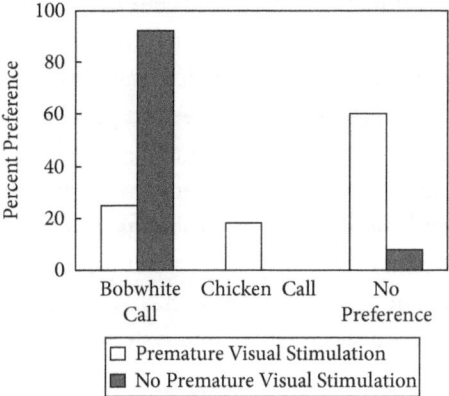

Figure 2.3. Percentage of bobwhite quail chicks that approached the bobwhite quail maternal call, approached the chicken call, or showed no preference as a function of premature visual exposure (based on data from Lickliter, 1990).

stimulation (57%) showed no preference, and some even approached the chicken call. Here, visual stimulation, received prior to when an animal can "normally" expect it, interfered with typical development. Other research has reported similar findings for other senses (for example, auditory stimulation can interfere with subsequent visual development in bobwhite quail, and extra visual stimulation can interfere with the sense of smell in rats). These and other results suggest that young animals do possess substantial brain plasticity early in life, but that patterns of brain development and sensory functioning are coordinated so that, in most situations, development goes according to plan. There exists a delicate, choreographed dance early in development between neural maturation, perceptual experience, and gene expression. The senses develop in a constant order in all vertebrates, and sensory stimulation is coordinated with brain development such that one sensory/brain system becomes established before others come online, insuring that one sensory system develops without competition from other systems.[7]

Although this dance is most easily demonstrated in species such as ducks and bobwhite quail, it also holds true for slower-developing mammals. Referring specifically to neonatal rats, which are functionally deaf and blind, developmental psychobiologist Norman Spear wrote, "If this animal could be made to see and hear, it seems at least as likely that severely maladaptive behavior would result due to distraction from the more conventional events (e.g., odors) upon which its survival depends."[8] This coordination between neural growth, perceptual experience, and gene expression means that an animal does not require a large number of genes to direct development. Rather, brains become organized in a species-typical way through the synergistic interaction among these factors. A few genes can go a long way when they are expressed in a species-typical environment.

I also need to note that when Lickliter gave early visual stimulation to bobwhite quail, resulting in auditory problems, it also caused acceleration of visual development. This clearly reflects neuronal plasticity, in that, presumably, brain areas normally devoted to hearing were recruited for vision, producing precocious development in one system (vision) and deficits in another (audition).

Although one cannot do experimental research with human fetuses and infants like those done with mallard ducks, bobwhite quail, and rat pups, there is at least one situation involving human babies somewhat analogous to Lickliter's experiment involving premature visual stimulation. Modern technology has resulted in the survival of babies born many months before their due dates. I imagine that many readers of this book know of at least one infant born more than a month early and weighing substantially less than 5.5 pounds (2.5 kg), which is the lower bound for "normal" birthweight in the United States. In technologically advanced countries today, infants can live when born as early as 24 weeks post-conception and weighing less than 2 pounds.

These infants can survive and sometimes thrive, but only through extensive intervention, being poked and pricked and having all of their sensory systems stimulated weeks or months before "expected." As in the research with quail chicks, premature stimulation might result in better performance later in some domains, but poorer functioning in others, sometimes leading to learning disabilities. According to Harvard neonatologist Heidelise Als,

> Social contexts evolved in the course of human phylogeny are surprisingly fine-tuned in specificity to provide good-enough environments for the human cortex to unfold, initially intrauterinely, then extrauterinely ... With advances in medical technology, that is, material culture, even very immature nervous systems exist and develop outside the womb. However, the social context of traditional special care nurseries bring with them less than adequate support for immature nervous systems . . . leading to maladaptations and disabilities, yet also to accelerations and extraordinary abilities.[9]

It seems clear that even behaviors and abilities that were once believed to be instinctive are, in fact, dependent on organisms having some prior experience, albeit experiences that nearly all members of a species can expect (unless you're a duckling hatched in Gottlieb's laboratory). Genes still play a role, yet genes are sensitive to and naturally intertwined with experience. Life is an interaction between nature (genes, biology) and nurture (experiences, culture), emerging over the course of development and evolution.

Gene × Environment × Development Interactions

There has long been evidence for an interaction between children's biological inheritance and their experience in influencing thought, emotion, and sociality. However, in the last several decades it's become possible to identify specific variants of genes and assess the connection of such genes with psychological outcomes. Of particular interest to us here, psychologists have looked at how aspects of children's early environments relate to the expression of specific genes and behavioral outcomes. I'll describe a couple of these studies here.

In a now-classic study, New Zealand psychologist Avshalom Caspi and his colleagues looked at the relation between childhood maltreatment and subsequent antisocial behavior as a function of specific genes. Earlier research had shown that a gene on the X chromosome is associated with aggressive behavior in both rats and humans. The gene has its effect by influencing the production of an enzyme called monoanamine oxidase A (or *MAOA*), which affects several neurotransmitters (chemicals that foster transmissions of electrical signals between neurons). People with one version of the gene have higher levels of *MAOA* than people with another variant, with low-*MAOA* activity being associated with elevated levels of antisocial behavior. Caspi and his team followed over 1,000 people from the age of 3 to 26 years, evaluating adolescent and adult antisocial behavior, such as convictions for violent offenses, conduct disorder during adolescence, and antisocial personality disorder at age 26, dependent on level of childhood maltreatment (none, probable, severe) in interaction with gene expression (low- vs. high-*MAOA* activity). This relation is shown in Figure 2.4. As you can see, for children who experienced no maltreatment, antisocial behavior was infrequent and was higher for those who probably experienced maltreatment. Importantly, antisocial behavior did not differ between the low- and high-*MAOA* people

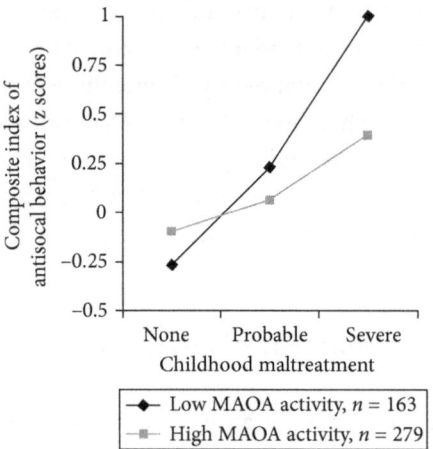

Figure 2.4. Relation between childhood maltreatment (none, probable, and severe) and *MAOA* activity (low versus high) on antisocial behavior. People with a genetic disposition (low-*MAOA* activity) for aggression were significantly more likely to show antisocial behavior than those with high-*MAOA* activity, but only when they grew up experiencing severe maltreatment. There were no differences in antisocial behavior between the low- and high-*MAOA* participants growing up in more favorable home environments.
Source: Caspi et al. 2002, with permission.

in the "none" and "probable" maltreatment groups: Levels of antisocial behavior were comparable whether individuals had the low-*MAOA* gene or not. The situation was different, however, when children experienced severe maltreatment. Levels of antisocial behavior were high for both *MAOA* groups, but especially high for people showing low-*MAOA* activity. Genes alone and the products they produced (here, *MAOA*) were not enough to cause children to become antisocial and aggressive; rather, genes in interaction with rearing environment predicted antisocial behavior in these children.[10]

In a more recent study including over 2,800 adults (2,038 who had schizophrenia) from five countries, researchers from the Lieber Institute for Brain Development at Johns Hopkins investigated the relation between genes, early life complications, and later schizophrenia. Researchers have identified a number of "small-effect" genes associated with schizophrenia, which alone do a poor job of predicting the disease. When the researchers looked at the *total* number of genes associated with schizophrenia in combination with the presence of prenatal and early life complications, however, they found that individuals with high genetic risk (a large number of small-effect genes) who also experienced early-life complications (during pregnancy and labor, at delivery, or shortly after birth) had a fivefold greater incidence of subsequent schizophrenia than individuals with comparable genetic risk but no prenatal/perinatal complications. Moreover, many of the high-risk genes were expressed in the placentas of babies who experienced complications. It seems that many of the genes associated with schizophrenia became turned on in the placenta because of complications, which then influenced brain development and the later incidence of mental illness.[11]

There have been hundreds of studies examining gene × environment × development interactions, not all as straightforward as these, and some with conflicting results. For example, other research by Caspi and his colleagues showed that children who were breastfed had higher IQs than children who were bottle-fed, but only if they had a particular combination of genes (called CC and CG) that was associated with processing fatty acids. Children with a third combination of genes (GG) had comparable IQs whether they were bottle- or breastfed. A follow-up study also found an interaction between type of feeding and genes on IQ, but in a different direction, with bottle-fed GG children having lower IQs than breastfed GG children.[12]

Such findings indicate that identifying the effect of any single set of genes on development may be difficult, and we should not expect simple explanations for how genes and environments interact at different times in development. What is clear, however, is that genes and environment *do* interact, and these interactions, especially early in development, can establish the life course a child will follow. This implies a high degree of neuronal, cognitive, and behavioral plasticity on the part of the child, with early experience determining to a large extent when certain genes are turned on and off. This plasticity is an evolved characteristic of humans. Although it is common to view evolutionary accounts of behavior as involving innate, hardwired, and "fixed" mechanisms, evolutionary developmental psychology emphasizes the flexibility of early learning and behavior. Plasticity, rather than being the antithesis of an evolutionary perspective, has actually been shaped by natural selection over the course of *Homo sapiens'* evolutionary history. We are the species of change, with children leading the way.

Plasticity in Human Development

Plasticity is central to the concept of development. At its most basic, *development* refers to change over time. Unlike *learning*, which refers to changes within individuals over short periods of time as a result of experience, development is a biological concept, describing species-typical changes from birth to death. This is in contrast to evolution, which also refers to changes typical of a species, but instead of taking place over a lifetime, evolution occurs over the course of many generations. In all species, but perhaps especially in humans, there is enough variability in the course and outcome of development to make it interesting. This variability is due to plasticity.

Children change. They go from helpless newborns, to babbling babies, unsteady toddlers, talking 2-year-olds, and eventually to temperamental teens before attaining adulthood. This universal change from infant to adult is a form of plasticity, but what interests us more here are variations in the people children become. Humans live in diverse environments, and children need the flexibility to adjust their behavior to those environments. Within a culture, some children benefit from a highly supportive early environment with plenty of physical and social resources, whereas others must make do with the meager pickings their parents and ecology can provide. How do children modify their thinking and actions to make the best of their conditions? Are there environments that are outside the range of human-typical situations that predictably produce pathology, and to what extent can the effects of such negative early experience be reversed by later experience?

Plasticity can be examined at a variety of levels—neural, cognitive, behavioral—and it is the latter two forms that will concern us the most. However, at day's end, all psychological plasticity is based in the brain, and I'll start this section with a brief discussion of neural plasticity.

Plasticity and Brain Development

Humans have big brains, far larger relative to body size than any other land mammal. (Some dolphin species come close, but that's for another discussion.) Our big brains take time to develop, with development of the prefrontal cortex (responsible for much "higher cognition") not being complete until the third decade of life. I'll have more to say about the causes and consequences of slow brain development in Chapter 4. Here I want to sketch brain development early in life, focusing on the role of experience in creating human brains. Brains will come up from time to time in this and other chapters, and it's necessary for readers to have some basic background of brain development, or developmental neuroscience.

In one sense, human newborns are brainy creatures. They have an excess of neurons, the basic unit of brains, many of which will be pruned to end up with the approximately 86 billion neurons for an average adult. Each neuron will make perhaps 10,000 connections (synapses) with other neurons, many more in the prefrontal area, resulting in perhaps 10 trillion connections overall. Although newborns have more neurons than they eventually will have as adults, their neurons are small in size and have relatively few connections. Over the course of several years, many neurons will die—a process of pruning called *apoptosis*, or *selective cell death*—while others will grow in size and in number of connections with other neurons. How a brain operates is dependent on the connections neurons make, and experience plays a major role in determining these connections.

In Chapter 1 I gave a few examples of how genes, neurons, and experience interact to produce "normal" vision. If you recall, if infants are born with cataracts over their eyes, their vision does not development typically once their cataracts are removed and they begin to receive normal stimulation. Despite being born with genes and neurons for vision, early experience is needed for brains to get hooked up properly. Vision improves for infants over time once they begin to receive "normal" stimulation, but the longer the period of deprivation, the less reversible the effects.

But most brains develop just fine to afford vision (or hearing, or most other psychological functions). Psychologist William Greenough and his colleagues[13] explained both the tendency for things to mostly "go right" and to sometimes "go wrong" with such basic sensory abilities by a mechanism they called *experience-expectant processes*. The nervous systems of animals (including humans) have been prepared by natural selection to expect certain types of stimulation, such as patterned light, a nursing mother (in mammals), and a three-dimensional world consisting of moving objects. These are experiences that nearly all of our human ancestors had, and human nervous systems have evolved to anticipate such stimulation, much as ducks and bobwhite quail have evolved to expect a vocalizing mother. Early experience is necessary for the visual system to become properly organized so a child can "see," but nothing more is needed for the brain to develop in a species-typical way. Neurons receiving species-expected stimulation live and become connected with other stimulated neurons, and those that do not receive such stimulation die or make connections with different neurons. Vision, per se, is not hardwired. What is hardwired is a susceptibility to certain environmental experiences rather than simply the circuitry for detailed behaviors themselves.

But what about the many differences between people that cannot be anticipated by natural selection? I can assure you, natural selection never anticipated a species of animal sitting in an air-conditioned enclosure, typing at a desktop computer, listening to strains of Beethoven over another device, while occasionally picking at chicken salad with a fork and checking his iPhone for a text that may ask him to stop by a grocery store to bring home a carton of cow's milk. Yet here I am, and there you are in a likely similar context. There are other *Homo sapiens* around the globe, however, who are eating their lunch with chop sticks and not a fork, bartering for basic essentials, sitting around a fire for warmth, gathering tubers for sustenance, and trying to keep track of the whereabouts and activities of several spouses. Despite the diversity of activities, each of us manages the requirements relatively well, granted, some better than others. How do we do it?

Greenough and his colleagues proposed that natural selection shaped another set of mechanisms they called *experience-dependent processes*, in which connections among neurons reflect the unique experiences of an individual rather than the experiences that all members of a species can expect to have. For both experience-expectant and experience-dependent processes, the excess neurons found in young brains enable children to make connections that reflect their specific environments. When certain experiences are not had—when the world does not cause certain neurons to be activated and synapses to form—the neurons and their connections die. As neurons die, plasticity is lost. Not totally lost, of course. We know that new synaptic connections are made throughout life—that you *can* teach old dogs new tricks.[14] Nevertheless, brain plasticity is greatest in infancy.

It's easy to see the loss of plasticity as a bad thing, and to some extent it is. It is more difficult to recover from the effects of a maladaptive environment when you're older and your brain is less able to make drastic changes. Yet there are good reasons for brains to become more specialized and less flexible with age. We dedicate neurons to important functions, such as vision and language, thereby reducing plasticity but increasing efficiency. It might be nice to be able to acquire a second and third language as an adult as easily as it was when you were a preschooler, but it makes more sense (and did so for our ancestors) to become really good at speaking and understanding one's mother tongue, likely the only language our forefathers and mothers every heard, rather than keep neurons "on the ready" for possible exposure to a new language at any age. Humans live a long time, and this necessitates that we retain the ability to learn and to change our behavior throughout life. Yet, a great deal in life does not change all that much, and people are best served by a nervous system that early in life commits neurons to basic survival-related functions.

Feral Children, Institutions, and Recovery

At its most basic, plasticity refers to the ability to change behavior (or cognition, emotions, or neural patterns) as a result of experience. As you can imagine, there's been much debate over the decades about the role of experience (and thus plasticity) in development, being the basis of the nature–nurture debate that just won't seem to go away despite overwhelming evidence of the interactive roles of biology and experience in shaping the people we become. One approach researchers have taken to make their point that "experience matters" is to demonstrate how early, species-*atypical* experiences can result in negative outcomes, such as intellectual, social, and emotional impairment and psychopathology. Plasticity comes into play when we ask to what extent these early environments can be reversed when children experience positive, supportive conditions. How long can babies be neglected before they are too far gone to become psychologically "normal"?

Feral Children

Perhaps the most extreme examples of children surviving in species-atypical environments come from tales and studies of *feral children*—children from an early age living apart from other humans "in the wild," sometimes alleged to being raised by dogs, monkeys, wolves, or other nonhuman animals. Feral children are things of legend (the purported founders of Rome, Romulus and Remus, were said to have been raised by wolves), but a number of cases have been well documented and reflect the extreme conditions human children can live in and still survive, as well as the limitations of plasticity. (For a listing of cases of feral children go to https://en.wikipedia.org/wiki/Feral_child.)

One well-documented case of feral children is that of Amala and Kamala, two girls who were perhaps 3 and 5 years old when they were found in a wolf's den, along with two wolf cubs, by the missionary Joseph Singh in India

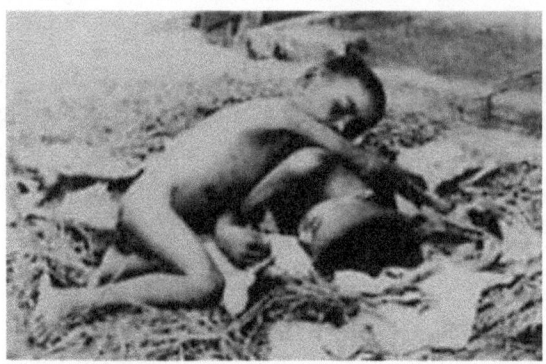

Figure 2.5. Kamala and her presumed sister Amala were found living in a wolf's den in northern India. Kamala lived for nearly 10 years after being discovered and learned to walk, acquired a limited vocabulary, and spoke in short, broken sentences. She had the estimated intelligence of a 3.5-year-old child.
Source: Alamy stock photos, with permission.

in 1920 (Figure 2.5). The girls walked on all fours, did not talk, would eat only raw meat, and balked at wearing clothes. Amala died shortly after being discovered, but Kamala, after nearly 10 years of rehabilitation, learned to walk, was toilet trained, and was able to speak in short, broken sentences. Kamala was examined by the prominent developmental psychologist Arnold Gesell when she was around seven, and he announced that she had the intellect of a three-and-a-half-year-old child. Kamala died of typhoid in 1929.[15] A similar account comes from South Africa, where a boy, named Saturday Mthiyane, was discovered at around 5 years of age living with a troop of monkeys. After 10 years of living with people, Saturday, like Kamala, had learned to walk but ate only raw fruits and vegetables and did not talk.[16]

There are many other cases of children being found living in the company of nonhuman animals, and, although one must remain skeptical of the claims that these feral children were, indeed, raised by wild animals, they reveal the limits of plasticity. On the one hand, the fact that children can presumably survive being raised by wolves and monkeys and can adapt to these wild animals' ways of life reflects an extraordinary ability to adjust to extreme conditions. Perhaps we shouldn't be so surprised. Humans frequently adopt abandoned infant animals and raise them much as children, or cross-foster animals of different species, often with great success. The Chinese psychologist Zing-Yang Kuo described many such successful cross-fosterings between species that are natural predators and prey, such as cats raising mice and chicken hawks raising chickens;[17] and, although they lack the scientific rigor of Kuo's experiments, hardly a week goes by that I don't see at least one Facebook video of unusual, and almost always charming, animal companions. (A hippo and a chicken is a recent video that comes to mind.)

On the other hand, once feral children are discovered, attempts to civilize them have imperfect success. In most cases, these once-wild children show some signs of human-typical behavior, learning to walk, wearing clothes, and displaying some social skills. Some form attachments with other people, but others never do. Many acquire a basic vocabulary, but few attain more than a rudimentary grasp of grammar. Feral children's difficulty learning language may be because the experience necessary to learn grammar—the rules by which words and parts of words are put together to produce meaning—must occur early, within the first two to four years of life. According to developmental psycholinguist John Locke, in commenting on the relatively large vocabulary but limited grammatical ability of Genie, a child who had been socially and linguistically isolated by her pathological father from the age of 20 months to 13 years: "This is not surprising, since . . . grammar has a narrowly circumscribed acquisition period—it should have begun almost exactly when her deprivation commenced in earnest—whereas her lexical [vocabulary] development is more open."[18]

Orphanages, Foundling Homes, and Fostering

Being raised by wolves or monkeys is extreme, as is being isolated in a locked room and strapped to a crib or toilet as in the case of Genie.[19] It's little wonder that children experiencing such conditions do not recover normal functioning. There is also the question of whether these children were abandoned by their parents because of some intellectual or emotional impairment. We know this was the case with Genie, whose father believed from early on that she was severely mentally impaired. There are less extreme situations in which children experience social, emotional, and intellectual deprivation early in life with later attempts at rehabilitation, and these are studies of children abandoned by their parents and placed in government- or church-run orphanages or foundling homes.

Ancestral parents who could not afford to care for their infants had few options. They could share what little they had among themselves, the infant, and their other offspring, hoping everyone would not die as a result, or they could abandon their new baby, using their limited resources to keep themselves and their other children alive. In Europe for much of the first and the early part of the second millennia, parents would sometimes leave their unwanted infants in public places in the hopes that someone would find the baby and raise it. Many European languages today have names reflecting children who were abandoned but were subsequently saved, such as *Esposito*, a common surname in Italian that in Latin means "to place outside" or "to expose." By the 1400s in Europe, parents could leave their infants, anonymously, at some churches, believing their babies would be taken care of. The outcome was usually less than hoped for. In the days before baby formula, infants were fed diets of mostly porridge, and death rates were often in excess of 60%.[20]

Orphanages and foundling homes for abandoned infants and children persisted from the 15th century until today. Although conditions in these homes have surely improved over the past 600 years, these institutions remained poor places for bringing up children through the present time. The conditions of "homes" in Europe, Asia, South America, and the United States during much of the 20th century were often described as being overcrowded and understaffed. Infants were kept in cribs for as long as possible and provided the minimal care necessary to keep them alive, at least temporarily. Death rates before the age of 2 in some institutions approached 100% due to the spread of infection. Mortality decreased with the advent of more hygienic conditions, but caretakers sometimes took their views of cleanliness to extremes, insisting that human contact with babies be kept to a minimum to avoid contamination. The result was a drop in death rates (although they still often averaged 30%), but children grew up to be emotionally, socially, and intellectually challenged.[21] And this is not ancient history. For instance, during the heyday of communism in Eastern Europe in the late 1900s, the Romanian government encouraged its citizens to have many children (five per family was the benchmark) in order to increase economic production. Birth rates skyrocketed, but economic production did not. As a result, many parents could not support all of their children, and the State developed a network of institutions that were at least as horrendous as any that existed in the United States during the Great Depression to handle the increase in abandoned children.[22] A 2006 report from the United Nations estimated that there were approximately 8 million children living in institutions, many as stifling as those from the early 20th century.[23]

The effects of such hands-off childrearing (referred to by some as *maternal deprivation*, and by others as *stimulus deprivation*) were often immediate and prolonged. For example, in a 1962 report, Sally Provence and Rose Lipton described 2- and 3-month-old institutionalized infants as feeling "something like sawdust dolls; they moved, they bent easily at the proper joints, but they felt stiff or wooden." And although, unlike feral children, they learned to talk and to socialize with others, as they got older their social, emotional, and cognitive problems grew. For instance, Provence and Lipton described institutionalized toddlers' emotional behavior as "increasingly impoverished and predominantly bland. . . . One gained the impression on watching them that they had largely given up on their efforts to initiate a contact with the adult."[24] When institutionalized infants were followed into childhood, adolescence, and adulthood, the outcomes were not encouraging. Study after study, conducted over at least six decades, similarly reported that "graduates" of these institutions had lower IQs, poorer memory functioning, a greater incidence of internalizing problems (such as anxiety and depression), externalizing problems (such as conduct disorder and excessive aggression), and attachment disorders than children who were never institutionalized, coupled with abnormal brain development. These effects tend to be long-lasting, persisting at least into adolescence.[25]

In an earlier book I wrote about a 13-year-old boy I knew in my childhood who came from foster homes and was adopted by a family in our small town. Johnny made friends, but he lost them just as fast. He'd lose his temper at the most minimal provocation, often leading to fights, that he inevitably lost. Despite his bravado, I remember him crying when he lost these fights, something 13-year-old boys in the company of other boys try not to do. He'd ride around town on his bicycle, joining groups of boys playing baseball, for example, but never quite fitting in. I remember feeling uncomfortable around him and not knowing why. Johnny didn't return to school the next year. The story was that his adoptive parents had "sent him back," to where I never knew, and no one in town, as far as I know, ever heard from him again.[26]

The deleterious effects of prolonged institutionalization on brain development are substantial. According to developmental neuroscientist Charles Nelson, "institutionalization appears to lead to a reduction in cortical brain activity . . . and to dysregulation of neuroendocrine systems that mediate social behavior." Consistent with Greenough's concept of experience-expectant processes, Nelson suggested that institutionalized children fail to receive the stimulation that developing brains have evolved to "expect." Nelson writes, "many forms of institutional rearing lack most elements of a mental-health-promoting environment. As a result, the young nervous system, which actively awaits and seeks out environmental input, is robbed of such input."[27] Based on findings from studies of Romanian institutionalized children,

Nelson proposed that too many neurons and synapses are lost in deprived children, most of which can never be replaced, suggesting a sensitive period from which these children cannot fully recover.

During the first decade of the 21st century, many Americans adopted children who had been raised for much of their lives in orphanages from Russian and other Eastern European countries. Many of the adoptive parents reported serious problems with their adopted children, and one such case actually caused an international incident. In 2010 a Tennessee woman placed her 7-year-old Russian adopted grandson on a one-way flight to Moscow, effectively returning a child who had become too difficult to handle. A letter accompanying the child stated,

> "This child is mentally unstable. He is violent and has severe psychopathic issues ... I was lied to and misled by the Russian Orphanage workers and director regarding his mental stability and other issues.... After giving my best to this child, I am sorry to say that for the safety of my family, friends, and myself, I no longer wish to parent this child."[28]

Russians were outraged by this and other problems with American-adopted Russian children (three other children had been murdered by their American parents, with about 20 suspicious deaths), and, despite the fact that many adoptions were quite successful, Russian officials froze adoptions to Americans, which as of this writing is still in effect.

The outrage was not limited to Russians, but to Americans as well. This once-abandoned child was being abandoned again, facing an uncertain future. Despite the criticism focused on the adoptive family, other parents who had adopted once-institutionalized children, while not condoning the actions, understood and felt sympathetic. A woman who had adopted two sisters, 5 and 6 years old when adopted, wrote 15 years later: "We have dealt with Post Traumatic Stress Disorder, Narcissistic Personality Disorder, Fetal Alcohol Effects, Reactive Attachment Disorder, arrests, drugs, failing out of school, lying, sneaking around, destruction of property—go ahead and name it ... we've been there."[29] I have a colleague who lost all control of her Russian-adopted son and resorted to removing knives from the house and locking all bedroom doors at night, in fear that her son might try to kill her, her husband, and their other children.

The future looks bleak for some children adopted from these institutions, but many of the "problem children" were not adopted until 5 or 6 years of age or later, and many other adoptions were quite successful. As I've emphasized, plasticity is greatest early in life. At what point can the effects of a truly deprived environment be reversed when children are placed in loving homes? One way of answering this question is to follow up on children who started life in institutions and see how they fare later in life as a function of how old they were when they were adopted. Psychologists Emily Merz and Robert McCall examined evidence of behavior problems in 342 children who were 6-to-18 years old and who had been adopted from Russian orphanages where they experienced unresponsive caregiving but received adequate nutrition and medical care. The researchers compared these adoptees to children who had never been institutionalized and to children in Romanian institutions who had experienced both psychosocial deprivation and inadequate nutrition and physical care, which the researchers referred to as *globally depriving institutions*. They found that children in the Russian orphanages who had been adopted before 18 months of age were similar to children who had never been in institutions in terms of behavior problems. In contrast, children who remained institutionalized beyond 18 months of age showed greater behavior problems than children who had never been in institutions, and these effects persisted into adolescence. Children in globally depriving institutions displayed even greater behavior problems, and these effects were found for children adopted after 9 months of age. Based on these and other findings, the authors concluded that "behavior problem rates increase for children adopted from globally depriving institutions after 6–9 months of age and for children adopted from psychosocially depriving institutions after 18–24 months."[30] Clearly, plasticity decreases with age, with children prior to their second birthdays being the most capable of recovering from early deprivation.

Similar results have been reported for intellectual functioning as measured by IQ. For example, researchers tested the IQs of children adopted from Romanian institutions by parents in the United Kingdom (U.K.) at ages 6 and 11 years. Some children had been adopted early (less than 6 months), and others later (6–24 months, or more than 24 months). They compared the IQs of these once-institutionalized children with those of children born in the United Kingdom and adopted by U.K. parents. The average IQs of children at ages 6 and 11 are shown in Figure 2.6. (IQ tests are constructed so that the average score is 100.) As you can see, Romanian children adopted before 6 months of age had IQs in the normal range, similar to those of the U.K. sample. Romanian children adopted between 6 and 24 months had

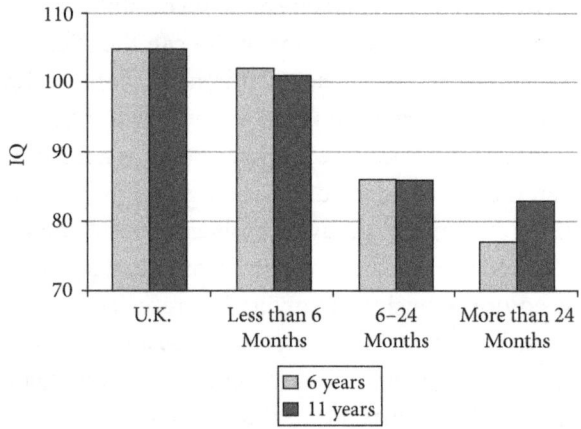

Figure 2.6. IQ scores for adopted Romanian children at 6 and 11 years of age as a function of their age of placement in adoptive homes. Also shown are the IQs for a group of U.K. adopted children.
Source: Adapted from data presented in Beckett et al. (2006).

IQs in the low-normal range, and children adopted after 24 months had the lowest IQs, averaging below 80 at 6 years but slightly higher at age 11. This slight increase in IQ from age 6 to 11 for the children who had experienced the longest deprivation suggests a possible catch-up effect: the longer children that live in supportive homes, the higher their intellectual functioning becomes.[31]

I do not mean to imply that children living in unsupportive environments past the age of 2 are destined for a life of social maladjustment and psychopathology. Maladjustment may be the most likely outcome for children living in the harshest conditions, but there is also evidence of great resilience in children who do not escape their deleterious situations until early childhood. For example, several studies have looked at Asian children, separated from their parents because of war or poverty, who were later adopted by middle-class American families. In one study, 25 children who had been adopted prior to 36 months were given IQ tests at an average age of 44 months. Although these children experienced both psychosocial and physical deprivation (16 were reported to have been malnourished during infancy, 14 so much so that they required hospitalization), by the time they had spent approximately 2 years in adoptive homes, their scores on IQ tests far exceeded American population averages.[32]

Studies of institutionalized children and children from war-torn communities reflect an extreme of possible rearing environments. Although as a result of war and poverty, millions of children today live in institutions, they are the exception to the human experience. Most children grow up with parents or other loving caregivers. Despite the extraordinary circumstances of institutionalized children, these observations tell us something important about developmental plasticity. During the first 9 months of life or so, children are highly resilient, even to environments lacking both social and physical resources. When children receive adequate physical care, they can rebound from social deprivation if they experience a supportive environment beginning around 18 or 24 months of age. Why this age? For one thing, children's cognitive abilities undergo substantial changes around this time. For example, children start putting words together into sentences, the beginning of true language. The eminent Swiss cognitive developmental theorist Jean Piaget proposed that this is a time when children's thinking becomes transformed from a hands-on, sensorimotor type of thought to a type involving mental (symbolic) representation. Although we now believe that this transition is a bit more complicated than Piaget initially proposed, the change in a child's thinking between about 18 and 30 months is substantial. Something's going on.

Consistent with these observations, some have proposed that human development is highly *canalized* during the first 18 or 24 months of life, meaning that all children follow the species-typical path "under a wide range of diverse environments and exhibit strong self-righting tendencies following exposure to severely atypical environments."[33] In other words, although infants and toddlers may be adversely affected by early negative environments, there is a tendency to return to a course of normalcy when they experience more supportive conditions. The earlier children can be rescued from these maladaptive situations, the greater the chance of reversing the ill effects of abuse and neglect.

One thing that the remarkable plasticity of young children does *not* mean, however, is that if you're lucky enough to have loving parents and socially and nutritionally beneficial conditions for your first 2 years of life, you're home free. Early positive experience is not an inoculation from the slings and arrows of later outrageous fortune. Early experience is important, but so is later experience. Just as a supportive later environment can compensate for the negative effects of an early impoverished one, the reverse is also true.

The psychological benefits of loving, supportive parents early in life can be reversed when conditions take a turn for the worse. As I write this, there is a great outpouring of emotion about the United States' policy of separating children, some breastfeeding infants, from their undocumented-immigrant parents. Experts in pediatrics, psychiatry, psychology, and neuroscience are warning of the toxic stress that children may experience from such traumatic events, including the long-lasting consequences that these experiences can have for children's subsequent mental health.[34] Children's extended plasticity can be a blessing, affording children the ability to recover from adverse early environments. But it also means that children are susceptible to the negative effects of later unsupportive environments.

Yet, we *are* talking about extremes here. Children did not evolve to be raised in institutions, removed from their mothers and other caring adults. What is a species-typical environment for a developing human child, and why is this question even relevant to our discussion of plasticity? In Chapter 1, I noted that members of a species, be they bobwhite quail, chimpanzees, or people, grow up to be much like one another because they each inherit not only a species-typical set of genes and biological mechanisms but also an environment that, beginning before birth (or hatching), is typical of their species and has been for thousands, perhaps millions, of years. Can we describe this environment for human children, and, importantly for the issue of plasticity, what is the range of environmental conditions that children can grow up in and still become "normal" adults?

Neontocracies versus Gerontocracies
We may be tempted to use our own 21st-century standards as the model for a species-typical environment for rearing children. In contemporary American culture, and those of other developed societies, children are highly valued for their own sake. They are viewed as innocent, requiring protection and nurturing, often at great expense to their parents. Although these may be the childrearing practices we're most familiar with, it takes only a little reflection to realize that children in other parts of the world today have very different experiences, yet they still seem to grow up to be functional adults. This culture-centered perspective is a problem not only when considering child development but also for all areas of psychology. Most psychological research has focused on people from WEIRD (Western, educated, industrialized, rich, democratic) societies, and although such research may be relevant to people living in those societies, it is not an accurate representation

of what is typical for our species as a whole, nor for the conditions in which *Homo sapiens* evolved.[35]

So what might a human-typical rearing environment be? Several scholars, notably anthropologist Melvin Konner, argue that the childhoods of hunter-gatherers, people who live nomadic lives much as our ancestors presumably did before the advent of civilization 10,000 years ago, should be the model for understanding contemporary children and their development.[36] Although there is variation in practices among different hunter-gatherer groups, infants typically stay in close contact with their mothers, nurse on demand, and are not weaned until 2 or 3 years of age. Once weaned, babies spend much of their day playing with other children; they have few chores, receive little or no formal instruction from adults, and have no prescribed bedtime. Children are loved and valued and little is demanded of them. Children can be treated this way because, unlike children from WEIRD societies, they have few options of what they will do when they grow up. They will become hunters and gatherers like their parents, and they will pick up the skills necessary to survive, mainly through observation and play, or they will die.

Despite the obvious differences between hunter-gatherer and WEIRD societies, anthropologist David Lancy has described these societies as *neontocracies*, in which "children have authority—lording it over their valet parents."[37] Before you start thinking that modern childhoods are pretty good models for children around the world and across time, consider that, since the advent of agriculture, neontocracies have been the exception rather than the rule. Lancy describes most societies, including many today, as *gerontocracies*, in which adults are the most valued members, with infants viewed as drains on resources and children seen as owing their parents for investing in them over the years. Let me provide a few examples Lancy (2015) gives of practices in gerontocracy societies from his book, *The Anthropology of Childhood*:

> Yoruba mothers feed children barely visible scraps compared to portions they give themselves. Good food might spoil the child's moral character. (p. 108)

> Pashtu mothers rarely make eye contact with their infants when nursing unless there's a problem. . . . This seeming indifference may be reinforced by custom whereby a mother is chastised by peers if she is overly fond of her child. (p. 121)

Like the Xhosa, [Gapun] mothers actively pit their three-year-olds (girls as well as boys) against each other, holding them in proximity and shouting orders to strike out at the opponent. Children are also encouraged and praised for hitting dogs and chickens. (p. 192)

Qualities we [Westerners] value, such as precocity, verbal fluency, independent and creative thought, personal expression, and ability to engage in repartee, would all be seen by [lower Tapajós] villages as defects to be curtailed as quickly as possible. (p. 200)

[From medieval times in Europe] parents sent their five- to seven-year-old children (who were, in their view, no longer actually children) to the homes of master-craftmen or merchants as apprentices, where the first decade of service might well be "scut-work" rather than the acquisition of a usable skill. (p. 151)

The Zulu of South Africa use a more direct approach [to accelerate walking]; they place the child on an ant's nest to motivate it to stand and walk. (p. 134)

Placing children on ants' nests to motivate walking!? How different from both hunter-gatherer and WEIRD societies can childrearing practices be? In many ways, practices in gerontocracies vary even more from those of our hunter-gatherer ancestors than those of modern societies. Although we may feel contempt at some of the childrearing practices of people in agrarian societies, they seem to have been adaptive—well suited (if not perfectly so) to the ecological conditions in which they live. Children in all of these cultures somehow grow up to be productive members of their group, capable of making a living, forming meaningful relationships with others, and producing children who, in turn, become competent adults. The demands and practices of human cultures vary so greatly that a narrow range of parenting practices could not be necessary to raise "competent adults," lest the species go extinct.

More than a quarter-century ago developmental psychologist Sandra Scarr made a similar assertion in the published version of her presidential address to the Society for Research in Child Development, and she caused quite a stir. Scarr wrote that, "ordinary differences between families have little effect on children's development, unless the family is outside of a normal developmental range. Good enough, ordinary parents probably have the same effect on their children's development as culturally defined super-parents."[38] Scarr proposed, based on evolutionary theory, that there existed an *average expectable environment*. Infants and children were prepared to respond to a relatively wide range of environmental situations in order to acquire developmentally appropriate knowledge, with environments falling outside this range failing to promote typical developmental patterns. Contemporary examples of such maladaptive environments are those involving abuse or neglect.

Scarr's critics were quick to point out that differences in parenting style and opportunities make a great difference in the eventual outcome of children and that "good enough" parents are just not good enough for a sizeable minority of children in our culture. In response, Scarr agreed that, within a society, individual differences in parenting styles and opportunities contribute to academic and economic success. But Scarr's focus was a broader one, concerned with how children become functioning, "good enough" members of their culture, whereas her critics were concerned with how individual differences among children within a culture result in differential societal success. Both are right, of course, though it is easy to see how the two camps could argue past one another, certain the other camp is missing the point, when in reality they are talking about different levels of human functioning.[39]

An evolutionary perspective is not limited to explaining how cultures that set babies on ant hills and those that enroll infants in academic preschools can both rear productive members of their respective societies. Within a culture such as ours, both early and later environments can differ widely. We may like to think that all Americans (or Brits, or Canadians, or Mexicans) want the same outcomes of economic success and happiness for their children, but, even if the desire is there, the opportunities are not. To become a successful adult in some modern-day subcultures involves different sets of skills, attitudes, and expectations than to become a successful adult in other subcultures, and this requires children making use of their evolved plasticity.

Contingent Life Strategies: Anticipating the Future Based on the Present (and on the Evolutionary Past)

Can children predict the future, especially their future? Can they "know" what psychological attributes would be best for them to develop in order to prepare themselves for life as an adult? Children grow up in different environments with different amounts of resources (think money and all that money can buy), social support, and predictability. Can early environmental conditions help children anticipate the type of world they will grow up in and, in turn, shape their developmental course to survive in that world?

The simple answer is "not perfectly," but children's evolved neural, cognitive, and behavioral plasticity can help them adjust the course of their development to one well suited to anticipated future environments (anticipated based on their early environments). Children develop contingent life strategies, or *conditional adaptations*, that enable them to succeed in a variety of contexts. However, such plasticity is constrained by the experiences of our ancestors, or what Melvin Konner referred to as *phylogenetic legacies*. The idea of contingent life strategies is an essential concept to evolutionary accounts of development, making it clear that one important thing that evolved in *Homo sapiens* was the ability to alter behavior in response to different and changing environments. As you might expect from our discussion so far, such plasticity is greatest early in development.

Contingent Life Strategies During Prenatal Development

When do children become sensitive to environmental conditions and, in turn, alter their life course? They begin do to so while still fetuses. Consider the effect of prenatal nutrition on children's later metabolism. Women who have poor nutrition during pregnancy give birth to lighter babies, but, somewhat counterintuitively, when these babies grow up, they have a tendency to be overweight. The reason for this outcome is that these infants produce higher levels of the appetite-regulating hormone leptin and store greater amounts of fat than children who had more nutritious prenatal diets.[40] These children's prenatal diet served as a signal that food was scarce, and as one's current environment is the best predictor of one's future environment, they developed a metabolism that held onto calories. This was likely highly adaptive for our ancestors but is less beneficial today, as even poor diets for children growing up in WEIRD cultures have high levels of sugar and fat, often leading to obesity.

Other research has shown that fetuses are responsive to stress their mothers experience, increasing their production of the stress hormone cortisol. Prenatal exposure to high levels of stress hormones is associated with poorer health outcomes later in life and influences aspects of how children's brains respond to stress. The result is often increased levels of impulsivity, risk-taking, anxiety, and antisocial behavior, which, on the surface, hardly seems to be adaptive. However, these are psychological features that may be beneficial for children growing up in high-stress environments, a topic we'll discuss in more detail in the next section.[41]

How do we know that children's levels of cortisol and subsequent ways they handle stress are due to prenatal experiences rather than genetics? Perhaps mothers' reactions to stress were driven by their genes, which they passed on to their children. I'd be surprised if individual differences in genetics do not play a role here, but it can't be the only factor. In a very clever study,[42] children's antisocial behavior when they were between 4 and 10 years of age was compared with prenatal exposure to stress between fetuses that were genetically related to their birth mothers and those that were not. How, you may ask, is this possible? Children in one group were conceived via in vitro fertilization (IVF), using the eggs of women unrelated to the birth mother. Children in a second group were also conceived by IVF, but with eggs from their birth mothers, and thus were genetically related to their birth mothers. Children's antisocial behavior was related to the amount of prenatal stress experienced by their birth mothers, regardless of genetic relatedness. Prenatal exposure to the stress of their birth mothers appears to be preparing infants for similar postnatal environments.

Anticipating Harsh and Unpredictable Environments

Although we may talk about a species-typical rearing environment, as we've seen, children across the globe grow up in a wide range of conditions, and they likely always have. Differences are found not only between cultures but also within them, with some children having it easier than others, and this probably has always been the case. If fetuses can be sensitive to the stress their mothers' experiences, why should this be any less true for infants and young children? Children's early life conditions are generally good predictors of what their later life conditions will be, and some psychological characteristics may be better suited to some environments than to others.

Natural selection could not have anticipated all possible environments children across the world and across time might be exposed to. Nonetheless, natural selection does seem to have focused on at least two broad factors central for survival: *harshness* and *predictability*. Harshness is an indication of stress in the environment, including rates of mortality, injuries, and illness;

presence of social support; and general access to resources, as reflected in modern societies by socioeconomic status (SES). Predictability refers to the stability of resources over time and to the dependability of important people in a child's life. For example, do economic conditions fluctuate, are neighborhood and family compositions stable, and are caregivers reliable? These are general factors that can be used for describing the environments of children from all types of cultures, WEIRD and non-WEIRD alike. Moreover, the psychological characteristics that are best suited for dealing with the different extremes of these environments (harsh and unpredictable vs. supportive and predictable) differ.

Life History Theory
Life history theory is used to explain why children living in different types of environments develop different styles of dealing with life. At its simplest, life history theory is concerned with how animals allocate bodily and behavioral resources as a function of their local ecology. Animals must make trade-offs between investing in developing their own bodies and behavioral abilities and investing in reproduction, including bearing and caring for children. To do so, they develop strategies that maximize their fitness, and the type of strategy they develop depends on qualities of the environment. Life history theory explains differences both between species and for individuals within a species.[43]

Life history strategies exist on a continuum from fast to slow (see Figure 2.7). A *fast life history strategy* is typical of short-lived animals (high mortality) or animals living in harsh and unpredictable environments. Under these conditions, it is adaptive (that is, it promotes survival and reproduction) to take an opportunistic versus a futuristic orientation, to mature and reproduce quickly (for tomorrow we may die), take risks, invest little in long-term relationships, and to have many offspring (think mosquitoes). In contrast, a *slow life history strategy* is typical of long-lived animals (low mortality) or animals living in environments with plentiful resources (nonharsh) and high predictability with reliable relationships (think elephants and people). Under these conditions it makes sense to develop more slowly (put more resources into developing one's body and behavioral skills), be risk prone, plan for the future (college, perhaps, or a retirement account), and invest more in relationships and in a small number of children.

In one of the first studies in developmental psychology to adopt this approach, Jay Belsky, Laurence Steinberg, and Patricia Draper proposed that:

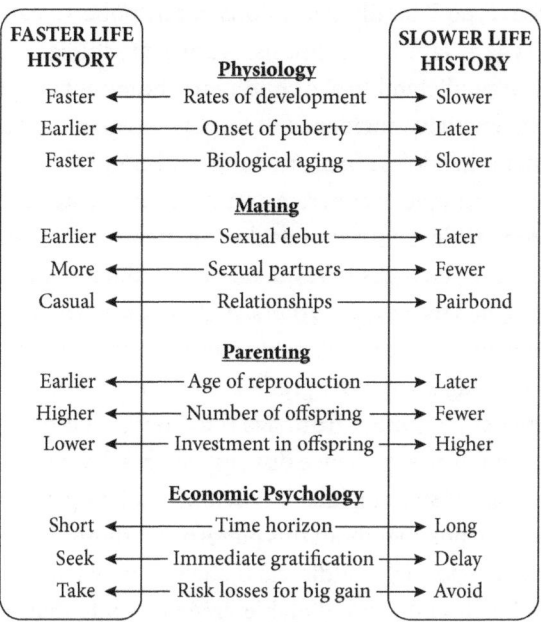

Figure 2.7. The fast–slow continuum of life history variation.
Source: Ellis et al., 2012.

a principal evolutionary function of early experience—the first 5–7 years of life—is to induce in the child an understanding of the availability and predictability of resources (broadly defined) in the environment, of the trustworthiness of others, and of the enduringness of close interpersonal relationships, all of which will affect how the developing person apportions reproductive effort.[44]

Belsky and his colleagues described two general patterns they called Type I and Type II that correspond roughly to fast and slow life history strategies. Type I families are characterized by high family discord, harsh parenting, and insecure attachment. As a result, children from Type I homes reach puberty and engage in sexual activity earlier, have unstable relationships, and invest relatively little in their children. Children from Type II families display an opposite pattern.

In the past two decades, research following life history theory has skyrocketed, and many of the hypotheses originally proposed by Belsky and his colleagues have been supported. For example, girls (although not boys) who experience Type I family conditions reach puberty earlier than girls experiencing Type II family conditions. Numerous studies have found that harshness and/or predictability of a child's early home environment is related to onset of sexual activity, incidence of teenage pregnancy, risk-taking, and antisocial behavior in adolescence or young adulthood.[45]

Let me provide a couple of concrete examples. In one study, children living in highly unpredictable environments during their first 5 years, reflected by parental job changes, changes in residences, and different adult males living in the household, had more sex partners, had their first sexual encounter earlier, and had engaged in more risk-taking and delinquent behavior at age 23 than children growing up in more predictable homes. In contrast, the quality of a child's home environment from age 6 to 16 was *not* related to later behavior, indicating it was experience during the preschool years that was primarily responsible for shaping later behavior.[46] At first glance, there doesn't seem to be anything positive about this pattern. Yet these behaviors, although generally frowned upon by middle-class society, may better serve children growing up in harsh and unpredictable environments than more cautious and culturally approved behaviors, which may be at odds with the everyday realities children in these types of environments must deal with.

Although most studies based on life history theory have examined children's social and emotional development, early experiences can also shape basic aspects of thought as well. For example, in one study people growing up in harsh and unpredictable environments were less apt to inhibit their thoughts or actions, although they were better able to shift attention between tasks than people growing up in more favorable environments, but only when testing was done in uncertain contexts. The researchers proposed that although inhibiting impulsive behavior and thought is important for attaining long-term goals—something someone following a slow life history strategy may be concerned with—it can be disadvantageous when local conditions favor opportunism. He who hesitates is lost, especially he who hesitates in a harsh and unpredictable environment. In contrast, the ability to shift effectively between tasks is critical for adapting to unpredictable circumstances.[47] Dutch evolutionary developmental psychologist Willem Frankenhuis and his colleagues proposed that children growing up in harsh and unpredictable environments possess "hidden talents"—enhanced cognitive and social abilities adapted to stressful or unpredictable conditions.[48] A fast life history strategy involves greater risk-taking and aggression, often with poor cognitive and mental health outcomes. Yet, from an evolutionary perspective a fast life history strategy affords potentially adaptive outcomes for children growing up in harsh and unpredictable conditions when it makes more sense to prioritize short-term success over what might be best in the long term.

I assume it's easy to see how an academic like myself would find this pattern interesting, but it has broader implications. I mentioned that people following a fast life history strategy often have poor mental health outcomes, frequently associated with impulsive and antisocial behaviors. These outcomes are expected by the *developmental psychopathology* model, the dominant model for explaining children's reactions to high-risk (harsh and unpredictable) environments: these stressful experiences disrupt normal development, adversely affecting children's well-being. Yet, stress has always been part of the human experience, and many of our ancestors had to deal with extremely stressful conditions, as do many contemporary humans today. From an evolutionary-developmental perspective, stressful early environments do not so much disrupt development as they direct or regulate development toward strategies that are apt to be adaptive (or were for our ancestors) under harsh conditions. Conversely, for children who experience supportive and well-resourced environments, development is directed toward strategies adaptive in those contexts.[49]

From an evolutionary-developmental perspective, the risky and sometimes violent behaviors of teens and young adults growing up in high-risk environments do not represent a form of psychopathology but, rather, an adaptive response to growing up in harsh and unpredictable conditions. Having unprotected sex, selling drugs, and using violence to compete for status and respect are still socially problematic and sometimes criminal. We do not have to accept such behavior, saying in effect, "It's part of human nature, and thus inevitable," or "It evolved, and therefore there's nothing we can do about it." This is nonsense. Just because something evolved does not mean that it cannot be changed (humans are highly plastic, after all), and more critically, being "evolved" or "biologically based" says nothing about its moral standing. This is the *naturalistic fallacy*, the false belief that if something is evolved (or is "natural") it must be "good" or "moral," or at least accepted as part of human nature. What an evolutionary-developmental perspective does tell us, however, is that early harsh environments prepare children for a life in later harsh environments, and understanding this should cause us to view the problematic actions of adolescents and young adults differently, to search for different types of solutions to solve these problems, and to take advantage of the strengths and abilities of people growing up in high-risk environments.[50]

Orchids and Dandelions

Although early environments clearly influence the type of life strategies children follow, this can't be the entire picture. Not all children growing up in harsh and unpredictable environments engage in risky behavior and have an opportunistic view of life, nor do all children who grow up with ample resources and loving parents take the slow-and-steady path through life. You likely know siblings who, despite growing up in the same house, followed different courses on their way to adulthood. So life history theory does not perfectly predict a child's developmental trajectory (nor does any other theory that I'm aware of). One factor that seems to modify the effect that circumstances have on children is their susceptibility to being influenced by outside forces. This is referred to as *differential sensitivity to context* and is another important factor in evolved plasticity.[51]

Some children have a greater tendency to modify their behavior in response to events that surround them than others, that is, they have greater plasticity, and this makes them more susceptible to the effects of both especially positive and especially negative environments. Let me tell a tale of two sisters, 4 and 9 years of age when the story begins. Four-year-old Emily had what her mother called a "difficult temperament" as an infant, but she also showed exuberant and infectious joy on her good days. In contrast, her sister Jill was always easygoing. Jill, as any child, had her own peculiarities. She was a fussy eater, was late to talk, but more even keeled than her younger sister. Personality differences between the two girls became exaggerated when their parents divorced. Emily had been a Daddy's girl, and she missed her father greatly. Her difficult temperament returned, along with difficult behavior. She would throw tantrums more typical of a 2-year-old. She would crawl under the bed and refuse to come out. She treated her mother's new boyfriends with contempt. Her parents and grandparents were frequently called to the school to help deal with Emily's latest outburst. Jill, by comparison, took the divorce, visitations with her father, economic hardship, and mother's new boyfriends in stride. Yes, she was upset at first but after a while learned to live with the new situation. When the girls' mother remarried and life settled down, so eventually did Emily. Emily went from a problem child that no teacher wanted in his or her class, to a favorite—a joy to have in class, and, when she put her mind to it, a top academic student. Jill did fine as well.

She was a good student, but the occasional C and even D did not bother her that much.

Emily and Jill reflect two ends of a continuum of sensitivity to context, sometimes called the orchid and the dandelion. Jill is a *dandelion child*. The flower (or weed) survives in nearly all environments. It may do a little better if given extra water or fertilizer, but it will also do OK in times of drought or deluge. Dandelion children are not all that sensitive to a range of both positive and negative environments; they'll do fine under most conditions, so long as they don't need to make drastic changes in their behavior. In contrast, Emily is an *orchid child*. Like the flower, orchid children are highly sensitive to their environments, tending to thrive in positive environments and suffer in negative ones. They are impacted by their environment both "for better and for worse" relative to dandelion children.[52] Although the dandelion–orchid distinction is actually a continuum, about 20% of children have biologies—as reflected by changes in heart rate, blood pressure, and cortisol levels, for example—that make them highly sensitive to environmental change, that is, orchid children.

Let me provide one research example to further illustrate the difference between orchid and dandelion children. In one study, researchers used a measure of heart rate variability with respiration that reflects the nervous system's response to stress and served as a measure of 5- and 6-year-old children's ability to biologically regulate reactions to environmental stimuli.[53] Children who had high levels of physiological reactivity (that is, orchid children) and who lived in high-stress homes as reflected by low family income, harsh parenting, and maternal depression, showed poor psychological adjustment (for instance, poor school performance, increased externalizing behavior), whereas highly reactive children from low-stress homes showed much more positive outcomes. That is, these orchid children flourished when early life conditions were positive but suffered when they were negative. In contrast, the less-sensitive dandelion children showed little change for most measures, regardless of the level of adversity in their home environment.

There are clues as to whether a child may be more on the orchid or dandelion end of the spectrum, and those include level of anxiety and temperament. On average, highly fearful and anxious children and infants with difficult temperaments are more likely to be orchid children, and thus highly sensitive to context, than less-anxious and more-easygoing children.[54] This pattern was found in a review of research that examined the findings of the relation between temperament and psychological adjustment in 84 longitudinal studies.[55] The authors reported generally good adjustment in terms of internalizing and externalizing behaviors and of social and cognitive competence for children with difficult temperaments (orchid children) growing up in supportive homes. In contrast, these highly reactive children fared less well when they experienced negative, harsh parenting. Children with easy temperaments (dandelion children) were less affected by differences in quality of parenting.

Children vary both in terms of their biologies and their experiences, and natural selection has been sensitive to these differences, producing different types of children with varying degrees of plasticity. By producing both orchid and dandelion children, parents can hedge their bets, so to speak, with parents having some children with a high degree of plasticity and sensitivity to context, and others who will thrive in the "expected" environment.[56] Parents cannot do this intentionally, but scientists have discovered that children's sensitivity to context is associated with variants of genes, and there is evidence that children's prenatal sensitivity to stress may increase their sensitivity to parenting effects.[57] Although natural selection is not forward looking, it has shaped children's biologies to be sensitive to early environmental conditions and has generated enough genetic diversity within the species to produce a range of potentially successful adults.[58]

Epigenetics

Children are changeable. In this chapter I have emphasized how children's evolved plasticity has afforded them the ability to adapt to a wide range of environments and to counter the effects of early negative ones. Such evolutionary explanations attempt to explain why, and perhaps how, through natural selection or other evolutionary mechanisms (for example, byproducts, or spandrels) children evolved the ability to adjust their development to aspects of their early environment. Natural selection does not possess precognition, that is, "knowing" what the future will bring. Based on what worked for one's ancestors, natural selection can select physiological, neurological, and psychological mechanisms that are responsive to early environments in anticipation of what a future environment might be like. If it worked for our foreparents, it might work for today's children.

Evolutionary explanations of why some behavior or thought pattern is the way it is are referred to as *distal* (as in "distant") *explanations*. How did some way of thinking, pattern of development, or behavior help our ancestors survive? Evolutionary explanations are incomplete, however. Natural selection gives us only the big picture, and we need to know the immediate causes of behavior, or *proximate* (as in "proximity") *explanations*. Depending on one's level of analyses, proximate explanations can be in terms of history of reinforcement (rewards and punishments), physiology (response to cortisol or other hormones), genetics (possessing one variant versus another variant of a particular gene), or brain structure and activity. Throughout this chapter I've alluded to some proximate causes for the plasticity children show in some contexts. These include physiological changes of how they manage stress, which combination of genes they possess, or changes in their brain structure or function. In recent years a new proximate level of causation has been identified, one that affects all other levels. The process is called *epigenetics* and explains how, at the molecular level, changes are mediated.

Epigenetics literally means "above genetics." According to developmental psychologist David Moore in his book *The Developing Genome: An Introduction to Behavioral Epigenetics*, epigenetics refers to "how genetic material is activated or deactivated—that is, expressed—in different contexts."[59] Just as we inherit DNA from our parents, we also inherit chemical epigenetic markers that regulate genes—turn them on at certain times, off at others, and determine how much protein they produce. It was once believed that epigenetic effects were active only early in development, turning off genes, for example, that were responsible for making fingers and toes. Once you have the full complement of 10, you don't need or want any more, and chemicals in the cytoplasm of cells cause the genes associated with producing the various digits to turn off and stay off. This epigenetic process assures that we don't have fingers growing from our livers, nor an extra pinky develop once our hands are fully formed. It would be useful if we could activate these genes sometimes when we lose a finger or toe due to an accident, but as yet we cannot. In recent years, scientists have discovered that epigenetic mechanisms occur not only in early development but also throughout life, and they seem to be the mechanism responsible for modifying genetic activity as a result of experience.

There are a variety of biochemical mechanisms involved in epigenetics. The one we understand best is *DNA methylation*. Chemicals from the methyl group (written CH_3 by chemists) exist in the cytoplasm of cells and can become attached to some of the nucleic acids (the chemical components of DNA), altering what a particular stretch of DNA "does," specifically, whether a gene will produce instructions for making proteins (which, essentially, is what genes do). Genes that are highly methylated shut down. Other cytoplasmic chemicals can become attached to stretches of DNA, effectively activating genes, a process called *acetylation* (see Figure 2.8).

DNA methylation can be measured through blood or even scrapings from the inside of a person's cheek. There are now dozens of studies showing that methylation, or other epigenetic mechanisms, is the primary mechanism by which experience modifies gene action and thus behavior. This led Dutch developmental psychologist Marinus van IJzendoorn and his colleagues to define child development as "experiences being sculpted in the organism's DNA through methylation."[60]

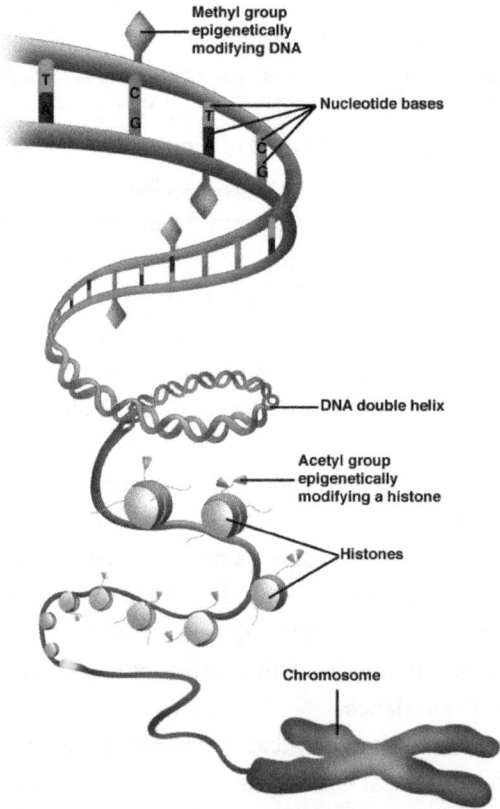

Figure 2.8. A schematic diagram of DNA, showing nucleic bases, the double helix, and methyl-group and acetyl-group epigenetic modifications.
Source: Moore, 2015, p. 40.

Much of this research in the area of child development has focused on the effects of early (sometimes prenatal) stress on later development. How does one decide which genes to investigate? One technique is to assess methylation for the entire genome. Humans have about 20,000 genes, with many genes having multiple "promoter" regions, which act as on–off switches (or more appropriately, dimmer switches) for gene action. For example, in one study assessing more than 470,000 promoter regions, significant relations were found between quality of parenting (measured in early adolescence) and DNA methylation at age 19 for nearly 24,000 regions, with a subset of these methylated regions showing positive relations with adolescent health (more supportive parenting associated with better health) and socioeconomic status (higher socioeconomic status associated with better health).[61]

Another technique for assessing epigenetic effects involves targeting specific genes known to be associated with particular psychological processes. The glucocorticoid receptor is one such gene (NR3C1), known to be associated with the regulation of the stress hormone cortisol. A number of studies have reported relations between early experience (especially stressful experience), methylation of the promotor region of this gene, and later psychosocial functioning.[62] For example, in one study, 11- to 14-year-old children who had experienced physical maltreatment showed greater methylation to portions of the NR3C1 gene and with a gene associated with nerve growth factor than children who had not experienced maltreatment. Given the association between the glucocorticoid receptor gene and stress regulation, the greater methylation of the NR3C1 gene may result in less than optimal functioning later in life. Other research has found a link between high levels of stress (including war stress) experienced prenatally and DNA methylation of the glucocorticoid receptor gene at birth, and these effects can persist for years.[63] For instance, in one study, pregnant women's ratings of hardship during the 1998 Quebec Ice Storm was related to levels of DNA methylation in their children's genes associated with the immune system 13 years later.[64]

Much more needs to be learned about how experiences influence gene expression, but the findings from the embryonic field of behavioral epigenetics make it clear that genes alone do not cause behavior—genes are as much affected by the actions of the organism, which is the vehicle for the genes, as they are responsible for generating those actions.

The study of epigenetics holds great promise. Perhaps the greatest benefits of an increased understanding of epigenetics will be in medicine. There are dozens of scientific journals and books dedicated to elucidating the role of epigenetic mechanisms in diseases from cancer to hair loss. However, one should not lose sight of the benefits that an understanding of *behavioral* epigenetics can provide, particularly with respect to the development of mental health associated with early-life stress. To quote developmental psychologist Elisabeth Conradt, "epigenetic research can advance research on early-life stress because epigenetic processes may help explain how early-life stress becomes biologically embedded and which children are most susceptible to this stress."[65] Epigenetics also has important implications for how species changes over evolutionary time, and we'll revisit the role epigenetics might have played in human phylogeny in the next chapter.

Changeable Children

It is a common misconception that evolutionary explanations of human behavior and thought imply an imperviousness to change: "It evolved, it's instinctive, and thus not subject to change." If that's what an evolutionary explanation actually implied, I wouldn't blame people for opposing it, and I would not be a fan of it myself. But evolutionary explanations do not imply this. All multicellular organisms evolved the ability to change in response to environmental conditions, but such plasticity may be greatest in humans, in part because of our long life spans (long-lived species need to be able to learn, and thus they retain some plasticity into old age), and in part because of the wide variety of ecological and cultural environments in which humans live. Plasticity is an evolved feature of *Homo sapiens*, and this is especially so early in life.

Evolution itself is a developmental concept; it involves change over long stretches of time, which requires plasticity at a different level of analysis—not over the course of a lifetime but over geological time. Moreover, the plasticity seen in the development of contemporary children was likely characteristic of our forechildren. Our ancestors not only evolved, but they also developed, and it was during their development that important changes took place, making us the species we are today.

3

Adaptable Ancestors

Developmental Plasticity and Evolution

If change in behavior over minutes, hours, or days is learning, change in individuals over a lifetime is development, and change in a species over geologic time is evolution, what do you call change in a population over decades? I don't know either, but a good example of it is the *Flynn effect*. The New Zealand psychologist James Flynn was the first to point out that in countries across the globe the average performance on IQ tests has steadily risen over the past hundred years or so.[1] IQ is intended to be a measure of general intelligence, and tests designed to tap IQ are deliberately constructed so that the average score is 100. The tests must be revised from time to time as the average score drifts from 100. One reason scores may drift is that items relevant to people in 1980, for example, may not be so relevant to people in 2020. For instance, one item on the Information subtest of the Wechsler Intelligence Scale for Children–Revised (WISC-R) published in 1974 is "Where does turpentine come from?" This may have been a reasonable item to ask someone 50 years ago, although I'd bet few people would know the answer today. (None of the 70 college students in my current class knew the answer.) However, having obsolete items like "turpentine" on the test would result in lower scores for contemporary people, not higher scores. Yet scores are getting higher.* Depending on which IQ test or subtest is examined, average scores increased from 3 to 15 points *per decade* (see Figure 3.1). This would mean that someone with an average IQ in 2020 would be in the "gifted" category in 1960 and off the genius charts in 1920.

This is not the place to get into a discussion of what IQ "really" measures— it has its champions and its detractors. Let's agree that it does measure some

---

* Modern versions of IQ tests still have an average of 100, but this is because they are periodically revised, making them more difficult relative to earlier versions. There are several ways of evaluating whether average IQ scores have changed over historical time. One is to examine the scores of many people who take the same test at different times (for example, in 1960 versus in 1980). Another is to give people today versions of earlier IQ tests, standardized on samples decades before.

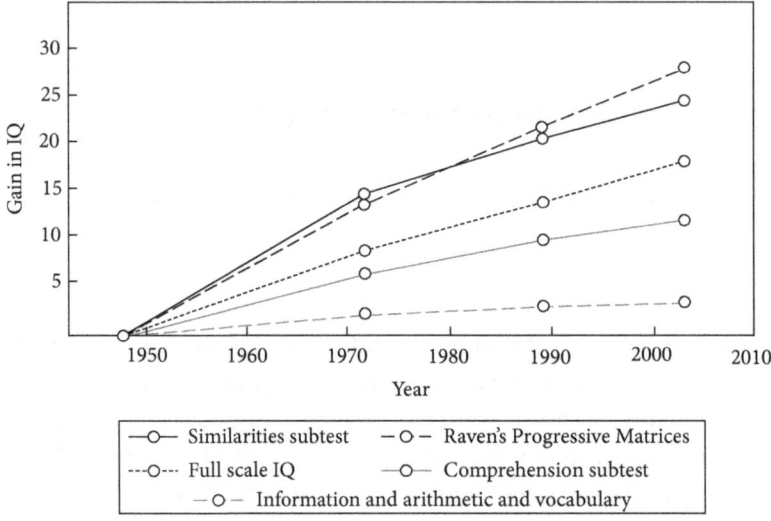

Figure 3.1. Examples of gains in intelligence test scores: Shown here are IQ gains from 1948 to 2002 in the United States as measured by Raven's Progressive Matrices, the Wechsler Intelligence Scale for Children (Full Scale), and several subtests of the Wechsler Intelligence Scale for Children. These are the gains that would have occurred if the tests were not made more difficult and the scoring systems were not adjusted at each test revision. (Adapted from Flynn, 2007, p. 8, with permission.)

important aspect of intellectual functioning, and a steady increase in our population's average scores over the decades suggests something important is going on both in the culture and in people's brains. One possibility is that more people are becoming more educated, and this is certainly true. One recent study examined data from over 600,000 people and reported that one year of education was associated with an increase of between 1 and 5 IQ points.[2] However, the greatest gains are found in subtests measuring a type of intelligence referred to as *fluid*—abilities that are thought to be biologically determined and reflected in tests such as memory span (for example, remembering sets of random digits in order) and most tests of spatial thinking (for example, *Block Design*, in which people reproduce designs shown to them using nine cubes, colored red on two sides, white on two sides, and red and white on two sides). Fluid abilities are supposedly less influenced by education or culture than are *crystallized* abilities, reflected in tests of general knowledge (for example, "What does democracy mean?") and verbal comprehension (for example, "What are some reasons we need soldiers?").

Crystallized abilities have improved as well, although not as much as fluid abilities. So what's going on here?

Greater educational opportunity surely is playing a role, and so is better nutrition and healthcare, but Flynn and others believe that the primary reason for the change in fluid abilities is the increasing complexity of modern life. Photography, picture magazines, billboards, and movies became commonplace in the early parts of the 20th century, followed by television, VCRs, DVDs, computers, the Internet, video games, and smartphones. Children today grow up inundated with visual information they must make sense of, and doing so may directly affect fluid intelligence. Flynn argues that greater use of technology, more people being engaged in intellectually demanding work, and improvements in education have led to a greater number of people dealing with abstract concepts than was the case in decades past, which, in turn, is responsible for elevated IQ scores.

Although there is great debate about what the Flynn effect means, one clear interpretation is that people within a culture have the plasticity to change how they think, not just in terms of things they know (for example, "selfies" versus "turpentine"), but in how they process information at a basic level and how they deal with abstract concepts. These differences begin in infancy and carry on through childhood and adolescence. For example, despite having more years of experience dealing with computers and electronic media than my children, grandchildren, and students, I am usually the one asking them for help with the new technology rather than the other way around. They are *digital natives*, and their proficiency with the media is not because of the number of years they've been involved with the digital world, but because they grew up with it. My cohort can function quite well in the digital world, thank you very much, although it's like we have been learning a second language. Because we didn't grow up with digital technology, we always "speak with an accent," so to speak.

Could these changes in thinking that happen in a population over decades become the target of natural selection? Possibly, although I'm not holding my breath that the next generation of children will be born knowing how to use Snapchat or how to navigate Netflix. (They could both be obsolete by then, anyway.) Needless to say, children who are digital natives clearly process information differently than children of earlier generations, and the result is population-wide changes in thinking. When environments change and members of the population have the flexibility to change with them, those changes can be "selectable," especially if the population is relatively small and the changes result in better chances for survival or reproduction. I don't see this happening for the 7 billion or more *Homo sapiens* inhabiting the planet now, at least not in the short run, but I can easily imagine it having happened for some of our hominin ancestors.

Developmental Plasticity as the Engine of Evolutionary Change

In the previous chapter we saw how children's evolved plasticity permitted them to adjust to a wide range of circumstances and to recover from the negative effects of an early environment. Humans, and other big-brained animals, remain plastic throughout life. It is plasticity that permits learning, and we never stop doing that, although our behavioral, cognitive, and neural flexibility does decline as we age. Plasticity is greatest in the young. Once a developmental path is taken, it can constrain future development, making it less likely that a totally new course can be traversed, or in the words of biologist John Paul Scott, "organization inhibits reorganization."[3]

What role might such developmental plasticity have played in evolution? Let me sketch the major premise. Because plasticity is greatest early in life, changes in development brought about through responsiveness to the environment produce behavioral changes in individuals, and these new behaviors become subject to natural selection. Individuals whose novel behaviors give them a leg up on other members of their group will be more likely to survive and will leave more offspring than their less-plastic compatriots. As these more-successful members of the species inhabit new ecological niches, they actively modify their environment, creating new selection pressures. Such niche construction may be especially potent early in development.[4] Genetic changes, either in terms of mutations or shifts in gene expression, follow. Once new forms or behaviors are produced in development, then and only then can natural selection operate to produce evolution. In the words of developmental biologist Mary Jane West-Eberhard,[5] "Adaptive evolution [improvement in a species due to selection] is a two-step process: first the generation of variation by development, then the screening of that variation by selection."

If you were paying attention in your high school or college biology courses, you might find the above explanation problematic. This is likely not what you were taught, and in fact, you may have been taught that this scenario is the antithesis of a proper Darwinian explanation of evolution. This is because the predominant view of evolution, initially formulated in the 1930s and termed the *modern synthesis* (or *neo-Darwinism*), explicitly eliminated any influence of development on evolution and viewed genetic mutations to be the cause of evolution. The modern synthesis integrated Darwin's theory of evolution by natural selection with the genetic theory of inheritance, made possible by the work of Gregor Mendel, the Czech Augustinian friar, whose research on pea plants was originally published in an obscure science journal in 1866 and rediscovered by several scientists in 1900. Although Darwin's theory could explain how animals with some traits survived and others died (that is, natural selection), Darwin did not have a proper theory of inheritance. In fact, he adopted French biologist Jean Baptiste Lamarck's *theory of inheritance of acquired characteristics*, which proposed that adaptive features gained during an organism's lifetime can be passed onto its offspring—think of giraffes stretching to reach leaves high in a tree and then passing on longer necks to offspring, or blacksmiths passing on their acquired muscles to their sons and daughters. With the discovery of Mendel's research, this theory seemed unlikely, and the German biologist August Weismann demonstrated the separation between what happens to the body during life and what is transmitted by the germ line (reproductive cells). For example, Weismann cut off the tails of infant mice and then bred tailless male mice with tailless female mice. After cutting off the tails of more than 900 mice over five generations, tails on newborn mice persisted. Weismann's simple experiment was hardly conclusive; nonetheless, it served as the death knell for Lamarckian inheritance and became part of the foundation of the modern synthesis. The simple message was that what happens during the lifetime of an individual (that is, across development) has no influence on evolution, which is caused only by random mutations. From this perspective, development is little more than an *epiphenomenon*—something that is very important to the individual but inconsequential to the evolution of the species.

The Baldwin Effect

Despite the dominance of the modern synthesis on evolutionary thought throughout the 20th century, there were always some scientists who continued to argue for a prominent role of development in evolution, while also arguing that such a role is fully consistent with a Darwinian perspective and not a backdoor way of rehabilitating Lamarckism. One of the earliest theories to make

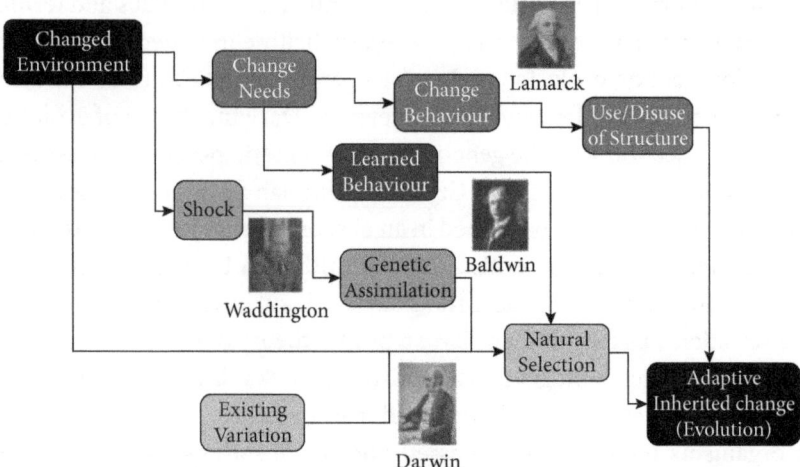

Figure 3.2. The Baldwin effect compared with Lamarck's theory of evolution, Darwinian evolution, and Waddington's genetic assimilation. All the theories offer explanations of how organisms respond to a changed environment with adaptive inherited change.

Source: From https://en.wikipedia.org/wiki/File:Lamarck_Compared_to_Darwin,_Baldwin,_Waddington.svg. This file is licensed under the Creative Commons Attribution-Share Alike 4.0 International license.

such arguments was put forth by developmental psychologist James Mark Baldwin around the turn of the 20th century.[6] (Similar theories were formulated about the same time by comparative psychologist Conway Lloyd Morgan and paleontologist Henry Fairfield Osborn, but Baldwin seemed to have the better press agent, and the phenomenon became known as the *Baldwin effect*; see Figure 3.2.) Baldwin proposed that individuals within a population gained reproductive advantages by engaging in novel behaviors and through learning, especially in social settings. Baldwin focused on an organism's response to stress, postulating that animals that have sufficient developmental plasticity, that is, who can modify their behavior in response to environmental stress, will be more successful than less-plastic animals and will pass this increased responsiveness to their offspring. Assuming future generations experience the same stressors, they, too, will be at an advantage. Over many generations, these once-acquired behaviors will become fixed and expressed without the need of a provoking environment. Baldwin called this process *organic selection*.

At first blush, organic selection seems to be a form of inheritance of acquired characteristics, yet this is not the case. Animals had to already have had the genetic propensity to adapt to specific predictable conditions (that is, plasticity), and following repeated generations in which this ability enhanced survival, those possessing the ability survived in greater numbers than those who did not, eventually to the point that natural selection eliminated variation in the trait, and all members of the group expressed the adaptive behavior. Thus, genes continue to remain important, although it is behavior that takes the lead in evolution. The reason is that behavioral expression is more susceptible to change (more plastic) than are genes or morphology (physical structure). That is, behavior has the greatest sensitivity to environmental influence, and behavior is especially plastic early in life. Some mainstream biologists recognized the advantage of an inheritance system that can respond quickly to environmental changes in nutrition, disease, climate, or predation, and referred to such a system as *soft inheritance* in contrast to the slower responding "hard inheritance" reflected by genetic mutation.[7] Yet, most biologists remained skeptical of soft inheritance, continuing to associate it with Lamarckism.[8]

Epigenetic Theories of Evolution

The Baldwin effect belongs to a class of *epigenetic theories* that hold that a developing organism's adaptability to environmental changes is an important mechanism for evolution. (We've run into the related concepts of both *epigenesis*—an emergent process by which an organism's structure and function change from relatively undifferentiated states to increasingly specialized, differentiated forms throughout development—and *epigenetics*—how genetic material is activated or deactivated in different contexts—in Chapters 1 and 2, respectively.) Baldwin's idea predated the modern synthesis, but related proposals emerged following the integration of Darwinian and genetic theory. For example, the Russian biologist Ivanovich Schmalhausen, like Baldwin, advanced the idea that individuals who were able to adapt to local environmental changes were more successful than those who could not, and the new adaptations eventually came under genetic control, being expressed without the environmental stimulation that initially began the process.[9] Schmalhausen proposed that this could happen because organisms have great genetic reserve that is only expressed under extreme conditions, such as climate change, new predators, or other drastic changes in one's life circumstances. In other words, organisms have many stretches of DNA that are not normally expressed but become so under certain stressful environments (or other stretches of DNA that become quieted). From here, the process follows the one proposed by the modern synthesis: Individuals with genes associated with survival and reproduction live and pass on these genes, whereas those without such genes die or, at least, produce fewer offspring. What's different with Schmalhausen's proposal from that of the modern synthesis is the idea that environmentally provoked adaptabilities have a genetic basis, consistent with Baldwin's ideas.

Despite the appeal of Baldwin and Schmalhausen's theories, there was little hard evidence to support their proposals. This was to change with studies performed in the 1950s by the British biologist Conrad Waddington.[10] In a now-classic experiment, Waddington exposed fruit flies (*Drosophila melanogaster*, a favorite research subject of geneticists) during the embryonic (pupal) stage to heat shock. Although this killed some flies, others survived, and some of these developed wings with few or no cross veins. Waddington selectively bred the no-cross-vein flies, exposed some of the resulting embryos to heat shock, and continued the experiment for 14 generations. Now, some of the surviving fruit flies showed the no-cross-vein pattern *without* being exposed to heat shock. That is, just as Baldwin and Schmalhausen predicted, a characteristic (here, lack of cross veins in the wings) became expressed in the offspring without the need of exposure to the initially provoking stimulus (here, heat shock) after multiple generations.[11] Waddington referred to this as *genetic assimilation*, which he defined as "the conversion of an acquired character into an inherited one; or better, as a shift towards greater importance of heredity in the degree to which the character is acquired or inherited."[12]

One shortcoming of this initial demonstration is that the "no-cross-vein wings" provided no adaptive benefit—they just happened to be associated with survival of heat shock but afforded no survival or reproductive advantage. Later studies addressed this problem. In one set of experiments, Waddington raised fruit flies on a high-salt medium and selectively bred flies that developed larger anal papillae (small rounded protuberances on their backsides) in response to the high-salt environment. Large anal papillae facilitate the excretion of salt from the body, making such a modification adaptive. After 21 generations of selective breeding, flies developed larger anal papillae without being exposed to a high-salt medium, demonstrating genetic assimilation for an adaptive trait.

Since Waddington's early experiments there have been many demonstrations of genetic assimilation on a large variety of plant and animal species.[13] One that always fascinated me is an experiment with the water flea *Daphnia cucullate*. This small (0.01–0.20 inch) flea develops a protective helmet when exposed to the larva of predators (a type of midge, *Chaoborus flavicans*), reducing its chances of being eaten, which is clearly an adaptation. The next generation of water fleas also develop the larger helmet, even when they are not exposed to predators in their environment. The authors of this study interpreted their findings as reflecting a form of maternally induced defense due to adaptive plasticity across generations.[14]

All of Waddington's examples, as well as that of the water fleas, involve a change in part of the body—wings, anal papillae, or protective helmet. What about changes in behavior? Central to Baldwin's claim is that changes in behavior, especially early in life, lead animals to solve new problems or to discover new niches to inhabit. A number of modern theorists have taken up Baldwin's banner, arguing that changes in behavior as a result of responses to novel environments are frequently the first step in evolutionary change, preceding genetic change.[15] Let me provide a few examples, some from over half a century ago, and others taking advantage of 21st century technology.

Two groups of researchers in the 1960s independently demonstrated transgenerational transmission of behavior in laboratory rats. In one study, infant rats were removed from their mothers and placed in a can partially filled with wood shavings for 3 minutes, once a day, for their first 20 days of life. The authors referred to this as *handling*, which is a form of stress for infant rats. Other rats were not handled but received typical laboratory experience with their mothers. The rats were then bred for two more generations. The grandpups of the handled and nonhandled female rats were subsequently tested for activity level in a novel environment, a 32-square-inch open field, which rats find stressful. The researchers reported that grandpups of the handled rats showed greater activity, reflective of greater exploration, in the open field than the grandpups of the nonhandled rats. This effect was especially large for the female pups: that is, experiences of the grandmothers affected the behavior of their grandpups.[16] In another experiment, pups from two strains of rats (called C57BL and BALD) were raised either by their natural mothers (C57BL pups raised by C57BL mothers, and BALD pups raised by BALD mothers) or cross-fostered (C57BL pups raised by BALD mothers, and BALD pups raised by C57BL mothers). The offspring and grandoffspring of these mothers were then tested for their ability to learn to press a bar to receive a reward in the presence of a visual stimulus. Learning was greater for rats of either the C57BL or BALD strain when they were raised by BALD mothers, and this effect persisted over two generations. There was something in the way the BALD mothers raised their pups that contributed to their ability to learn. The researcher could not identify the mechanisms involved but suggested that "a nongenetic system of inheritance based upon transmission of parental influences is potentially available to all mammals."[17]

We have a much better idea of the mechanism involved in soft inheritance today, namely methylation and other epigenetic mechanisms. Recall from Chapter 2 that gene expression becomes modified as a result of experience, with methylation generally shutting down gene expression and acetylation activating genes. Contemporary research by neuroscientist Michael Meaney and his colleagues, also looking at the effects of maternal behavior in rats on dealing with stress, illustrates this nicely. Meaney and his associates showed that rat pups who are licked a lot by their mothers tend to show less stress as adults in an open-field setting than rat pups who are licked less often. When the female pups become mothers themselves, they show the same licking patterns as their mothers, along with the same epigenetic (methylation) markers. This is not a simple effect of inheriting a low-licking versus a high-licking gene, for the effect is still found when rats are cross-fostered (for example, a rat whose biological mother was low-licking and whose foster mother was high-licking): As adults, the female rats show the same licking behavior toward their pups and the same epigenetic markers as their *foster* mothers, not their *biological* mothers.[18] According to Meaney, "Individual differences in behavioral and neuroendocrine responses to stress in rats are, in part, derived from naturally occurring variations in maternal care. Such effects might serve as a possible mechanism by which selected traits are transmitted from one generation to another."[19]

The case for inherited epigenetic effects is less clear in humans, although several studies have reported evidence of epigenetic inheritances for some physiological functions in *Homo sapiens*.[20] Perhaps the best documented (though still controversial) evidence for epigenetic inheritance in humans comes from research looking at the children and grandchildren of women who were pregnant during the Dutch Hunger Winter of 1944–1945. In the latter years of World War II, poor weather and Nazi policies resulted in extreme famine in the Netherlands. Women who were pregnant during the famine experienced not only a lack of calories for themselves, but also for their unborn babies. Researchers followed the children who were conceived during the famine as well as the next generation. Women who suffered severe malnutrition early in pregnancy gave birth to children who showed lifelong changes in methylation markers for genes linked with growth, development, and metabolism.[21] What is fascinating is that when these female babies became mothers themselves, their offspring had lower birthweights and ponderal indices (ratio of length to weight) than the offspring of adequately nourished mothers. That is, experiences of the grandmother while pregnant influenced the development of her *grandchildren*.[22] A similar phenomenon of the effects of malnutrition has been reported for *men*; a grand*father's* malnourishment during childhood affected the growth rate and health (susceptibility to cardiovascular disease) of his grandchildren.[23]

***

Epigenetic theories of evolution emphasize the role of development in generating novel behaviors or responses to extreme environments, and some scientists have viewed such arguments as the antithesis of Darwinian evolution. However, developmental variation and natural selection are not competing explanations for evolution but, rather, should be seen as two aspects of a single process. Weismann's contention of the separation of the somatic (body) and germ line is basically correct. Nonetheless, the experiences of an animal over the course of development are also important to evolution. According to anthropologist Melvin Konner, "At the leading edge of adaptation, experience during individual lives can establish a foothold for a new local dynamic of natural selection . . . Experience, far from being wasted because of the independence of the genome from the rest of the organism, pioneers what may become fundamental genetic changes."[24] And because juveniles are the most plastic, curious, and playful members of social species, including humans and presumably our hominin ancestors, children will often be the ones to discover new solutions to old problems or to investigate, construct, and inhabit new niches, setting the stage for natural selection to "do its thing."

One can romanticize the idea of children leading the way in evolutionary change—imagining fearless juveniles daring to boldly go where no hominin has gone before. Chances are, however, that many of the innovations discovered by juveniles that led to evolutionary change were accomplished in the presence of their mothers. In fact, because of the intimate relationship they have with their offspring, especially in mammals, mothers, more often than not, may have been the "environment" that these enterprising infants and juveniles were responsive to.

Mother Knows Best

A few readers of this book may recall the 1950's TV series *Father Knows Best*, depicting the everyday life and adventures of an American Midwestern middle-class family. The title reflects the paternalism of the era, with the wise father handing out advice to his children. In reality, although fathers have always been important, they are not nearly as important as mothers.

Mothers as Primary Caretakers

The greater importance of mothers relative to fathers in development is likely not a surprise. It may be politically correct to say that men are as capable of caring for children as women are, and this may even be true, if men's lactation deficiencies are ignored. But historically, and presumably prehistorically, fathers have provided only a paltry amount of childcare compared with mothers.[25] There are more single fathers raising children today than there were in the past, and they seem to be doing a decent job—an indication that men *can* be effective caretakers. In gender-egalitarian societies, men are spending far more time in childcare than their fathers and grandfathers did, and they are approaching parity in childcare with women. Throughout time and across cultures, however, it is women who have been principally responsible for childcare, and thus who have had the greater impact on their children's development and evolution. According to Konner, there is not a single traditional society in which fathers devote more time to childcare than mothers.[26]

To some extent, women's greater time and effort in parenting—in investing in their children—is a matter of being a mammal. In all mammals, a certain amount of female investment is necessary, or obligatory. Conception and prenatal development occur internally in the female, although it doesn't have to be so. For some seahorses, females deposit their eggs in the sacs of males, who then inseminate them, with the baby seahorses developing within the males' bodies. It doesn't work that way for mammals, however. Once born, mammals require substantial care to survive, and some of this care can come only from mothers. I'm referring, of course, to nursing. The biological class "mammals" (or "Mammalia") gets its name from the glands that provide milk to infants, and this is something only females can do (or only females could do before the invention of baby formula). There is a long history of exclusive female childcare in mammals. In 95% of mammal species, fathers provide no care to their offspring once they are born.[27] It's not that these fathers are deadbeat dads, abandoning their mates when they should be lending a helping hand (or paw). Rather, females have evolved to do all the parenting. Males of these species are simply not needed and are essentially just sperm donors.

Humans are among the 5% of mammals for which fathers provide some childcare, although selection pressures have been much stronger on mothers. As the current and previous chapters have emphasized, we are a flexible species, having the plasticity to alter our behavior in response to novel environments, and this is true for how men and women invest in their offspring. Biology does not dictate that women have the role of caring mothers or that men have the "bring-home-the bacon-but-let-your-spouse-handle-the-children" role. Nonetheless, natural selection has biased women to be more concerned with children and childcare than men. The experience of being pregnant, of nursing, and of caring for a dependent infant fosters emotional bonds between mothers and their infants that set the stage for greater involvement in childrearing even after children have been weaned.

Mothers Are Really Important

Women's greater role in childrearing has also affected other aspects of men's and women's psychology. For example, evolutionary psychologist Anne Campbell proposed that although both men and women compete with members of their own sex (intrasexual competition), men tend to compete more vigorously, engaging in more risky and violent behavior than women. One reason for this sex difference is essentially that women are more important than men, at least when it comes to the survival of children.[28] In traditional societies a child without a father usually fares less well than a child with a father, the latter accruing more resources and higher social status; but children without mothers often don't make it to adulthood at all, and if they do their social standing is greatly diminished.

Women not only tend to take fewer risks than men and are less violent in their intrasexual competition, but they also usually live longer. This is surely no surprise to readers, although what might be surprising is that this greater longevity may be tied to women's greater efforts in childcare. Neuroscientist John Morgan Allman looked at the relation between female-to-male longevity and the amount of male care provided to offspring among groups of

Table 3.1. Female/male survival rates as a function of degree of paternal care for selected primates (adapted from Allman, 1999, with permission)

Primate	Female/Male Survival Ratio	Male Care
Chimpanzee	1.42	Rare
Spider monkey	1.27	Rare
Orangutan	1.20	Rare
Gibbon	1.20	Pair living, but little direct role
Gorilla	1.13	Protects, plays with offspring
Human	1.05–1.08	Supports economically, some care
Goeldi's monkey	0.97	Both parents carry infant
Siamang	0.92	Carries infant in second year
Owl monkey	0.87	Carries infant from birth
Titi monkey	0.83	Carries infant from birth

primates. His results are shown in Table 3.1.[29] Chimpanzees are at the top of the list with a female-to-male survival ratio of 1.418, meaning that, on average, females live about 40% longer than males. Male chimpanzees provide little or no care to their offspring. This is due, in part, to not knowing whose child is whose (paternity uncertainty). Chimpanzees have a promiscuous mating style; females when in estrus (or "in heat") copulate with different males. High-ranking males may get more mating opportunities than low-ranking males, but, basically, nobody knows for certain "who's your daddy?" Males, thus, have no need to invest time or resources in offspring that may not be genetically related to them, and female chimps have evolved to do all the parenting. Male spider monkeys, orangutans, and gibbons similarly devote little or no care to their offspring, and females outlive males in these species by about 20%. Male gorillas, who have a high degree of paternity certainty because of their harem-like mating strategy, play with and protect their offspring, and they do slightly better, longevity-wise, with females outliving males by about 12%. The remainder of the list includes males who provide some care and/or economic support for their offspring, beginning with humans (the data here were based on Swedish samples, with women living between 5% and 8% longer than men), and ending with monogamous owl and titi monkeys, in which the males carry the babies from birth. These

South American monkey fathers actually spend more time caring for their offspring than the mothers, and they live about 15% longer than their female partners. The take-away message is that caring for children matters, and those that do the bulk of it live longer, perhaps because they have evolved less-dangerous lifestyles that increase the chance that they will be around to foster their offspring's development. In nearly all mammals, including humans, it is the female who devotes more time to childcare and who also lives longer. It is the exceptions that prove the rule, however, with the fathers in the few species in which they spend more time in childcare than mothers outliving their female mates.

Mothers as the Environment for Evolutionary Change

The idea that "mothers matter," especially for mammals, is not a novel one. Its relevance here is that the early experiences of infant mammals are mostly determined by their mothers. In a certain sense, mothers *are* the environment of infant mammals. If the young of a species, including humans and our ancestors, had the plasticity to change their behavior in response to environmental conditions, mothers were likely an essential part of that environment. There is substantial research on mammals illustrating how mothers affect the acquisition of important behaviors in their offspring, from knowing what to eat and avoiding predators, to responding to stress and mating preferences.[30] Research and theory on the impact of mothers on child development is similarly enormous. At least since the time of Freud, mothers have received both the credit and the blame for their children's psychological outcomes, some of it possibly deserved and some of it not. Might mothers also be responsible for some of our evolved psychological characteristics?

Some of the examples of the transmission of behavior across generations provided earlier can be attributed to mothers. For example, the work of Meaney and his colleagues on the role of mother rats' licking of their pups, and their grandpups' subsequent response to stress, points clearly to maternal effects. In the paragraphs to follow, I outline briefly one line of research that suggests that differences in how chimpanzees are raised can affect aspects of their social cognition, proposing one possible route our ancestors may have taken on the road to a human form of social cognition. (I will discuss this and related work in greater detail in Chapter 6.)

Like humans, chimpanzees are social creatures, and there is strong evidence that they acquire forms of greeting, grooming, and tool use through social learning: that is, chimpanzees learn from others, often through simple observation.[31] There are multiple forms of social learning, however, and chimpanzees raised in the wild or by their mothers in captivity seem not to engage in true imitation, in which the observer both understands the goal of the model's actions and then copies those actions to achieve that goal. Consider a chimpanzee that watches as another chimp rolls a dead log to expose ants, which she then eats. True imitation would involve the observer replicating the actions of the model (rolling the dead log) to achieve the goal (eating ants). Most chimpanzee social learning seems not to involve imitation, but rather *emulation*, in which the goal is recognized (getting some ants to eat) but is attained using other means than the one used by the model (for example, jumping up and down on a log). The exception to this pattern is for *enculturated* chimpanzees that have been raised by humans much as children are raised. These animals are talked to, their caretakers point out people and objects to them, and they are cared for, as much as possible, as human infants and young children are. Under these conditions, when tested beyond the age of 2 years, enculturated chimpanzees imitate the specific behaviors shown to them (for example, clapping cymbals together, putting plastic pegs in a pegboard and hitting them with a hammer), much as human children do, both immediately after observing someone engage in the behavior and after a significant delay.[32]

The point I want to make here is that young chimpanzees have the cognitive plasticity to modify their social cognition in response to a species-*atypical* environment, so that their behavior is more similar to that of a human preschooler than to a mother-reared chimpanzee. Contemporary chimpanzees, which themselves have gone through 5 to 7 million years of evolution since sharing a common ancestor with humans, will never attain the cognitive abilities of modern people, regardless of their early rearing environment. "Planet of the Apes" is purely science fiction and not a prediction of what could happen under certain rearing circumstances. However, assuming our common ancestor with chimpanzees also had such plasticity, changes in the behavior of mothers could have resulted in changes in their offspring's social cognition, giving their progeny an advantage with respect to social learning. These individuals could then mate with other similar animals, resulting in a second generation of imitators. Following the precepts of the Baldwin effect, animals with greater social learning would continue to have an advantage, and this would produce new selection pressures. Over many generations, the once–environmentally induced phenomenon now becomes genetically assimilated, with all (or nearly all) mothers engaging in interactions with their babies that promote advanced forms of social learning.

* * *

There really is no question that mothers are important. I don't want to place mothers on a pedestal, glorifying their role in development or evolution, although I don't think it is overstating the case to say that mammal mothers, on average, contribute more to their offspring's development than fathers do. Mothers serve as a filter or buffer by which their young experience the environment, exposing them to hormones, immune factors, and other chemicals, initially through the placenta and later through milk. As a consequence, a mother contributes greater than 50% of an infant's inheritance than would be predicted by her genetic contribution.[33] Infants who have the plasticity to respond to individual differences in their mothers' actions may develop new, adaptive behaviors without the need of immediate genetic change, leading the way to eventual new species-level behaviors or cognitions. In this scenario, plasticity needs to be features of both mothers and infants. As I wrote elsewhere,

> Note that the plasticity needed for such a scenario must lie both within the infant and the mother. For mammals, many aspects of early environment are interpreted through mothers, making infant mammals especially sensitive to variations in maternal behavior. It is mothers who are the first responders to environmental change.[34]

Do "Smarts" Make You Evolve Faster?

I opened this chapter with the Flynn effect, the steady increase in IQ over the past century. I interpreted this increase as reflecting humans' plasticity, or responsiveness to their environments. As cultures change and new tools for communicating and thinking are developed, children (and to a lesser extent, adults) change as well. If we had IQ tests going back several hundred years, before the advent of universal education, electricity, and credit cards, imagine what the change in IQ would look like. Of course, what constituted intelligent functioning in 1620 may be different than what constitutes intelligent functioning four hundred years later, and each age has had its own intellectual heavy hitters. Few modern *Homo sapiens* could hold a cognitive candle to the likes of political theorists such as Benjamin Franklin, Thomas Jefferson, or Alexander Hamilton; or scientists such as Isaac Newton, Galileo Galilei, or Gottfried Wilhelm Leibniz (imagine inventing calculus from scratch!); or composers such as Johann Sabastian Bach, Wolfgang Amadeus Mozart, or Ludwig von Beethoven (I can't fathom how these composers could write such complex music for so many instruments without the use of a computer). Every epoch has likely had its share of geniuses, although these great minds were the exceptions for their ages. We may not always think well of the intelligence of our fellow man or woman, but if the Flynn effect is any indication, I think it is undeniable that the thought processes of the general population today are far different than that of our counterparts two, three, and four hundred years ago.

We are able to adjust and change (mostly in a positive, more intellectually sophisticated way, I'd argue) to new environments due to our plasticity, but is this plasticity dependent on having a big brain? Other species make adjustments to changes in their world as well, but might the advent of language and symbolic representation—if not unique to humans, at least expressed most profoundly in humans—be responsible for the rapid rate of change in response to environmental circumstances shown by *Homo sapiens*? In other words, are we as a species able to take advantage of our plasticity to develop (and evolve) novel responses to changing environments because we start out so smart to begin with compared with other species? The answer seems to be a qualified "yes."

There is, in fact, a relation between brain size and rate of evolution, at least with respect to anatomical changes. Biologist Jeff Wyles and his colleagues looked at the rate of anatomical change (per million years) in groups of land vertebrates in relation to changes in brain size (relative to body size). As you can see in Table 3.2, members from the *Homo* line (*Homo sapiens* plus our extinct relatives, including *Homo erectus* and *Homo habilis*) and our ancient relatives, the hominoids (apes and extinct species such as *Australopithecines*, excluding *Homo*), show both the highest relative brain sizes and the fastest rates of anatomical change. The rest of the animal groups examined followed suit: as relative brain size increases, rate of anatomical change over evolutionary time also increases.[35] Why the strong relationship? Wyles and his colleagues speculated, consistent with

Table 3.2. Brain size in relation to rate of anatomical evolution (from Wyles, Kunkel, & Wilson, 1983, p. 4396, with permission)

Taxonomic Group	Relative Brain Size	Anatomical Rate
Homo	114	>10
Hominoids	26	2.5
Songbirds	23	1.6
Other mammals	12	0.7
Other birds	4.3	0.7
Lizards	1.2	0.25
Frogs	0.9	0.23
Salamanders	0.8	0.26

our earlier arguments, that behavior can be a major driving force of evolution, and animals with big brains are able to deal with novel environments through innovation and social transmission of information better than less brainy animals. At least one study has confirmed this relationship in mammals: bigger-brained (relative to body size) species were more successful when introduced to new environments than smaller-brained species.[36]

Humans have the largest brains relative to body size of all animals, and we use much of this oversized organ to think, learn, and in general, adapt to changing environments. Might some of humans' cognitive advancements have been especially important in altering the course of human evolution? Some theorists think so, and this is likely best articulated by biological anthropologist Terrance Deacon. Deacon argued that the advent of symbolic representation—being able to think abstractly and use signs and symbols to represent objects, people, and ideas—transformed humans' connection to their environment, with language being the ultimate symbolic tool. According to Deacon:

> Stone and symbolic tools, which were initially acquired with the aid of flexible ape-learning abilities, ultimately turned the table on their users and forced them to adapt to a new niche opened by these technologies. Rather than being just useful tricks, these behavioral prostheses for obtaining food and organizing social behaviors became indispensable elements in a new adaptive complex ... Once symbolic communication became even slightly elaborated in early hominid societies, its unique representational

functions and open-ended flexibility would have led to its use for innumerable purposes with equally powerful reproductive consequences.[37]

Among the purposes of ancient humans' new abilities were the invention of material culture, the sophisticated construction and use of tools, and the transmission of knowledge between individuals and across generations via social learning. As we'll see in later chapters, none of these abilities are wholly unique to humans, yet no other species comes close to using them as effectively as most 4-year-old children do, to say nothing of adults.

You may imagine that it was our adult *Homo* and hominin ancestors who did the bulk of the talking and using of symbolic representation, and this was probably the case. However, language and thinking in symbols have their origins in infancy and childhood, and I will have much to say about big brains, social learning, and development in later chapters. The point I wish to make here is that the plasticity so characteristic of our species is mediated by an oversized brain and the enhanced cognitive and communication abilities a big brain provides. Such brains are not only important for today's children and adults, but they also afforded our ancestors the plasticity they needed to change their behavior and in the process alter the course of human evolution. I'll have more to say about how humans' big brains evolved in the next chapter.

Adaptable Ancestral Children

Plasticity is an evolved feature of our species. For mammals in general, and humans specifically, it is children who display the greatest sensitivity to environments and thus the greatest propensity for change. This is not only true for children growing up in the world today, but also for the children of our hominin ancestors. To be a descendant of people living today, our foremothers and forefathers had to procreate and raise children to maturity. Before ever beginning the mating and parenting routines, however, our foreparents had to get through infancy and childhood themselves, often modifying their behavior or cognition to adapt to ecological conditions. Our ancestors not only evolved, but they also developed. In the process they created new structures and functions and inhabited new niches, all creating new pressures for natural selection to work on. Although traditional thinking has mostly ignored the role of development in evolution, and sometimes even deemed it heretical, theories both old and new have incorporated the idea of developmental plasticity as an engine of evolutionary change, all while remaining within the bounds of Darwinian theory. Development is not only important for the individual, as we've always known, but has also been vital for the evolution of the species, something we seem to have only recently rediscovered.

4

Embryos and Ancestors

Several years ago my students and I had the chance to conduct some social-learning studies at a sanctuary for chimpanzees and orangutans in central Florida. During that time, I struck up a friendship with Grub, a 9-year-old human-reared chimpanzee (Figure 4.1). Maybe it was not exactly a friendship, but more of a friendly acquaintance. After our work routine was completed each day, Grub and I played a game of his invention involving tag and chase. He would begin the game by sticking two fingers through the heavy fence in his outdoor enclosure, and I would tag them, causing him to run clockwise along the side of the enclosure while I ran in the same direction on the outside. Then he would stop and extend his fingers again, I would tag him, and we would run again. We did this until Grub tired of it, and it soon became a pleasant part of my visits.

One day, after a few rounds of tag and run with Grub, I decided to switch things up a little. When I tagged his fingers and he started running clockwise, I started running in the opposite direction. It turned out that Grub did not like surprises. As soon as he realized I had changed the game, he ran full-force at me, lunging his body against the enclosure, hair standing on end and canine teeth bared, all while howling. I quickly went into flight mode until I realized I was safely outside the enclosure. Grub's caretaker came over and reprimanded him, much like a human mother would do. Grub lowered his head and walked to the other side of the enclosure. I was just beginning to relax when Grub slowly walked back to our side of the enclosure, pressed his face against the fence, and drenched me with a mouthful of water from about 20 feet away. I thought that was funny until *I* received a reprimand from the caretaker for encouraging Grub's unacceptable behavior with my laughter. As Grub went to the other side of the enclosure and began climbing his rope ladder, I was convinced HE was laughing at ME!

I am quite deliberately attributing human emotions and motives to Grub, in opposition to the century-long scientific commandment: "Thou shalt not anthropomorphize animal behavior." One should explain the actions of nonhuman animals only in terms of behaviors, avoiding all attributions of

Grub at the Center for Great Ape's sanctuary in Wauchula, Florida. With permission from Patti Ragan.

Figure 4.1. Grub. It's almost impossible to look into the eyes of an ape and not feel a human connection.

human-like emotions and cognitions. This may be easy to do with fruit flies and lab rats, but it is almost impossible to do with our close genetic cousins, chimpanzees. In my "tap-fingers-and-run" game with Grub, I saw play, joy, surprise, anger, shame, deception, and revenge. Grub may be special in that he was raised by people, much as a human child would be, until he became too big and strong for a human to safely interact with him. But I challenge anyone who views close up chimpanzees or the other great apes (bonobos, gorillas, and orangutans) not to come away with the feeling that they are, indeed, "like us." Queen Victoria in 1842 had such an insight after seeing an orangutan at the Zoological Gardens in London, writing in her diary that the orangutan was "frightful, and painfully and disagreeably human."

Despite seeing glimpses of ourselves in the eyes of the great apes, we are clearly different from them, both in terms of our physiques and, especially, our cognitions. Grub's charging the enclosure with canines flashing clearly reminded me of his nonhuman propensities. Ever since Darwin, people have pondered how humans and chimpanzees are related, and how *Homo sapiens* evolved our unique suite of characteristics from a common ancestor with chimps over the last 5 to 7 million years. There is, of course, not a single answer to this question, but in the last couple of decades it has become increasingly clear that changes in early development made important contributions to the forms and functions of many animals, including modern humans.

In this chapter I introduce the field of *evolutionary developmental biology*, or *Evo Devo*, which examines how different developmental mechanisms affect evolutionary change. One such mechanism is termed *heterochrony*, which refers to genetic-based differences in developmental timing. One particularly important form of heterochrony for human evolution is *neoteny*, which refers to the retention of infantile or juvenile traits into later development. Humans, as it turns out, are a neotenous species, with many characteristics of adult humans being similar to those of juvenile chimpanzees, and presumably to juvenile members of our common ancestor with chimps. In particular, humans owe their large brains in part to the retention of a rapid prenatal brain growth rate that continues well past birth. In a final section, I examine *Homo sapiens'* slow road to adulthood, the invention of new stages of development, and how these stages may have contributed to the evolution of the modern human mind.

Evo Devo

> Embryos undergo development; ancestors have undergone evolution, but in their day they also were the products of development
> (Gavin de Beer, 1958, p. 1)

In the years between the publication of *The Origin of Species* and the formulation of the modern synthesis in the 1930s, *embryology*—the study of the early stages of development in multicellular animals—was closely associated with evolutionary theory. Major theorists often disagreed about how development and evolution were related, but evidence of structures characteristic of "more primitive" species in the embryos of "more advanced species" (for example, tails and gill slits in human embryos) suggested a connection. For example, 19th-century theorists such as German biologist Ernst

Haeckel proposed that evolution was the cause of development. This is reflected in the mellifluous phrase I learned in 10th-grade biology, "ontogeny recapitulates phylogeny," or the development of the individual (ontogeny) goes through, or repeats, the same sequences as the evolution of the species (phylogeny). Others, including British biologists Walter Garstang and Gavin de Beer, argued, essentially, the opposite—that variations in development were the engines of evolutionary change, with Garstang going so far to write, "Ontogeny does not recapitulate phylogeny, it creates it."[1]

Although Garstang and de Beer were on the right track, the idea that development played a role in evolution fell out of favor with the advent of the modern synthesis. As discussed in the previous chapter, Weismann's principle that modifications made during an animal's lifetime cannot make their way into the germ line made development and embryology personae non grata in evolutionary circles. Species changed as a result of random genetic mutations coupled with the actions of natural selection. Mutations that promoted survival or reproductive success were maintained, whereas mutations that had deleterious consequences were eliminated. Development had no role.

Knowledge of the workings of DNA and technologies to "read" and manipulate the genomes of different species exploded in the latter part of the 20th and early decades of the 21st centuries, and as they did, so did the realization that differences among species involved more than differences in protein-coding genes. The substantial differences in the morphology, behavior, and cognition among mice, men, and meerkats belie the relatively small differences in their genomes. The discrepancy between differences in body and behavior and differences in genes is perhaps even more striking between humans and chimpanzees, who share roughly 98.8% of their DNA.[2] The solution to this conundrum was to be found in development as revealed by the field of *evolutionary developmental biology*, or *Evo Devo*. Evo Devo examines the developmental process of different animals to infer their phylogenetic relationship and how different developmental mechanisms affect evolutionary change. Evo Devo reintroduced embryology to the modern synthesis, integrating it with molecular genetics and paleontology. Most of the developmental processes investigated by Evo Devo researchers occur early in life, during embryological development, and are concerned with the timing of the expression of genes and their influence on the formation of animal bodies. Thus, before delving further into Evo Devo, it's necessary to provide a brief primer on the mechanisms of DNA inheritance. I then examine some of the core principles of Evo Devo: modularity; the ancient origins of master genes; the role of regulatory genes in the evolution of body form; and heterochrony—genetic-based differences in developmental timing.*

What Is DNA and What Does It Do?

I've written about DNA, genes, and genetics in earlier chapters, especially Chapter 2 when discussing plasticity, and I'm confident that most readers of this book have a basic understanding of the molecular basis of inheritance. But because so much of Evo Devo is related to genetics and gene action, I think a short tutorial is in order.

At the core of genetics is *DNA, deoxyribonucleic acid*. In 1953 James Watson and Francis Crick famously discovered how this complex molecule copies itself, leading the way to a new understanding of inheritance and the genetic foundation of life. In short, DNA is the basis for all life on earth, from *E. coli* to elephants. DNA consists of long chains of nucleotide pairs (or base pairs) strung together to form chromosomes found in the nuclei of cells. The nucleotides of DNA come in four types: adenine, thymine, guanine, and cytosine (abbreviated A, T, G, and C, respectively). Humans have 46 chromosomes that contain roughly 3 billion nucleotide pairs, with some stretches of these base pairs constituting genes. The traditional definition of a *gene* is a sequence of DNA that codes for one of the approximately 25,000 proteins in our bodies. Using this definition, humans have approximately 20,000 genes, about the same number as mice and chimpanzees.[3]

Perhaps somewhat surprisingly, only a minority of a person's DNA codes for proteins, as low as 1.5%. What, then, is the other 98.5% doing, if anything? Scientists once referred to noncoding DNA as "junk," because they believed it had no purpose. More recent research indicates that about 80% of DNA serves some function, although other estimates put this number much lower, below 10%. All Evo Devo researchers agree, however, that the most important function of noncoding DNA is regulating the activity of the coding DNA.[4] *Regulatory genes*, which account for between 3% and 8% of the genome, activate or suppress specific coding genes and thereby influence development.

---

* For an amusing 4 minute and 46 second summary of Evo Devo sung to the song "Despacito," I recommend going to Evo-Devo (Despacito Biology Parody) | A Capella Science—YouTube, https://www.youtube.com/watch?reload=9&v=ydqReeTV_vk

Modularity

One important finding from Evo Devo research is that animals are made of units, or *module*s, that are relatively independent from one another, with unique genetic specification. This may seem obvious, in that the vertebrate skeleton is distinct from the nervous system, the liver is distinct from the heart, and the visual system is distinct from the auditory system. The important implication of modularity is that natural selection can operate independently on different modules at different times. According to pioneering Evo-Devo researcher Rudolf Raff, modularity is "an ineluctable feature of biological order. It is arguably the most crucial aspect of order in living organisms and their ontogenies, and is the attribute that most strongly facilitates evolution."[5]

Ancient Origins

Evo Devo researchers investigate a wide range of organisms, from bacteria to humans. Different researchers use different *model organisms* to investigate what they are really interested in. For example, the fruit fly (*Drosophila*) has been a favorite subject of geneticists, not because the scientists are fascinated with fruit flies for their own sake, but because fruit flies have only four pairs of large chromosomes and reproduce rapidly, making them ideal subjects for studying genetics. Scientists are interested in the processes of genetics or development, and fruit flies, mice, and salamanders are convenient species for studying the processes they really want to learn about. One result of Evo Devo researchers' use of different model organisms is that data exist permitting comparisons between different animals, some that have last shared a common ancestor only recently (for example, humans and chimpanzees), and others whose common ancestor dates back hundreds of millions of years (for example, fruit flies and humans).

Perhaps the most remarkable finding of Evo Devo is the existence of a common set of master genes associated with building the bodies of animals as diverse as *Drosophila* and *Homo sapiens*. Termed *Hox* genes, they control an embryonic animal's body plan from head to tail. They produce proteins that determine the generation and location of different appendages—legs, antennae, and wings in fruit flies; and arms, legs, fingers, and vertebrae in humans and other animals with backbones. Mutations in *Hox* genes can result in an antenna growing where a leg should be in a fruit fly or extra fingers or toes in vertebrates. What is truly amazing is that these master genes have been conserved (that is, remained virtually unchanged) over the course of evolution, dating back perhaps to the earliest bilateral (symmetrical) animals more than 650 million years ago. This predates the evolution of insects by perhaps 100 million years. According to evolutionary developmental biologist Sean Carroll, "The discovery that the same set of genes controls the formation and pattern of body regions and body parts with similar functions (but very different designs) in insects, vertebrates, and other animals has forced a complete rethinking of animal history, the origins of structure, and the nature of diversity."[6]

Although scientists were at first quite surprised to find similar master genes in species that hadn't shared a common ancestor in more than 550 million years, upon reflection it perhaps should not be so startling. Natural selection works with what is available, and once a solution to a general type of problem is discovered, it makes sense to use that solution to solve similar problems. There is no need to reinvent the wheel (or placement of limbs) when a solution already exists. In fact, conservation of master genes may have been necessary for evolution to produce the wide range of diversity that it has. According to Raff,

> if each new species required the reinvention of control elements [master genes], there would not be time enough for much evolution at all, let alone spectacularly rapid evolution of novel features observed in the phylogenetic record. There is a kind of tinkering at work, in which the same regulatory elements are recombined into new developmental machines.[7]

You may think some of these findings are a bit perplexing. If the master genes are essentially the same across species as diverse as fruit flies and people, why do people have fingers and toes but fruit flies have wings and antennae? Even when mutations occur, one does not find an antenna sprouting on the head of a mouse or vertebrae forming in the back of a fly. The answer, in part, is because the context in which these genes are expressed is as important as when, during development, they are expressed. The *Hox* genes in question may determine body plan from head to tail, but they are not the only things evolving. Natural selection has produced fly bodies, mouse bodies, and human bodies, independent of the *Hox* genes (recall the principle of modularity). Thus, whereas the *Hox* genes in a fruit fly may produce a wing, the corresponding genes in a mouse will produce a vertebrate or a leg.

Evidence that similar master genes produce species-specific forms is illustrated in research by Swiss geneticist Walter Gehring and his colleagues examining variants of the *Pax-6* gene, called *eyeless* in fruit flies, *Small eye* in mice, and *Anirida* in humans. Each of these genes is involved in the formation of eyes. Eyes have evolved independently between 40 and 60 times in the animal kingdom, but despite the wide variety of kinds of eyes and the type of animal they develop in, all seem to use a variant of the *Pax-6* gene. When the *Small eye* mouse gene was introduced into a fruit fly larva, it produced eyes on wings or legs, depending on where in the embryo it was placed. But the eyes were those of a fruit fly, not a mouse.[8] Based on this and related research, Raff concluded that

> eyes great and small, primitive and specialized, use *Pax-6* in a great demonstration of the long conservation of the function of this gene in development of animal neural systems and photoreceptors. This commonality doesn't mean that the compound eyes of insects and the camera eyes of vertebrates are homologous, but that the photoreceptors share a long-conserved master regulatory gene present in the ancestral neural precursor of eyes.[9]

Eyes may have been invented many times over the past 650 million years, but the genes controlling the underlying photoreceptors may have arisen only once and been conserved in species from fruit flies to humans.

Regulatory Genes

If the master genes are essentially the same in a wide range of species, how is it that species differ so much in body form? One explanation is duplication: genes controlling a portion of a body (spinal vertebrae in vertebrates, for example) can duplicate, resulting in animals with differing numbers of vertebrae or ribs. Snakes, for instance, have between 200 and 400 vertebrates and ribs, whereas humans have 33 vertebrates and 24 ribs. But the most critical factor in producing different body types from a common set of genes is developmental timing. Regulatory genes determine when and whether a *Hox* gene (or other genes) is activated and how much protein it produces. According to Carroll, "It is the switches [regulatory genes] that encode instructions unique to individual species and that enable different animals to be made using essentially the same tool kit."[10] Changes in developmental timing are responsible for changes in body form and have been for hundreds of millions of years.

Some biologists have proposed that changes in regulatory genes rather than changes in coding genes themselves are the principle engine of evolution, and research tends to support this claim.[11] With respect to differences between humans and chimpanzees, recent research comparing the DNA of the two species suggests that some of the largest genetic differences between chimps and humans lie in certain regulatory genes that affect the development of the brain.[12] For example, research by Singapore geneticist Shyam Prabhakar and colleagues identified 992 noncoding DNA sequences (and presumed to be regulatory genes) associated with neural adhesion (chemical or mechanical links between brain cells that facilitate cell migration, signal transmission, and tissue repair) that differed between mice, chimpanzees, and humans. Chimpanzees and humans both showed a large number of noncoding sequences near neuronal cell adhesion genes, but almost no overlap between them, suggesting independent neuronal evolution in these regulatory genes between the two species.

Heterochrony

Regulatory genes determine whether, when, and how much protein a coding gene produces, and phylogenetic changes in regulatory genes have played a substantial role in the evolution of body form, including for humans. Especially potent effects of regulatory genes include determining when in development sets of genes will be activated and the rates at which different parts of an organism develop. Development is not uniform across different parts of an organism. In other words, there is not a single developmental schedule, with all parts of an animal following the same time course. Development is not like blowing up a balloon, in which all areas of the balloon (or all parts of the body) increase in size and complexity at the same time and rate. Rather, different organs or cell types follow different developmental timetables, unrelated to the schedule of neighboring organ systems. From an evolutionary perspective, genes associated with the development of a certain part of the body can be activated or suppressed, turned on sooner or later, for a longer or shorter period, all independently of what happens to other body parts. Genetic-based differences in developmental timing are referred to as *heterochrony*.[13]

To get an appreciation of heterochrony, consider our own species' evolutionary history. There is no evidence of a rapid, instantaneous change in human body form over the past 5 million years. Rather, according to Carroll,

> the picture of hominin evolution is a mosaic pattern, with different traits appearing at different times and evolving at different rates in hominin history . . . the development of different structures was evolving in a patchy, nonlinear way over a long course of time. [O]ur history involved quantitative shifts in brain size, body proportions, skull size, gestation time, juvenile development, and more—assimilated over tens of thousands of generations.[14]

Heterochrony is not only a description of development but can also be a powerful mechanism of evolutionary change, and this is afforded by modularity. Recall Raff's comments on the importance of modularity as "the attribute that most strongly facilitates evolution." Different parts of an animal can develop at different rates, and these rates may be retarded or accelerated relative to the developmental rates experienced by a species' ancestors and can produce modifications in behavior or form that will then be subject to natural selection.[†]

In the days before the modern synthesis and the integration of Darwin's idea of natural selection with genetic theory, heterochrony was believed by some to be the principle mechanism of evolutionary change. Specifically, German biologist Ernst Haeckel's *biogenetic law* (or *recapitulation theory*) proposed that evolution proceeded by accelerating development, with new features being added to the embryonic endpoint of an immediate ancestor. From this perspective one can get a nearly complete picture of evolution by studying embryology. The problem with the theory is that it just doesn't fit the facts. For instance, the order in which a feature appeared in evolution does not always correspond to the path it takes in development. Teeth, for example, appeared earlier in evolution than tongues, but teeth appear later in the embryological development of present-day mammals than tongues.[15]

[†] Technical note: Following McKinney and McNamara (1991), there are three types of heterochronic retardation: (1) *progenesis*, or earlier onset of some aspect of development; (2) *neoteny*, or reduced rate of development; and (3) *post-displacement*, or delayed onset of development. For ease of reading, I do not differentiate between these three types of retardation here, often using the term *neoteny* to refer to retardation of development in general. McKinney and McNamara also identified three forms of heterochronic acceleration: (1) *hypermorphosis*, or delayed offset of development; (2) *acceleration*, or increased rate of development; and (3) *pre-displacement*, or earlier onset of growth (from Bjorklund, 2007a, p. 44).

Although it may sound counterintuitive, scientists began to realize that evolutionary advances can sometimes be achieved through the slowing of development, or the retention of infantile or juvenile traits into later development, which is referred to as *neoteny*. I introduced the concept of neoteny in the early pages of Chapter 1 when discussing Konrad Lorenz's idea of *Kindchenschema*, or baby schema, the features of young infants that adults find so appealing. I mentioned then that some theorists have proposed that neoteny played an important role in human evolution, a topic I will take up in the next section. Moreover, heterochrony, and particularly neoteny, has been viewed by many as having an important role in the evolution of many species.[16] For instance, anthropologist Ashley Montagu proposed that "the evolutionary history of many groups, nonhuman and human, is characterized by delayed development, prolongation of the youthful stages into phases of sexual maturity, and the discarding of the old adult phase."[17] Neoteny may be a good strategy for evolutionary innovation, permitting an organisms to take a step backward, so to speak, with the potential to redirect its development. On a similar note, paleontologist Stephen Jay Gould wrote that "the early stages of ontogeny are a storehouse of potential adaptations, for they contain countless shapes and structures that are lost through later allometries. When development is retarded, a mechanism is provided (via retention of fetal growth rates and proportions) for bringing these features forward to later ontogenetic stages."[18]

As an example of neoteny, consider the salamander axolotl, also known as the Mexican walking fish. Similar to frogs and other amphibians, axolotls start life as water-dwelling tadpoles (their larval state), getting oxygen via gills. Some tadpoles metamorphose into land-dwelling, air-breathing reproductive salamanders. Others, however, attain sexual maturity while still tadpoles. That is, the development of the axolotl's reproductive system is independent of the development of its respiratory/body form systems. Under some conditions, it maintains a juvenile/larval body while its reproductive system matures, becoming a sexually active tadpole.[19]

The evidence that neoteny has played a role in the evolution of many species is well documented[20] but must be inferred from fossil records or from contrasts of differences in body form, physiology, or rates of development among different animals. There is at least one well-documented example, however, in which neotenic changes in a population of animals over decades has been observed via *selective breeding* (also called *artificial selection*). Darwin was well aware that farmers and animal breeders selectively bred animals with desired features to produce over a matter of generations dogs with longer legs or meatier cattle, for example. Darwin assumed that natural selection worked in a similar way, though much more slowly. In 1959 Russian zoologist Dmitry Belyayev began a program of selective breeding of wild red foxes (*Vulpes vulpes*) with the goal to make them doglike pets, replicating the process that had converted wolves into domesticated dogs. The project continues to this day under the supervision of biologist Lyudimila Trut.

Belyayev's attempt to domesticate foxes began as he classified captured animals into three categories: Class III foxes fled humans or bit when stroked or handled; Class II foxes permitted themselves to be petted but showed no signs of friendliness toward people; and Class I foxes were friendly to humans, wagging their tails and whining. Class I females were bred with Class I males, and after only six generations a new classification was required, "domesticated elite"—foxes that were eager for human contact. These elite pups acted much like dogs, sniffing and licking humans and whimpering to gain attention, some as early as 1 month old. By the 20th generation, 35% of the foxes were "domesticated elites."[21] Domesticated animals, in general, share many of the behavioral features of Belyayev's foxes. Domesticated dogs (*Canis familiaris*), sheep (*Ovis aries*), and goats (*Capra hircus*), for example, are typically less aggressive toward one another and toward humans and more responsive to human cues and instructions. It was only through domestication of the wild bezoar ibex (*Capra aegargus*) that goat yoga is possible (see Figure 4.2).

Figure 4.2. The increasing popularity of goat yoga is only possible through the domestication of the wild bezoar ibex (*Capra aegargus*) into much tamer and playful domesticated goats (*Capra hircus*).
Source: Photo by Julie Earls, with permission.

One unanticipated side effect of this selection for tameness was associated changes in body form. Generation after generation, as the researchers produced increasingly tame animals, the domesticated foxes also changed in appearance, retaining into adulthood many of their puppy-like features, including shorter and wider heads, floppy ears, and shortened legs, tails, snouts, and upper jaws. Trut and her colleagues commented that "The shifts in the timing of development brought about by selection of foxes for tameability have a neotenic-like tendency: the development of individual somatic [body] traits is decelerated, while sexual maturation is accelerated."[22]

* * *

It's hard to minimize the significance of Evo Devo in modern evolutionary thinking. According to Sean Carroll, "Evo Devo constitutes the third major act in a continuing evolutionary synthesis. Evo Devo has . . . provided a critical missing piece of the Modern Synthesis—embryology—and integrated it with molecular genetics and traditional elements such as paleontology."[23] The discovery of the importance of regulatory genes and the rediscovery of the role that changes in developmental timing (heterochrony) can have in the form and function of animals put development front and center in any explanation of the evolution of species. This is as true of humans as of other animals. In fact, although human evolution has involved both the acceleration and slowing of developmental rates relative to our ancestors, a number of theorists over the past hundred years or so have proposed that humans owe much of their unique morphology and behavior to developmental retardation. We are primarily a neotenous species, and I devote the next section to investigating these claims.

Humans as a Neotenous Species

> If I were to express the basic principles of my ideas in a somewhat strongly worded sentence, I would say that man, in his bodily development, is a primate fetus that has become sexually mature. (Louis Bolk, cited by Gould, 1977, p. 361)

This somewhat disturbing quote from a 1926 publication, depicting humans as sexually mature primate fetuses, is reminiscent of the axolotl, the salamander that sometimes becomes sexually mature during its larval stage. The quote is from Dutch Professor of human anatomy Louis Bolk, who recognized, as had others, the flaws in Haeckel's biogenetic theory, particularly with respect to human evolution. Bolk looked at human development in comparison with that of other primates and concluded, in exact opposition to Haeckel, that human evolution had not proceeded by acceleration relative to ancestral forms, but rather by retardation. Bolk noted that many physical characteristics of modern humans resemble fetal or juvenile features shared with other primates that have become permanent in adult *Homo sapiens*. Bolk believed that the primary difference between humans and our simian relatives was our species' slow rate of growth. According to Bolk's *fetalization theory*, humans are apes who, physically, never grew up. In Bolk's words, "There is no mammal that grows as slowly as man, and not one in which the full development is attained at such a long interval after birth... What is the essential in Man as an organism? The obvious answer is: The slow progress of his life's course."[24]

Some of the features Bolk listed as reflecting human fetalization (or neoteny, in more contemporary terms) include peoples' flat faces and rounded skulls, reduction of body hair, and how the skull connects to the spine permitting upright walking, among others. Table 4.1 presents an abbreviated list of human neotenous traits.

Bolk's fetalization theory involved more than a description of neotenous human features but assumed, among other things, that *all* of human evolution was characterized by slowed development. This was not an unreasonable proposition in the days before the modern synthesis and Evo

Table 4.1. Some neotenous functional traits in humans (adapted from Bolk, 1926; Montagu, 1989; Skulachev et al., 2017)

Rapid growth of brain well into third year
Low birth weight
External gestation
Prolonged immaturity
Prolonged dependency
Infant's great need of fluids (150 ml per day)
Fetal rate of bodily growth, weight, and length during first year
Prolonged growth period
Ends of long and finger/toe bones remain cartilaginous for years
Late development of reproductive maturity
Small nose
Longer legs than arms
Absence of baculum (penis bone)

Devo, but we now know this is not the case. The modular nature of animals' bodies means that different systems can be accelerated or retarded relative to one's ancestor, independent of other systems. Even if Bolk were correct in assuming that slowed development is an essential feature of humans, all systems did not experience the same retardation in development simultaneously. Bolk, although being an ardent believer in evolution, did not buy into Darwin's idea of natural selection. For Bolk, evolution was not primarily governed by an animal's adaptation to local environments but by internal factors—in the case of retardation, brought about through modifications in the endocrine (hormone) system. Despite Bolk's often-extreme and now discredited views, his research set the stage for later theorists to examine both human physical and behavioral features as reflecting slowed, or neotenous, development, and I'll examine some of these claims in the following sections.

Some Human Neotenous Features

First, let me emphasize that Bolk's idea that all aspects of *Homo sapiens* reflect a slowing, or retardation, of development relative to ancestral species is wrong. Heterochrony seems to clearly have played an important role in human evolution, but in some cases development is seemingly accelerated with respect to our common ancestor with chimpanzees, not retarded. For instance, human brain and cognitive development clearly exceed that of other primates, although as we'll see later in this section, some of this was achieved by retaining fetal brain growth rates postnatally. Other accelerated features of human development include the early fusion of bones in the wrist and early descent of the testes.[25] Yet, Bolk seemed to be on the right track in noting that humans are a slow-developing species compared with their primate relatives and that some characteristics of *Homo sapiens* were achieved via a retention or extension of fetal or juvenile features.

Some Examples of How Neoteny Operated on Physical Form. In the early days of paleontology, scientists believed that the hallmark of human evolution was a gradual but steady increase in brain size, with other physical features, such as upright walking, evolving later. As more fossils were found, however, it became apparent that this scenario had it backward: Early hominins, such as the 3.2-million-year-old *Australopithecine* Lucy, had a skull about the size of a modern chimpanzee but walked on two legs, much as contemporary people do. Evolving bipedality required many adaptations to multiple parts of the body, but one of then—how the spine connects to the base of the skull—involved neoteny.

Most mammals are quadrupeds, locomoting on all fours. Although you've likely seen a number of YouTube or Facebook videos of dogs or cats doing amusing things while walking on their hind legs, they don't do it easily and can't do it comfortably for any length of time. This is because in most mammals, the angle at which the spine connects to the skull (called the *cranial flexure*) is such that the head is facing forward when the animal is on all fours. This is different in humans. The cranial flexure for *Homo sapiens* is such that we are facing forward when we are standing on two feet. Many of you, I'm sure, have served as a "horsie" for a young child, crawling on your hands and knees while bending your neck so you can look forward. You can only maintain this posture for so long before you get a sore neck. Although the cranial flexure is different between humans and other mammals in adulthood, it is essentially the same for all mammals during embryonic development. The flexure changes, however, over the course of development in the dog more so than in the human. This adaptation—retaining an embryonic relation between the spine and the skull—resulting in the head sitting atop the spine, permitted upright walking in our hominin ancestors.[26]

Another physical difference between humans and other mammals brought about by neoteny that may have had important differences in human evolution is the orientation of the vagina. In adult chimpanzees and in most (if not all) other mammals, the vagina is sloped toward the back of the body. As a result, males typically "mount" females, with copulation being done from the rear. Humans can also engage in "doggie-style" sex, but intercourse can also be easily done face to face. This is because the orientation of the vagina in humans is sloped toward the front of the body. As with the cranial flexure, the slope of the vagina is similar in all embryonic mammals, oriented toward the front of the body. This changes in dogs and chimpanzees, but not in humans. Again, humans retain an embryonic characteristic (development is retarded), resulting in an important physical difference in adulthood. Why might the slope of the vagina be important in human evolution? Unlike chimpanzees and bonobos, which are promiscuous breeders, humans are a marginally monogamous/marginally polygamous, species, with men and women falling in love and forming emotional pair bonds. Stable "families," promoted by love and sex between women and men, may have served to keep mother and father together long enough to raise a slow-developing and costly offspring, and looking your lover in the eyes may have been one adaptation that facilitated long-term bonds and commitment.[27]

Behavioral Neoteny: The Taming of Homo Sapiens. Earlier in this chapter I discussed the work of Russian zoologist Dmitry Belyayev, who established a breeding program to domesticate wild foxes. Belyayev selectively bred foxes for tameness and over the course of 20 generations produced foxes that interacted comfortably with humans, much as puppy canines do. One impressive finding of Belyayev's project was that the tamed foxes also possessed a suit of neotenic, juvenile physical characteristics, including shorter and wider heads, floppy ears, and shortened legs, tails, snouts, and upper jaws. Equally remarkable, however, is that tameness itself is a neotenic trait, which likely played a major role in human evolution.

When we speak of tameness in domesticated animals, we are usually referring to a reduction in "wildness," especially a tolerance for humans, an increase in compliance, and a decrease in aggressiveness. When we use the term in reference to members of our own species, we similarly mean it to represent increases in agreeableness and a decrease in aggression. Thus, in Shakespeare's play, Petruccio uses a variety of tactics to tame the shrewish Katherine into becoming an obedient wife. Medieval obedient wives aside, humans have seemingly become increasingly tame over their evolution, showing an impressive ability to interact with often large numbers of people with relatively little conflict.

Humans have sometimes been referred to as a domesticated species; however, it is a species that was not tamed by another animal but by itself, that is, through a process of *self-domestication*.[28] Self-domestication could have resulted when natural selection favored prosocial and cooperative relations among group members (or "survival of the friendliest" to use primatologist Brian Hare's phrase) as opposed to aggression, producing a "tamed" animal. What brought about this tameness was a form of behavioral neoteny, a retention of juvenile characteristics for interacting with other members of the species with greater tolerance and less aggression than that shown by our ancient ancestors. In particular, humans show relatively low levels of *reactive aggression*, sometimes referred to as impulsive or "hot" aggression. (Reactive aggressive is contrasted with *proactive aggression*, or instrumental or "cold" aggression, which is premeditated.) Reactive aggression occurs in response to a real or perceived threat. An individual is provoked to aggress.

You might be surprised that humans, especially human males, are considered to display relatively low levels of reactive aggression. Volumes have been written about elevated levels of aggression and violence in human males, especially adolescent and young adult males, who are in the midst of establishing manhood and finding and maintaining a mate.[29] For example, bar fights or their equivalent are common in all cultures, often occurring in response to minor insults to one's manhood or perhaps to features of one's girlfriend or one's mother. Disputes among men while playing sports can easily end up in fisticuffs, and in some sports such as hockey, fights are part of the game. Despite human adult males' reputation for high levels of reactive aggression, compared with chimpanzees, they are almost a docile species. Primatologists have repeatedly documented high levels of reactive aggression in chimpanzees and other primates.[30] The life of a chimpanzee is one of frequent conflict, with very little provocation needed to incite aggression. The primatologist Sarah Hrdy notes that humans regularly pack themselves into crowded spaces such as airplanes for extended periods of time with rarely a serious fight breaking out. A similar flight packed with chimpanzees would produce a constant melee, with severed appendages and a few deaths highly likely.[31]

One mechanism for reduced aggression and greater docility in humans relative to our simian predecessors is increased *inhibition*, the ability to *not* to respond to an immediate stimulus. Humans' enhanced sociality required that individuals within a group not respond to every sexual or aggressive urge that hits them, but rather to inhibit such responses, thus enabling cooperative social interaction. The idea that *Homo sapiens*' ancestors evolved superior inhibitory skills relative to their immediate ancestors has been proposed by a number of theorists,[32] including America's most influential philosopher of the early 20th century, John Dewey. Dewey proposed that, unlike other animals, humans possess *reflective thought*, which

> converts action that is merely appetitive, blind, and impulsive into intelligent action. A brute animal, as far as we know, is pushed from behind; it is moved in accordance with its present physiological state by some present stimulus . . . If a man's actions are not guided by thoughtful conclusions, then they are guided by inconsiderate impulse, unbalanced appetite, caprice, or the circumstance of the moment. To cultivate unhindered unreflective external activity is to foster enslavement, for it leaves the person at the mercy of appetite, sense, and circumstance.[33]

Enhanced inhibition abilities would result not only in reduced reactive aggression but also smoother relations between males and females, as males were able to exert greater control over their sexual urges; better social skills as individuals were increasingly able to deceive others to gain social advantages; and improved parenting for slow-developing and long-dependent offspring, as parents (particularly mothers) were increasingly able to delay their own gratification and aggressive reactions in response to needy and often "difficult" children.[34]

But perhaps the greatest advantage that enhanced inhibition and reduced reactive aggression produced was an increased ability to cooperate with fellow group members. Cooperation involves different individuals working together to achieve a common goal, which many think is the hallmark of *Homo sapiens*, and this requires controlling emotions and especially inhibiting impulsive aggressive reactions. I will have much more to say about the role of increased prosociality and cooperation in Chapter 6. The important point here is that these abilities, which go far beyond anything seen in other animals, were enabled by a retention of a juvenile feature (reduced reactive aggression) from our common ancestor with chimpanzees.[‡]

Brain Development. Perhaps the quality that differentiates humans from our simian relatives more than anything else is our intelligence, and this is afforded by our big brains. The *encephalization quotient* is a measure of how much "brain" a species has beyond that which is needed to run the body. The bigger the brain, the "smarter" the animal, and the higher the encephalization quotient. Chimpanzees have an impressive encephalization quotient of about 2.7, meaning they have about 2.7 times "more brain" than necessary to operate their bodies, which is pretty impressive. Humans exceed this value by a factor of nearly 3, having an encephalization quotient of about 7.6.[35]

[‡] Note: Primatologist Richard Wrangham (2018, 2019) has recently championed the position that humans' reduced levels of reactive aggression were, indeed, brought about through the process of neoteny (or paedomorphism, to use his term), and that this, along with the advent of language that afforded effective communication, provided the opportunity for groups of males (in particular) to cooperate. A central problem males cooperated about was control of overly aggressive dominate males. Wrangham proposed the *execution hypothesis*, in which groups of males would engage in proactive aggression in order to kill bullies and other individuals who violated group norms. The result was an overall more harmonious group with established social and moral norms, but one that was maintained by the threat of ostracism or death for those who violated the norms. Humans compared to chimpanzees and other social mammals display reduced levels of reactive aggression but elevated levels of proactive aggression, resulting in what Wrangham called the *Goodness Paradox: The Strange Relationship Between Virtue and Violence in Human Evolution* (the title of his 2019 book). Robert Trivers (1971) had earlier proposed that murder might have been used to eliminate social cheaters from the group to a similar effect (that is, enhanced social harmony).

We are brainy creatures, indeed. But size isn't everything. Human brains, at both the level of the neuron and the overall organization of the brain, are more complex than those of chimpanzees, and our brains have provided us learning, communicative, and symbolic abilities that far exceed anything achieved by chimpanzees. How might these changes in brain size, organization, and function have come about? And what role might neoteny have played in some of these changes?

Before addressing this question, a (very) brief tutorial on human brain development may be in order. The basic unit of the brain is the *neuron*, a specialized cell that transmits electrical information to and from other neurons. Neurons consist of a cell body that contains the nucleus. Extending from the cell body are many projections, one of which is called the *axon*, a long fiber that carries messages away from the cell body to other cells, and more numerous fibers called *dendrites* that receive messages from other cells. Dendrites from one neuron do not actually touch dendrites from another neuron but, rather, transfer electrical signals via spaces between them, called *synapses*. Chemicals in the synapses, called *neurotransmitters*, facilitate the transmission of signals from one neuron to another. Adults have about 86 billion neurons, and because each neuron has many dendrites, there are perhaps a trillion or more synapses.[36]

Developing an adult brain takes time, however. Most of the neurons that a person will ever have are produced by the seventh month of prenatal development in a process termed *proliferation*, or *neurogenesis*, although recent research has shown that neurons in at least one area of the brain (the hippocampus) continue to be produced well into adulthood. Once neurons are born they need to migrate to what will be their permanent position in the brain, where they will extend their dendrites to make connections with other neurons, a process known as *differentiation*, or *synaptogenesis*. Neurons also increase in size over the course of development and grow sheaths of a fatty tissue called *myelin* on their axons, which serve to insulate the axons, much as coating on an electrical wire insulates the wire. The result is faster transmission of nervous signals and a reduction of interference from the activity of other neurons. Many of the neurons an infant develops will die, a process that begins late in the prenatal period and continues throughout life, called *apoptosis*, or *selective cell death*. Many of the synapses between surviving neurons also die, a process termed *synaptic pruning*.

How did human brains get so large relative to those of their presumed ancestors? Although there is not a single answer to this question, it seems clear that neoteny played an important role. Both the greater number of neurons that humans have relative to chimpanzees (and seemingly to the ancestor we have in common with chimpanzees and bonobos) and the structure and organization of neurons are a result of humans' retention of fetal rates of brain development well past the time of birth. Brain development is rapid during the prenatal period for all primates, but this rapid growth rate is extended in our species. Consider neurogenesis, the formation of new neurons. This process is extended in humans during the prenatal period, resulting in more neurons than for our simian cousins (approximately 86 billion for humans versus 28 billion for chimpanzees as adults).[37]

Although human infants' brains at birth are larger than those of the other great apes, they are actually smaller as a proportion of their eventual adult weight compared with those of chimpanzees, bonobos, gorillas, and orangutans. Human babies' brains are about 28% of the weight they will be as adults; in comparison, the weight of the brains at birth of the other great apes is between about 40% and 45% of their eventual adult weight.[38] This means that more brain development occurs after birth for humans than for the other apes. Brain growth slows down quickly after birth for other primates, but not for humans, who continue the rapid pace of brain development through the second year of life and beyond. Although most neurogenesis is complete by birth, neurons continue to grow in size, axons become myelinated, and neurons form connections with other neurons after birth. By 6 months the human brain weighs 50% of what it will in adulthood; at 2 years, about 75%; at 5 years, 90%; and at 10 years, 95%, with the final 5% of growth not being completed until late adolescence or early adulthood. In contrast, chimpanzees reach their adult brain size by about 5 years of age.[39] So the brain, which grows rapidly before birth, continues its rapid development after birth. Thus, even when we develop "more brain" than other primates, we do it by retaining fetal growth rates months and years after birth.[40]

Why, you may ask, didn't humans retain the great ape brain developmental schedule and build a bigger brain before birth rather than postpone so much brain development until after being born? The principle reason seems to be limitations of how large a neonatal head can grow and still fit through the birth canal of a bipedal woman. Human babies need to be born early relative to infants of the other ape species because if they delayed birth until their brains were about 40% of their eventual adult size, as is the case for the other great apes, their heads would not fit through the birth canals of their mothers.[41] Some have estimated that human infants are essentially born up to a year or more prematurely relative to the other great apes. As a result, the evolutionary pressures that resulted in an enlarged brain required that the period of pregnancy be relatively short and that much brain development be done after leaving the womb. Human babies' early exit from the uterus means that they have experiences—such as seeing a three-dimensional world, clearly hearing sounds, having to deal with the force of gravity, eating, and interacting with other members of their species—while their brains are still growing. In contrast, chimpanzees and bonobos have such experiences only after their brains are more fully developed.

Such experiences, happening earlier than would be expected given the typical great ape schedule, have substantial implications for social and cognitive development. Recall our discussion of Robert Lickliter's bobwhite quail chicks in Chapter 2. When these birds were exposed to light several days before hatching, it changed their brains and interfered with auditory attachment behaviors (some chicks approached the maternal call of a chicken as opposed to that of a bobwhite quail) but enhanced their visual abilities. As mentioned in Chapter 2, something similar happens with human babies who are born months prematurely and are exposed to sights, sounds, and other sensations in the neonatal intensive care unit that they would not normally receive until much later. Some of these infants show signs of delayed or impaired development (learning disabilities, for instance), although others display enhanced functioning in some areas (mathematics, for example).

Scholars have long recognized that human infants' gestation is extended into postnatal life and have referred to this period by a number of terms, including, *exterogestate fetus, extrauterine spring, exterior gestation, exterogestation,* and *the fourth trimester*.[42] The significance of extending gestation into postnatal life is that the infant experiences not the constant and protected environment of the womb but, rather, a stimulating and variable sensory, social, and cultural world during a time when the brain continues to develop rapidly. The result is a very different organism from one who would have not experienced the external world until 8 or perhaps 12 months later. German zoologist Adolf Portmann argued that it is this *extrauterine spring* that is responsible for the special nature of human development that leads to the extraordinary intellectual and social abilities of our species. Imagine, Portmann asks us, "the developing human spending the important maturation period of its first year in the dark, moist, uniform warmth of its mother's womb . . . It will gradually become clear that world-open behavior of the mature form is directly related to early contact with the richness of the world, an opportunity available only to humans."[43]

Neoteny not only played a role in extending the *rate* of brain development in humans but also influenced the evolution of individual neurons. The process of synaptogenesis is responsible in large part for cognitive and behavioral plasticity, and such plasticity is greatest early in development. However, neuronal metabolism and synaptic activity peak later in humans than in other primates, thus extending neural plasticity into adulthood. Researchers have identified a number of genes associated with synaptogenesis in the cerebral cortex that are expressed in both chimpanzees and humans. Such gene expression peaks in chimpanzees sometime before their first birthdays but does not peak in humans until about 5 years of age. In addition, levels of gene expression associated with cortical synaptogenesis are similar in adolescent and adult humans to those observed in juvenile chimpanzees.[44] Also, the process of *myelination*—the coating of axons with a fatty tissue that results in faster nerve transmission with less electrical interference—is slower during human childhood and extended later in development relative to chimpanzees.[45] As a result of these differences, humans retain substantial levels of plasticity throughout life compared with their simian relatives. According to neuroscientists Enric Bufill, Jordi Agustí, and Rafael Blesa in their review of neuronal neoteny,

> human neurons belonging to particular association areas retain juvenile characteristic throughout adulthood, which suggests that a neuronal neoteny has occurred in *H. sapiens*, which allows the human brain to function, to a certain degree, like a juvenile brain during adult life... Neuronal neoteny contributes to increasing information storage and processing capacity throughout life, which is why it was selected during primate evolution and, to a much greater extent, during the evolution of the genus *Homo*.[46]

* * *

Chimpanzees, bonobos, and gorillas have impressive brains, which were likely similar to the brains of the last common ancestor we shared with our great ape relatives. But the brains that reside in the skulls of modern *Homo sapiens* are more impressive still, and they are associated with intellectual and cultural accomplishments that are qualitatively different from those of the other great apes. Relative to chimpanzees, human brains are nearly three times greater in volume, have more cortical white matter (myelinated fibers), higher metabolic activity, and faster growth extending into infancy, among other features. There is no single cause for these changes, but one is alteration of the rate of development (heterochrony) relative to chimpanzees, and presumably to our common ancestor with chimps. Some of these changes are due to acceleration, but others—the ones I've emphasized here—are due to neoteny. Humans retain the rapid rate of brain and neuronal development well past birth, which, as a consequence, provides the possessors of these brains greater learning experiences early in life and the ability to change their thoughts and actions well into adulthood. In many ways, these changes in rate of development were responsible for the evolution of the modern human mind.

Extending Development

As we've seen in the preceding paragraphs, humans take proportionally longer to attain adult neurological status than chimpanzees and the other great apes. But brains aren't the only part of humans that develop more slowly relative to other apes; their bodies, teeth, and reproductive systems are also slower to develop than those of apes. In fact, the human model of delayed sexual maturity is actually the extreme end of a general primate pattern. The closer the common ancestor is to *Homo sapiens*, the longer the period of reproductive immaturity: in lemurs, approximately 2 years; in macaques, approximately 4; in chimps, approximately 8; and in humans, approximately 15 years.[47] Setting human reproductive maturity at age 15 is actually a bit misleading, for although females can become pregnant around this age, first births in most hunter-gatherer cultures, and likely for our ancestors, are typically delayed until about 19 or 20 years.[48]

Waiting 15 or 20 years before reproducing has its risks. Although people in contemporary cultures can anticipate living decades past their reproductive prime, such longevity is a modern phenomenon. Life expectancies in many impoverished countries today barely reach 40 years and were similarly low in the United States and Europe as little as 150 years ago. For our ancestors, delaying parenthood when life expectancy at birth likely ranged from about 21 to 40 years[49] was highly risky, with many people dying before they had the chance to reproduce. In biology, when costs are very high (in this case, the likelihood of death before reproducing), the associated benefits must also be high; otherwise, they would have been eliminated by natural selection. What might be the adaptive benefit afforded by delaying maturity so long? There is not a single answer to this question, but one favored by many scholars is that ancestral humans evolved in an ecology that placed a high premium on learning the technological and, especially, the social skills associated with one's culture, and this required an extended time in which to learn them.

Inventing New Stages of Development

Perhaps we should not be too surprised that humans take their time growing up. Mammals that have long life spans also tend to develop slowly. The life expectancy of elephants, for example, is about 65 years, and they do not reach sexual maturity until about 11 years of age. But humans have not simply stretched out the time it takes to become sexually mature; they have also invented new stages of development relative to other mammals. All mammals go through at least three postnatal stages of development: *infancy*, which extends from birth to weaning; the *juvenile period*, which follows weaning when young animals now must generally fend for themselves, including finding food and shelter, but are not yet sexually mature; and *adulthood*. According to anthropologist Barry Bogin, our ancestors added two new stages of development: *childhood*, the time between weaning and the juvenile period (about 3 to 7 years), and *adolescence*, a period following menarche (the first menstrual period) in girls, with rapid growth spurts for both boys and girls.[50] Both of these new stages have their own distinct physical and psychological features that were associated with the evolution of the human mind and behavior.

When we use the term *childhood* in everyday parlance, we typically mean it to refer to children who are weaned and past the toddler stage but who have not yet reached puberty. Psychologists typically make finer distinctions, often in line with Bogin's classification. Educators, psychologists, and people in general often refer to children between about 3 and 6 years of age as "preschoolers," reflecting that, in literate societies, these children are not yet ready for formal education. In contrast, the ages between about 6 and 12 are often described as "middle childhood" by psychologists. This distinction is relevant not only for children growing up in developed cultures but also for children living in traditional cultures and likely for our ancient ancestors.

Children are typically weaned by age 3 in most hunter-gatherer societies, but it will be several years before they are able to fend for themselves even minimally. These children still have their baby teeth, meaning many foods need to be specially prepared for them, and they lack the strength and dexterity to forage or hunt. Also notable, preschool-age children have limited cognitive abilities. Of course, in comparison with infants they can be viewed as mental giants, especially as reflected by their use of language, acquiring the basic grammar and vocabulary of their mother tongue in a relatively brief period of time. However, their reasoning and problem-solving abilities are greatly limited, making it impossible for them to live independently even if they had the physical abilities to do so.

Pick up any child- or developmental-psychology textbook and you're likely to see the better part of a chapter devoted to the theory of Swiss psychologist Jean Piaget. Piaget[51] identified four major stages of cognitive development: *sensorimotor*, extending from birth to about 2 years of age, in which infants understand their world in terms of sensations and actions; *preoperations*, describing children between the ages of about 2 to 7 years; *concrete operations*, reflecting the thinking of children between about 7 and 11 years; and *formal operations*, acquired between 11 and 16 years and, once attained, reflective of adult thinking. For the preoperational child (someone in Bogin's childhood stage), thinking is symbolic (they have language), but it is intuitive, lacking the logical operations that older children possess. For example, if the water in a short, stout glass is poured into a tall, thin glass as they watch, preschool children often claim that there is now "more water" in tall glass than there was in the short glass. They cannot ignore the difference in the height of the water in the two glasses and fail to understand that they can just pour the water back into the original short glass to prove the amount of water is equivalent. Children in the concrete operational stage (a child in Bogin's juvenile period) have no trouble with this simple task. Although more recent research findings have questioned much of Piaget's original interpretations, his description of preoperational children as cognitively unsophisticated has generally been supported. Compared with older children, preschoolers can only keep limited amounts of information in mind; do poorly on many reasoning and problem-solving tasks; have difficulties regulating their thought, emotions, and behaviors; and perform poorly in social situations requiring both cooperation and competition.[52]

Contemporary children in Bogin's juvenile stage remain dependent on adults for survival (as they do in contemporary hunter-gatherer societies),[53] but they are much closer to being able to take care of themselves than are preschool children. Secondary teeth begin to replace their baby (or milk) teeth, they increase in strength and manual dexterity, and their cognitive abilities begin to increasingly resemble those of adults. They lack the knowledge and experience of adults, but they are able to better regulate their behavior, can retain more information for longer periods of time, and use many of the everyday reasoning abilities that adults use to solve problems. In many cultures, children of 6 or 7 years were said to enter "the age of reason," capable of making a religious commitment (taking communion in the Catholic Church, for instance) or being responsible for their actions (in British Common Law, the age at which children may be said to commit a crime). Juveniles around the world are given responsibility for important tasks, including babysitting and meal preparation. In the United States and other postindustrialized nations, many juveniles make their way home safely from school each afternoon without adult supervision and operate the microwave, refrigerator, and television sufficiently well to "survive" while not harming themselves or burning down the house in the process. More telling are the millions of children living independently on the streets of cities, towns, and villages on every continent. Without adult support, juveniles band together to manage to eke out an existence under conditions of extreme poverty.[54]

The second new life stage Bogin identified was adolescence, with rapid growth spurts for both males and females and a period of low fertility for females. More recently, research has shown substantial brain reorganization during adolescence.[55] For instance, the amount of gray matter (reflective of neuronal cell bodies) decreases from the juvenile stage to adolescence, while the amount of white matter (reflective of myelination of axons in the frontal cortex) increases. The distribution of neurotransmitters, such as dopamine and serotonin, changes between the juvenile and adolescent stages in both the frontal cortex and the limbic system, an area of the brain associated with emotion. In addition, many structures in the limbic system reach adult levels of functioning before the prefrontal lobes (the area involved in higher-order cognition as well as inhibition and self-regulation of behavior), causing what some researchers refer to as a mismatch in maturation.[56] Although subadult animals of other species are often referred to as "adolescents," no other species displays the rapid growth spurt and brain reorganization typical of humans, although chimpanzees (*Pan troglodytes*) and bonobos (*Pan paniscus*) apparently do have a post-menarche period of low fertility.[57]

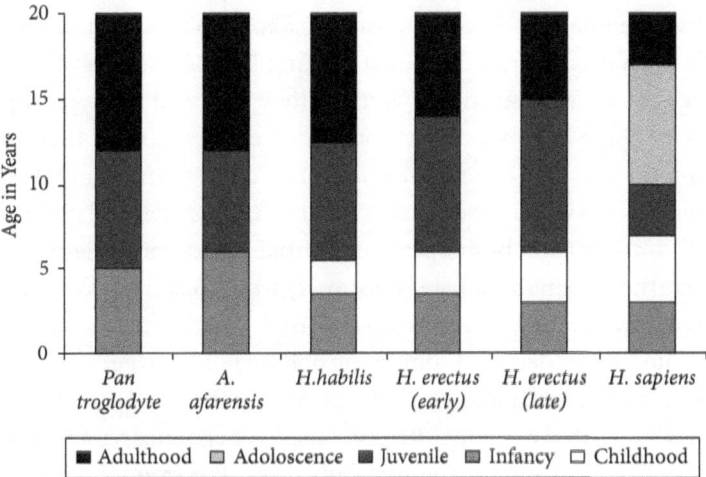

Figure 4.3. Evolution of human life history stages. According to Bogin, humans evolved two new life stages: childhood and adolescence.
Source: Bogin, 2001. Reprinted with permission.

Based on fossil evidence of dental development and skeletal size and structure, Bogin[58] proposed that humans developed these new life stages gradually over the course of hominin evolution. Figure 4.3 presents the proposed life stages for modern chimpanzees (*Pan troglodytes*), *Australopithecus afarensis*, *Homo habilis*, early and late *Homo erectus*, and *Homo sapiens*. As you can see, Bogin identified the first evidence of the childhood stage in *Homo habilis*, which became extended in *Homo erectus* and *Homo sapiens*; he identified adolescence only in *Homo sapiens*.

Psychological Abilities Associated with New Stages of Development

If an extended period of development, coupled with a large brain, was necessary to learn the complexities of human social life, why was it necessary to add new life stages? What adaptive value, if any, is provided by the evolutionarily new stages of childhood and adolescence? We cannot know for sure, but it is possible that humans' different life stages permitted the acquisition of new cognitive abilities, which in turn changed the nature of the species. In actuality, human infancy can itself be regarded as a qualitatively different stage than the infancies of other primates. Recall that human babies are essentially born prematurely, such that the first 8 or 12 months of their postnatal life would be spent in the womb if they followed the typical primate schedule of being born when their brains were about 40% of their eventual adult size (the so called *extrauterine spring*). Because so much rapid brain development occurs while experiencing a world full of social and physical stimulation, human infants' brains get a substantial "head start" relative to chimp brains. By the time human babies normally would just be leaving the comforts of the womb, they have developed complex social interactions, learned to locomote, and understand something of human language.

The new stage of childhood begins with a brain that continues to grow rapidly and is associated not only with continued dependence on adults, but also with motor and, especially, cognitive advances. For example, infants show the first signs of *counterfactual thinking*—creating something that is "counter to the facts." Beginning around 18 months, children engage in pretending, for example, using a shoe as a mobile phone. Counterfactual thinking improves substantially by 3 years of age when children typically begin to engage in *sociodramatic play*, in which they take on different roles and follow a storyline as if they were in a theatrical performance. Children of this age also find some counterfactual assertions very humorous. For example, one 3-year-old we know, after being read a book before her nap by her grandmother, thought it was hilarious when asked if two cats sleeping side by side on the bed might have similarly read a book to one another. For some months, this child's idea of a joke was to make counterfactual statements, mainly about animals performing some human-unique activity, such as one cat reading a book to a second cat before nap time. (I'll have more to say about play in Chapter 5.)

Children's ability to imitate the actions of a model also show improvements and changes around age 3, with children now engaging in *overimitation*—copying all the actions of a model, even those that are irrelevant to achieving a task goal. Imitation is an especially powerful form of social learning, which, although not unique to humans, is, according to some, the basis of *Homo sapiens*' ability to acquire and transmit cultural knowledge across generations.[59] Language also blossoms during childhood, with 3- and 4-year-old children becoming, essentially, linguistic geniuses over a very short period of time. Developmental psycholinguist John Lock and Barry Bogin argued that language was especially important for survival during childhood, as it improved communication between young children and their parents at a time when children are particularly in need of assistance.[60] (I'll have more to say about social learning in Chapter 6 and the evolution of language in Chapter 5.)

The transition to the juvenile period brings with it continued advances in cognitive and social-cognitive abilities. Brain development slows down, as does growth in general. Late during this period the first pubic and underarm hair appears, as do differences in the voices of boys and girls, both spurred by secretions from the adrenal glands (known as *adrenarche*). During this time children's interactions with peers increase. In most cultures, these interactions occur in sex-segregated groups with boys and girls often engaging in different activities, for example, pretend play parenting for girls and an increase in rough-and-tumble play for boys. Evolutionary developmental psychologist Marco Del Giudice and his colleagues proposed that many forms of peer social interactions (competition, coalition building) are first practiced at this time and can influence a person's future social standing, as well as set the stage for future reproductive strategies.[61]

Although adolescence is associated with increased cognitive abilities, it is more commonly thought of as a time of emotional instability, increased self- and social awareness, and increased risk-taking and the seeking of novelty, behaviors adults often find troubling. These characteristics, however, are likely adaptive, as the emerging adults seek independence from their parents, experiment with new environments, and establish a place in their social group.[62] (I'll have more to say about adolescence in Chapters 5 and 7.)

* * *

Although development changes continuously and gradually over time, it is often convenient to think of life as consisting of a series of stages, so that functioning within one stage is qualitatively different from functioning in earlier or later stages. The transition from infancy to childhood is distinguished by the cessation of nursing and, in humans, by differences in thinking and communication. The term *infancy* comes from the Latin *infantia*, meaning "not able to speak." The transition from childhood to the juvenile period seems to be governed by adrenarche, and the transition from juvenility to adolescence by menarche (in girls) and maturity of the reproductive system and brain more generally. These biologically based changes reflect differences in how children think, behave, feel, and are perceived. Each stage serves to adapt children to their current niche and to foster the expression or acquisition of skills important both for their immediate and their future survival. Could development proceed without stages? Surely, but if it did it is likely that many of the achievements of youth would be hampered and the final product (the "adult") would be a different animal than it is now. Humans take longer to develop than any other mammal, but this was accomplished not only via an extension of the great ape patterns of development, but also through the invention of new life stages.

Development and Evolution

We may have evolved from our ancestors, but each of our ancestors also developed, and it is development that creates the new forms and functions that serve as the grist for the mill of natural selection. Changes in patterns of development, such as extending the period of prenatal brain growth, extending the age of sexual maturity, or reducing reactive aggression, produced new selection pressures, leading eventually to a species that—though recognizable as a relative of our genetic cousin, the chimpanzee—evolved social and cognitive abilities that have resulted in ecological dominance of the planet. Bigger brains, for example, necessitated early birth, which produced a highly dependent infant who experienced an increasingly stimulating social and physical world, which influenced the subsequent social and cognitive skills of the developing child. These changes occurred in a highly social species, and the confluence of large brains, delayed development, and social complexity resulted in an intelligent animal capable of learning the nuances of any culture in the world and transmitting that culture to members of the next generation.

Perhaps somewhat surprisingly, many of the features that set humans apart from the other apes came about through neoteny, the retention of infantile or juvenile characteristics into later life. The focus of this chapter has been primarily on neotenous physical features, primarily as they relate to brain development. The brain is the organ that generates cognition and behavior, and as we'll see in the next chapter, there are many features of young humans that can be described as reflecting *cognitive neoteny*. In many cases, immature behavior or cognition are not things that children must grow out of, the faster the better, but may have value in themselves.

5
The Adaptive Value of Immaturity (or The Benefits of Being Young at Heart)

It didn't happen after Newtown, arguably the most heartbreaking school shooting in U.S. history, with 20 first graders and six teachers gunned down by a 20-year-old with a semi-automatic rifle. The parents of the murdered children petitioned and pleaded for gun control legislation, and although they generated debate for a while and sympathy from the general public, they received little more than thoughts and prayers from the political class. Parkland was different. The campaign led by teenagers had better results— the National Rifle Association lost some corporate support, more than a million marchers took to the streets across the country a month after the shooting, and some gun legislation was enacted in the state of Florida, sometimes referred to as the "gunshine state." The teens continued their advocacy through the 2018 midterm elections and by all accounts changed some minds and some votes.

There is a confluence of reasons why this particular mass shooting produced greater traction for gun control than others, but central is the people who organized it: students from Marjorie Stoneman Douglas High School. These were adolescents, no longer children but not fully adults. The leaders were articulate and charismatic, but likely no more so than the adult leaders of the Sandy Hook groups. They were *digital natives*, intuitively savvy with social media and able to communicate their ideas and organize their actions with millions of people of all ages. But it was their very youth that gave them a leg up relative to the adult protestors of campaigns past. A little more than a year later, a shy but persistent Swedish teenager, Greta Thunberg, gained the attention of the world with her protests about the lack of government response to climate change. The immediate result was school strikes across the globe involving over 4 million people in September 2019, followed by a United Nations Summit on Climate Change later that same month.

The Parkland teenagers and Greta Thunberg possessed the unrealistic optimism of youth, not recognizing how difficult the battle for change would be and thus not deterred from engaging those who disagreed with them. Their youth also provided them with a second advantage: adults are prepared by natural selection to view them positively, to be sympathetic to young people who show both signs of distress and flowering independence. Of course, context matters. Adults are less likely to be positively disposed when encountering a group of teenage boys hanging around a poorly lit street corner late at night.

Development is usually thought of as a progression from small to large, incompetence to competence, and immaturity to maturity. We get *better* as we develop, becoming more coordinated, stronger, smarter, and socially and emotionally capable. From this perspective, immaturity is a necessary evil, something to get over on the way to adulthood. Such a perspective misses an important point, however. Not all features of infancy and childhood are incomplete or miniature versions of adult features. Some serve to adapt the young to their current ecological niche and not to prepare them for life as an adult. In Chapter 1 I defined *ontogenetic adaptations* as mechanisms that promote survival at a specific time in life and disappear when they are no longer needed. The placenta and umbilical cord are clear examples of structural ontogenetic adaptations, whereas the sucking and rooting reflexes are behavioral examples. Human infants and children likely possess many other ontogenetic adaptations, features of a young animal that promote its survival or success at a particular time in development but then disappear when they are no longer needed. For example, just as adults are prone to view favorably an adolescent's not-quite-grown-up appearance and behavior, at least in some contexts, so are adults biased to view infants' immature physical and behavioral characteristics in a positive light, increasing the chances that the highly dependent infant will be cared for and survive. Other aspects of immaturity can be thought of as examples of behavioral or *cognitive neoteny*—youthful features of behaving or thinking that, rather than hinder development, may actually facilitate development or be necessary for later mature functioning.

In this chapter I first look at the role that infants' immature facial features has on adult attachment and caregiving and how other signs of immaturity may continue to foster caregiving from adults for older children. The next section examines cognitive neoteny and the adaptive impact children's immature cognition sometimes has on their behavior. I then look at how some aspects of immaturity may contribute to the learning and evolution of language, perhaps the most prototypical of all human abilities. The final section examines the very serious phenomenon of play and its role in human evolution and development.

You've Got the Cutest Little Baby Face

Children and their parents have a shared interest: having children survive and become adults so they, too, can have children. To this end, parents invest time and resources into their children, much to their children's benefit. However, such a shared interest goes only so far. For children, surviving is everything, and thus they want as much investment from their parents as they can get. For parents, investment in a child must be weighed with respect to that child's chances of reaching adulthood, the amount of resources (including social support) a parent has available at the time, and the cost of investing in that child relative to investing in other children the parent currently has or may have in the future. Natural selection has provided parents with adaptations for evaluating the fitness of their offspring, helping parents make good investment decisions about when and how much to invest in any given child. However, children are not passive participants in this game of survival but have evolved "psychological weapons in order to compete with their parents."[1]

Infancy is perhaps the most critical time in a person's life for gaining the nurturing needed for survival. Until relatively recently, only about 25% of children born survived to their first birthdays, with nearly half dying before puberty.[2] As I've noted in earlier chapters, human infants are especially helpless for an extended period of time relative to our simian cousins and require substantial care, often from a multitude of people. In many traditional and hunter-gatherer societies, newborns are evaluated for signs of health and are abandoned or killed if found lacking.[3] What can infants do to increase the chance of obtaining the care they need from their parents to survive?

The Benefits of *Kindchenschema*

Natural selection has provided infants with a number of features to promote caregiving from adults. British psychoanalyst John Bowlby, the father of attachment theory, noted that adults are particularly sensitive to babies' cries, smiles, and movements, and infants displaying such behaviors are likely to be attended to and cared for.[4] Another powerful cue that babies possess to get investment from adults is their immature facial features. Recall from the opening pages of the first chapter the photo of my granddaughter, Amelia. At 5 months of age, she displayed features that adults find difficult to ignore: fat cheeks, flat nose, rounded head that is large relative to body size, and large eyes relative to head size. These are characteristics that Konrad Lorenz called *Kindchenschema*, or *baby schema*, or, more colloquially, *babyness*.[5] Compared with adult faces, people's attention is attracted to infant faces, and everything else being equal, they prefer to look at the faces of infants rather than those adults.[6] But it's not just greater attention that *Kindchenschema* evokes: Lorenz proposed that baby faces evolved to generate positive feelings and nurturance from adults, all in the quest of surviving the dangerous stage of infancy. One possible reason for adults' preference for babyness is that these cues are relatively honest signs of health and the general fitness of infants.

The results from over 100 studies in the past 70 or so years have generally confirmed Lorenz's hypothesis: Using a host of measures, infants with cuter faces (that is, faces with greater degrees of babyness) are associated with greater interest and caring than less-cute infants. Adults rate baby-faced infants as more attractive, friendlier, more sociable, easier to care for, and more helpless and powerless than less-baby-faced infants.[7] A baby-faced schema has a positive emotional influence on adult–child interactions. Adults show more affectionate interactions with and display greater empathy for cuter than for less-cute infants and are also more likely to express greater motivation to care for cuter than less-cute infants as well as make favorable hypothetical adoption decisions.[8] For example, in one study, evolutionary developmental psychologist Anthony Volk and his colleagues asked adults to rate 12 different photos of children ranging from 6 months to 6 years of age in terms of cuteness and later to make a hypothetical adoption decision for each child. The researchers reported that adults were more likely to rate the more immature-looking child as cute, and these ratings were correlated with their likelihood of making an adoption decision—the more baby-faced a child looked, the greater the likelihood that people made a positive adoption decision.[9] This bias toward cute infants in not limited to babies of one's own ethnic group but extends to infants from members of different races (for example, Caucasian adults respond similarly to cues of cuteness in Caucasian, Asian, and African infants), and as any kitten or puppy owner knows, we even respond to cuteness cues in other species.[10]

Let me provide one research example demonstrating how adults view cute versus less-cute babies. Behavioral biologist Melanie Glocker and her colleagues[11] experimentally manipulated the degree to which infant faces reflected babyness, thus controlling for possible confounding factors such

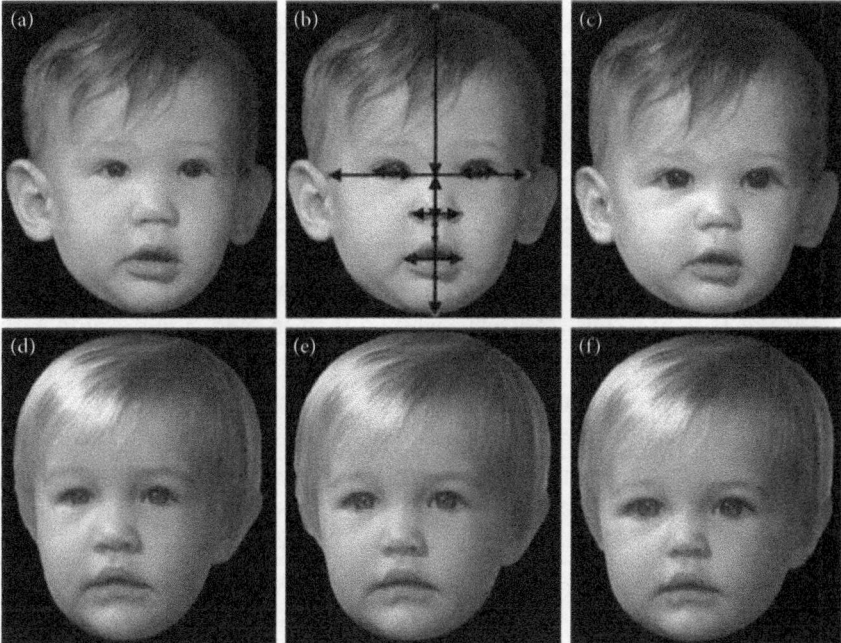

Figure 5.1. Photographs can be manipulated to produce infants with low (photos a and d) or high (c and f) baby schema features, relative to unmanipulated photos (b and e).
Source: Glocker et al., 2009a, with permission.

as hairstyle, eye color, or facial symmetry. Figure 5.1 shows two infant faces and how they were manipulated to make each face reflect high or low baby schema. The photos in the middle are unmanipulated portraits of infants. The photos on the left reflect changes made to produce low baby schema (more mature looking), while the photos on the right reflect high baby schema (more immature looking). As you can see, subtle differences in the roundness of the cheeks, the length and width of the head, distance between the eyes, length and width of the nose, width of the mouth, and distance between the nose and mouth produced cuter (photos c and f) and less cute (photos a and d) infants. One group of college students rated a total of 60 high- and low-baby schema photos as well as unmanipulated photos in terms of cuteness ("How cute is this infant?") on a 5-point scale from "Not very cute" to "Very cute." Another group rated the same set of photos on a 5-point scale in terms of how interested they would be in taking care of each infant ("How much does the infant make you feel that you would like to take care of it?"). For both the Cuteness and Caregiving tasks, the young adults gave the highest ratings to the high-baby-schema infants and lowest to the low-baby-schema infants, with ratings for the unmanipulated infants in the middle.

Sex Differences in the Effects of Baby Schema

Both men and women are susceptible to the positive effects of babyness, but these effects tend to be stronger in women than in men.[12] For example, in one study researchers varied the baby-schema properties of infants' faces and asked men and women to judge the cuteness of the different faces. Women, in general, were more sensitive to differences in cuteness than men, but this differed with the women's age and reproductive status. Young women between 19 and 26 years of age were the most sensitive to cuteness cues, followed closely by women 45 to 51 years of age. In contrast, women 53 to 60 years of age performed more poorly compared with the younger women, and were indistinguishable from both younger (19 to 26 years) and older (53 to 60 years) men. The authors suggested that this pattern reflects a hormonal link between infant cues for cuteness and motivation to provide care, with younger women being especially sensitive to the baby-schema cues. Consistent with the idea that some portion of this sex effect was due to hormones, premenopausal women were more sensitive to cuteness cues than postmenopausal women, who were comparable to men.[13] Other research has found that women tend to choose to look at cuter babies when ovulating.[14] The stronger effect of babyness in women should not be surprising, as historically and prehistorically the bulk of childcare has fallen on women, making it both to a baby's and a mother's advantage for women to be sensitive to infants' cues of dependence.

Consistent with the idea that sex difference in sensitivity to babyness might be related to changes in hormones comes from research looking at age differences when this bias for baby-faced infants is first seen in development. Several researchers have reported that preference for high-baby-schema faces, especially in girls, is not found until adolescence.[15] For instance, in one study 12- and 13-year-old girls, half of whom had had their first period (post-menarcheal) and half of whom had not (pre-menarcheal), were shown slides of infant and adult faces and asked to choose which face they preferred. The post-menarcheal girls preferred the infant faces significantly more often than the pre-menarcheal girls. In a second study, pre- and post-menarcheal girls and same-age boys rated photos of infants, peers, college students, and 30- to 50-year-old adults in terms of liking. Post-menarcheal girls displayed the highest preference for infant faces, with pre-menarcheal girls showing less of a preference for infant faces and the same preferences as the boys, suggesting that this preference may be related to the onset of puberty and possible parenthood, at least in girls.[16] Although most studies report that the preference for baby faces doesn't appear until adolescence, several researchers have reported that 3- to 6-year-old children, and even 5- to 15-month-old infants, look longer at more attractive and cuter infant faces than less attractive infant faces, suggesting that the bias for babyness has early developmental origins and that a "preparation-for-parenthood" explanation may be only part of the story.[17]

Baby Schema and the Brain

In the last two decades, advances in neuroscience have made it possible to link important psychological behaviors to functioning in the brain, and the effects of baby schema are no exception. At one level, it should not be surprising that the effects of babyness correspond to differences in brain activity. Science has long known that mind and behavior are governed by the brain. It would be startling if neurological activity were *not* related to important psychological phenomena. What is important, however, is understanding what regions of the brain are related with the various babyness effects and the types of psychological functions these brain areas are typically associated with. For example, although there is great overlap between brain regions that process both adult and infant faces, infant faces generally produce more rapid neural responses than adult faces and recruit additional brain regions.[18] Viewing baby faces has also been shown to elicit strong reactions in brain areas associated with processing emotion, causing neuroscientist Lizhu Luo and colleagues to conclude that "overall infant faces evoke [from adults] both stronger arousal and enhanced responses to both positive and negative cues from the infant."[19] Other studies have found that baby faces are associated with greater activity in brain regions associated with empathy, reward, attachment, and motor behavior.[20] The extensive activation in motor areas when viewing infant faces may cause adults to be extra careful when interacting with babies. This is supported by studies showing that viewing cute infants increased adults' fine-motor abilities and that adults reported more positive affect, tenderness, and calmness after viewing infantile faces of puppies and kittens.[21] Other research has reported that mothers show stronger activation of numerous brain areas when viewing their own baby versus another infant.[22] In general, the evidence indicates that viewing infant faces with high baby schema evokes greater activation in brain areas associated with processing faces, emotion, and attention than viewing low-baby-schema faces.[23]

Becoming Cute and Not-So-Cute

The effects of babyness can have a powerful impact on how adults view and interact with infants, with cuter infants seemingly evoking more positive affect and interactions with adults than less-cute infants. But we do not stay forever cute. At what age do the effects of babyness emerge, when are they the greatest, and when do they start to decline?

From an evolutionary perspective, one might think that infants would be their most adorable at birth. This is a time of great vulnerability, and it would be in infants' best interests to evoke as much love and attention from adults as they can. However, as anyone who has ever seen newborns can attest, they often fall short of the highest standards of baby schema. (As Winston Churchill, the World War II Prime Minister of Great Britain, is attributed as saying, "All babies look like me. But then, I look like all babies.") Many newborns have misshapen heads from their trip through the birth canal, and infants born prematurely have lower body weight and more atypical features than full-term babies. Although many newborns can rightfully be called cute, on average, the features most associated with high baby schema are not in full bloom until between 3 and 6 months of age.[24] This may not be to the neonate's advantage, yet it may provide some benefits to adults. Ancestral parents had to make tough decisions about whether to invest in a newborn or not, with abandonment or infanticide being an option if an infant was not likely to survive, especially when resources were limited. So although it may not have been in newborns' best interest for their parents (most probably their mothers) to be objective in evaluating the health and fitness of an infant, it likely was to the parents' advantage.

These age differences in perceptions of babyness were confirmed in research by evolutionary developmental psychologist Prarthana Franklin and her colleagues.[25] Franklin and company showed a group of adults photographs of newborns and of 3- and 6-month-old babies and asked them to rate the babies in terms of cuteness, happiness, and health, and to make hypothetical adoption decisions about the babies. They reported that newborns received lower ratings than 3- and 6-month-old infants for each measure, confirming that adults do, indeed, feel more favorable toward slightly older infants relative to newborns. I should note that ratings on a 5-point scale were all above 3 for the newborns (average ratings ranged from 3.06 for happiness to 4.08 for adoption decision), so that adults' perception of newborns was generally positive, just not as positive as for older infants.

When do the benefits of babyness decrease? Adults rate other adults and older children with babyish facial features as less intelligent, more socially dependent, more honest, warmer, and physically weaker than their more mature-looking peers, suggesting that the effects of babyness continue to influence adults' judgments long past infancy.[26] Other research indicates, however, that the positive effects of baby schema persist only to about 4 to 5 years of age, after which adults' judgments of attractiveness and likeability for children's faces do not differ from their judgments of adult faces.[27] Relatedly, neuroscience research indicates that some brain responses to photographs vary as a function of the age of the person depicted in the photograph, with photos of infants showing the greatest activation, followed by photos of prepubescent children, and the least activation for photos of adults.[28]

Cues of Immaturity Beyond Infancy

Children are most vulnerable and in need of care during infancy, but they still have many years before they are self-sufficient. Are there any properties children beyond the earliest years of life display that may serve as signs of immaturity to adults and thus cues to provide nurturance? My Spanish colleague, evolutionary developmental psychologist Carlos Hernández Blasi, and I have conducted a number of studies looking at this question. One feature of preschool-age children that seems to promote positive affect from adults is their voice. In one study, adults listened to pairs of voices of 5- and 10-year-old children and were asked to make judgments about which child (or which voice, actually) best reflected attributes of positive affect (for example, cute, friendly, nice, likeable), negative affect (for example, sneaky, likely to lie, feel more irritated with), intelligence, and helplessness. The researchers reported that adults expressed more positive affect and helplessness attitudes toward the voices of 5-year-olds, attributed greater intelligence to the voices of 10-year-olds, and showed no bias toward either the younger or older voices for negative affect.[29] It should probably not be surprising that adults use young children's voices as cues to their maturity and dependence. Language typically blooms between children's second and third birthdays, transforming how children communicate and interact with people and making the medium of their messages (that is, their voices) important and likely honest cues of their developmental status.

But *what* young children say might be as important and useful cues to their maturity as the voices they use to say it. In related research using similar methods to the "voices" studies, adults were asked to judge which of two hypothetical children, the one expressing mature cognition or the one expressing immature cognition, reflected best a series of adjectives and statements for positive affect, negative affect, intelligence, and helplessness. Results were consistent for males and females, parents and nonparents, people with little versus much experience with children, and Spanish and American participants: children expressing immature cognition were selected more often for positive affect and helplessness and less often for negative affect and intelligence compared with children expressing more mature cognition. When cognitive statements were paired with more versus less mature faces (reflecting children of about 5 and 9 years, respectively) the level of cognition (mature versus immature) was more important in influencing peoples' decisions than the faces.[30] Similar to research using infant faces, the positive effects for some types of cognitive immaturity is not observed until late adolescence, suggesting that the bias may be influenced by hormones and related to the possible onset of parenthood.[31]

It's worth noting that in these studies demonstrating the benefit of cognitive immaturity on adult judgments, not all forms of cognitively immature statements had a beneficial effect. Positive effects were only found for immature cognition that reflected what the researchers referred to as *supernatural thinking*, reflected in statements such as "The sun's not out because it's mad," or "Mountains have big peaks for long walks and small peaks for short walks." Statements manifesting equally immature cognition that reflected *natural thinking*, as expressed by overestimation of one's abilities ("I can remember all 20 words") or poor inhibition ("I had to peek, even though I was told not to"), did not provide any benefits and, in fact, were associated with higher ratings of negative affect. As a coauthor of these studies, I admit we were initially perplexed by the beneficial effects being found only for the immature supernatural statements. Upon reflection, however, we realized that supernatural thinking is not limited to childhood but typifies the thinking of most adults in traditional societies, unschooled adults, and most educated adults in pre-Renaissance Europe.[32] Supernatural thinking is observed under some circumstances among educated adults today, outside of the realm of religion. For example, more than 31% of American and 25% of British adults believe in astrology, and about 40% of both U.S. and British adults believe in haunted houses;[33] even professional biologists take longer to decide whether plants versus animals are living things.[34] We argued that some forms of supernatural thinking may represent a default way of understanding some "natural" phenomena, and that supernatural thinking itself is not limited to childhood but is also a feature of adult thought. As we noted, "If scientific geniuses such as Newton, Copernicus, and Kepler could believe in angels, astrology, and alchemy, such thinking, by itself, can hardly qualify as a form of immature cognition . . . One explanation [for adults' and older adolescents' preferences for children expressing immature supernatural thinking] may be due to the historical and evolutionary newness of scientific thinking. Although scientific thinking is emphasized in modern society, such thinking is an evolutionary novelty, and adults and older adolescents still favor the more intuitive supernatural thinking, at least when expressed by children."[35]

***

Infancy is a perilous time, and natural selection has provided babies with a number of psychological "weapons" to increase the chance that their parents will attend to, care for, and fall in love with them. One such cue is the *Kindchenschema*, with natural selection shaping adults, and especially fertile women, to be captured by an infant's immature facial features. These cues not only serve the infants, but also seem to be signs to parents about the health and viability of an infant. Cuter babies may be healthier babies, and ancestral parents sometimes had to make difficult life-and-death decisions about how much or whether to invest in their young offspring. As children get older, other cues, including their voices and some of their expressions of cognitive immaturity, replace facial features as reliable indicators of children's need for attention and care. Lorenz and other scientists have noted that the young of other species often display signs, such as special coloration, to signal their immaturity and need for care. In some sense then, humans are little different from silvered leaf monkeys, whose newborns are the color of carrots, which seems to foster interest in females of the group to promote caregiving; however, humans' extended period of dependence requires that they evoke care from adults for a longer period of time, necessitating the evolution and development of additional cues to immaturity.

Cognitive Neoteny

Perhaps the greatest champion of humans as a neotenous species was the British-American anthropologist Ashley Montagu. Montagu was a public intellectual who was forced to leave a university position at Rutgers in the 1950s after the McCarthy hearings. He was the author of more than 60 books, including *Man's Most Dangerous Myth: The Fallacy of Race*, *The Natural Superiority of Women*, *On Being Human*, and *Elephant Man: A Study in Human Dignity*. Although attracting less attention from the general public than some of his more controversial publications, his book *Growing Young* was, according to a book-jacket testimonial by renowned Harvard paleontologist and evolutionist Stephen Jay Gould, "The best statement ever written on the most important, neglected theme of human life and evolution." Montagu wrote that, for humans,

> evolution has consisted of a shedding of the adult traits of our ancestral forms, and an increasing retention and development of the juvenile traits of those forms ... [W]e are designed to fulfill the bountiful promise of the child; to grow and develop as children, rather than into the kind of adults we have been taught to believe we ought to become ... In other words, the spirit of the child is, in the profoundest sense, the spirit of humanity, an adaptive trait of the greatest biological value.[36]

Montagu identified 27 "basic behavioral needs" that he believed appeared early in development and that he regarded as neotenous.

Montagu may have waxed a bit poetic about the neotenous nature of children, especially by current scientific standards, but I believe that his emphasis on the extension of juvenile characteristics into adulthood as features of *Homo sapiens* was generally on point. Although many of the basic behavioral needs that Montagu identified as being neotenous are highly questionable (for example, love, friendship, need to work, need to organize, dance, song), others I believe hit the mark, including flexibility and resiliency (both reflective of plasticity); explorativeness, need to know, need to learn, curiosity, experimental mindedness (reflective of humans' continuous quest for information/knowledge); play, joyfulness, imagination (each related to the extension of play, particularly fantasy play, beyond the juvenile period); and optimism.

In this section I extend Montagu's perspective, though looking at childhood features of cognition a bit differently. As mentioned earlier, development is usually thought of as progressing from immaturity to maturity, with adult form and function being the ultimate goal. From this perspective cognitive immaturity is something we need to get over, the sooner the better. Yet, some aspects of youth may not be impediments to be overcome but, rather, adaptations suited to a particular time in development that disappear or are replaced by more mature forms of behavior or cognition later in life.[37] Here I discuss several aspects of infants' and children's immature cognition that serve adaptive functions early in development and pave the way for more mature forms of cognition. Most of what I describe in this section can be seen as ontogenetic adaptations, defined in Chapter 1 as adaptations that adjust infants and children to their immediate environment and not necessarily to a future one. I begin examining children's self-centered perspective (egocentricity), followed by immature but adaptive aspects of children's memory, the "design stance" with respect to tool use, and finally overestimation of one's abilities.

Egocentricity

I recall a childhood encounter with a neighbor boy who was curious about the ages of my parents.

"How old are your mother and father?" Maurice asked.

"I don't know," I replied, "but I know that my mother is older than my father."

"That's impossible," Maurice said, "and illegal! Fathers are *always* older than mothers."

That night I checked with my parents and was told that my mother was, indeed, a few months older than my father, and that this was perfectly legal in the state of Massachusetts. I didn't realize it at the time, but one reason for Maurice's insistence that fathers are always older than mothers was that his father was 15 years older than his mother, and he believed that this must be true for all marriages.

Maurice's self-centered view concerning age differences between mothers and fathers reflects what the Swiss psychologist Jean Piaget called *egocentricity*. Preschool children, in particular, tend to have difficulty taking the perspective of others, assuming others see and understand things the way they do themselves.[38] This is not a personality defect such as narcissism but, rather, reflects the fact that much of children's thinking is centered around themselves. They, of course, are not as self-centered as infants, who behave as if objects that are out of their immediate perception no longer exist, nor does a self-centered attitude totally disappear in adulthood. Subsequent research found that preschool children are not quite as egocentric as Piaget initially proposed; however, egocentricity does seem to typify preschool-age children and does decline with age.[39]

The Benefits of Talking to Yourself. Such overly self-centered cognition would appear to be a serious hindrance for effective functioning, and it is; any adult who was as self-centered in his or her perspective as the typical 4-year-old would likely find completing everyday tasks difficult. Yet, given the niche that young children inhabit, an egocentric perspective can sometimes have its benefits. For example, young children's egocentrism has been proposed to facilitate early peer interactions during play. Preschool children often engage in *parallel play* (which is perhaps better described as *parallel interaction*), in which two or more children play near one another, sometimes in the same activity, but not actually *with* one another. During such play, children often talk about what they're doing. For example, one child playing in a sandbox might say "I'm making a big road with my bulldozer," while another child says "I'm racing my car down the road and banging through the wall." Although, on the surface, this appears to be a conversation, it is not; there is no obvious turn taking, and what one child says is independent of what the other child is talking about. Piaget referred to such exchanges as *collective monologues*, a reflection of young children's egocentric orientation, with children talking *with* one another but not really *to* one another.[40] Several researchers have proposed that there may be some benefit to these self-centered interactions. Such semi-social play may make it easier for young children with minimal social skills to move into more cooperative play. Children who did not talk to themselves in a group setting may be less likely to later find themselves in true social play with peers.[41]

Although older children are less likely to talk aloud to themselves when in public, they still engage in what the Russian psychologist Lev Vygotsky called *private speech* (and what Piaget referred to as *egocentric speech*) when solving certain problems. Vygotsky proposed that people use language to guide their behavior. Whereas older children and adults use covert language (talking "in their heads") to help them solve problems, younger children lack the cognitive abilities to do so; rather, they talk out loud to themselves, using their private speech as a *cognitive self-guidance system* (for example, when working on a puzzle saying aloud to themselves, "Now I need a corner piece that's mostly blue to fit in here"). With maturation, young children's overt speech goes "underground" as covert verbal thought.[42] Although adults sometimes still talk aloud to themselves when faced with a difficult problem, it is questionable whether such speech actually helps their performance.[43]

Research has generally supported Vygotsky's theory of private speech development, with a number of studies showing that children's use of private speech when solving school-type tasks decreases between the first and third grades, is positively associated with performance for younger but not older children, is more apt to be used for more difficult than less difficult problems, and goes "underground" as covert verbal thought earlier for brighter than less bright children.[44] Talking aloud to oneself—using overt language to initiate and sometimes inhibit action—is, indeed, a reflection of immature cognition, although a type of cognition that may help children solve otherwise insolvable problems. Telling a young reader, for example, to "Read quietly to yourself!" may not be worthwhile, as beginning readers may not be able to read quietly "in their heads."

The Benefits of Self-referencing. Not only do young children assume that others perceive the world as they do, or are sometimes unaware that their speech is falling on deaf ears, so to speak, but their egocentric perspective also results in their referencing events and objects to themselves, and such promiscuous self-referencing may have benefits for learning. For instance, not only children but also adults tend to remember information better when they can reference the information to themselves. This was illustrated in research by psychologist Charles Lord, who showed adults a series of adjectives and asked them to determine whether each word was either like their fathers, a famous person (Walter Cronkite, a news anchorman, who at the time was the best-known person in America), or themselves. People who related the adjectives to themselves later remembered more of the words, demonstrating that self-referencing enhances learning.[45] This effect is also found in children, who have a "natural" tendency to reference everything to themselves. For example, in one study preschool children showed higher levels of recognition memory for self-referenced items, including actions attributed to a cartoon character with the child's name.[46]

Why might self-referencing benefit learning and memory? Self-referencing results in greater elaboration of memory representations, making it easier to retrieve that information later on. The self is likely the most elaborated of representations, and young children's bias toward self-referencing results in richer encoding of information and thus greater likelihood of remembering the information at a later time. For an organism with limited memory skills, an egocentric perspective, though a reflection of immaturity, has its advantages.

Egocentricity in Adolescence. Egocentricity can also provide some benefits to people with more substantial memory and reasoning abilities. Piaget noted that adolescents' concerns about how they fit into an emerging adulthood, their future in society, and how they may impact that future brings with it its own form of self-centeredness. For Piaget, the advent of formal operational thinking—the ability to deal with what is possible and hypothetical, not just what is "real"—gives adolescents a new sense of intellectual power, often believing that their ideas are unique to them and certainly superior to the "stodgy and simple-minded" ideas of their elders. This sense of intellectual uniqueness, however, is accompanied by an increasing concern about what others are thinking about them. As a result, adolescents often have the mistaken belief that other people are as concerned with their feelings and actions as they are, which only enhances their self-consciousness. Adolescents feel they are constantly "on stage," playing to what developmental psychologist David Elkind called an *imaginary audience,* feeling that they are the primary focus of other people's attention. More related to the idea that egocentricity may provide some adaptive advantage for adolescents is Elkind's proposal that teenagers' egocentrism leads to what he called the *personal fable,* a belief in one's uniqueness and invulnerability.[47] A number of researchers have reported that belief in personal invulnerability (that is, the personal fable) during adolescence and young adulthood is associated with increased risk-taking and sensation-seeking in both males and females. Tests of invulnerability, assessing beliefs in both physical invulnerability (for example, "Taking safety precautions is far more important for other people than it is for me"; "There are times when I think I am indestructible") and psychological invulnerability (for example, "What people say about me has no effect on me at all"; "It is just impossible for people to hurt my feelings"), are associated with the likelihood of teens and young adults engaging in a number of well-known high-risk behaviors, including tobacco use, suntanning, driving while drinking, texting while driving, parkour tricks on rooftops, and drug use, among others.[48] Although there are some inconsistencies in the research findings, most agree that the effect of the imaginary audience and personal fable peaks during early adolescence, although feelings of invulnerability can persist into young adulthood.

Many of the things parents of teenagers spend sleepless night worrying about can be attributed, in part, to adolescents' sense of invulnerability and subsequent risk-taking. There are obviously potentially negative consequences of adolescent egocentricity. What, then, might be the benefits? Feelings of invulnerability during adolescence are accompanied by adolescents' increased optimism about themselves and their future, with both occurring at a time in life when children are developing an adult identity and an increasing sense of independence, and such optimism is often associated with positive psychological outcomes (see discussion in following section).[49] Although the increased risk-taking behavior of adolescents can be worrisome, risk has not only costs but benefits. Young people who attempt new tasks, who take risks and succeed (and even who fail, so long as failure doesn't result in long-term detriments or death), increase their separation from their parents, learn important lessons that will be useful to adult functioning, and may hasten entry into adult life.[50] In addition, adolescents' sense of psychological invulnerability ("I won't get my feelings hurt," "I don't care what other people think") seems to promote positive coping and adjustment mechanisms.[51]

Adolescents' sense of invulnerability and sensation seeking make them susceptible to the potential glories of war. War for adolescents can provide adventure, mean serving a higher cause, be a rite of passage, and be seen as fulfilling their fantasies about becoming heroes. Adolescent and young-adult males are also especially likely to engage in aggression, risk-taking, and competitive behavior, which are means of achieving status and impressing women (the young-male syndrome), further increasing their likelihood of becoming warriors. In some military contexts, adolescents' beliefs in their uniqueness and invulnerability make them ideal soldiers in contrast to older men who are apt to have a better notion of their mortality. Societies have long enlisted adolescents, and even children, as soldiers. Thousands of young teens served in both World War I and II, and approximately 20% of the combatants in the American Civil War were under 18.[52] The willingness and ability of adolescents and young men to put themselves in harm's way was surely beneficial to the survival of many ancient human groups. Many invulnerable-feeling ancient teenagers may have benefited from becoming warriors in terms of gaining status and mates, but in modern warfare they often do not make effective soldiers and may be particularly susceptible to the traumas of war. In 1990 the United Nations adopted *The Convention on the Rights of the Child*, which prohibited conscription of children under 18 years, volunteers under 16 years, and 16- and 17-year-old recruits from taking a direct part in combat.[53] The UN resolution is obviously not being followed in many conflicts around the globe, with many children (defined as someone under 18 years of age) suffering the consequences.

Memory

There can be little question of the significance of memory for our lives. Our memories of past events and "facts" determine, to a large extent, how we behave. Memory is critical in determining who we are. In some nontrivial respect we *are* our memories. Nearly all acts of cognition involve memory in one way or another. Memory can refer both to the repository of knowledge one has (one's "memories," such as the Christmas the family went to stay with Grandma and Grandpa, what you had for breakfast this morning, or the definition of "breakfast") and to the act of remembering, that is, the process by which one recognizes or recalls specific people, events, or facts. Each of these types of memory develops and each evolved.

Perhaps of greatest significance for human evolution is the distinction between implicit and explicit memory. *Implicit memory* (or implicit cognition) is an evolutionarily older form of representation. It is not available to consciousness (self-awareness) and is reflected by knowledge of procedures, learning via classical and operant conditioning, and the intuitions people have. For example, I'm sure each reader knows how to tie a bow or ride a bicycle, but this knowledge is likely implicit. It's difficult to tell someone how you perform these acts without going through the physical motions. Implicit memory is contrasted with *explicit memory*, which is memory for events that can be brought to consciousness—these memories can be declared through language and, thus, are sometimes referred to as *declarative memory* (telling someone about that Christmas at Grandma's, for instance). Most researchers argue that explicit memory is unique to humans, or found in other species in only limited situations, and that it provided our species with a substantial adaptive advantage. With declarative memory we can engage in "mental time travel," thinking about the past and anticipating the future.[54] The memories of human infants are believed to be entirely implicit in nature, with explicit forms of memory developing beginning in the second and third years of life.

The emergence of explicit memory would seem to be a major accomplishment, and, at first blush, it is difficult to see how *not* possessing explicit memory could provide infants or children with any advantage. Yet, developmental psychologist Katherine Nelson suggested just that. She proposed that the near total dependence infants have on adults should cause them to be especially attentive to recurring social events in their lives; acquiring memory representations of important people, places, and things in their environments can be adequately accomplished by implicit (unconscious) memory systems, making explicit memories of little use to infants and young children. According to Nelson, "building in complex cognitive goals, and the mechanisms such as explicit or declarative memory for achieving them, appears burdensome and likely to interfere with the primary requirements of this period of life."[55]

On a speculative level, the well-known phenomenon of *infantile amnesia*—the inability of people to remember specific episodes the happened much before the age of 3 or 4 years—may have some adaptive benefits. The favored explanation for infantile amnesia is that events are encoded differently (or at least not as elaboratively) during infancy and early childhood than they are later in life, making it difficult or impossible for the adult brain to retrieve information encoded earlier in life.[56] Yet, the general inability to recall details from childhood may have its benefits. Many experiences of infancy and early childhood are relevant only to that time in life, and remembering these events may interfere with and contradict the knowledge that is needed to function in later environments. This is similar to an argument that Brandi Green and I made with respect to slow and inefficient information processing characteristic of infants and young children:

> Because little in the way of cognitive processing can be automatized early . . . , children are better prepared to adapt cognitively to later environments . . . Cognitive flexibility in the species is maintained by an immature nervous system that gradually permits the automatization of more mental operations, increasing the likelihood that lessons learned as a young child will not interfere with the qualitatively different tasks required of the adult.[57]

Other aspects of young children's cognition seem to help them learn and later remember events. In the previous section we saw how young children's persistent self-referencing resulted in enhanced learning and memory in some contexts. Are there any other seemingly immature aspects of cognition that may have a counterintuitive memory benefit? One that has been suggested is the ease with which young children's recollection of events can be influenced by the suggestions of adults. There is an extensive body of research showing that preschool children in particular are apt to change their testimony about what they have witnessed, and in many cases seemingly change their memory for events, when asked leading questions by an adult interviewer.[58]

Such elevated levels of suggestibility are typically viewed as a problem, not an adaptation, especially in forensic settings. From an evolutionary perspective, however, it makes sense for young children to be attentive to the suggestions of their parents and other significant people in their lives. Parents are especially important sources of information for young children, and interpreting novel events from a parent's perspective likely has adaptive value for children, resulting in the acquisition of culturally relevant knowledge. Failing to remember events the way adults do could lead to less efficient learning of valuable skills and knowledge, particularly for children with limited technical and social experience.[59]

Consistent with this interpretation are findings that children from about the age of 3 will frequently copy all aspects of a model's behavior with respect to using a tool or engaging in other complicated behavior (for example, "rituals"), even when some of the modeled actions are obviously unnecessary, such as tapping a stick on the table before using it to retrieve an out-of-reach toy.[60] This is referred to as *overimitation*, which was discussed briefly in Chapter 4 and will be discussed in greater detail in Chapter 6. One interpretation of overimitation is that it is an adaptation that promotes social learning. Children view the actions of an adult or older peer as *normative*—this is how *we* perform this task or behave in this situation.[61] When watching someone use a tool in a particular way, children assume, usually correctly, that the adult knows what he or she is doing, and copying all actions, even seemingly unnecessary ones, is an adaptive way of acquiring important technical and social information. Preschool children seem to be especially likely to overimitate actions performed by their mothers, even if an unfamiliar adult model is identified as an expert for a particular task.[62] In some cases, irrelevant actions may interfere with solving problems, but children can later refine their behavior through experience.

In general, children seem biased to believe in the credibility of kindly adults. This can sometimes lead to false memories and inefficient problem solving, but more often than not this was likely adaptive for our ancestors and continues to be adaptive for children today.

The Design Stance in Tool Use

Humans life is full of artifacts—objects constructed by humans for specific purposes, such as cups for drinking, spoons for eating, and computers for a seemingly infinite number of purposes. More than any other species, humans need to know how to deal with the plethora of artifacts their culture provides. We call some artifacts *tools*, and children seem to have been specially adapted by natural selection to learn to use tools.

Tools are used to solve problems, and one adaptation that, on first inspection, may appear to hinder problem solving is what philosopher Daniel Dennett called the *design stance*.[63] The design stance refers to people's belief that a tool was designed for a specific purpose. The reason that it is sometimes viewed as a detriment to problem solving is that it can inhibit innovation. In the early part of the 20th century, Gestalt psychologist Karl Duncker developed the *candle problem* (see Figure 5.2). He gave adults a corkboard, a candle, a book of matches, and a box of thumbtacks; their task was to affix

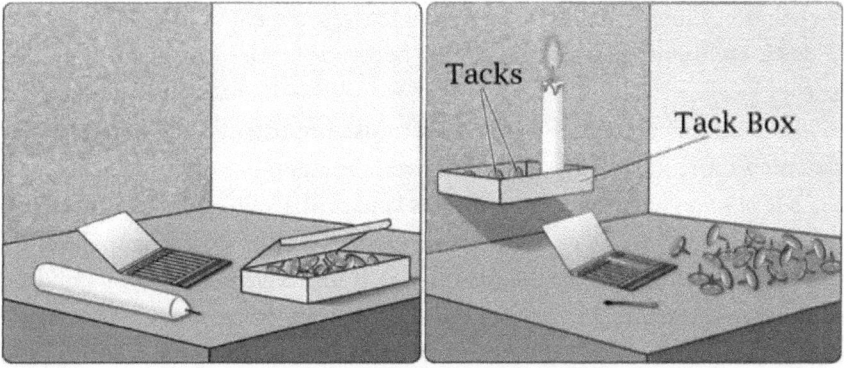

Figure 5.2. Duncker's candle problem. Adult participants were asked to affix a lighted candle to the corkboard so that it did not drip on the table below. People had a difficult time using familiar objects in a novel way, a phenomenon called *functional fixedness*.
Source: Lu et al., 2019, with permission.

a lighted candle to the cork board so that it did not drip on the table below. People had a hard time solving the problem, although the solution was relatively easy once you knew it: attach the box to the upright cork board using a thumbtack, then put the lighted candle in the box. What made this task difficult was that people had to find novel uses for the objects, and this required *not* thinking of how objects are typically used (thumbtack boxes are used for holding thumbtacks). Duncker referred to this phenomenon as *functional fixedness*, the tendency not to identify alternative uses for familiar objects (thumbtacks boxes can serve as a shelf to hold a candle).[64] The design stance would seem to exacerbate rather than reduce functional fixedness and, thus, would seem to be a hindrance to effective tool use.

The design stance is found early in development, displayed by infants as young as 12 months of age. Infants and toddlers understand that spoons are used for eating and hammers for hitting, for example, and when shown how to use novel tools they display functional fixedness, being less likely to use a tool for a purpose other than one they had been shown. For example, 3-year-old children believe that an object designed for one purpose (for instance, catching bugs) is, indeed, a "bug catcher" even though it can also be used for another function (collecting raindrops).[65]

Given that the design stance often leads to less flexible tool use, how can it be seen as an adaption? The answer is quite straightforward: although the design stance may increase functional fixedness, more often than not it is going to lead to acquiring a proper use of an important human artifact, especially for young children who have a lot to learn about life. Beginning in infancy, children believe that people's behavior is based on intention (that is, they perform actions "for a reason"), and this includes how people use tools. Children can quickly learn how to use important human artifacts by watching more knowledgeable adults who, much more often than not, will use a tool in an adaptive way. This bias is part of a suite of adaptations children seemingly have evolved for learning about tools. According to developmental psychologists Krista Casler and Deborah Kelemen, "young children exhibit rapid learning for artifact function, already possessing an early foundation to some of our most remarkable capacities as tool manufacturers and users."[66] One of these adaptations is something that on the surface may appear to be a handicap and a reflection of immature cognition. The design stance may be unique to humans, as tool-using chimpanzees, bonobos, gorillas, and monkeys show no evidence of it.[67] (I will have more to say about the role of object play on tool use later in this chapter.)

The Advantages of Thinking You're Better than You Are

The first-grade class was getting fidgety. There were a few minutes left before the bell rang, so the teacher decided to fill the time with some entertainment. "Can anyone sing a song for us?" she asked, and several children gave renditions of their favorite tunes. "Can anyone dance?" she asked. I felt that this was my time to shine. "I can tap dance!" I answered. I walked to the front of the room and proceeded to shuffle my feet, trying my best to imitate the dancers I had seen on TV. Well, the result *was* entertainment, but strictly comedy. My classmates roared with laughter and even the teacher was unable to hide her amusement. Fortunately, the bell rang soon and the children lined up to go home, so my stint in the spotlight was short lived.[68]

This experience, seared in my memory from early childhood, is not atypical. Young children are the optimists of the world, especially when it comes to their own abilities. Relative to older children and adults, preschool and early school-age children are convinced they have better memories, greater physical abilities, know more about how things work, and are smarter, stronger, tougher, and of higher social standing than they actually are.[69] Young children's elevated self-evaluations are not due to a general inability to make accurate judgments about someone's skills or characteristics. When asked to evaluate other children on a host of features, they do a reasonable job.[70] Their overly positive appraisal is limited to themselves, and some have argued that young children's excessive optimism is an adaptation, protecting them from the negative consequences of failure or negative evaluation at a time when most of their physical and intellectual abilities are quite limited.[71] Following the theorizing of developmental psychologist Albert Bandura, young children's overly positive evaluation of their own abilities and characteristics may serve to foster the sense of *self-efficacy*—beliefs about their having control over their own lives.[72] Bandura proposed that people with high levels of self-efficacy behave as if they have some control over what happens to them, which results in more effectual actions. Although preschoolers may be expert singers, tap dancers, bakers, and baseball players in their own minds, in reality their physical, intellectual, and social skills are quite limited, and accurate self-appraisals could result in low levels of self-efficacy and eventual failure to master important tasks.

Children's optimism about their abilities provides them with the motivation to persist at tasks on which children more in touch with their abilities might quit. This is consistent with psychologist Martin Seligman's view of the role of optimism in young children: "The child carries the seed of the future, and nature's primary interest in children is that they reach puberty safely and produce the next generation of children. Nature has buffered our children not only physically—prepubescent children have the lowest death rate from all causes—but psychologically as well, by endowing them with hope, abundant and irrational."[73]

A number of studies have examined the potentially adaptive nature of young children's overestimation of their abilities. In an early study I did with colleagues Jane Gaultney and Brandi Green, we assessed what we called *meta-imitation* in preschool children. *Meta-imitation* refers to children's knowledge of their own imitative abilities and is a form of *metacognition*, people's knowledge of their own cognitive abilities. Meta-imitation is quite poor in preschool-age children. In a first study, we had parents ask their young children how well they thought they could imitate the actions of a model during daily activities, to observe their children's attempts at imitating actions, and to query their children afterwards about how well they thought they had done. These young children consistently overestimated their ability to copy a model's action (57% of all observations) and almost never underestimated their attempts (5%). When asked afterwards how well they thought they had done, they were a bit more accurate, overestimating about 40% of the time, but again, almost never underestimating their imitative efforts (2.5%). A similar pattern of results was found by preschool teachers during school activities. Let me provide a couple of examples from mothers of their children's imitative attempts:

> I was putting on make-up and Tricia [age 3 years, 3 months] said she wanted to put on "lickstick" too. I asked her how well she thought she would do it and she answered "pretty good." She did get some on her lips, but also on her face and her hands. I asked her to look in the mirror and tell me how well she did. She was very pleased. "Just like you, mommy!"
>
> Cara [age 3 years, 8 months] was watching her sister Megan (8 years) jump rope. I asked her if she could jump rope like Megan. She replied that she could. Cara did not actually jump rope. She hopped up and down a few times while she shook the rope. Afterward, she seemed very proud of her accomplishment.[74]

Metacognition improves with age, and, for older children and adults, high levels of metacognition are typically associated with high levels of cognitive performance.[75] This does not seem to be the case, however, for very young children. In our final study, 3-, 4-, and 5-year-old children watched a model

THE ADAPTIVE VALUE OF IMMATURITY 147

perform two tasks with different levels of difficulty: juggling one, two, or three balls, and throwing balls in a basket from 1.5, 3, and 7 feet away. The children were asked to predict how well they thought they would do on each task and later were asked how well they thought they had done (postdiction). Children were also administered a test of verbal intelligence. Again, children overestimated their abilities for both the intermediate (juggling two balls, throwing from 3 feet) and difficult (juggling three balls, throwing from 7 feet) tasks, both for predictions and postdictions, with the 4- and 5-year-olds being more accurate than the 3-year-olds. We then correlated children's overestimation scores with the verbal IQ measure, and these values are presented in Figure 5.3. Higher correlations mean that children's rate of overestimation was positively associated with IQ; that is, the more children overestimated,

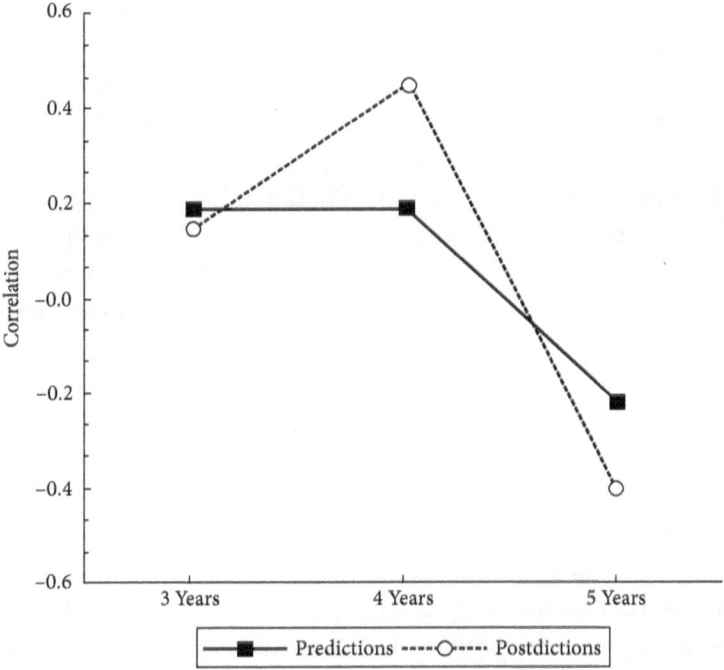

Figure 5.3. Correlations between prediction and postdiction overestimation scores on a meta-imitation task for 3-, 4-, and 5-year-old children. Correlations were positive for the 3- and 4-year-old children, implying that being out of touch with one's imitative abilities is associated with greater competence (at least higher verbal IQ scores) for younger children. In contrast, correlations were negative for the 5-year-olds, suggesting that, for older children, good meta-imitation is associated with higher IQ scores. (Based on data from Bjorklund et al., 1993.)

the higher their IQ scores were. Negative scores mean that high rates of overestimation (that is, poor meta-imitation) were associated with lower IQs. As can be seen in the figure, overestimation was negatively related to IQ for the 5-year-old children, typical of what is found for other types of metacognition for older children. In contrast, correlations between IQ and overestimation were positive for the 3- and 4-year-old children, implying that being out of touch with one's imitative abilities is associated with greater competence (at least higher verbal IQ scores) for younger children.

In other work from our lab, kindergarten, first-, and third-grade children were given lists of words printed on cards that they were to sort into groups, any way they wanted, and then remember as many as they could. Children received five memory trials, with different sets of categorically related words (for instance, different examples of animals, furniture, tools) on each trial. Before each trial, children were asked how many words they thought they would remember. We classified children as either a high or low accuracy based on how accurate their predictions were on the early trials. We then looked at changes in memory performance from early trials (1 and 2) to later trials (4 and 5). Kindergarten and first-grade children who overestimated more (the low-accuracy group) generally showed greater positive changes in recall and strategy use than the more accurate (high-accuracy group) children; the opposite pattern was found for the third-grade children.[76] Thus, at least for younger children, overestimating one's abilities on early trials was associated with greater gains in cognitive performance than for children who were more in touch with their cognitive abilities. These findings are consistent with Bandura's arguments that young children's overestimation biases foster improvements in their abilities by motivating persistence and promoting self-efficacy.

Task persistence is not the only way in which overly positive self-evaluations can impact children's behavior. For example, developmental psychologist Kristi Lockhart and her colleagues proposed that children possess high levels of *protective optimism*, believing that their physical and intellectual abilities will improve over time rather than decline, and that people have a good deal of control in changing their traits. In one study, for example, 5- to 7-year-old children were more likely to believe that they would gain greater knowledge in the future than 8- to 12-year-old children and adults.[77] Given young children's limited physical and psychological abilities, such optimism leads them to believe that they will eventually become competent, serving a self-protective function.

Young children's enhanced sense of accomplishment causes them to believe they are achieving goals, either goals set by adults or their own goals, where a more objective assessment might suggest otherwise, and as a result, they experience feelings of mastery. Given young children's belief in their own abilities, educational psychologist Deborah Stipek argued that instead of trying to make young children's judgments of their abilities more accurate, we should "try harder to design educational environments which maintain their optimism and eagerness."[78]

Developmental psychologist Harriet Rheingold said that the child's job in development is to "render the novel familiar."[79] Children do this by exploring their environment, attempting new and sometimes "dangerous" tasks. Although there are clearly individual differences, young children can be seen as adventurers, whose ignorance of how difficult some tasks are gets them to go where a more knowledgeable person may fear to tread; their overestimation of their actual performance results in their persisting on tasks until their performance actually does improve. Such overestimation has its benefits, but it also has it disadvantages. Some tasks really are dangerous, and young children require guidance from parents as they explore their niche. As developmental psychologist Jodi Plumert wrote, "The developmental dilemma, therefore, is to continually aspire to trying new and different things but not to try things that might have dangerous consequences."[80] The role of parents is to guide this development, monitoring their children's behavior, encouraging some activities, discouraging others, and scaffolding still others.

* * *

The examples of cognitive neoteny I've examined in this section are not neoteny in a literal sense: they do not represent features of ancient juvenile ancestors that have been retained in contemporary *Homo sapiens* adults. Rather, they are examples of what are usually thought of as immature or poor cognition that actually may have an adaptive value for children at a particular time in development. However, many of these immature features persist to some extent into adolescence and adulthood, resulting in grown-up humans possessing some childlike features, which, I argue, also provides them with some benefits. Teenagers' belief in their invulnerability, reflected in the personal fables discussed earlier, can be seen as a form of unrealistic optimism. As adults, we never totally get over our self-centered perspective of the world, and, like children, we learn and remember information better when we can reference it to ourselves. Adults' memory for events is influenced by the suggestions of high-status people, adults are apt to imitate irrelevant actions of a model when learning a new task,[81] and they continue to display the design stance when using tools, as well as functional fixedness. In addition, overestimating one's characteristics and abilities is not something limited to preschool children; psychologically healthy adults also generally believe they possess better skills and qualities than an objective observer might infer. Moreover, such optimism actually increases in old age, with older adults generally being more emotionally positive about their own lives than are younger adults.[82] A meme I came across while writing this chapter reflects, I think, adults' recognition and admiration for the optimism of childhood: "Whatever you're doing today, do it with the confidence of a four-year-old in a *Batman t-shirt*."

From the Mouths of Babes

Language is a marvelous thing. It allows humans to communicate with one another as no other species can. Language can displace the speaker and listener from the here and now, to talk about the past, plan for the future, or direct attention to people, objects, and actions in distant places. Language permits a type of cognition unavailable to other animals. Language may not be the equivalent of thought, but for many, thought without language is unthinkable.

Perhaps even more remarkable is children's *development* of language. Every biologically typical member of the species acquires his or her mother tongue over a relatively brief period of time. The transition from first words, to first sentences, to true linguistic genius is rapid, accomplished following a species-typical timetable in similar ways for children over the globe learning vastly different languages. How children acquire their native language has been the topic of great debate, central to the classic nature–nurture controversy. As for most psychological phenomena, the answer surely lies in complex interactions between biology and experience. But in another way, language is 100% part of a child's biological nature, as much as walking is and perhaps even seeing. According to linguist Derek Bickerton, children's acquisition of language is comparable to a spider building a web, a beaver building a dam, or a bat using echolocation: "the biological program for what the species does best simply sets itself in motion when stimulated by the words around it."[83] Yet language is also 100% environmental. There is no universal, innate human language. Children learn to speak the language that surrounds them at birth, with any child being able to acquire any of the world's 6,000 or so languages through only exposure to and interaction with other speakers. In the words of developmental psychologist Michael Tomasello, "Human linguistic competence defies pigeonholing. It is clearly an evolved capacity of the human species, but it is totally learned. It is a fundamental cognitive capacity, but it is totally social. It is mastered and practiced by individuals, but it is culturally normative through and through."[84]

There continues to be much debate about how children acquire language, but no serious scholar doubts the joint contribution of biology and experience in the process.[85] There has also been much ink spilled concerning the evolution of language, whether it can be explained by natural selection or not, and if so (as most theorists today believe) what its immediate benefits were. Among the many proposed evolved functions of language include benefits to social life through gossip, grooming, or group solidarity; use as a mental tool; or to facilitate mating, hunting, or toolmaking, among many others.[86]

I will not review various accounts of either language development or language evolution here, nor will I examine the many factors that influence how children and our ancestors learned to speak. My focus will be only on how some aspects of children's immaturity may contribute to learning one's mother tongue and the possibility that, although language may have been central to survival and to social and mating success in ancient adults, it made its first appearance in the mouths of babes.

Children Are Biologically Prepared to Learn Language

It seems obvious that children's ability to learn improves with age. Our school curricula reflect this common-sense belief. Children are taught their colors, shapes, letters, and numbers during the preschool and early school years, move on to reading and arithmetic, and eventually graduate to topics such as biology, chemistry, psychology, and computer programming. This increased complexity in curriculum is correlated with improvements in children's cognitive abilities, including being able to stay on task and to reason, as well as the neurological architecture that underpins such abilities. But there are exceptions, the most notable being language. Children are biologically prepared to process the linguistic environment around them and to develop in the course of just a few years the phonology (sounds), semantics (meaning), and syntax (rules for structuring words and sentences) of any of the world's languages, several of them if they are exposed to more than one language as young children. The task of learning either a first, or more commonly, a second, language after childhood is more difficult and seems to involve different brain mechanisms than those involved in learning a language early in life. This should be obvious to anyone who has tried to learn a second language as an adult. I have made such attempts a number of times and have always come up short. Even those who are successful in acquiring a second language as an adult rarely achieve the same mastery in vocabulary and syntax as they do of their first language and almost always speak with an accent. The ability to process the sounds of a specific language starts early. Six-month-old infants are able to tell the differences between the sounds (phonemes) in all known languages, at least of those that have been studied. (Most languages have between 30 and 60 phonemes, but some as few as 11 and others as many as 141.[87]) By 12 months of age, however, they become better at discriminating among the sounds they hear frequently (the sounds of the mother tongue) and gradually lose the ability to distinguish (and produce) the sounds not heard in their language.[88]

One reason for this pattern is that the brains of infants and children are highly plastic, able to be modified as a result of experience. In Chapter 2 I introduced the concept of *experience-expectant processes,* in which the brain has been prepared through evolution to "expect" certain types of experiences. When children receive species-typical experiences—such as exposure to a three-dimensional world, sound in the range human auditory organs can process, and socially responsive adults—development proceeds "normally," adhering to a species-typical schedule. When a child's early experience does not follow a species-typical pattern—when they do not get the type of stimulation their brains have evolved to "expect"—development proceeds abnormally. Infants with cataracts have altered vision even after cataracts are removed, and children brought up in stultifying institutions display social, emotional, and cognitive deficits even when moved to better environments. Experiences later in life, after neural patterns have become established and the brains less plastic, have a reduced effect on functioning.

Hearing speech is something young human brains have evolved to expect. When they hear speech early in life, as almost all members of the species do, evolved mechanisms within the brain take that information and produce language. With time and experience, children get better at understanding and producing their own language but lose the plasticity to easily acquire other languages. As with other functions that are central to survival, such as vision and hearing, dedicating neurons to a specific language made sense for our ancestors. Becoming proficient in communicating with other clan members trumped retaining plasticity for the possibility of acquiring a second or third language at the expense of expertise in one's mother tongue.

But regardless of how plastic young children's nervous systems are, plasticity in itself cannot explain how readily children learn their native language. All serious scholars of language acquisition recognize that young children have a biological readiness to acquire language, although they debate the nature of that readiness.[89] I have no intention of examining the various proposals for how best to describe the evolved capacities that permit children around the world to acquire language. Rather, I want to focus on what I believe is compelling evidence of children actually *inventing* new languages under some circumstances, based on the not-quite-true-language words and signs that surround them.

Pidgins and Creoles. The first evidence of children inventing language comes from the work of linguist Derek Bickerton, an expert on *pidgins* and *creoles*.[90] Pidgins are communication systems that develop when people who speak different languages live and work together. This occurred throughout the world in the 17th and 18th centuries as Europeans (mostly) established plantations in the Caribbean or the Pacific and brought in laborers from different countries to work the fields. Pidgins combine the language of the "bosses" with the different languages of the workers to produce a way for people with diverse backgrounds to communicate with one another. Pidgins typically have highly variable word order, little in the way of a grammatical system, and are not considered true languages. In fact, Bickerton proposed that pidgins might be similar in form to the *protolanguages* spoken by our ancestors. You can think of a pidgin as being similar to the "language" some tourists speak in a foreign county. They know a handful of words, often use only the present tense, may not know how to make nouns plural, and sprinkle their prose with words from their own language. Such "language" will often be successful in getting directions to a nearby museum, for example, but, in my experience, it sometimes results in laughs or sympathetic expressions from native speakers. (After about a month of frequenting the same small grocery store in Germany one summer and doing my best to communicate in pidgin German, I recall the employees gradually changing their opinion of me, treating me less like an ugly American and more sympathetically, like an intellectually challenged German.) *Creoles*, in contrast, develop over time from pidgins, becoming new "true" languages such as Haitian Creole—a combination of French, other European languages, Taíno (a language of indigenous people of the Caribbean), and West African languages; Louisiana Creole—a combination of French and a variety of West African languages; and Hawaiian Creole—an English-based language combined with native Hawaiian and other European and Asian languages.[91]

Although pidgins can take some time to develop into creoles, Bickerton provides evidence that they can actually develop in a single generation in the hands (and mouths) of children. On most plantations, preschool-age children were cared for in nurseries as their parents worked. As children got older, they did menial jobs, again, usually with other children. They may have been exposed to their parents' languages at home, but most of the day they dealt with their "bosses" and other children from diverse backgrounds. Bickerton documents that from these interactions children developed a true language, a creole, and did so within a single generation. Rather than learn their mother tongue, these plantation children *created* a language. One interpretation of these findings is that children possess an intuitive grammar and use it to modify the fragmented pidgin spoken by their parents and convert it into a true (and new) language.

From the Fingers of Children. The second piece of evidence that children will invent their own language when a well-established one is not available comes from research following several cohorts of deaf children in Nicaragua. Because of civil war in the country, schools for the deaf closed for many years, only reopening in the 1970s. During this time, deaf children had little contact with one another but, rather, lived with their hearing parents and siblings, communicating mostly through gestures. When a school for the deaf opened in the capital Managua, children were not taught sign language, in part because there was no recognized form of Nicaraguan Sign Language for them to be taught. Rather, children were taught to read written Spanish and to read lips. Despite the lack of specific instruction in signing, the children developed a true sign language over the course of several years, Nicaraguan Sign Language (*Idioma de Señas de Nicaragua*; Figure 5.4). Psychologist and language researcher Ann Senghas and her colleagues studied several cohorts of deaf children at the school and documented changes over time in the sign language they used. They found that Nicaraguan Sign Language was systematically modified from one cohort of children to the next, with children aged 10 years and younger generating most of the changes. In other words, over several "generations," children created a new sign language based on the incomplete forms used by their predecessors.[92]

THE ADAPTIVE VALUE OF IMMATURITY   155

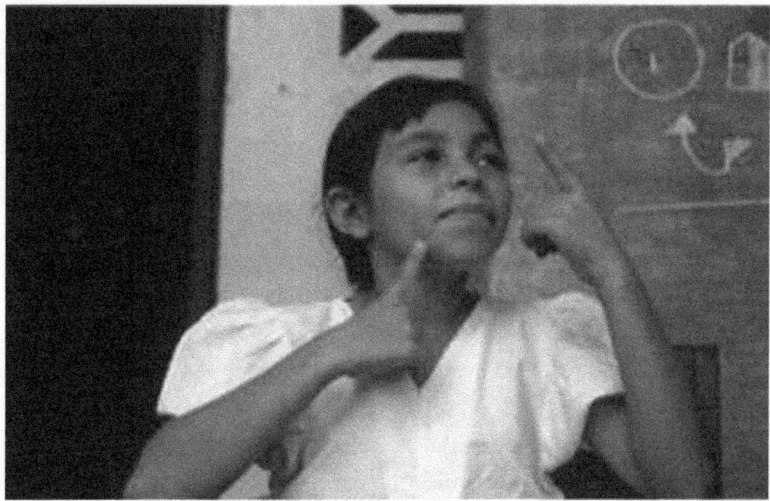

Figure 5.4. Deaf children developed Nicaraguan Sign Language (*Idioma de Señas de Nicaragua*) over the course of several cohorts of children.
Source: Photograph from BBC News. Pro.magnumphotos, with permission.

Additional support for children's facility for creating sign language comes from a recent experimental study by developmental psychologist Manuel Bohn and his colleagues. In a series of studies, pairs of children between 3 and 8 years of age were placed in separate rooms and saw one another, live, via video displays but could not hear one another. One child had to communicate the content of a picture (sometimes a concrete object such as a brush or a hammer, sometimes the abstract concept "empty" or "nothing") to the other, and all children did so by using gestures. Children were generally successful in their attempts at communicating with one another via gestures, and over the course of 30 minutes children developed arbitrary and conventionalized signs that were grammatically structured (and not structured according to their spoken language, German). The authors concluded that their results suggest, consistent with the findings from deaf children inventing Nicaraguan Sign Language, "that children have the basic skills necessary, not only to acquire a natural language, but also to spontaneously create a new one."[93]

The Benefits of Language for Children. Most of the time, of course, children do not need to invent or create their own language from fragments of a protolanguage they hear. The fact that they can, however, suggests that children have, indeed, been especially prepared by natural selection to make sense of vocal and gestural information for the purpose of communicating. It also seems possible that, although adults likely came up with words for important things and actions to communicate with one another, it was children, probably through play, who used their evolved and biologically based abilities to combine them into phrases and sentences, eventually creating a true language.

When looking at the many hypotheses about the evolved function of language, almost all refer to selective advantages it provided *adults*—for hunting, mating, cooperation, toolmaking, and so forth. But it is also likely, in fact, probable, that language afforded some benefit to the children who (from the current perspective) invented it. Developmental psycholinguist John Locke and anthropologist Barry Bogin[94] recognized this and proposed that language afforded young children (from about 3 to 7 years) better communication with their parents and, thus, greater chances of survival. Based on the practices of modern hunter-gatherers, our ancestral children were most likely weaned by 3 years of age but still required support from their parents. Recall that the power of the baby schema, discussed earlier in this chapter, is reduced around 4 or 5 years of age, so that just looking cute may not be enough to evoke care and affection from adults. However, recall also that children's voices and some expressions of cognitive immaturity now serve as cues to children's dependent state and, thus, to adults' motivations to view such children positively.

Immature Cognitive Processing and Language Development

The theme of this chapter is that aspects of children's neural, cognitive, and behavioral immaturity may be adaptive. By definition, young children have immature nervous systems, and the fact that they seem to be especially good at acquiring language lends some support for the contention that an immature system does a better job of acquiring a particularly human ability in a relatively brief period of time. However, you may be reluctant to think of a young nervous system designed by natural selection for developing (and perhaps even creating) language as "immature." A more compelling argument for the role of cognitive immaturity on language would include evidence of a general cognitive limitation that actually facilitates language acquisition. There is some evidence, albeit indirect, for this position.

Developmental psycholinguist Elisa Newport[95] proposed that young children's facility in acquiring language is not due so much to advanced cognitive abilities, but, somewhat counterintuitively, because of certain cognitive limitations. In Chapter 2 I mentioned briefly the phenomenon of sensory stimulation being coordinated with brain development so that the development of one sensory system does not interfere with the development of other sensory systems. Newport proposed that something similar might happen with language acquisition, suggesting that young children's cognitive limitations simplify the body of language they process, in turn making the complicated syntactical system of any human language easier to learn. Newport referred to this idea as the *less is more hypothesis*. In other words, children's limited cognitive abilities, reflected by slower speeds of processing and smaller working memories, reduce the complexity of what they must make sense of, resulting in easier initial stages of language (mainly syntax) acquisition. As they make progress in understanding and producing language, maturationally paced abilities gradually increase, as does language learning.

Newport noted that children's learning during early stages of language acquisition begins slowly, more slowly, in fact, than for adults learning a second language. Children's early language learning must be slow, in part because their limited cognitive abilities allow them to perceive and hold in mind only parts of complex linguistic stimuli. Their early language typically includes single words (usually a single syllable), with the number of words and the complexity of sentence structure they are able to use increasing with time, reflected both in their spontaneous speech and in their ability to imitate the language of others. Children's immature cognitive abilities limit the complexity of the language they can make sense of, making the job of learning language easier. In comparison, adults learning a second language get off to a much faster start than young children because their greater cognitive abilities permit them to deal with a greater number of words and more syntactic complexity. This advantage is short lived, however. Adults have more new language to work with, but they now must analyze all this information at once, which can result in acquiring some aspects of language in only a rotelike fashion, limiting their eventual proficiency.

To test her hypothesis, Newport developed a computer simulation that essentially limited how much the computer program could keep in memory at any one time. This is essentially equivalent to varying the size of a child's *short-term store*, the amount of information children can keep in mind at any one time. The capacity of children's short-term store increases gradually over childhood, and Newport similarly increased the amount of information that her computer simulation could process over time. Newport found that limiting the computer program's memory produced early deficits in language learning (for instance, whole words were often lost), but that word endings that denote plurals and verb tense were more apt to be retained. There was also an improvement in signal-to-noise ratio (that is, the ratio of relevant linguistic information to irrelevant background information) and loss of irrelevant accidental co-occurrences of words and phrases. This means that when starting with a larger short-term memory (as adults do), many language-irrelevant associations were kept, which hindered rather than facilitated language learning. Newport concluded, "overall, then, a learning mechanism with a restricted input filter [smaller short-term memory] more successfully acquired a morphology [syntactic structure]; the same learning mechanism with a less restricted filter [larger short-term memory], or with no filter at all, entertains too many alternative analyses and cannot uniquely determine which is the better one."[96] Psychologist Jeffrey Elman,[97] using a very different type of computer simulation, reached a similar conclusion and used the metaphor *the importance of starting small* to describe his findings. Preliminary evidence for Newport's and Elman's hypotheses comes from research showing that adults learn an artificial grammar faster when presented with smaller rather than larger units of the language.[98]

Children's limited cognitive abilities are not the only thing that results in young children processing less complex language than older children and adults. Parents, grandparents, older siblings, and random strangers in grocery stores talk to infants and young children in a simplified form, using a special type of speech that is *not* used when talking to adults. This "baby talk," or *child-directed speech* (or *infant-directed speech* when addressed to babies), involves simple words, many repetitions, and many questions, uttered using high-pitched tones and exaggerated modulations. Although there is great cultural variation in the extent to which child-directed speech is used, it is universal,[99] with American middle-class mothers being among the most frequent users. For an example, consider the following monologue overheard of a woman speaking to her infant son: "Hi, big boy! How is my little man? Huh? How is Mama's big boy? Did we just go for a walk? Did you and Mommy just go for a walk? Did we? Did you see the doggie? Huh? Did we see a little doggie?" Her son did not answer any of her questions, or utter anything other than a coo or two, but he was attentive to his mother and smiling. And who knows what was going on inside his head.

One reason people use this form of speech is that infants and children are more attentive to adults who use it, and infants are better able to tell the difference between words spoken in infant-directed speech than in normal adult-directed speech.[100] Using infant-directed speech also supports social interactions between babies and their caregivers, further promoting language development.[101]

Ann Fernald[102] speculated that infant-directed speech might have evolved initially as a way for mothers to communicate to their babies (for example, convey approval or disapproval, request attention, and comfort infants) as well as to regulate the emotions of their infants. Consistent with Fernald's hypothesis, research has shown that rhesus monkey mothers use special vocalizations with their infants that attract and engage their babies' attention, much as human mothers do.[103]

* * *

Language is perhaps one of the most complex things that humans acquire and, quite ironically, it is mastered by children who usually do not know their home address, cannot tie their shoes, and often can't count beyond 10. Young children have been especially prepared by natural selection to acquire, and perhaps even invent, language. Rather than being a hindrance, children's limited cognitive abilities and the simplified speech directed to them results in a less complex body of language from which they extract the sounds, words, and grammar of their native tongue. From this perspective, language acquisition seems to be a conspiracy between children's developing (and evolved) nervous system and adults whose speech to children seems to match the processing abilities and limitations of infants' brains.[104]

"Play Is the Work of the Child"

This quip, attributed to innovative educator Maria Montessori (but can probably trace its roots to Frederick Fröbel, who coined the term and the concept *kindergarten*, and before that to the philosopher Jean Jacques Rousseau in his 1762 book *Emile*), reflects the central role of play in children's lives. To these pioneering educators, play was serious business. There is much to like in this perspective, seeing play as having a central role in children's lives, much as work has a central role in the lives of adults. But one must be cautious not to equate too literally children's play with adults' work. Play, by definition, in *not* serious stuff, at least not to the children who are doing it. Play is something engaged in voluntarily that, by definition, has no purpose other than its own activity. Children do not play in order to learn, to improve their skills, or to become socially adept. All these things may happen through play, but playing is its own reward, not an intentional means to an end, and certainly not work. Philosopher John Locke recognized this, writing in his 1693 book, *Some Thoughts on Education*:

> Children should not have any thing like work, or serious, laid on them; neither their minds, nor bodies will bear it. It injures their healths; and their being forced and tied down to their books in an age at enmity with all such restraint, has, I doubt not, been the reason, why a great many have hated books and learning all their lives after. 'Tis like a surfeit, that leaves an aversion behind not to be removed.[105]

Play is a characteristic of young animals, and, although by definition it is "purposeless," almost every person who has studied it—including giants of developmental psychology such as Jean Piaget, Lev Vygotsky, and Jerome Bruner—recognizes its importance for development. This was identified by one of the pioneers of play research, German philosopher and psychologist Karl Groos, who wrote, "animals cannot be said to play because they are young and frolicsome, *but rather they have a period of youth in order to play.*"[106]

In some respect, human children are like other juvenile animals: they play for the sake of playing. Like kittens, they may run around in circles, smiling and laughing as they do; they may chase one another, perhaps wrestling when one child catches the other; infants, toddlers, preschoolers, and elementary school children will explore objects (a precursor to true play) and manipulate them, perhaps to produce some perceptual outcome (such as banging objects together to make noise), to build something, or to pretend one object is something else (such as making believe a shoe is a phone); or they may engage in fantasy play, either alone (or perhaps with an imaginary friend) or with other children, taking turns playing different roles (you be the mommy and I'll be the baby; or you be Ironman and I'll be Wolverine). Of course, the play of other animals never becomes as complex as that of human children. Kittens, puppies, and juvenile tigers, monkeys, and chimps engage in locomotor play, chasing and wrestling with one another, perhaps taking turns being the "winning" and "losing" partner in a bout, but they do not have the social or cognitive capacity to partake in fantasy, or pretend play, at least not to the extent that human children do. And importantly, although the adults of some mammals are known to play in the context of courtship or parent–child interaction,[107] there is no other animal that extends curiosity and play into adulthood to the extent that our species does. This point was made by the historian Johann Huizinga, who described humans as *Homo ludens,* or "playful man," writing, "Play is older than culture, has not been essentially changed by civilization, and has permeated from the beginning 'the great archetypal activities of human society.'"[108]

What Is Play?

We seemingly all know play when we see it, but defining it precisely is a bit more tricky. First of all, play—in human and nonhuman animals and in children and adults—is engaged in voluntarily. When an adult tells a child to "go outdoors and play," the directive is to leave the house, but if the activity is to be considered play, what exactly the child does is up to him or her. Play is fun, often accompanied by laughter and a "play face," requires some effort, is not serious (that is, it is not like work), and has no obvious immediate purpose; rather, it is done for its own sake. Children may engage in other enjoyable activities, such as reading a book, watching television, or mastering the intricacies of making a peanut butter and jelly sandwich, but these activities are not play. Despite substantial differences in the lives of children from diverse cultures, play follows a species-universal developmental course, making it an excellent candidate for a feature that has been influenced by natural selection and evolved to serve an adaptive function, much as infant–mother attachment or language has. According to developmental psychologist Paul Harris, "the stable timing of [play's] onset in different cultures strongly suggests a neuropsychological timetable and a biological basis."[109]

On the surface, a child at play is not producing anything useful, not doing anything to enhance his or her status, nor gaining any resources, which, from an evolutionary perspective, would seem to be a waste of time and energy. Yet, the deep structure of play includes the practice and honing of skills—some of which may be important for future success in adulthood—and serves both immediate and deferred functions. In play, children can explore the world, other people, and one's self in a safe environment without taking on too great of a risk. Importantly, humans' extended period of immaturity provides children the time to play to prepare them for the challenges of adulthood; surely play served a similar function for our ancestors and may have been necessary for the evolution of *Homo sapiens*' unique set of social-cognitive abilities.

Types of Play and Their Development

Play comes in a variety of types and can be described in a variety of ways. A child can play alone (*solitary play*), side by side with another child but not directly interacting with that child (*parallel play*, or *parallel interaction*), or with other children (*cooperative*, or *social, play*).[110] Play can involve vigorous activity (*locomotor play*), including wrestling and play fighting (*rough-and-tumble play*), manipulation of objects (*object play*), or make believe, performed either alone (for example, pretending to fly a spaceship to Mars) or with other children (for instance, playing house, school, cops and robbers, or superheroes). The latter type of play is called *pretend play*, *fantasy play*, or *symbolic play* and involves an "as-if" orientation toward objects, actions, and other children. As discussed in Chapter 4, it requires a cognitive system capable of *counterfactual thinking*, representing objects and people in a form other than what they really are. Many bouts of play will include several of these components, such as fantasy play with objects like dolls or action figures, or locomotor play involving make-believe characters, as might be the case when pretending to be superheroes or developmental psychologists (well, it *could* happen). Each type of play is observed in varying degrees in all cultures, follows a common developmental schedule, has some value for the players, and may have had an important role in human social-cognitive evolution.

Locomotor Play. I assume that many readers of this book have fond memories of high-energy outdoor games when they were children. My favorite was a variant of tag we called "Wolves and Pigs," which I described in an earlier book:

> It started with one child being the wolf and running to catch the other children, the pigs. Once the first child was "caught," he or she too became a wolf and the two of them chased the other children until the last pig had been caught by one of the now many wolves. We played this on summer evenings until it became too dark to see, both boys and girls ranging in age

from 6 or 7 to their early teens. I remember running in my parents' backyard, especially the quick turns and dodging I'd do to avoid being tagged. I particularly remember running in an arc to escape an oncoming wolf; my recollection is of making turns and being nearly parallel to the ground, held up by centrifugal force. I'm sure that neither my speed nor my violation of the laws of physics were as impressive as I recall them, but it's my memory and I'm sticking to it.[111]

Games like Wolves and Pigs are not only played in suburban backyards, but also in crowded cities and in hunter-gatherer communities. You can see early variants of chase games as 2- and 3-year-old children entice their older siblings or parents to chase and catch them. Running itself is enjoyable, but the real fun seems to be in getting chased (or chasing), often with some physical contact (pretend wrestling or being tickled) following the "capture." Locomotor play (sometimes called *physical play*) includes running, climbing, wrestling, and play fighting; it is often social, involving other people, or can be a solo activity, such as climbing a tree. Locomotor play is common during the preschool years, peaking around 4 or 5 years, accounting for about 20% of all observed behaviors of children during preschool and decreasing thereafter, being replaced by fantasy play (which often co-occurs with Locomotor play).[112] Similar levels of locomotor play are observed out of school and in traditional and hunter-gatherer cultures, with boys typically engaging in greater levels of such play than girls, especially the more vigorous rough-and-tumble play. Locomotor play is also observed in many mammals, again, with males engaging in more wrestling and play fighting than females.[113]

Locomotor play uses up a lot of calories and might appear to be a substantial expenditure of energy with no benefit other than having fun, which would seem to have little in the way of survival value for children. But that is only on the surface. Research examining the locomotor play of both human and nonhuman juvenile mammals reports a number of benefits to locomotor play. These include fostering muscle, skeletal, and coordination development, obtaining information about the local environment, facilitating the development of spatial cognition, and, when performed with other children, learning about social interaction, including skills that might be useful in adulthood.[114] For example, some researchers have speculated that the play fighting of boys is similar to adult fighting in hunter-gatherer societies. Other research with monkeys showed that juvenile animals that were prevented from engaging in play fighting when they were in superordinate (the one who pins) or subordinate (the one who gets pinned) roles grew up to be "bullies" and "sissies," respectively, indicating the important role that such rough-and-tumble play might have in social animals.[115] And, of course, many adults continue to engage in high levels of physical activity that provides health and, when done with other people, social benefits, and the origins of these beneficial activities can be seen as extensions of childhood play. Such activity is often done in the context of competitive games, which have clear goals and, thus, are not truly "play" as typically defined. People do gain recognition and status by being good tennis, basketball, softball, golf, or pickleball players, but the greater benefit, I believe, in addition to that afforded by the exercise itself, is in the social interaction the games afford. I play basketball several days a week with men (and sometimes women) of advanced age, and although being recognized as a valued player has some rewards, winning or losing is not as important as the social interaction during the game and perhaps on the bench before and after the games. For this we can thank our evolved childhood disposition toward the pleasure of exercise play.

Object Play. Lots of animals play with objects. We have two cats in our home, and although much of their day involves just lying around, a good deal of it involves play, especially when they were kittens. They frequently chase one another, sometimes resulting in brief wrestling matches, a form of locomotor play. Much of their play, however, is with objects, from balls, to skeins of yarn, to pieces of paper, and the occasional small lizards that live on our pool patio. Human infants and children also play with objects, but their play becomes much more detailed and complex than that of cats and dogs (or chimps and monkeys). In part, this is because of the nature of the objects they play with. As I mentioned earlier in this chapter, human life is full of artifacts, many of which are tools, and researchers have speculated how children's object play leads to tool mastery. According to British developmental psychologist Peter Smith, object exploration and play help prepare children to use tools "over and above what could be learnt through observation, imitation, and goal-directed practice."[116]

As infants' manual dexterity improves, they increasingly explore objects, learning what objects do and, importantly, what can be done to them. Over the course of the first year, infants grasp, mouth, shake, and generally manipulate objects, learning their *affordances*—the quality or property of an object that defines its possible uses: for instance, a chair is for sitting, a hammer for grabbing and hitting, a box for putting things into. Infants learn about tools first by exploring them and then by playing with them.

According to developmental psychologist Jeffrey Lockman, "the origins of tool use in humans can be found during much of the first year of life, in the perception-action routines that infants repeatedly display as they explore their environments."[117] Object play continues to increase in frequency and complexity into the preschool years, accounting for between 15% and 30% of preschool children's activities in the classroom, with boys typically engaging in more object play than girls. This pattern is found across cultures, including in traditional and hunter-gatherer societies. It is interesting that juvenile chimpanzees also spend about 10% to 15% of their time in object play. Although chimpanzees do not use tools with anything near the frequency that humans do, they use tools more than any other of the great ape species, using sticks for ant and termite fishing, rocks to crack nuts, and leaves to shield themselves from rain, for example.[118]

Although the importance of object play for subsequent tool use seems obvious, hard data proving this connection is difficult to come by. A number of studies reported that children showed superior problem-solving behavior when they had a chance to play with the objects/tools before being asked to solve a problem with them. They performed even better than children who watched a model use the tools to perform the task but did not play with the objects beforehand. However, other researchers failed to replicate these findings.[119] In one study examining a connection between object play and tool use, developmental psychologist Jeffrey Gredlein and I observed 3-year-olds while they played with objects and documented how much of their time involved object play versus other activities, for example, simple contact (just holding an object) or fantasy play. One week later children were seen again and given a lure-retrieval problem, in which they could select among a series of objects to help them get an out-of-reach toy. Some of the objects were too short and others the wrong shape to reach and retrieve the toy, whereas others were "just right." Boys did better than girls on this task (although girls did just as well after being given a hint), and there was a strong positive relationship between success on the lure-retrieval task and how much time children spent in object play a week earlier (with objects that were different from those used in the lure-retrieval task), although this relationship was found only for boys. Boys who spent more time in object play a week earlier were more likely to select the correct tool to retrieve the toy than boys who spent less time in object play. There was no effect of object play on later tool use for girls.[120]

Why this sex difference? As mentioned in Chapter 1, evolutionary developmental psychologist David Geary proposed that infants enter the world with a small set of *skeletal competencies* specialized to process information relating to the physical, biological, and social worlds. These abilities get fleshed out with experience, here experience playing with objects. Geary and others argue that sex differences in early behavior interact with inherent but still developing skeletal competencies, producing different outcomes for boys and girls, and that young human males may be especially sensitive to actions on objects, benefiting more from object play than girls.[121]

Children are "fiddlers." Their juvenile tendencies draw them to explore and play with objects, and in the process they learn about the objects, their affordances, and how these objects are used by members of their society as tools. They seem to share this tendency with great apes, especially chimpanzees, who also play with objects as juveniles and use tools as adults, although much less so than humans. Children will learn much about tools through observation, imitating what other more learned members of their culture do with objects. But the origin of sophisticated tool use can be found in infants' and young children's object play, and it is doubtful that humans would be the artifact-using species we are without children's youthful tendencies to engage in "purposeless," playful actions on objects.

Fantasy Play. Play fighting and using Lego blocks to construct buildings or twigs to make "stick men" are all important features of children's play, but the prototypical human play involves fantasy—pretending some objects are things they are not (the kitchen spoon is a magic wand, *object substitution*) or making believe that you and your friends are superheroes saving the world by combating evil villains (*sociodramatic play*). The evolutionary roots of locomotor play run deep in mammalian history, and simple object play is frequently observed in chimpanzees. But fantasy play, the hallmark children's play, is rarely observed in any of the great apes, and when it is, it is limited to mostly object substitution. For example, there have been several observations of juvenile chimpanzees in the wild carrying a log and treating it is as if it were a baby. Several captive chimpanzees and gorillas, who had been reared as much as possible as human children (enculturated apes) and are often trained in sign language or other forms of linguistic communication (for example, using geometric tokens as word substitutes), treated dolls as if they were babies, carrying them and pretending to feed them, for example. There is no convincing evidence, however, of great apes engaging is sociodramatic play, something human children spend much time doing beginning around their third birthdays. After reviewing the existing evidence of fantasy play in great apes, primatologists Juan-Carlos Gómez and Beatriz

Martín-Andrade concluded that such play is rare, more likely to be observed in enculturated or language-trained apes, and, unlike human children, is not a typical behavior pattern of apes. That there is a glimmer of fantasy play in the great apes, especially in enculturated animals, suggests that they may possess rudimentary symbolic abilities that are only (or mostly) expressed when they experience a species-*atypical* environment, one more like that experienced by human children.[122] This argument is identical to one presented in Chapter 3 when discussing imitation in enculturated apes. Human-like sociocognitive abilities are only expressed when the animals are reared in a human-like environment.

What sort of underlying abilities would children need to transform a chimp-like style of play to the rich fantasy play displayed by human children? In short, they need *symbolic* or *mental representation*. Developmental psychologist Judy DeLoache has referred to the knowledge that an entity can stand for something other than itself as *representational insight*, and she has shown, for example, that young children's ability to understand that a photograph represents the depicted object—in addition to being an object itself—develops around 2 years of age, with the ability to separate what an object looks like and really is, such as a refrigerator magnet that looks like a cookie, continuing to develop past the age of 3 years or so.[123] Under some conditions children as young as 15 months can understand that pictures are representations of objects,[124] and this capacity permits them to pretend, for instance, that a banana is a phone or a bowl is a hat.

Beginning around 3 years of age, children are increasingly able to invoke imaginary situations that are distinguished from reality. They are able to engage in *counterfactual thinking*, representing objects and people in a form other than what they really are, and taking an "as-if" stance.[125] Children of this age not only are able to pretend that a stick is a knife but also begin to engage in sociodramatic play, often with other children, taking on pretend roles and staying in character all while the play session continues (see Figure 5.5). The Australian developmental psychologist Mark Nielsen argued that counterfactual thinking is a central feature of human childhood that played a critical role in the evolution of human cognition. Nielsen proposed that "by pretending children thus develop a capacity to generate and reason with novel suppositions and imaginary scenarios, and in so doing may get to practice the creative process that underpins innovation in adulthood."[126]

Fantasy play, in particular, may have especially potent effects on subsequent learning and cognitive development. Fantasy play functions as an

Figure 5.5. Beginning about 3 years of age, children engage in sociodramatic play, which requires *counterfactual thinking*, representing objects and people in a form other than what they really are, and taking an "as-if" stance.
Source: Shutterstock, with permission.

experience-expectant process, stimulating the brain for focused learning. A number of studies have reported that children who engage in high levels of fantasy play show more positive outcomes in other areas, including perspective taking, language development, and executive-function abilities (including working memory, inhibition, and cognitive flexibility—I'll have more to say about fantasy play and executive function in Chapter 7).[127] In a pair of retrospective studies, German developmental psychologist Werner Greve and his colleagues reported that the amount of free play adults engaged in as children was positively associated with later self-esteem, friendship, and general psychological and physical health, and that these effects of childhood free play on adult outcomes were mediated by greater adaptivity (flexible goal adjustment).[128]

* * *

Play is a characteristic of young mammals, including humans. It is during play that juveniles practice and acquire the skills necessary for survival. Human children, however, have so much more to learn than the young of other species. *Homo sapiens* is a tool-using and tool-constructing species, and children's object play is more elaborate than that of other tool-using animals such as chimpanzees and gorillas. Humans' social lives are also more complicated than those of other animals, and it is during play with other children—especially fantasy play—that children acquire many of the skills they will need to succeed as adults. Although modern children learn much important cultural information in school, children in traditional societies learn through observation (adults in traditional cultures do little direct teaching) and through play with other children. The role of children's play as a means for our ancient ancestors to acquire the social, technological, and intellectual skills necessary for survival cannot be minimized. Play may not have been the only means of knowledge acquisition for our ancestors, but research strongly suggests that play evolved as an important principal learning mechanism in our species.

One marvelous thing about humans, however, is that play is extended beyond the juvenile period and into adulthood. Granted, some adults have a more playful attitude than others, and there have been (and likely still are) some cultures that do the best they can to beat the urge to play out of all but the youngest of society's members. Nevertheless, the innovation and creativity observed in varying degrees in all cultures owes much to the extension of play into adulthood. By continuing to play, adults foster and cement social relations, but perhaps most important, it is through play that adults create novel and useful artifacts (think the wheel, the Swiss army knife, the digital computer), produce imaginary scenarios to entertain others (think novels, poetry, Broadway plays), and come up with innovative solutions to problems. What academics like me do for a living can be thought of as "playing with ideas." Playful dispositions and the products and ideas they produce are not limited to scientists, engineers, or novelists but are important in the everyday functioning of most people. In many ways, play is children's (and evolution's) gift to adults, fostering not only the cognitive means for solving problems, but also the joy of imagination, discovery, and building things. Play may be childish and a reflection of immaturity, but it is not frivolous. Rather, it reflects an adaptive process that played an important role in human evolution and continues to be important in human development.

The Benefits of Youth

We owe much to our younger selves in becoming the adults we are. We also owe a debt to our youthful ancestors, for it was primarily during early development that the roots of many of humans' most important psychological adaptions arose. Of equal significance, however, is the extent to which our species retained many aspects of youthful, some may say immature, cognition into adulthood. We clearly become smarter and more in control of our actions as we age, which is necessary if we are to accomplish the many tasks of adulthood. Yet, to a significant extent, much of what humans have achieved has been because of a youthful approach toward life. This is reflected in statements made by two of the greatest scientists who ever lived:

> I do not know what I may appear to the world; but to myself I seem to have been only like a boy playing on the seashore, and diverting myself now and then finding a smoother pebble or a prettier shell than ordinary, while the great ocean of truth lay all undiscovered before me.[129] (Sir Isaac Newton)
>
> I sometimes ask myself how it came about that I was the one to develop the theory of relativity. The reason, I think, is that a normal adult never stops to think about problems of space and time. These are things which he has thought of as a child. But my intellectual development was retarded, as a result of which I began to wonder about space and time only when I had already grown up. Naturally, I could go deeper into the problem than a child with normal abilities.[130] (Albert Einstein)

Few ever accomplish intellectual feats comparable to Newton or Einstein, but most of us have retained to varying degrees the curiosity, wonder, and playfulness of youth, and these childlike characteristics have given our species, for better or worse, dominion over the globe and affected greatly not only the grandest accomplishments of *Homo sapiens* but also our mundane interactions. As Ashley Montagu proposed, many of the traits that make for a successful adult are remnants of childhood functioning, making "the spirit of the child . . . an adaptive trait of the greatest biological value."

6
Developing the Evolved Social Brain

I was a child of the cognitive revolution. I started college the year Ulric Neisser published his discipline-defining book, *Cognitive Psychology*, and my graduate-student days included discussions of how the cognitive revolution freed psychology from the stranglehold of behaviorism. As developmentalists, we had lively debates about the pros and cons of Piagetian versus information-processing accounts of children's thinking and the impact of cognitive development on children's social behavior. Social development was increasingly seen as being due to age-related changes in more general cognition. Lawrence Kohlberg's theory of moral development, first published in 1969, emphasized social-cognitive reasoning and dominated the field of moral development for 40 years. Kohlberg's theory of gender identification, also first published in the late 1960s, similarly dominated research and theory on that topic for several decades.[1] By the 1980s cognitive development had become the explanatory mechanism for social development, capstoned by the publication of Kenneth Dodge's social-information processing theory and Albert Bandura's renaming and reformulation of his social-learning theory to social-cognitive theory.[2] In the first and subsequent editions of my *Children's Thinking* textbook, I wrote,

> As a cognitive psychologist, I tend to believe that most aspects of human behavior are a function, to some significant degree, of one's cognition. I find this especially easy to believe of the social behavior of children. A child can only be as social as his or her level of cognitive functioning will permit.[3]

From this perspective, canonical through the latter part of the last century, children's emerging cognitive skills—developed to deal mainly with the physical world—are applied to social relations and situations. "Cold" cognition is primary, with social (or "hot") cognition simply being the application of general intellectual abilities to the social realm.

Gradually over the decades I began to see the light and came to believe that social cognition was an entity unto itself—not simply a derivative of more general cognitive functioning—and that it perhaps preceded the more general type of cognition that developmental psychologists had so thoroughly studied. I had come to believe that social-cognitive development during the early months and years of life—both in contemporary children and in our ancestors—is the essential foundation of our humanness.

Humans are a social species, but then again, so are wolves, chimpanzees, most monkeys, zebras, and gazelles, among many others. But humans' sociality is extreme—we are hypersocial (or *eusocial*) in much the same way as termites and ants are. Humans' *hypersociality*, of course, is different from that of the social insects. We don't have a queen who does all the reproducing or a caste of sterile females who do all the work, but we do show a remarkable degree of cooperation with one another to get a job done and the ability to function effectively in large groups with people we do not know personally. The social-cognitive abilities necessary for this human hypersociality originated in the childhoods of our ancestors and continue today to foster learning and efficient functioning in social groups both small and large.

Don't get me wrong. I'm not saying that humans always cooperate with one another and put the interests of others ahead of their own. We may be a social species, but we are also a selfish one. Evolutionary theory dating back to Darwin has emphasized the role of competition. Selfish individuals (or genes, depending on your focus) that outcompeted other members of their species were more apt to survive and reproduce. Cooperation, in which one individual expends time, resources, and reproductive potential to help another, is, on the surface, the antithesis of competition, the central mechanism of natural selection. Cooperation is what some scientists refer to as a Darwinian puzzle, something that typifies the species but apparently reduces fitness. Moreover, Darwin emphasized that selection operates at the level of the individual, not the species or the group, and this has been the principal perspective of mainstream evolutionary theory since its inception. Yet even Darwin had difficulty explaining some aspects of human functioning from the perspective of individual selection, specifically morality. Darwin suggested that perhaps in the case of *Homo sapiens*, natural selection sometimes operated for the good of the group. How else can one explain *altruism*, people engaging in actions that benefit others at some cost to themselves? Over the decades scientists developed explanations to make sense of the sometime self-sacrificing behaviors of people and other species while still maintaining the basic tenets of Darwin's theory.

For example, evolutionary biologist William Hamilton proposed *kin selection* as one mechanism for explaining altruism and cooperation.[4] Animals will sometimes behave against their personal self-interest if it helps one's relatives, that is, individuals who share some of one's genes. For Hamilton, passing on genes to future generations was the key to evolutionary success. Animals could increase their *inclusive fitness* by fostering the development and reproduction of kin—siblings, grandchildren, and cousins, for instance—in addition to, or sometimes instead of, fostering their own development and reproduction. But this does not explain altruism expressed toward nonrelatives. To do this evolutionary biologist Robert Trivers proposed the theory of *reciprocal altruism*, in which nonrelated individuals within a group help one another with the expectation that good deeds will be paid back in the future.[5] Perhaps the clearest example of reciprocal altruism in nonhumans is food sharing in vampire bats. These nocturnal mammals live in large social groups and feed on the blood of horses and cattle. As you can imagine, the equines and bovines are not willing participants in this process, and bats sometime return to the home cave without getting a blood meal. When this happens, bats who had had a successful night will regurgitate some of their blood to an unsuccessful cave-mate. These exchanges are not random, however; only bats who were observed to spend time together and/or who had shared blood meals with them in the past (bat friends, if you will) shared with one another. You can think of this as a tit-for-tat or "you scratch my back I'll scratch yours" arrangement, with help, in this case a possibly life-or-death meal, being given because of past behaviors or the expectation that the recipient will make similar sacrifices in the future.[6]

Of course, people also commit acts of kindness to others with no expectation of getting anything back from the recipient for their largess, with actions as mundane as holding a door for a fellow pedestrian or making donations of time, money, or other resources to help people in another community, such as a donation to the Red Cross to help earthquake victims on another continent. What possible benefit could such behavior have for the giver? One explanation is that others in the community occasionally observe such acts of generosity, and the altruist gains a reputation as a cooperative and kind person and is treated accordingly by group members.

Incidences of kin selection and reciprocal altruism are easily recognized in humans, as well as many social species, but human sociality goes far beyond what is observed in other animals. Specifically, humans are remarkably cooperative, analogous to the eusocial insects. However, the hypersociality of most termites, ants, bees, and naked mole rats (the only eusocial mammal comparable to the social insects) can be explained by their high degree of genetic similarity (that is, by kin selection). Humans, in contrast, show high levels of cooperation with nonrelatives, and they achieve this through a suite of cognitive and motivational mechanisms. These mechanisms have their roots in infancy, develop with experience, and are the basis of *Homo sapiens'* current hegemony of the earth.[7]

Trying to explain cooperation from a classic Darwinian perspective has often befuddled evolutionary scientists, but cooperation is actually responsible for major transitions in the history of life on the planet and is well within the domain of explanations based on natural selection. The first life forms on earth were bacteria and bacteria-like Archaea, single-celled organisms lacking a nucleus and other organelles (*prokaryotic cells*). A major transition occurred with the advent of *eukaryotic cells*, in which mitochondria, the nucleus, and other organelles, with their own sets of RNA and DNA, gave up their independence and cooperated to produce new life forms. A later transition resulted when different eukaryotic cells assembled into multicellular organisms, with only some of those cells being engaged in reproduction. Eusocial species, including termites, ants, naked mole rats, and humans, are simply the end result (for now) of a cooperative process extending back more than a billion years.[8]

But more is needed to explain human cooperation than kin selection, reciprocal altruism, and reputation enhancement; what is needed is some form of group selection. That is, rather than propose that natural selection operates solely at the level of the individual or the individual's genes, group selection proposes that natural selection can also operate at the level of the group. Recall that Darwin himself proposed that this may be necessary to explain some features of our own species, and various theories of group selection have been proposed since then. Modern theories, most particularly *multilevel selection theory*, propose that natural selection operates at a variety of levels, the group being one of them. Specially, groups of individuals that function more efficiently than other groups are more apt to survive and thrive. This is not your grandfather's group selection theory. Gone are ideas such as the feeble zebra "sacrificing" itself to the lions for the good of the herd. Instead, groups that function effectively have a competitive edge over groups that function less effectively, and effective functioning arises because of cooperation among group members.[9] This does not mean that selfishness doesn't have its advantages; it clearly does within a group. The benefits of altruism are apparent, however, when groups compete. According to evolutionary biologists David Sloan Wilson and E. O. Wilson, "*Selfishness beats altruism within single groups. Altruistic groups beat selfish groups.*"[10] Furthermore, the logic of multilevel selection theory is not inconsistent with the gene-based logic of modern evolutionary theory. According to E. O. Wilson, "*For group-level traits as for individual-level traits, the unit of selection is the gene that prescribed the trait. The targets of natural selection, which determines whether genes do either well or poorly, are the traits prescribed by the genes* [italics in the original]."[11] For our species, these traits include cooperation, which led to better group organization and functioning.

Humans are the most social and the most cooperative of all mammals, and the genesis of this hypersociality is in infancy. Infants' early orientation to others serves primarily to keep them alive at a time when they are highly dependent on adults for their survival. But infants' social cognition soon morphs into an awareness that other people have intentions, feelings, and thoughts, which, coupled with language, results in children understanding that others in their immediate environment are "like me" and that they are also "like them." Natural selection has endowed infants and children with the seeds for a type of cognition that inexorably leads to identifying with social groups, morality, advanced forms of social learning, and cooperation. Competition and selfish motivations do not disappear, but from an early age they exist alongside cooperative, prosocial motivations. Except at the most general of levels, natural selection has not dictated what social groups should accomplish or what constitutes moral (good) or immoral (bad) behavior. These are determined by the cultures in which children live, but natural selection has ensured that neurotypical children living in species-typical environments will identify with group members, develop a sense of right and wrong, and cooperate with people who are viewed as "like me."

Although hypersociality is rare in the animal world, its evolution within the line that led to *Homo sapiens* is, in retrospect, not surprising. Recall the neotenous nature of humans. Human infants' oversized brains mean that, compared with other primates, they are helpless and dependent upon adult care for an extended period of time. Developing strong social relations with their caretakers surely increased infants' and young children's chances of survival. The self-domestication of *Homo sapiens* (discussed in Chapter 4), particularly the reduction in reactive aggression, led to less conflict among individuals and greater cooperation. Of course, relations among brain size, self-domestication, an extended pre-reproductive period, and hypersociality are multidirectional. One factor (reduced reactive aggression, for example) cannot be said to have caused increased sociality, or the vice versa. These and most certainly other factors interacted synergistically to produce the modern human mind. But one thing that seems certain is that most of these advances were brought about by changes in development and through the experiences of infants and children.

In this chapter I first examine the *social brain hypothesis*, the idea that increased social cognition was a (perhaps *the*) driving force in human evolution and was afforded by the interacting factors of increased brain size, slow development, and increased social complexity. I next look at infants' orientation to social stimuli, which all but guarantees that babies will form social relationships with the important adults in their lives, enhancing their chances for survival. In the final section I examine the evolution and development of human hypersociality, loosely following Michael Tomasello's theory of *shared intentionality*. I present research and theory on the development of children's social cognition and contrast it with that of great apes, including treating others as intentional beings, empathy, social learning, social normativity, prosociality, and collaboration.

The Social Brain Hypothesis

There has not been a lack of theories about the principal causes of human evolution. Anthropologists, psychologists, paleoanthropologists, and biologists have generated hypotheses about important selective pressure that transformed African apes into *Homo sapiens*, including cooperative hunting, cooking and eating meat, warfare, tool invention and use, thermoregulation of the brain, climate change, and bipedality, among others. We've run into several theories about human origins in earlier chapters of this book (neoteny, for example). There is, of course, no single cause for human evolution, and surely many interacting factors contributed to the rise of a species with the social, technical, and intellectual abilities that are qualitatively (or at least massively quantitatively) different from those of all other animals. Nonetheless, scientists rightly look for phenomena that may have had extraordinary influences on human evolution, and many scholars today look at humans' social nature as the engine that drove cognitive evolution, and this perspective is the basis of the *social brain hypothesis*,[12] discussed briefly in Chapter 1. Humans evolved from social animals, who themselves required substantial skills to navigate the social hierarchies of their groups. As the social environments of our human ancestors became more complex, so did their need for social intelligence, what psychologists Richard Byrne and Andrew Whiten called *Machiavellian intelligence*, after the 16th century author of *The Prince*, a small book advising leaders how to acquire and maintain political power.[13] As the size and complexity of social groups increased, so did the pressure to effectively compete and cooperate with fellow group members. The evolutionary biologist Richard Alexander went so far as to propose that humans invented their own selective pressure—themselves.[14]

It may seem a bit counterintuitive to nominate social skills as the epitome of human intelligence. After all, advances in human civilization seem to be measured chiefly in terms of technological advances—from stone tools to locomotives to digital computers, and from grass huts to pyramids to skyscrapers—or intellectual artifacts such as alphabets and number systems, or the theories of general relativity and evolution by natural selection. Aren't these the things that reveal humans' true genius? Yet, according to one early proponent of the social brain hypothesis, psychologist Nicholas Humphrey, such intellectual feats are rare and do not reflect the intelligence of most members of the species. Humphrey suggested that a space alien following Albert Einstein around for a day would likely conclude that he, like his fellow earthlings, had a humdrum technological mind. Even if we decided that humans' ability to master technological skills from building domiciles to brewing craft beer is a more realistic measure of true human intellect, such skills are most readily acquired via humans' exceptional social-learning abilities.[15] Rather than display technological brilliance, it is during social interactions when people, including Einstein, show their real intelligence.[16]

Big Brains, Slow Development, and Social Complexity

Exceptional social intelligence requires a big brain as well as an extended period of time in which to acquire the skills needed for successful group living. Humans inhabit a vast range of ecologies and cultures, so a big brain by itself is not sufficient to develop effective social intelligence. Because of the diversity of human cultures, children cannot possess a narrow range of adaptations for living successfully in social groups. Rather, they need plasticity to adjust their behavior to their specific context, as well as the time to learn the ins and outs of their culture. The combination of a big brain capable of learning, living in socially complex groups, and an extended period of immaturity (and plasticity) may be the ingredients necessary to produce an animal with high levels of intelligence.[17] Other big-brained, slow-developing, and socially complex species include elephants, cetaceans (dolphins and whales), and chimpanzees, which are all animals regarded as "intelligent." As I mentioned in an earlier chapter, both the course of human brain development and humans' extended period of reproductive immaturity are extensions of more general primate patterns, and these factors are further related to social complexity. This is reflected in research by anthropologist Tracey Joffe, who compared the size of the neocortex (the "thinking" part of the brain), social complexity (measured in terms of size of the group), and the length of the juvenile period for 27 different primate species, including human hunter-gatherers. Joffe reported a strong relation among these three factors: the bigger the brain, the larger the social group, and the longer the juvenile period tended to be.[18]

Other factors, such as a change in diet—for example, increasing the amount of animal protein consumed afforded by the control of fire—likely led to more efficient use of calories, permitting greater brain development.[19] Evolutionary anthropologist Robin Dunbar further proposed that control of fire afforded early humans more social time together by sitting around the campfire in the evening.[20] Recent research with traditional hunter-gatherers indicates that conversations around a fire at night are usually social in nature, in contrast to daytime conversations that are more likely to be about functional matters (norm regulation, economic matters).[21] Dunbar proposed that this extra social time was necessary in order to increase the size of the community; as brain and community size increased over hominin evolution, social time had to increase as well.

Again, it is not the case that one of these factors (social complexity, for example) is directly responsible for changes in the other factors (brain size and length of juvenile period). As brain size increased it permitted enhanced social cognition, which selected for a longer juvenile period in which to acquire social skills, which served as a selection pressure for increased brain size, and so on. Brain size, social complexity, and the length of the juvenile period became entwined in feedback loops, producing increased social intelligence. And although this evolutionary pattern was not limited to *Homo sapiens*, it did find its most extreme expression in our species.

Young Infants' Orientation to Social Others: Forming Attachments

It goes without saying (although I'm sure I've said it repeatedly in this book) that human infants are highly dependent on their parents, particularly their mothers, for survival. As for all mammals, humans form attachments, the especially close emotional relationships between children with their primary caregivers, usually their mothers, who are typically infants' sole source of nutrition for some months. Unlike other mammals, however, babies' dependency on adults extends years past weaning (about 3 years of age in hunter-gatherer communities). As discussed briefly in Chapter 1, this includes *alloparents*—people other than mothers, including fathers, older siblings, grandparents, and unrelated helpers—who frequently provide some care for infants. Because human adults are highly responsive to social cues, it behooves young infants to get adults' attention and to develop positive social relations with them, increasing the chances of receiving caregiving and thus surviving babyhood. Human newborns' immature nervous systems, however, prevent them from playing much of a deliberate role in establishing and maintaining social relations with adults, although they are not passive participants in the social give-and-take between infant and parent.

Early-Developing Perceptual Biases

As I mentioned in Chapter 5, infants have evolved "psychological weapons" designed by natural selection to garner attention and caregiving from adults. One important weapon discussed in the previous chapter was the *Kindchenschema*, or *baby schema*—immature facial features that adults find attractive and that promote caregiving. But once infants get an adult's attention, how do they maintain it? Adults are responsive to the social cues of infants—making eye contact, responding to the utterances or facial gestures they make to an infant—and infants who respond to adult cues tend to prolong and strengthen social interactions. Infants with developmental delays or who are later diagnosed with autism are less socially responsive to adults, and parents of such infants are correspondingly less responsive to their infants, setting up a transaction that can result in insecure attachment and lower-quality parent–infant social relationships.[22] To promote social interaction when infants' neurological state prevents them from intentionally directing

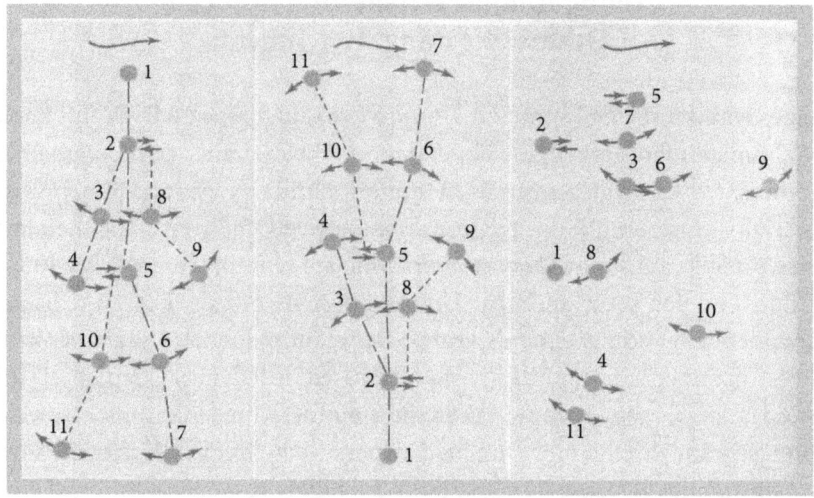

Figure 6.1. Examples of light displays showing normal walking (biological motion), the same figure upside down, and random movement. Research has shown that young infants will look longer at displays of natural biological motion (the upright walker) than the upside-down or random display.
Source: Bertenthal, Proffitt, & Kramer, 1987.

their behavior, young babies possess a few early-developing biases* that can serve to establish and maintain attention to social others.

One such bias is attention to biological motion. Living things do not move in random ways. Arms and legs have joints at elbows and knees and are attached at shoulders and hips, and when an animal moves it does so in a particular way. People have a tendency to look at "normal" biological motion, and this can be demonstrated by showing people light displays in which lights are attached to joints (for example, at knees, hips, elbows, and shoulders) and then looking at how much people attend to such displays when they are upright, upside down, or when lights just move randomly. Figure 6.1 shows examples of three light-display stimuli: a right-side-up walking person, the same person but presented upside down, and random movements of lights. Newborns and young infants spend more time looking at a right-side-up

---

* I use the term *biases* here in a neutral, not pejorative, way rather than adopt the more commonly used term *preferences*. Preference implies a conscious liking for one thing over another—for sushi versus salmon, for example—and I do not wish to put such meaning into babies' minds. The word "bias" should be interpreted merely as infants consistently attending to one class of stimuli more than another.

display of biological motion than at random or upside-down displays, which may help promote social interaction from early in life.[23] However, although infants spend more time looking at displays showing biological motion, they do not seem to treat it as a person until about 9 months.[24]

Newborns are also attentive to faces, especially eyes, again a bias that would enhance face-to-face interaction between infant and parent.[25] Such biases do not mean that newborns have a concept of "faces." Although natural selection may have provided infants with some notion of faces and their importance, other evidence suggests that newborns and young infants' attention to faces is related to a set of low-level perceptual biases, as discussed briefly in Chapter 1. These include tendencies to attend to: moving stimuli, areas of high contrast, curvilinear relative to linear stimuli, and top-heavy stimuli, which have more elements on the top than the bottom (such as two eyes above a single nose and mouth).[26] These are all features of human faces. With experience, infants' attention to different components of faces and their ability to discriminate between faces improves, especially for the type of faces they see regularly (for example, female faces if their primary caretaker is female; faces from their own ethnic group).[27]

Newborns also seem especially sensitive to human speech. For example, in one set of studies newborns showed activation in some language areas of the brain (anterior temporal areas) to both the language they heard in the womb and to a foreign language, but not to a whistled form of vocal communication.[28] Other research has shown that newborns prefer to listen to—and that their brains respond differently to—the language spoken by their mothers, which they heard in utero, rather than to a foreign language. This suggests not only a preparation for acquiring language, but also for attending to the most significant person in their lives, their mothers.[29]

Another early-appearing social behavior that may foster social interaction is *neonatal imitation*, discussed briefly in Chapter 1 in our discussion of ontogenetic adaptations. When adults makes a face at a newborn, for example, sticking out their tongues or pursing their lips, babies will (sometimes) make a face back at them.[30] Recent research has shown that babies do not necessarily make the same facial gesture as the one they saw, but they will make *some* facial response (sticking out their tongues, for example) more frequently than expected by chance.[31] Although the initial interpretation of neonatal imitation was that babies were showing evidence of social learning right out of the womb, a more likely interpretation is that newborns' reactions to viewing adults' facial gestures evolved as a reflex-like mechanism to promote infant–mother interaction during a time when infants are unable to intentionally control their own behavior.[32] Support for the position that neonatal imitation is not a form of social learning comes from the fact that it disappears around 2 months of age when higher-cortical brain areas are able to influence infants' intentional actions, suggesting that neonatal imitation is under the control of subcortical regions of the brain, unlike the "true" imitation observed in older children. For instance, newborns who were later shown to be cortically blind were still able to visually orient to objects in the first month of life before losing their ability, suggesting that early visual processing is done primarily by subcortical brain regions.[33] Evidence that neonatal imitation serves to promote social interaction between infant and mother at a time when infants cannot control their own social behavior comes from research by developmental psychologist Mikael Heimann. Heimann reported that infants who showed high levels of imitation at birth had better quality social interactions with their mothers 3 months later than infants with low levels of neonatal imitation. A more recent study found that macaque monkeys that showed high levels of neonatal imitation displayed greater amounts of gaze-following 7 months later.[34] These findings suggest that neonatal imitation is best thought of an ontogenetic adaptation that serves to promote social interaction between young infants and their parents at a time when infants cannot control their own social behavior; it further sets the stage for later social interaction and disappears when new neurocognitive abilities emerge.

Attachment: The First Relationship

Each of these early-developing abilities facilitates infants' orientation to social others and promotes attachment, usually to their mothers. Although attachment may be influenced by some early perceptual and cognitive abilities of infants, it is at its core a biologically based *motivational* system that evolved to protect children from danger while motivating caregivers to provide care.[35] Life for primates includes a constant web of relationships, including peer relationship, sexual relationships, sibling relationships, and father–offspring relationships, but the first relationship is attachment, usually between an infant and its mother. Young infants have evolved tendencies to orient to people (especially their faces) and to engage in interactions with them. For example, in addition to the "unconscious" perceptually based biases newborns have toward orienting to faces, discussed in the previous section, beginning about 2 months of age, infants begin to respond to adult behaviors during face-to-face interactions. Infants and mothers engage in what psychologist Colwyn Trevarthen called *protoconversations*, taking turns uttering sounds, making faces, and generally sharing positive emotions.[36] Infants' smiles and laughs encourage continued interaction by adults, all serving to foster attachment. When a mother does not respond as expected but merely maintains a "still face" while looking at her baby, the infant initially increases his or her actions, attempting to provoke mother to respond, but quickly becomes disturbed, stops responding, and orients away from the mother.[37]

Many theorists have proposed that attachment is the model for all future relationships. For example, researchers have described different styles of attachment, both in infancy between babies and their mothers, and in adulthood between romantic partners. In work initially with 1-year-old infants, pioneering attachment researcher Mary Ainsworth and her colleagues described three types of attachment: *secure* (infants explore novel environments and are easily soothed by their mothers when distressed); *insecure-resistant* (infants are anxious, do little exploration of novel environments, and may be ambivalent or show anger when mother tries to soothe them); and *insecure-avoidant* (infants show little distress when left alone by their mother, avoid contact when mother later returns, and show little wariness of strangers). Evolutionary psychologist Lee Kirkpatrick develop a similar classification scheme to describe adult *romantic* relationships: *secure* (characterized by comfort), *anxious* (characterized by excessive worry about love or lack of it from the partner), or *avoidant* (characterized by little expression of intimacy or by ambivalence about commitment).[38] Using these and other measures, researchers have found continuity between people's descriptions of their adult romantic attachments and their recollections of their childhood relationships with their parents.[39] Most attachment researchers view these and other results of continuity between early attachment and later social behavior and relationships as support for John Bowlby's theory that people form *mental models* of close relationships based on their early experiences with their primary caregivers and then carry those models into their adult relationships.[40] Attachment theorists further claim that quality of early attachment predicts later social and emotional behaviors, with infants who have secure attachments to their parents showing high levels of social competence and low levels of internalizing and externalizing behaviors later in child in childhood. Recent meta-analyses (statistical reviews of a number of research reports) seem to confirm these relationships.[41]

Jealousy Protest in Infancy

A relatively recent discovery by attachment scientists is evidence of jealousy during the first year of life. Jealousy has typically been thought of as a secondary emotion, such as embarrassment, shame, and guilt, not seen until around children's second birthdays. According to conventional beliefs, such emotions require an advanced cognitive system, such as that described by Piaget as preoperational thought. This type of thinking involves mental representations that go beyond those of the sensorimotor period (birth to about 2 years in Piaget's theory). To feel embarrassment, shame, or jealousy one must be able to take the perspective of another. (Why feel embarrassed or ashamed when you cannot see yourself as others see you?) Jealousy was viewed similarly. Jealousy is not the same as envy, desiring what someone else has, but is an emotion evolved to protect relationships. In adult romantic relationships, you feel jealous when you believe your significant other is involved with or interested in someone else, threatening your relationship. Jealousy can be adaptive, causing one to re-evaluate the relationship and perhaps do things to strengthen it.[42]

Infants may not experience jealousy the same way or by using the same psychological mechanisms that adults do, but there is evidence that, under some circumstances, they are aware of threats to their relationships with their mothers and they behave accordingly. Research by developmental psychologist Sybil Hart and her colleagues has shown that infants will display *jealousy protest* by at least 9 months of age. In a series of studies, babies watched as their mothers talked and paid attention to either a realistic baby doll ("Oh, what a cute baby!") or to pictures in a book ("Oh, how delicious this cake looks!"). How did babies respond? Infants showed greater signs of distress, requests for mother's attention, and heightened physiological arousal when their mothers paid attention to the doll than to the book (Figure 6.2). It's not just the loss of attention babies are complaining about but their mother's attention to another infant—a competitor.[43]

Hart proposed that jealousy protest is an evolved adaptation and is first seen at an age (9 months) when a sibling could have been born. Infant mortality was high for our ancestors, and the birth of a new baby would mean

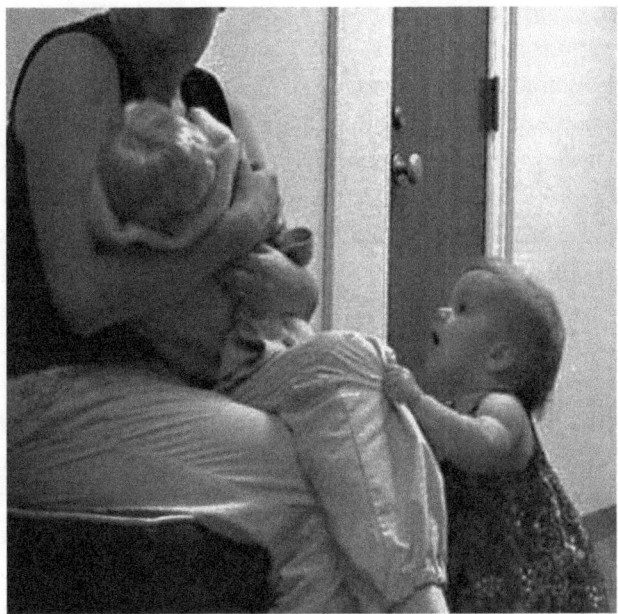

Figure 6.2. A 10-month-old female infant displays distress and mother-directed approach behaviors while maternal attention is directed toward a rival.
Source: Hart, 2015, with permission.

losing exclusive access to the mother for nursing and nurturing at a time when infants were still highly dependent on their mothers for survival. I find it likely that the psychological mechanisms underlying jealousy protest in infants and those underlying sibling jealousy a couple years later are not the same. Rather, infant jealousy protest is probably an ontogenetic adaptation, disappearing when no longer needed and in this case replaced by a different (though functionally similar) emotion governed by different neurological mechanisms. But jealousy protest is an adaptation, nonetheless, one that increases the likelihood that an infant will not lose the attention and resources it needs to survive babyhood.[44]

The Development and Evolution of Human Hypersociality

Human infants' orientation toward others, especially parent figures, shows an adaptive preparation for sociality. However, other infant mammals have similarly evolved dispositions toward social others. They must have if they are to survive. No other primate, however, seems to engage in anything equivalent to protoconversations, which may be precursors of more sophisticated dyadic interactions between infant and caretaker found in human, but not great ape, infancy. In addition, although there are a number of mammal species, including some monkeys, which, like humans, are cooperative breeders—being cared for by individuals other than their mothers—mothers are typically the exclusive caretakers of their infants for the other great apes. It seems possible that some of human infants' promiscuous sociality early in life is related to their need to form social relations with adults other than their mothers.

Human sociality extends far beyond attachment, however, leading eventually to levels of social learning, group identification, cooperation, and morality that differentiate *Homo sapiens* from all other primates. These species-unique forms of sociality begin in infancy and early childhood and have their deep origins in the infancies and childhoods of our ancestors. To understand human adults' extraordinary hypersociality it is necessary to understand its development and to contrast it with the development of our close genetic relatives, chimpanzees and bonobos, who are the best models we have for what our last common ancestor with these animals may have been like.[45] Darwin himself realized that mental abilities, just like physical features, have an evolutionary history. New forms of thinking do not arise fully formed but, rather, change gradually over human phylogeny, and the best way to get an idea of what these changes may have been is by examining those abilities in the great apes. And as we have come to increasingly understand, perhaps the most important evolutionary changes occurred in the young of our ancestors. According to primatologist and developmental psychologist Michael Tomasello, "if we wish to explain how uniquely human psychology is created, we must focus our attention on ontogeny, and especially on how great ape ontogeny in general has been transformed into human ontogeny in particular."[46]

Although psychological research with chimpanzees and other great apes dates back more than 100 years, such research, involving both laboratory and field studies, has exploded in the past several decades, and some of this work has explicitly looked at behavioral and cognitive differences between chimpanzees and human children.[47] There has even been some research done contrasting ape and human development. In this section, I briefly review six related aspects of social-cognitive development, each of which reflects a unique type of human social intelligence, and contrast its development (or its end state in adults) with chimpanzees. These aspects are: treating others as intentional beings, empathy, social norms, social learning, prosociality, and collaboration. I do this loosely following Michael Tomasello's *shared intentionality theory*.[48] In the following section I outline the major ideas in Tomasello's theory, followed by a closer look at each of the six aspects of social cognition. Tomasello also identifies communication, specifically language, as a unique type of social cognition. Although I concur with Tomasello about the uniqueness and importance of language for human social intelligence, I discussed aspects of the evolution and development of language in Chapter 5. I will not cover it in detail here, other than to note that there is no evidence of conventional linguistic communication (that is, language) in great apes, but such communication is unique to humans.

Shared Intentionality Theory

Michael Tomasello spent 20 years as Co-Director of Developmental and Comparative Psychology of the Max Planck Institute of Evolutionary Anthropology in Leipzig, Germany. There he had access to a captive group of chimpanzees, plus each of the other great ape species (bonobos, orangutans, gorillas). Along with a team of colleagues and students, Tomasello studied aspects of human and great ape social cognition and developed a theory of human social-cognitive development and evolution that aims to explain *Homo sapiens*' unique form of sociality.

Tomasello describes his theory as neo-Vygotskian. Lev Vygotsky was a psychologist working in the former Soviet Union in the early part of the 20th century who developed a theory of social-cognitive development. Vygotsky argued that children's cognition develops in cultural contexts that determine largely how, where, and when interactions between children and adults take place and what *tools of intellectual adaptation* are available to them. Tools of intellectual adaptations, or what others have called *cognitive artifacts*,[49] are methods of thinking and problem-solving that children internalize from their interactions with more competent members of society. These tools permit children to use their basic mental functions more adaptively.[50] Cognitive artifacts can be physical in nature, such as written documents, computers, and maps, or mental in nature, such as literacy, mathematics, and scientific reasoning. Tomasello, like Vygotsky, argues that children's social cognition is largely structured by the cultural context in which children grow up, but unlike Vygotsky, Tomasello emphasizes that infants and young children are biologically prepared to develop a suite of social skills that, in interaction with their cultural environment, produce a unique type of human sociality.

Tomasello proposed that there are two types of unique human capacities that emerge during infancy and childhood. These capacities have their roots in great ape cognition and sociality, but their particular form is unique to humans. The first capacity is *joint intentionality*, which is the "the cognitive capacity to create a joint agent 'we' with other individuals, creating the possibility of taking the perspective of others,"[51] or seeing things from another's point of view. This first emerges in *shared attention* around 9 months (for example, mother and infant sharing attention about a third object), with infants motivated to socially affiliate with others by sharing attention, emotions, and knowledge with them. The second capacity is *collective intentionality*, which develops between about 3 and 5 years of age. Children now have the ability to establish a *group-minded "we"* with other people, which improves their perspective-taking ability and results in children being attentive to social conventions and norms. This includes identifying members of in-groups and out-groups and conforming to expectations of in-group members. Children view others in certain social groups as being "like me," which serves as a motivation to be attentive to and learn from these social compatriots.[52] Tomasello's collective intentionality is similar to the historian Yuval Noah Harari's concept of *intersubjective meaning*, in which people are able to communicate with many other people based, not on shared interactions, but on similar beliefs and feelings.[53] In either case, this is a type of cognition that is necessary for high levels of cooperation among unfamiliar individuals to occur.

Tomasello proposes that human social cognition evolved from sophisticated social and cognitive skills of great apes, but that human skills are qualitatively different from those of the apes. To anticipate the difference between chimpanzee (*Pan troglodyte*) and human social-cognitive development, let me describe two studies that evaluated species differences in (1) solving physical problems dealing with space, quantities, and tools, and (2) solving social problems dealing with imitation, nonverbal communication, and reading the intentions of others. In one study developmental psychologist Esther Herrmann and her colleagues contrasted large samples of adult chimpanzees and orangutans with 2.5-year-old children and reported no difference between the children and great apes on the physical tasks but substantial differences on the social tasks, with the children consistently outperforming

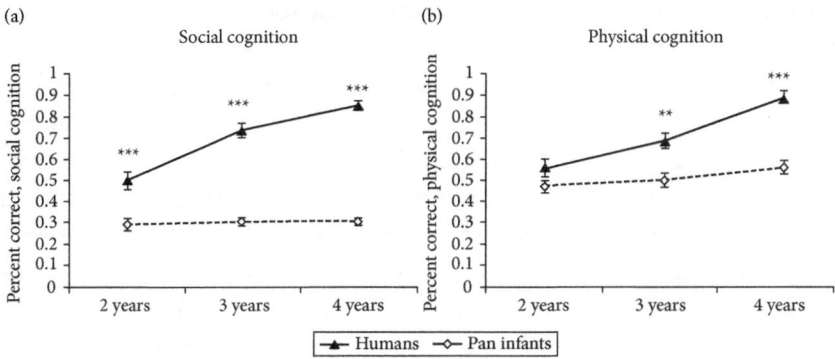

Figure 6.3. Developmental changes in performance on social and physical cognition tasks by children and chimpanzees (*Pan*). Children improved on both sets of tasks with age, whereas chimpanzees' performance remained unchanged from 2 to 4 years.
Source: Wobber et al., 2014, with permission.

the apes.[54] In a second study, developmental psychologist Victoria Wobber and her colleagues assessed sets of physical and social-cognitive tasks in both 2-year-old children and 2-year-old chimpanzees and retested both the children and the chimps one and two years later. The results of this longitudinal study are shown in Figure 6.3. As you can see, as in the earlier study, at 2 years of age the children and the chimpanzees were comparable in terms of physical cognition, but the children exceeded the chimps in social cognition. The children continued to improve their performance at 3 and 4 years of age, whereas the chimps' performance remained stable for both the social and physical tasks.[55] As I noted in Chapter 4, children's brains continue to grow through the preschool years; in contrast, chimpanzees' brains at age 2 are nearly 90% complete. Children's prolonged brain development while living in an artifact-rich and socially complex environment provides them with the opportunity to develop forms of both physical and social cognition not available to the faster-developing chimpanzees.

Treating Others as Intentional Beings

I'm sure readers have witnessed and very likely participated in face-to-face "conversations" between babies and adults where the adult talks and points things out to the baby, and the baby, in turn, looks to where the adult is pointing, possibly even uttering some sound or expressing some emotion (a smile?) in turn. What's going on in such interactions is *shared* (or *joint*) *attention*, a triadic interaction between an infant, an adult, and some object, possibly another person, but also possibly an inanimate object such as a cup. Mother may say, "Oh, look sweetheart, there's your cup! Do you want some more juice?," and baby may respond by following mother's pointing or her gaze, by pointing to the cup and by making some sound, perhaps switching attention between mother and the cup. Mothers and other adults may have been pointing things out to infants in these protoconversations for some months, but it is not until about 9 months of age that babies truly become engaged partners.[56]

On the surface, such shared attention may seem to reflect only a minor change in how infants and adults interact, but in reality it is a big cognitive deal. It represents a major change in how infants understand their social world. They now explicitly treat others as *intentional agents*, people who do things intentionally, or "on purpose." To put a 10- or 12-month-old infant's understanding into words, "Mother is pointing something out to me because she wants me to see it. I can also direct her attention to something I see but she does not." Infants' ability to interpret the referential attempts of others is captured by philosopher Daniel Dennett's concept of the *intentional stance*, in which people appeal to the mental states of others when attempting to explain what they do.[57]

There are hints of shared attention in the protoconversations observed in younger infants, with baby and adult sharing emotions, but it is not until 9 months that infants begin "triangulating" attention between themselves, another person, and a third object. Shared attention increases over the second year of life. Between 12 and 18 months infants will point to adults to inform them about things the adults don't know, will point to objects to direct an adult's attention to something he or she is searching for, and will use others' eye gaze as a cue to direct their own attention.[58] Around this time, babies also begin to engage is *social referencing*, using a parent's tone of voice, gesture, or facial expression to determine how they should react to an ambiguous situation, such as falling while running ("Is this a cry-worthy fall or not?").[59] Joint *visual* attention seems to peak around 14 months, as language takes an increasing role in directing others' attention.[60]

The developmental pattern of shared attention is universal, being found for a broad range of tasks in diverse cultures, even in cultures in which adults direct little attention to young infants.[61] This suggests that the development of shared attention is highly influenced by species-typical biological maturation and will reliably emerge when infants experience a species-typical environment. Although chimpanzees and other great apes will follow the gaze of another, there is no evidence that they engage in shared attention equivalent to what 9- and 10-month-old human babies do.[62]

As Dennett's concept of the intentional stance indicates, shared attention implies that infants are aware, at some level, that others have a mental life—that people's behavior is based on their knowledge and motivations. Psychologists have described such an understanding under the broad concept of *theory of mind* and have studied extensively how children come to understand that people's behavior is influenced by their beliefs and desires.[63] The gold standard for demonstrating theory of mind is passing *false-belief tasks*. In one classic task, children view a scenario involving two children and the hiding and moving of an object (see Figure 6.4). For example, in one

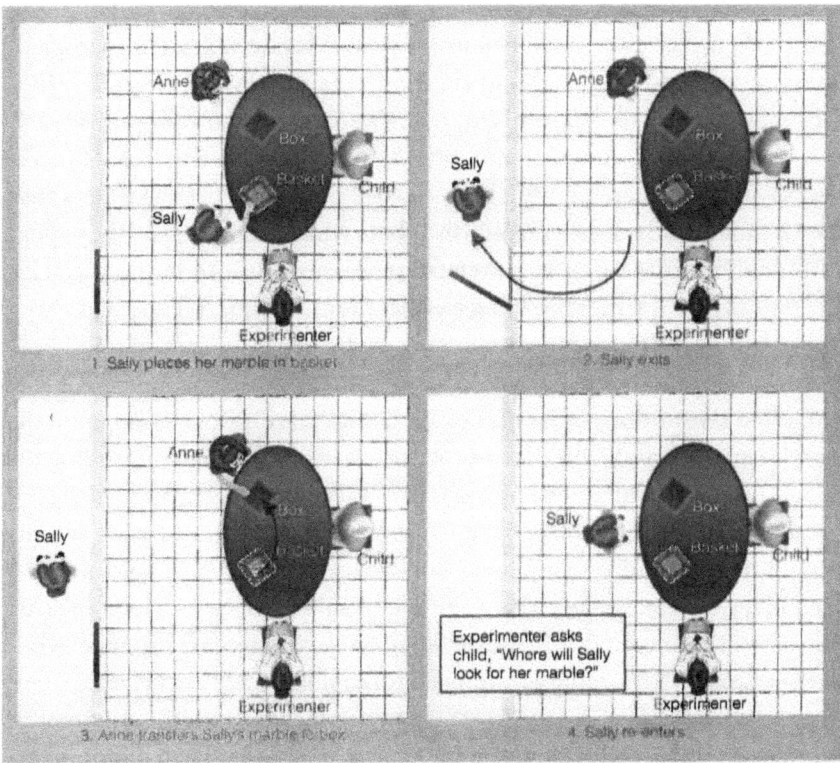

Figure 6.4. The Sally–Anne version of the false-belief task. Children have to judge whether Sally can have a false belief. When the marble is moved to a different location when Sally is out of the room, will the child understand that Sally still believes, incorrectly, that the marble is in the basket, where she last saw it?
Source: Bjorklund & Hernández Blasi, 2012, p. 288, with permission.

scenario a child, let's call her Sally, watches as a marble is hidden in a basket. Sally leaves the room and then another girl, let's call her Anne, enters the room, removes the marble from the basket, and places it the box. Sally then returns and goes to retrieve the marble. Where will Sally look for the marble? Where she saw it hidden a short while ago, in the basket, or where it really is, in the box? To answer this question correctly requires a form of *counterfactual thinking*. The *fact* is that the marble is in the box, but Sally has a false belief and will look where she erroneously thinks it is, in the basket where she last saw it. Perhaps somewhat surprisingly, children do not reliably get the right answer until about 4 years of age. Although the timetable for passing false-belief tasks varies somewhat across cultures,[64] the general developmental pattern appears to be universal and found even for the children of Baka Pygmies living in the rain forests of Cameroon.[65]

Children perform better when, instead of evaluating what another person knows, they must evaluate what another person feels or likes. For example, in one study 14- and 18-month-old children were asked which treat they liked the best—broccoli or Goldfish® crackers. The children naturally preferred the crackers. An adult expressed an opposite preference to children—broccoli over Goldfish®. When the adult later asked children to please give her a treat, the 12-month-olds gave her Goldfish®. That's what they liked, and they apparently couldn't imagine anyone preferring raw vegetables to the tasty cracker. In contrast, the 18-month-olds gave the adult the broccoli she had earlier expressed a preference for, recognizing that their own likes were different from those of another person.[66] Although other researchers have not always replicated this finding, by 3 years of age children are able to understand that people can have conflicting desires, about a year ahead of understanding that people can have conflicting knowledge.[67]

Other research has shown that children at much younger ages will display an understanding of another's knowledge on false-belief tasks if, rather than being required to *tell* where Sally thinks the treat is, a simpler measure if used: where the infants first *look* when Sally returns. For instance, when, in the example, Sally returns, young children fail the false-belief task, *saying* that she will search where the treat actually is (the box), but the children will first *look* to where Sally last saw it, in the basket. This has been interpreted as an *implicit* understanding of false belief.[68] At an unconscious level, the children *know* that Sally has a false belief, but they are not yet able to explicitly act upon that knowledge. Using simplified situations in which children's visual attention is used to reflect an understanding of false belief, infants as young as 7 months "pass" the tasks.[69] One can argue about what such looking behavior actually reflects. Some make the claim that infants and toddlers understand that other people's behavior is based on their own beliefs and that sometimes those beliefs can be false;[70] in contrast, others suggest that infants' looking behavior reflects remarkable statistical learning skills and biases to attend to faces and motion and not an understanding of false belief, per se.[71] Consistent with this latter interpretation, one study has shown that 3- and 4-year-old children's performances on implicit and explicit false-belief tasks are not related to each other, and that explicit false belief is related to children's performance on language and executive function tasks, whereas implicit false belief is not. These patterns suggest that different psychological mechanisms underlie implicit and explicit false belief.[72] Regardless of how one interprets these findings, it is not until about 4 years of age that children's *actions* are influenced by their understanding of false belief.

What about chimpanzees? Do they have a theory of mind? One set of experiments suggests that chimpanzees at least understand that if someone is looking at an object they *see* that object, that is, have knowledge of it. In a series of studies by primatologist Brian Hare and his colleagues, pairs of chimpanzees were put in competition with respect to some desired food. In these studies, one chimp was socially dominate relative to the other. When the submissive chimp could see the treat but also could see that the dominate chimp's vision of the treat was occluded, he or she would retrieve the food and then run back to safety. If the submissive chimp saw that the dominant chimp could see the location of the food, he or she didn't bother going to get the treat. The dominant chimp would either get there first or forcibly take the treat away from the lower-ranking chimp. That's the way chimp social hierarchies work. In a food competition situation, chimps behaved as if seeing is knowing, a seemingly necessary component of theory of mind.[73] However, in another situation, in which chimps had to make begging responses for a food treat to one of two people—one whose eyes were open and another whose eyes were occluded (by wearing a blindfold, for example)—the apes chose randomly.[74] This suggests that chimpanzees' understanding that eyes have knowledge is limited to species-typical situations (competing for food) and not generalizable across situations as it is in children (Figure 6.5).

What about false-belief tasks? When using variants of the Sally–Anne and similar tasks described earlier, chimpanzees consistently fail them.[75] However, at least two studies using looking behavior suggests that, like infants and toddlers, chimpanzees may have an implicit understanding of

Figure 6.5. Chimpanzees are highly social animals, but their social cognition is qualitatively different from that of *Homo sapiens*.
Source: Shutterstock, with permission.

false belief, but also like infants and toddlers, they are unable to act upon those beliefs.[76] In other words, if chimpanzees do have an implicit understanding of false belief, it does not affect their actions.

The foundational ability of human sociality is understanding others as intentional agents, beings who have a mental life and whose actions are based on what they know and what they want (termed *belief-desire reasoning*). The first glimmer of such thinking is found in human infants at around 9 months of age in shared attention and expresses itself several years later in the ability to understand that others can have false beliefs and that people sometimes act on those erroneous beliefs. Nearly all other forms of human sociality are based on an understanding that other people's actions are a function of their knowledge and motivation. Such understanding is necessary for people to effectively compete, cooperate, and learn from one another. Both the earlier shared attention and the later false-belief reasoning are unique to humans, at least in their explicit forms, but their roots can be found in the social cognition of chimpanzees.

Empathy

Much like the emotion of jealousy described earlier, *empathy* is usually thought of as a secondary emotion that requires a certain level of cognitive sophistication not available to children much before the age of 2. At its broadest level, empathy refers to the ability to recognize, perceive, and feel the emotion of another. At a minimum, empathy requires the ability to take the perspective of another. Perspective taking is not an all-or-none thing, however, but develops gradually over infancy and childhood. For example, babies need some level of perspective taking to participate in shared-attention routines with adults, beginning around 9 months of age. Yet the ability to take the emotional and cognitive perspective of another continues to develop well into the childhood years as evidenced, for instance, by children's failure to pass conventional false-belief tasks until about the age of 4. As children's perspective-taking skills improve, so does their ability to experience empathy.

One early-developing forms of empathy is seen in newborns. Several studies have reported that infants as young as 3 days old will begin to cry and show signs of distress when they hear the cries of another infant, although not when they hear an artificial simulation of a baby's cry.[77] During the toddler years, children are able to recognize and often react to the distress of others, although they do not fully understand the internal state of others and assume it is the same as their own. For example, a 2-year-old boy may give his tearful mother a teddy bear because it comforts him when he is sad. With age and improved perspective-taking abilities, children are increasingly able identify the emotions others are expressing and to realize that other people's perspectives and feelings may be different from their own.[78]

What about apes? Primatologists Stephanie Preston and Franz de Waal proposed that there are different types of empathy, some of which are shown by great apes. The type of empathy that typifies humans, in which someone recognizes another person's emotional state, is referred to as *cognitive empathy*; it requires advanced perspective-taking skills, and this seems not to be expressed by chimpanzees and the other great apes. Yet, Preston and de Waal propose that great apes display simpler forms of empathy, such as emotional contagion (similar to that shown by newborns hearing the cries of other babies), sympathy, and, in some contexts, even cognitive empathy.[79] As an example, de Waal relates an incident in which an 8-year-old female gorilla helped a 3-year-old boy who fell into the primates' cage at the Chicago Brookfield Zoo, and another in which a long-time human researcher at the Stuttgart Zoo introduced her newborn baby to the bonobos, upon which the alpha female left briefly and returned with her own newborn.[80] Yet, in laboratory settings chimpanzees seem to be indifferent to the welfare of others. For instance, chimpanzees usually fail to provide food to other familiar but unrelated chimps, even though there is no material cost to themselves.[81]

Apes are not without the capacity for empathy, but they seem to display it sparingly. Anthropologist Sarah Hrdy believes that empathy is a critical component in what it means to be human and something that differentiates *Homo sapiens* from the great apes, writing, "What makes us humans rather than just apes is the capacity to combine intelligence with articulate empathy."[82] It seems that the ability to put oneself in someone else's shoes—to take the perspective of others—is a necessary component for empathy, and perhaps the ability to see others as intentional agents, with feelings and thoughts guiding their behavior, almost necessitates experiencing empathy.

"Promiscuous Normativity"

Humankind's grandest accomplishments, as well as its most horrendous tragedies, have not been achieved by lone-wolf individuals but by people in groups. Throughout this book I've emphasized that humans are a social species, but this, in itself, is not unusual. Sociality is common among mammals and birds. In social species, individuals develop relationships with other individuals. They form friendships and may even have enemies. Chimpanzees, monkeys, wolves, and most social mammals will sometimes help friends and attack enemies. Animals in most social species compete for status, with some such as chimpanzees forming coalitions to compete for resources and dominance.[83] Male chimpanzees even form something equivalent to war parties and attack and sometimes kill members of other chimpanzee troops.

So what's so different about human social groups and their development? Human children, like chimpanzees, form relationships with peers, engage in reciprocal interactions, and sometimes compete with other groups of children for access to resources, such as exclusive control of the dress-up area in a preschool or the jungle gym on the playground. Such group behavior, however, is based on dyadic, one-on-one, interactions, with each individual in the group knowing and collaboratively interacting with each other member of the group. Group behavior is based on individual, personal experience. This begins to change starting about the age of 3 and progressing into the early school years. Now children begin to develop a sense of group-mindedness; they make implicit, and sometimes explicit, distinctions between in-group and out-group members, with group membership no longer being based solely on personally knowing and interacting with others. Children are beginning to develop what Tomasello called *collective intentionality*, and this will transform the children's (and the species') social life.

Although 3 years of age may represent the beginning of collective intentionality, children make distinctions between social groups much earlier, with distinctions on the basis of race, gender, and language being found before their second birthdays. For example, 9-month-old infants associate faces from their own race with happy music and other-race faces with sad music.[84] In other research, 18- to 20-month-old children associate sex-stereotypic objects with the "appropriate" gender (for instance, toy cars and trucks for boys, dolls for girls) and selectively imitate same-sex stereotypic behavior (for instance, building a house for boys; putting diapers on a baby for girls) by about 2 years of age. These effects tend to appear earlier and be more extreme in boys than in girls.[85] And 11- and 14-month-old infants were more likely to imitate the gestures of a native speaker than a foreign speaker (with associated differences in brain activity), suggesting an early implicit in-group/out-group distinction with social-learning consequence.[86] Thus, children seem to have the cognitive capacity to make in-group versus out-group distinctions early, setting the stage for collective intentionality.

The first signs of group-mindedness are seen when children start to enforce social norms on others. Social norms reflect what one is "supposed" or "ought" to do; it reflects the group's expectations for individual behavior. For example, my fashion-conscious daughter at about 4 years of age informed me that I could not wear a pink shirt to work. Pink was for girls. Blue, yellow, and even purple were OK, but pink violated what she perceived to be a social norm. Young children sometimes vigorously enforce social norms on other children. This can be seen in tattling among preschoolers. Developmental psychologists Gordon Ingram and Jesse Bering observed the incidence of tattling among groups of preschoolers and reported that children tattled an average of about 1.25 times per day and were generally truthful in their negative reports about others. Tattling was used mostly by dominant children, and most tattling was for rule violation. The authors suggested that tattling serves as a form of *cheater detection*, preventing other children from breaking social contracts.[87] In other research, children as young as 3 (but more reliably by 5 and 6 years) will sacrifice some of their own resources to punish a selfish player or one who violated rules of a game;[88] children are also more apt to punish out-group than in-group members.[89] In an interesting study, researchers created morphs between doll (inanimate) and human faces; they then showed a set of ambiguous morphs to 5- and 6-year-old children and asked them to rate each image in terms of "humanness." In one experiment, some morphs were of the same sex as the child (in-group), whereas others were of the opposite sex (out-group). In a second study identical morphs were shown on one of two backgrounds, one depicting a city in which the children lived (in-group) and one depicting a city "far away" (out-group). In both studies, the 6-year-old (but not 5-year-old) children rated the morphed images from the out-group (opposite gender, different city) as less human than images from the in-group (same sex, same city).[90]

One research technique that shows how easily children can come to identify with a social group is the *minimal groups paradigm*, originally developed with adults,[91] but which has also been frequently used with children. In a minimal groups paradigm participants are assigned to one of two groups based on some arbitrary and inconsequential feature, such as the color shirt one wears. For example, in one study 5-year-old children were randomly assigned to wear either a red or blue T-shirt and then asked to view photos of other children (also wearing red or blue T-shirts). Children were first asked to rate on a 6-point scale how much they liked each child. The children were then told of either a positive or negative behavior and were asked to decide which child—the one wearing the blue shirt or the one wearing the red shirt—most likely engaged in the target behavior. Children were also asked to distribute five coins between a red-shirted and a blue-shirted child. The authors reported that children expressed greater liking for and gave more coins to in-group than to out-group members (Experiment 1) and were more likely to attribute bad behavior to out-group children and good behavior to the in-group children (Experiment 2).[92] Other research using the minimal groups paradigm has shown that preschool children care more about how in-group versus out-group members evaluate them, care about how others perceive the reputation of the group (as well as their own reputation), and display more liking, sharing, helping, and trust to in-group than to out-group members.[93]

Social norms, however, expand beyond well-defined groups to one's society in general. My daughter's insistence on what color shirts I could and could not wear was based on, what to her, was a universal social norm. For instance, 5- and 6-year-old children watched as a puppet distributed stickers to a sticker-poor and a sticker-rich child. The children complained when the puppet gave more stickers to the "rich" kid, which violated the social norm of fairness.[94] Although younger children (3- and 4-year-olds) in this experiment did not protest when the puppet distributed stickers unfairly, they will call out rule violators under some circumstances. For example, in one study 3-year-old children agreed upon arbitrary rules for playing a game with puppets. When a puppet later violated a rule, the children only enforced the rule when a puppet had previously agreed to the rule, but not when a puppet was unaware of the rule. That is, following a norm was only required for those who had agreed beforehand to follow the rule.[95] In other research, 3- to 5-year-old children corrected a puppet that omitted unnecessary actions on a tool-use task previously performed by an adult, protesting that the puppet was "doing it wrong."[96]

As Tomasello put it, young children are *promiscuous normativists*. Between the ages of 3 and 5 years, children begin to develop a more sophisticated sense of "we." According to Tomasello, children between the ages of 3 and 5 years are "beginning to feel solidarity with in-group members, typically identified as those who resemble them in behavior and appearance."[97] This means the size of the group to which children identify can expand beyond the number of people they actually interact with to larger social groups composed of unfamiliar people. These groups may include one's school, religion, race, gender, culture, and even humanity writ large. Children's sense of group-mindedness continues to develop past the age of 6, of course, and will vary depending on specific cultural norms. However, young children's sensitivity to groups, in-group/out-group distinctions, group norms, and the importance of obeying and enforcing (sometimes through third-party punishment) such norms is not found in our nearest living relatives, chimpanzees or bonobos;[98] such promiscuous normativity lays the foundation for a human-type sociality and surely did for our ancestors.

Social Learning

Two-year-old Shayne and his father walked hand in hand from the car to the supermarket. As they approached the automatic door, Shayne raced into the store and stepped onto the scale in the lobby. Once on the scale, he stood very still, his arms to his side and his head pointed upward, staring at the face of the scale. After a few moments he looked at his father, smiled, and stepped down. His father then repeated the same routine.[99]

Although on the surface, this may appear to be a father imitating his young son, in actuality, it is the reverse. Shayne had accompanied his father to the grocery store on many occasions and watched as his father stepped onto the scale to check progress on his most recent diet. Shayne knew the routine by heart, and although he had no clue as to what the moving hand on the scale face meant, he knew it was something his beloved father did, and so he did it, too. This is an example of social learning.

At its most basic, *social learning* refers to situations in which one individual comes to behave like others. Most social mammals and birds display some degree of social learning, but none to the degree that humans do. Humans acquire not only important technical knowledge via social learning, such as how to use tools from knives and spears to computers and cars, but also vital social knowledge, such as when to say "please" and "thank you" and the proper way to perform karaoke or to praise God. Human social learning sometimes has no instrumental outcome, such as learning to use a tool or being fed but, rather, a strictly social one. Shayne's copying of his father's behavior serves no purpose other than to enhance the sense of belonging or identification between Shayne and his father. For a highly social species such as *Homo sapiens*, this can have profound implications.

Humans' facility for social learning permitted our ancestors to pass knowledge from one individual to another with great fidelity. All animals learn from their own experience, but by being able to learn from the experiences of others, an individual need not start from scratch to learn a new skill. No need to reinvent the wheel. Such social learning has implications not only for the individual but also for the group; each generation can begin where the last one left off, which results in the rapid accumulation of cultural knowledge. Tomasello referred to the cumulative character of human culture as the *ratchet effect*, in which an invention, skill, or idea can jump from one mind to another, permitting the entire group to acquire a new trait.[100] Humans' vast material and intellectual culture was, and continues to be, achieved through social learning, and this begins early in life.[101]

Types of Social Learning. There are different forms of social learning, with each involving different levels of cognitive abilities. The most basic form is *local* (or *stimulus*) *enhancement*, in which an individual observes others engaging is some activity at a particular location (for example, a chimpanzee rolling a log to reveal some tasty ants), moves to that location, and, through trial and error, achieves a similar outcome, perhaps using a different method (for instance, jumping on the log to get at the ants). A somewhat more sophisticated form of social learning is *mimicry*, where the individual copies the behavior of a model without any understanding of the goal of that behavior, such as a 2-year-old boy stepping on a scale, looking at the scale-face, and stepping off, just like Dad does. More cognitively involved yet is *emulation*, in which an individual identifies the goal of a model but does not necessarily copy the exact behaviors to achieve that goal. For example, a child watches someone sifting sand through her fingers to get seashells, but, instead of sifting, she tosses sand in the air to reveal the shells. True *imitation* (or *imitative learning*) involves the individual understanding the goal of the model, as in emulation, but using the same or similar behaviors to achieve that goal. In the sifting seashell example, the observer would use the same actions (sifting sand through her fingers) as the model to achieve the same goal (getting seashells). The most sophisticated form of social learning is *teaching*, or *instructed learning*, in which one individual (the teacher) modifies his or her behavior only in the presence of another (the student), without the teacher getting any immediate benefits.[102] Humans are not the only animals that engage in the more advanced forms of social learning (imitation and teaching), but no other animal does so to the extent that humans do.

Social Learning in Children. Social learning has its origin in babies' more general social orientation. The Swiss psychologist Jean Piaget called the earliest form of social learning *mutual imitation*, in which an infant emits some behavior that is then mimicked by an adult, which, in turn, activates the baby to continue that behavior.[103] Piaget described one such interaction with his 3-month-old daughter: "I noted a differentiation in the sounds of her laughter. I imitated them. She reacted by reproducing them quite clearly, but only when she had already uttered them immediately before."[104] Infants are not actually learning anything new here but, rather, are engaging in social give-and-take with an adult, involving behaviors that they already possess. Babies apparently enjoy these bouts of parent–infant "imitation." For instance, 3.5-month-old infants vocalize and smile more during and immediately after being imitated by their mothers than they do for nonimitative behaviors.[105] A similar facilitating effect on social interaction of being imitated has been reported for rhesus monkey infants.[106] Beginning around 8 months of age, Piaget noted the first signs of true social learning (that is, in which infants acquire some new behavior), as infants copy sounds and bodily movements, including facial gestures, observed in others. For example, in one study in which parents kept diaries of their children's imitative behaviors, 12-, 15-, and 18-month-old infants learned, on average, one or two new behaviors a day simply by watching.[107]

Much of toddler social learning is in the form of emulation rather than imitation. Children seemingly understand the goal but often use other techniques to achieve that goal.[108] Consider a study by Hungarian developmental psychologist György Gergely and his colleagues,[109] where 14-month-old infants watched as an adult turned on a light by pressing a button with her head. In one condition, the adult's arms were wrapped in a blanket, preventing her from using her hands, a more typical body part for turning on a light. In a second condition, the adult's hands were free. When later given the opportunity to turn the light on themselves, those toddlers who saw the adult whose hands were free also used their head to turn on the light, displaying imitation. However, those who watched the adult whose arms were wrapped in a blanket used their *hands*, not their heads, to turn on the light. Gergely and his colleagues reasoned that the toddlers figured that the arm-restricted adult had no choice, so they copied not the exact behavior of the model (using their heads) but, rather, a different but more typical action, pressing the button with their hands, to achieve the same goal (emulation). Gergely and his colleagues referred to this behavior as *rational imitation*. Other researchers have similarly shown that infants as young as 7 months will copy the *intended* actions of a model (for example, pulling off the end of a barbell, even though the model's hand slipped when she demonstrated the action) rather than the actual outcome (having one's hand slip from the end of the barbell).[110] This reflects the fact that infants are treating others are intentional agents, as discussed earlier.

Beginning around 3 years of age, children's social-learning strategy seems to change. Where previously they would sometimes use different behaviors than a model to achieve a goal (that is, emulation), they now persistently engage in imitation to the extent that they will copy the obviously irrelevant actions of a model as well as the relevant one. This is referred to as *overimitation*, and I alluded to it briefly in Chapters 4 and 5. For example, in one study preschoolers watched as a model performed a series of actions on a puzzle box to get a toy that had been locked inside. Some of the actions were obviously irrelevant to opening the box, but even when warned to avoid "silly," unnecessary actions, the children copied them anyway.[111] There have now been dozens of studies examining overimitation,[112] and although the extent to which children will copy irrelevant actions varies somewhat with context (for instance, when they have some knowledge of the model's intention; whether a high- or low-status person serves as the model; when the model speaks a different language; as they become more familiar with specific tasks),[113] it is not too much of an exaggeration to say that young children are almost slavish imitators. Overimitation is not limited to children in WEIRD societies but has been reported across cultures, including 2- to 6-year-old Kalahari Bushman children.[114] And preschoolers are not the only people who overimitate; overimitation persists into adulthood in some contexts, including among the hunter-gatherer Aka of the Central African Republic.[115]

Why should children imitate even the obviously irrelevant actions of a model? Rather than view overimitation as a reflection of immature cognition, many scholars view it as an adaptation. As noted in the previous section on social norms, one reason children overimitate is that they believe the model is reflecting a social norm: that's the way "we" do it, and a child will correct someone who skips irrelevant actions previously demonstrated by a model.[116] Overimitation may be adaptive in acquiring vital cultural information, including rituals that may have no apparent goal other than their own execution but are valued by group members.[117] This *normative account* holds that children may understand that not all actions are necessary for completing a task, but they believe all of the actions are important for the "bigger overarching action sequence," and that performing both relevant and irrelevant actions is important for aligning oneself with one's cultural in-group.[118] According to evolutionary developmental psychologist Mark Nielsen, "Children show they are prepared socially and cognitively to adopt the ritualized behaviors of those around them in many ways . . ., the most compelling of which is overimitation."[119] Consistent with this argument, preschoolers are more likely to imitate meaningless actions made by in-group than by out-group members.[120]

Other researchers have proposed that overimitation is an adaptation for learning about cultural artifacts and their uses.[121] As mentioned previously, humans are an artifact-creating and using species. Tools in one form or another are everywhere, and humans have evolved adaptations for learning how to use tools and how to treat artifacts. (See discussion of the design stance in Chapter 5.) For example, psychologist and primatologist Andrew Whiten and his colleagues[122] argued that an efficient way to learn about artifacts (for example, using tools, how to treat sacred objects) is to copy exactly the actions of others, even if some irrelevant actions are acquired along the way. In a related vein, developmental psychologists György Gergely and Gergely Csibra proposed that children's overimitation is a human adaptation permitting fast and accurate transmission of information between individuals, which they refer to as *natural pedagogy*.[123] They argue that when learning to use objects by watching adults, children apply an *assumption of relevance*, presuming that all actions an adult performs are necessary for achieving a goal. After all, surely the grown-ups know what they're doing.

Teaching, or instructed learning, is the most sophisticated form of social learning, although it is not limited to humans. Effective teaching requires some component of theory of mind. According to Michael Tomasello and his colleagues, "To learn from an instructor culturally—to understand the instruction from something resembling the instructor's point of view—requires that children be able to understand a mental perspective that differs from their own, and then to relate that point of view to their own in an explicit fashion."[124] Similar to imitative learning, children must internalize the adult's instruction and understand the goal of the behavior—the adult's purpose when he or she initially taught the behavior. It is likely no coincidence that overimitation, the ability to learn from instruction, and collective intentionality, as reflected in children's discovery of social norms as discussed earlier, come online at about the same time. According to Tomasello, "The major ontogenetic transition occurs at around age three, when young children go from just imitating and culturally learning from others to a full understanding of adult pedagogy as the cultural transmission of objective knowledge."[125]

Social Learning in Great Apes. Humans' social-learning skills are truly remarkable and are dependent on the shared intentionality abilities discussed earlier in this chapter. We saw then that infants' and young children's capacity for shared attention was an extension of abilities observed in our close primate relatives and, thus, likely characterized our last common ancestor with chimpanzees and bonobos. What about social learning? Chimpanzees and bonobos live in socially complex groups that require considerable interpersonal skills. How is human children's social learning different than that of great apes? Earlier in this chapter we discussed studies that showed that 2-year-old children displayed superior social-cognitive skills relative to both adult and 2-year-old chimps, with the children's social skills increasing with age, whereas the social abilities of the chimpanzees remained stable.[126] What, more specifically, are the social-learning abilities of chimpanzees, and how do they differ from those of human children?

As I mentioned earlier, social learning has permitted humans to establish a rich material culture via the ratchet effect, transmitting information across generations, with each generation potentially adding to the knowledge of the prior generation. Great apes also transmit nongenetic information across generations, which some scholars refer to as evidence of culture, whereas others are content to refer to such transmission as *traditions*. Chimpanzees and orangutans have been observed to pass along forms of greeting, grooming, tool use (as used in cracking nuts or "fishing" for termites), as have some cetaceans (dolphins and killer whales).[127] However, there is no evidence of a ratchet effect in these nonhuman social learners. Chimpanzees, for example, do not display generation-by-generation improvements in the tools or techniques they use to crack nuts or fish for termites. As a result, great ape culture remains static.

In the laboratory, chimpanzees often display considerable social-learning skills, but most of their learning is done by emulation, not by imitation. In an early study, chimpanzees and 2-year-old children were shown a desirable out-of-reach object and watched as a human experimenter used a rake to retrieve it. The 2-year-old children mostly imitated, using the same actions as the model did to retrieve the object, even when there was a more effective way of getting what they wanted. Chimpanzees, in contrast, ignored the inefficient method used by the model and, instead, used a more straightforward method to achieve the goal. That is, they emulated rather than imitated, and more recent studies have produced similar findings.[128] In general, emulation seems to the primary form of social learning in chimpanzees and the other great apes. Given that these apes rarely engage in imitation, it is not surprising that there is no evidence of overimitation in these animals.[129]

What about teaching? There are a number of observations of chimpanzees in the wild in which mothers seem to engage in teaching with their young offspring.[130] For instance, primatologist Christophe Boesch reported mother chimpanzees making slow, exaggerated movements while cracking nuts when in the presence of their infants, which he interpreted as teaching. Such behavior is rare, however, and teaching does not seem to be a major avenue of social learning in chimps.

There are a few interesting exceptions to the pattern of great ape social learning presented here, and those involve apes, mostly chimpanzees, that are raised as closely as possible like human children. Michael Tomasello, Sue Savage-Rumbaugh, and Ann Kruger speculated that one reason for chimpanzees' impoverished social cognition is that "unlike human children, they do not develop in a social environment in which adult conspecifics are constantly encouraging their attention to objects, intentionally teaching them how to use objects as tools, and rewarding them for imitating actions on objects."[131] When apes experience a human-like rearing environment, including language, shared-attention attempts, and explicit teaching by their human caretakers, will it also change aspects of their social cognition, specifically, their social learning? The *enculturation hypothesis* proposes that such chimpanzees will develop some social-cognitive abilities more similar to those of human children.[132]

I briefly presented evidence of imitation in enculturated apes in Chapter 3. In the first study of social learning in enculturated chimpanzees, Michael Tomasello and his colleagues showed enculturated chimpanzees, mother-reared chimpanzees, and 18- and 30-month-old human children a series of actions on objects (for example, placing a sifter on one's head, clamping an object with a clamp). The researchers gave the apes and the children the opportunity to interact with the objects either immediately or after a 2-day delay.[133] For the immediate imitation task, the enculturated apes imitated the modeled actions as well as the children, and both had greater performance than the mother-reared chimps. The enculturated chimps actually outperformed the children on the 2-day delayed imitation task. Other researchers have reported similar findings of human-like imitative abilities in enculturated great apes.[134] With respect to teaching, primate researcher Roger Fouts reported that the enculturated and language-trained chimpanzee Washoe taught about 50 signs to her adopted son Loulis, which he used both with Washoe and with her human caretakers[135] (see Figure 6.6).

In discussing some of this research earlier in Chapter 3 and some of the research on fantasy play in chimpanzees in Chapter 5, I argued that glimmers of human-like social-cognitive abilities are seen in apes that have experienced a species-*atypical* environment, one more like that experienced by a human child than a juvenile ape. This illustrates that chimpanzees possess some latent social-cognitive abilities that could certainly serve as the starting point for the evolution of a more human-style form of social learning.

* * *

It is difficult to overestimate the role that social learning has in human development, human culture, and human evolution. Enhanced social learning by itself, of course, is not "the cause" of human psychological evolution, nor the only reason for our species' extraordinary accomplishments. Enhanced symbolic and communication abilities, in combination with superior social-learning skills, have resulted in *Homo sapiens*' dominance of the earth. The foundation for humans' social-learning abilities can be found in the joint intentionality of infants and later in the collective intentionality of preschool children. These abilities emerged in the ontogeny of our ancestors and were

Figure 6.6. The social cognition of enculturated (human-reared) chimpanzees often more closely resembles that of human preschool children than that of mother-reared chimpanzees.
Source: Shutterstock, with permission.

built upon variations in the development of great ape social-learning skills; these skills not only provided immediate survival benefits to our forechildren, but also, as they continued to develop, gave ancient adults ways of improving their own lot and the invention and expansion of human material culture.

Prosociality

Compared with other primates, *Homo sapiens* is a nice species, at least toward members of their in-group. Don't get me wrong. Within-group competition can get nasty and even violent, and between-group competition much more so. But recall our discussion in Chapter 4 that one neotenous feature of humans was a reduction in reactive aggression. In comparison with chimpanzees, for example, humans are less aggressive and more tolerant of one another, permitting the development of a greater degree of cooperation than anything seen in the great apes. Accompanying this decrease in reactive aggression, and perhaps necessary for enhanced cooperation to evolve, was a tendency toward positive, or *prosocial*, behavior with respect to our fellow conspecifics. This prosociality manifests itself in helping, sharing, and a sense of fairness, and each of these has its origins in infancy and early childhood.

The coexistence of selfish and prosocial behavior is illustrated in research by evolutionary psychologist Patricia Hawley.[136] Hawley has documented different ways that individual children and adults gain resources and status within a group, and she finds that high-status people use a combination of both aggressive/selfish and affiliative/altruistic techniques. Some people attain status and resources mainly through coercive behaviors, others through mainly prosocial behaviors, and others through a combination of the coercive and prosocial actions. Hawley refers to the latter groups as *bistrategic controllers*, and these tend to be the most successful/socially dominate people. Bistrategic controllers have been found at all ages, beginning in the preschool years.

Being prosocial means differentiating good from bad behavior and friend from foe, including telling the difference between people who help versus hinder another person's goal. There is evidence that such a distinction is found during the first year of life. For example, developmental psychologist J. Kiley Hamlin and her colleagues showed live "morality plays" to infants, with one puppet trying to achieve a goal (for instance, trying to reach the top of a hill) and other puppets either helping (bumping the protagonist up the hill) or hindering (bumping the protagonist down the hill) the goal-striving puppet. Later the infants were given the opportunity to reach for either the Helper or Hinderer puppet. Infants consistently reached for the Helping puppet as early as they were able to make reaching responses (about 4.5 months).[137] Although other researchers have suggested that these results can be explained on the basis of strictly perceptual mechanisms,[138] Hamlin and her colleagues argue that these and related findings reflect a core, evolved understanding of an aspect of morality that is expressed early in life and not, at this stage in development, much influenced by socialization.[139]

In the remainder of this section, I look at three types of prosocial behavior in young children and great apes: helping, sharing, and a sense of fairness. As we'll see, rudiments of each of these behaviors require the ability to treat others as intentional agents; more sophisticated forms of helping, sharing, and fairness are more complicated, requiring what Tomasello calls *collective intentionality*.

Helping. Toddlers like to help. Many a household project would be done more quickly if a 2- or 3-year-old child did *not* offer assistance. In one study, developmental psychologist Harriet Rheingold asked the parents of 18- to 30-month-old children and other adults to perform some common household tasks and to record the children's reactions. Rheingold reported that children spontaneously and promptly helped the adults in most of the chores they did, regardless of whether the adult was the child's parent or an unfamiliar person.[140]

Young children's tendencies to help is seen even among preverbal toddlers. For example, in a now-classic study, 18-month-old children watched with their mothers as an unfamiliar adult performed a series of tasks and sometimes required help to complete the task. For instance, the adult dropped a marker he was using or was unable to open a cupboard door to put some books away. In these conditions, the children usually helped the adult, picking up and handing the adult the marker or opening the cupboard door. Importantly, children did not offer help when the adult intentionally threw the marker on the floor, for instance. Their behavior was motivated by a need in the adult, and they could tell the difference between an adult in need and one who required no help. When tested under similar circumstance, mother-reared chimpanzees showed no inclination to help, although, interestingly, some human-reared chimps did help, providing further support for the enculturation hypothesis discussed earlier in this chapter with respect to social learning.[141]

Many similar studies have been done with children using variants of this paradigm, with mostly similar results. Among some of the findings: toddlers are more likely to help a familiar than an unfamiliar person; 15-month-olds are more likely to help an unfamiliar person when encouraged by their mothers; 2-year-olds are equally likely to help an unfamiliar adult whether their mother is present or not; and 2-year-old children display the same level of satisfaction and prosocial arousal when achieving a goal (throwing wooden marbles in a sound-producing apparatus) as when helping someone else achieve the same goal.[142] As they grow older, children help other children as well as adults, and their helping is unaffected by whether they are rewarded for helping or not.[143] In fact, children who are rewarded for helping subsequently help *less* than children who receive no rewards. Similar patterns of the emergence of helping are found across cultures.[144] These findings all lead to the conclusion that helping in infants and young children is intrinsically motivated and, during the preschool years, seems not be greatly influenced by socialization practices.[145]

This is not to say that helping behaviors develop independently of experience. Despite often substantial differences in childrearing practices across the globe (see Chapter 2), most infants and children grow up in positive, supportive environments of social interactions, and it is through these interactions that all social behaviors emerge, including helping. Some theorists have proposed that the children's motivations for helping during infancy and early toddlerhood are not based on a prosocial motives but on desire for social interaction. This changes into the preschool years, with children now motivated by a desire to promote the welfare of others.[146]

Developmental psychologist Felix Warneken proposed that helping in young children was selected for over the course of human evolution because it fostered children's survival by providing assistance to adults. Although toddlers can rarely perform useful tasks in any culture, by the age of 3 years children in traditional subsistence cultures can and do contribute to the family economy by fetching water, collecting firewood, or relaying messages, among other tasks. As such, helping behavior may have been a target for natural selection, although this likely could only have been achieved once children understood that other people are intentional agents with a different perspective from their own.[147] Beginning around the age of 3, children would also recognize the normative nature of their helping—it's what children in their culture do, and thus something that they also strive to do.

Sharing. Toddlers are not known for their propensity to share. Once young children have a desired object, they want to keep it and often complain loudly if asked to share. One study of 21-month-olds reported that 84% of all disputes between children involved struggles over toys.[148] As it turns out, young children's selfish motivations are accompanied by equally generous motivations, at least under certain circumstances. For instance, when children do not possess valued objects beforehand, they are more likely to share the objects equally. In one study, pairs of 18- and 24-month-old children were shown some marbles that could be used in a game. A researcher explained how the game was played and then let the children play themselves. On each trial, the children had four marbles. The 18- and 24-month-old children distributed the marbles equally 44% of the time (two marbles to each child), unequally 37% of the time (3 to one child, one to the other), and monopolized the marbles, taking all four, only 19% of the time.[149]

Children make increasingly even distributions of resources (toys or food) with age.[150] For example, in the *Dictator Game*, a child is given some resource, such as stickers or candy, and told he or she can share some of the resource with another child. In these situations, younger preschool children typically share fewer resources than older children, although even

4-year-olds will share some (usually very few) resources with a peer, indicating some rudimentary notion of altruism in young children.[151] As they get older, children also become more selective with whom and how much they share. For example, 3-year-olds (but not 2-year-olds) are more likely to share with someone who had previously shared with them;[152] 3-year-olds are more likely to divide resources evenly with friends than nonfriends;[153] and 5-year-olds are more sensitive to social norms than 3-year-olds, sharing more when given information that sharing is what other children do in these situations.[154]

Like helping, children's sharing seems to be intrinsically motivated, in that it does not increase (in fact, it decreases) when children are given rewards for sharing.[155] Children's sharing, at least in its early stages, also shows similar patterns across a wide range of cultures.[156] With increasing age, sharing varies according to cultural norms, reflecting the importance of experience in children's prosocial behavior.[157]

In one interesting study, 18- and 25-month-old children stood at a table and could reach and pull one of two handles: one delivered a snack for themselves, whereas the other delivered a snack for themselves *and* for an adult who sat on the opposite side of the table. When the adult sat silently, both the younger and older children pulled the handles randomly, delivering the snack to both themselves and the adult about half the time. However, when the adult stated her desire for a snack ("I like crackers. I want a cracker."), the 25-month-olds pulled the "sharing" handle about 70% of the time, while the 18-month-olds continued to pull the handles randomly. That is, when there was no increased cost to the child and a potential recipient expressed a desire for the snack, 2-year-old children were more than happy to comply with her wishes; 18-month-olds, in contrast, didn't seem to see the point.[158]

This study was modeled on similar experiments with chimpanzees. When pairs of chimpanzees could pull two ropes, one that gave them a treat and the other that gave treats both to them and to another chimpanzees, the apes chose randomly. Despite there being no cost to sharing, the chimpanzees responded indiscriminately.[159] In the wild, chimpanzees that have caught a monkey or other animal will sometimes allow other chimps to take some of the carcass after being persistently harassed by the recipients, a form of reluctant sharing referred to as *sharing-under-pressure* or *tolerated theft*.[160] Research with captive chimpanzees confirms that chimps that vigorously beg or harass another ape that has resources are more likely to be shared with than a less-harassing chimp; chimpanzees are also more likely to share with relatives, high-ranking (more dominant) chimps, and "friends," than with nonrelatives, lower-ranking chimps, and nonfriends.[161] Thus, although chimpanzees are reluctant sharers, they, like 3-year-old children, share more with friends than nonfriends; but, unlike 2-year-old children, they will not bother to make an effort to share with a fellow ape by pulling one rope over another, even when there is no cost to themselves.

Fairness. Perhaps the foundation of prosociality is a sense of fairness. Are some people getting more than they deserve and others getting less? Most early investigations of children's sense of fairness suggested that it was not until about age 5 that children distribute valued resources fairly, that is, equally.[162] Children as young as 3 clearly recognize when they are getting less than they deserve but seem not to recognize the unfairness of the situation (or at least not to protest it) when they receive a larger portion.[163] More recent research indicates that young children will distribute resources fairly under some circumstances, and that even preverbal infants have some implicit notion of what is fair.

Researchers using infants' looking behavior have found that infants as young as 10 months of age will look longer at a display in which someone receives an unfair distribution of some resource (1 versus 3) than when resources are divided evenly (2 for each) between two individuals.[164] By itself, these findings could reflect simply a perceptual bias and not be an indication of any sense of fairness. Other research, however, has shown that 15-month-old infants choose to receive toys from and play with fair rather than unfair actors, suggesting that infants' biases are, indeed, related to a sense of fairness.[165]

Other research indicates that young children's sense of fairness reflects more a sense of equity than equality. In a study by Katharina Hamann and her colleagues, 2- and 3-year-old children were shown how to use an apparatus that had ropes on two ends of a platform. In one condition, children found an unequal (3:1) distribution of treats on their respective platforms as they walked into the room, making it unnecessary for them to pull the ropes; the lucky child rarely offered to share any treats with the unlucky child, seemingly being content with the unfair distribution. In a second condition, when a child pulled on the rope it moved a board and delivered some treats. Sometimes one child got more treats than the other, and the lucky 3-year-old (but not 2-year-old) child occasionally shared his or her treats with the unlucky child. In a third condition, both children had to pull the rope simultaneously to move a board that produced some treats. When there was an unequal distribution of treats (for example, one child received three, whereas the other child received one), the lucky 3-year-old (but not 2-year-old) child shared with the unlucky child nearly 80% of the time. These findings show clearly that by 3 years of age children are sensitive to the effort another person puts into a task and realize that rewards should be shared fairly.[166] Hamann and her colleagues performed a similar experiment with chimpanzees. Like human 2-year-olds, chimpanzees rarely shared any treats they gained as a result of collaborating with another individual.

In other research, children played modified versions of the *Ultimatum Game*, in which, like the Dictator Game mentioned earlier, one participant (the proposer) has some resources (say, four gummy bears) that he or she can share with a second person (the responder). The difference here is that the players only get to keep the reward if the responder accepts an offer. If the responder refuses the offer, neither player gets any treats. In adults from Western countries, offers much less than 30% or 40% are rejected, indicating that people prefer to receive no reward than to settle for an unfair distribution. Like adults, children 7 years and older tend to make non-zero offers and to reject unfair offers when the proposer has the option to offer more.[167] Five-year-old children, in contrast, behave rather selfishly when they are the proposer. In one study, 5-year-olds made zero offers 65% of the time; 5-year-old responders consistently rejected zero offers but also frequently rejected unfair (3:1) offers when the proposer could have made a fair (2:2) offer, demonstrating a sense of fairness.[168] From a strictly rational point of view, responders should accept any non-zero offer; they have nothing now, and they'll have at least one reward if the say "accept." The fact that they don't reflects their sense of fairness: They'd rather get nothing than accept an unfair offer. In similar studies with chimpanzees and bonobos, the great apes behaved rationally, never rejecting any non-zero offers. Unlike 5-year-old children, they seemed unconcerned about issues of fairness and certainly saw no reason to reject "free food."[169] Based on these and related findings, Tomasello stated that "the only reasonable conclusion . . . is that dividing resources with a sense of fairness is just not something that nonhuman great apes do."[170]

Despite Tomasello's contention, nonhuman primates may have some limited sense of fairness. Primatologists Sarah Brosnan and Frans de Waal proposed that many apes and monkeys display what they call *inequity aversions*, protesting against an unequal distribution of some resource, usually food, and always complaining that they, and not their partner, are getting less than their fair share.[171] In a now-classic experiment, Brosnan and de Waal had pairs of female capuchin monkeys exchange small rocks for food rewards with an experimenter. Initially, both monkeys swapped their rocks for slices of cucumbers. After several rounds of trading rocks for cucumbers, one of the monkeys was given grapes, a favorite treat, in exchange for the rocks, while the other monkey continued to get only cucumber slices. Under these conditions, some cucumber-receiving monkeys stopped performing the task and others continued to trade rocks for cucumber slices but refused to eat them. Much like 3-year-old children, the monkeys were averse to getting a worse deal than their partners.[172] It is doubtful that the motivation behind the monkeys' behavior was one of social injustice, but these findings suggest that the roots of evaluating fairness in some social contexts lie deep in our evolutionary history.†

* * *

Human selfishness coexists with human niceness and does so from the earliest stages of life, changing as social-cognitive abilities (joint attention, group-mindedness) develop over infancy and the preschool years. Following the tenets of mainstream evolutionary theory, selfish behavior is expected and observed in (almost) all individuals in (almost) all species, but prosociality is rarer. Hints of "niceness" can be seen in our simian relatives, and its early emergence in *Homo sapiens* strongly implicates changes in great ape ontogeny as the source of human prosociality.

Collaboration

The epitome of human sociality is cooperation, which requires that individuals sacrifice some immediate possible gain for the attainment of some greater group-defined goal. Although cooperation is not unique to humans, no other species displays the wide range of cooperative actions as *Homo sapiens*, with such behaviors being evident in children as young as 3 years of age. Cooperation among children, most readily seen in collaborative activities, is dependent on the cognitive accomplishments described in previous sections of this chapter and may be an emergent property of earlier expressed

---

† To see how capuchin monkeys react to inequality, visit Frans de Waal's TED talk at https://www.youtube.com/watch?v=meiU6TxysCg.

developments, including joint attention, perspective taking, prosociality, and "we mindedness."

Collaboration—coordinated activity in which the participants continuously try to solve a shared problem—is observed to varying degrees in our great ape relatives, both in the wild and in controlled laboratory situations. For example, male chimpanzees appear to coordinate their actions when hunting monkeys. However, upon closer examination, group hunting is less cooperative and more opportunistic, with one chimpanzee initiating the chase as others move to locations to give them the best chance to capture the prey themselves. There appears to be no plan or communication among the hunting party. Chimpanzees cooperate to achieve individual advantage. According to anthropologists Martin Muller and John Mitani, contexts of cooperation among chimpanzees are related to male competition and that "competition . . . frequently represents the driving force behind chimpanzee cooperation."[173]

In controlled laboratory experiments, chimpanzees will work together to achieve a common goal. For example, in research by Hamann and her colleagues described in the previous section on "fairness," chimpanzees will collaborate with one another, each pulling separate ropes so that both receive equal food rewards. Chimps will go so far as to open a door for their partner to join them in the joint activity and to select a partner with whom they had worked successfully a day earlier.[174] Some research indicates that chimpanzees in these situations will help another chimp obtain food, although, unlike children, a chimp's likelihood of providing help is not related to whether it had worked with the other chimp in a collaborative activity or not.[175] And unlike 3-year-old children, when joint effort in a collaborative task leads to unequal outcomes, the lucky ape does not divide the spoils evenly but takes the lion's share for itself.[176] According to Tomasello, "The overall picture is thus that in the group activities of chimpanzees, the individuals are not working together as a 'we' in the sense of having a joint goal and individual roles within it; rather they are operating in what Tuomela (2007) calls 'group behavior in I-mode.'"[177]

Most children under 3 years of age are no better cooperators than are chimpanzees. Recall the results of the studies by Hamann and her colleagues, in which children pulled ropes together to receive treats. When the children had to collaborate to get the treats, 3-year-olds usually shared the treats equally, even when one fortuitously received more treats than the other. In contrast, 2-year-old children (like chimpanzees) did not. By 3 years children are increasingly able and willing to collaborate with one another and to understand that collaboration requires a commitment to another person to perform the task as previously agreed upon. For instance, 3- and 5-year-old children will protest if a partner deliberately quits playing a game and are less likely to take a bribe to end a game when they had explicitly agreed to collaborate with a partner than when no explicit commitment had been made.[178] In other research, 60% of pairs of 5-year-old children, with no direction from adults, coordinated their actions over a series of trials, taking turns being the "winner" and "loser" in a game of chicken in which one partner must swerve his train to avoid a crash. (Not all children cooperated, however. In some pairs socially dominant children were reluctant to ever swerve, resulting in unequal distribution of rewards. Collaboration may be the norm, but selfish, competitive behavior coexists with cooperative behavior.)[179]

Collaboration typically involves attaining some instrumental gain as a result of working together, but collaboration is also necessary for playing a social game where there is no material reward other than playing the game itself. Several studies have reported that children as young as 18 months are able to coordinate their actions with an adult to play a social game and that they protest when the adult suddenly stops, trying to re-engage their partner so the game can continue.[180] Children will even protest when they can continue the game without the help of the adult, clearly indicating that it's the social interaction that they are trying to reinstate, not merely the completion of the game.[181] Young children's social view of collaborative activities is not restricted to Western cultures and has been found with similar frequencies and at similar ages across diverse cultures.[182] In contrast, chimpanzees make no protest when a partner ceases to play a strictly social game (that is, one without a food reward).[183]

Collaboration clearly requires that children be able to treat their partners as intentional agents, with knowledge and goals that may be, and sometimes may not be, similar to their own. They must be able to take the perspective of others and to form a *group-minded "we"* with a collaborator. This requires what Tomasello referred to as *collective intentionality*. With experience, children become more skilled collaborators, and individual differences are found reflecting children's adoption of cultural norms.[184] These findings are consistent with Tomasello's neo-Vygotskian view that there is a significant maturation component to children's early cooperative motivation and skills that become fleshed out by specific cultural experience.

* * *

Sometime between when humans last shared a common ancestor with current-day chimpanzees and bonobos and the emergence of fully modern *Homo sapiens*, changes occurred in the ontogeny of our ancestors' social-cognitive abilities, permitting the evolution of hypersociality. Without such changes during the early years of development, the panoply of social-cognitive skills that uniquely define our species could not have occurred. Adaptations central for adult social life arose first in our forechildren, based on modifications of great ape ontogeny. A list of some of the human-unique social-cognitive abilities is presented in Table 6.1.

Early adaptations for shared attention, empathy, normativity, social learning, prosociality, and collaboration are highly *canalized* over the first 3 years of life, such that children follow a species-typical path under a wide

Table 6.1. Partial list of uniquely human social-cognitive abilities, evolved from changes in great ape ontogeny, discussed in this chapter

Protoconversations: Infants taking turns uttering sounds, making faces, and generally sharing positive emotions in face-to-face interactions with an adult.

Treating others as intentional beings: Treating others as people who do things intentionally, or "on purpose"; appealing to the mental states of others when attempting to explain what they do.

Joint (shared) attention: Beginning around 9 months, a triadic interaction between an infant, an adult, and some object, possibly another person. Involves treating others as *intentional agents*.

Social referencing: Infants using a parent's tone of voice, gesture, or facial expression to determine how they should react to an ambiguous situation.

Explicit false-belief task: Being able to say that a person can believe something that is factually false, as in the Sally-Ann task. This requires *counterfactual thinking*.

Perspective taking: The ability to take the perceptual, emotional, and cognitive perspective of another.

Cognitive empathy: The recognition of another person's emotional state, which requires advanced perspective-taking skills.

Collective intentionality: The ability to establish a *group-minded "we"* with other people. This includes identifying members of in-groups and out-groups, conforming to expectations of in-group members, and enforcing social norms on others.

Overimitation: Copying all actions of a model, both relevant and irrelevant.

Instructed learning: Teaching, in which learners must be able to understand a mental perspective that differs from their own and then relate that point of view to their own in an explicit fashion.

Prosociality: Increased prosocial behavior relative to great apes, reflected in increased helping, sharing, and a sense of fairness/justice.

Cooperative problem solving: Collaborating with another to achieve a goal and, unlike great apes, distributing resources fairly.

range of diverse environments. Later in development, with increasing experience and cognitive capacity as reflected by enhancements in executive functions, children are better able to modify their social behavior in line with expectations of their culture. As children's social-cognitive abilities improve and they are able to establish a group-minded "we," they can better appreciate the point of view of others; they are able to constrain their selfish motivations in some contexts and to behave prosocially more selectively, discriminating whom to imitate, help, share with, collaborate with, or treat fairly.

The Moral Species

Jean-Jacques Rousseau and Thomas Hobbes had differing views about the inherent goodness or brutishness of humans. Are humans born essentially good and innocent and become corrupted by society, or are they born essentially evil and must be civilized by society? New research in evolutionarily informed developmental psychology may actually be able to address this long-standing philosophical debate.

As other animals, *Homo sapiens* have a long history of natural selection favoring selfish actions and selfish genes. This leads to competition between individuals for access to status and resources, with aggression often being used to achieve one's goals. Infants and children are no different. Babies and young children are demanding of attention from their parents, are reluctant to share food or toys already in their possession, and express hostility to outgroup members, all supporting a Hobbesian perspective. Yet, we see that ancient humans evolved some neotenous features resulting in reduced reactive aggression and, under some circumstances, a tendency beginning early in life to take the perspective of others, to help others, to share with other people, to acquire a sense of fairness, and to collaborate, consistent with a Rousseauian interpretation of humankind.

The entire concept of morality only makes sense in a hypersocial species. In fact, a strong argument can be made that cooperation is the basis of morality. This is a position taken by anthropologist Oliver Curry and his colleague, who reported evidence that seven cooperative behaviors—helping kin, helping your group, reciprocating, being brave, deferring to superiors, dividing disputed resources, and respecting prior possessions—serve as the foundation for moral rules across a diverse set of 60 societies.[185] Michael Tomasello makes a similar argument, hypothesizing "that the evolutionary and ontogenetic roots of human morality lie in cooperative activities for mutual benefit."[186]

Human hypersociality and morality have their origins in the earliest stages of development. Changes in the ontogenies of great apes led to a species whose youngest members were prepared to be social. The ability to view others as intentional agents, as simple as it may seem, set the stage for cognitive empathy, belief-desire theory of mind, normativity, highly efficient social learning, prosociality, and collaboration. These social-cognitive abilities cannot be created de novo in adulthood but must develop. They do so with a strong, evolved maturational basis in the early years of life, and in an organism that remains plastic long after other faster-developing animals become set in their ways, permitting the diversity of human cultures.

7
Evolutionary Mismatches in the Development of Today's Children

Lenore Skenazy got her 15 minutes of fame (or perhaps infamy) in 2008, pilloried by the press and many parents as "America's Worst Mom." What did Skenazy do to warrant such scorn? Did she leave her children in a hot car while she played slot machines in a casino or lock them in a dark cellar as punishment for not doing their chores? No, her crime was that she permitted her 9-year-old son Izzy to ride the New York City subway by himself. Izzy was equipped with a MetroCard, a subway map, a 20-dollar bill, and some quarters to make a phone call if needed. The 45-minute trip was uneventful but joyful for Izzy. Then the journalist-mother wrote a column about her son's adventure and her reasons for letting him have it in *The New York Sun*,[1] and the accusations of negligence and child abuse poured in.

Why the hubbub over what, to an earlier generation of New York City children, would be a mundane experience? Because in the decades prior to Izzy's wild ride, Americans had become obsessed with their children's safety. This was prompted, in part, by reports of kidnapped and murdered children, with 24-hour news stations informing people in Portland, Maine, what awful thing might have happened to a child in Portland, Oregon. Never mind that child kidnappings and murders by nonrelatives are statistically rare; they do happen, and when they do, no matter where in the world they occur, we hear about it. The message is: *How would you feel if your child was abducted while walking home from school alone?* Americans had become obsessed with what First Amendment lawyer Greg Lukianoff and social psychologist Jonathan Haidt in their book *The Coddling of the American Mind* called *safetyism*—an excessive concern for the physical and emotional safety of children.[2] In the years since Skenazy's indictment as "America's Worst Mom," many people have come to her defense or realized that they must give their children more freedom. Skenazy herself wrote a book, runs a popular blog (both titled *Free-Range Kids*), and cofounded the group Let Grow: Future-Proofing Our Kids and Country, all aimed at fighting the culture of overprotection. She's not alone in this pursuit, but it may seem as if she's fighting an uphill battle, for in many ways the trend toward safetyism has increased over the past decade.

I was especially attentive to the controversy that Skenazy provoked in 2008 because I had published a book a year earlier that focused on the many aspects of childhood in the early 21st century that were at odds with how our ancestors grew up, and this was causing problems for contemporary children. At that time, my major concern was that adults were rushing children through a childhood that has purposes of its own, often by using developmentally inappropriate techniques for educating children. I viewed adults' overscheduling and overprotection of children as reducing free play, which is an important component of healthy development. I was less attentive to the possibility that Americans were infantilizing their children by prolonging their period of dependency. With the benefit of hindsight and following a decade of "a smartphone in every teenager's pocket," I now believe that the development of many contemporary children is being both rushed *and* delayed—rushed by academic acceleration that can turn children off to the natural joy of learning and by exposure to adult content and issues, and delayed because of safetyism, trying to protect children from the slings and arrows of everyday experiences and as a result postponing independence and reducing resilience. Poor psychological adjustment can result in either case, both due to a mismatch between children's evolved adaptations and their current environments.

I discussed the *mismatch hypothesis* briefly in Chapter 1. Our human ancestors evolved in very different environments from those of today, and as a result some adaptations shaped to deal with Stone Age culture may not be good matches for contemporary children. Early *Homo sapiens* lived in small groups as nomadic hunter-gatherers. As discussed in Chapter 2, most hunter-gatherer communities were *neontocracies*, valuing children and giving them a good deal of autonomy in their daily lives. Babies stayed close to their mothers until weaned, around 2 or 3 years of age, and then spent much of their time playing with other children. Little was expected of them in the way of chores; there was no formal schooling and little formal instruction. Through observation and play, they learned how to be hunter-gatherers. There were really no other career opportunities for them.

If the childhoods of hunter-gatherers should be the model for understanding modern children and their development, as many scholars believe, life for children in WEIRD (Western, educated, industrial, rich, democratic) societies is vastly different from those of our forechildren. Formal education—with groups of same-age children sitting quietly at desks most of the day, being instructed by an unfamiliar adult on topics of no immediate survival value—is an evolutionarily novel phenomenon, and it is little wonder that many children find school boring and burdensome, tolerable only because of the social interaction they have with their peers. But the lives of children and adults have been diverging from those of hunter-gatherers for at least 10,000 years, starting with the advent of agriculture and animal domestication and continuing through the establishment of cities, nations, systems of justice, and corporations. People also have had to adjust to advances in material and intellectual culture, from the wheel and metallurgy to writing, mathematics, and the Internet. One amazing thing about our species is that we, and especially our children, have the neural, cognitive, and behavioral plasticity to adapt to such changes—to deal with the mismatch between the environments in which our ancestors evolved and current ones. We saw in Chapter 2 that many traditional cultures—*gerontocracies*—treat children harshly, valuing them for their economic contribution to the family, very different from both ancestral hunter-gatherer environments and our own. Yet such cultures still manage to produce successful and reproductive adults. So does our culture, but this does not mean that adapting to environments highly different from those of our ancestors does not have psychological costs. Perhaps we can better construct our ecologies to take advantage of the fruits of modern life while minimizing the consequences of the mismatch between current and ancient environments.

Modern human culture is full of mismatches. Evolutionary mismatches occur when there is an *adaptive lag* such that the ancient environment in which an adaptation evolved changed more rapidly than the once-functional adaptation. In particular, human cultural change outstrips human biological change, causing many mismatches. For example, our preference for sweet and fatty foods evolved in an environment when nutritious meals had to be caught, dug out of the ground, or picked from fortuitously found trees and bushes. Because of the recent prevalence of fast-food restaurants and supermarkets, these evolved preferences for high-caloric food put many contemporary people at risk for diabetes and obesity. Modernity, in general, has resulted in substantial changes in how people make a living, spend their time, raise their children, and relate to one another, and some scholars have argued that the high levels of depression and other mental-health problems suffered by contemporary people is the consequence. My concern here is not with the entire panoply of mismatches between the environments of our ancient ancestors and those of WEIRD nations today but, rather, with those mismatches that are mainly associated with a particular time in development. For example, hunter-gatherer infants, and presumably our ancient ancestors, were nearly always in close contact with their mothers or other caregivers and were breastfed on demand for the first 2 or 3 years of life. This is very different from the practices of WEIRD societies, and some people argue that this produces a mismatch with infants' evolved needs, having consequences for emotional and social development.[3]

Natural selection has operated at all life stages, such that children are well adapted to the particular developmental niche in which they live. When environments change, including cultural environments, mismatches can occur. I focus here on mismatches in two stages of life, adolescence and childhood. Adolescence extends from the onset of puberty until young adulthood, although it is impossible to set specific ages for this stage. It is a time when young people seek greater independence from their parents and develop their adult identities. They are particularly sensitive to social relations, risk-taking, and sensation seeking, and this is accompanied by neurological changes.[4] Three cultural changes that cause mismatches with adolescent development are (1) a prolongation of dependency, fostered in part by safetyism; (2) the widespread use of social media; and (3) hyper-individualism. In contrast, childhood, following anthropologist Barry Bogin's classification of children between about 3 and 7 years of age,[5] represents a time of much learning. Children in the past seemingly educated themselves, using their evolved social-learning abilities to acquire the technologies and social conventions of their culture, mostly through play with other children. Formal schooling in WEIRD countries is vastly different from the environments in which our ancestors learned, and these mismatches may be especially consequential during childhood.

I need to make clear at the beginning of this chapter that I am not arguing that a mismatch is always a bad thing—that any deviation from ancestral environments is "bad" and living as much as we can as our ancestors did is "good." This is an example of the *naturalistic fallacy*, mentioned briefly in Chapter 2, which is the false belief that if something is evolved (or is "natural") it must be "good," or at least accepted as part of human nature. Many of the evolutionary mismatches are the result of advancements in modern technology that make life more worth living (or permitting us to live a longer life), and we must keep in mind the positive features of these mismatches as well as their negative ones.

How *Slow* Can You Go?

More than any other mammal, *Homo sapiens* follow a *slow life history strategy*, investing heavily in a few slow-developing offspring. (See discussion of life history theory in Chapter 2.) There is, however, variation in the speed that individuals move through life, with differences in the resources and support available when growing up resulting in children adjusting their life course trajectory. Compared with children growing up in resource-rich and predictable environments, children living in harsh and unpredictable environments develop faster, engage in risky behavior, have sex earlier and with more partners, and, as adults, invest less in more offspring. They essentially develop an opportunistic lifestyle. Children growing up in more favorable and predictable environments show an opposite pattern, developing a futuristic lifestyle. Natural selection has been sensitive to the early environments of youth, and children have enough plasticity to adapt aspects of their development to an anticipated future (current environments being the best predictor of future environments).

One way a mismatch can occur is when children living in harsh and unpredictable environments follow fast life history strategies, which may have been adaptive in ancient ecologies but result in youth engaging in dangerous and sometimes delinquent behaviors in many of today's societies. Such behavior may still be adaptive in a Darwinian sense, while putting children and adolescents at odds with economic and criminal-justice systems in first-world nations. I discussed in Chapter 2 how life history theory can be used to understand and possibly deal with the risky and sometimes violent behaviors of adolescents and young adults who grow up in less-than-optimal environments, and I won't revisit that issue here. Perhaps a more pressing issue is the mismatch caused by children following an increasingly slow life history strategy, which typifies many children living in WEIRD societies today.

Following a (Really) Slow Life History Strategy

In many affluent cultures, life for children has never been better or safer. Their parents had relatively few children, fostered in large part by reliable birth control (a mismatch itself from ancient environments), as well as the resources to invest intensely in them. Low birth rates and substantial investments in children are not limited to North America but are found worldwide. The fertility rate (number of children per woman in her childbearing years) in 2019 throughout Europe and in many South American and Asian countries was less than 2 per woman, below the replacement rate.[6] Once born, life expectancy for children is high, bolstered by government systems that ensure good public health (clean water, good sanitation) and availability of high-quality medical services. Granted, these services are not equally available to all citizens of developed countries, but the likelihood of surviving to adulthood for children born in WEIRD countries today is greater than it's ever been. Such high investments by parents should cause children to follow a slow life history strategy, which most do, and this is wholly consistent with evolutionary logic. So where's the mismatch? The mismatch is that many children today are following an *exaggeratedly slow life history strategy,* promoted by their safety-conscious parents, producing young adults less prepared for adult life than previous generations.

Safetyism

I earlier defined *safetyism* as an excessive concern for the physical and emotional safety of children. According to Lukianoff and Haidt (2018), safetyism began in the 1980s, peaked in the 1990s, especially among educated parents, and continues at high levels today in the United States and other WEIRD countries. Whereas children of earlier generations were often encouraged to "get out of the house and go play," presumably with neighborhood children (Skenazy's free-range kids), this is foreign for many of today's youth, who instead have formal play dates, made and supervised by their parents. As a mundane example, consider a typical school day when I was a child and one for many children today. In the morning I waited at the end of a neighbor's driveway with other children for the school bus. The only time we'd have a parent join us was for the first few days of school for a kindergarten child. After school I walked home alone from the bus stop, then after a snack and change of clothes, I left the house and played with other kids in the neighborhood until supper time. Today, when I drive from home to work in the morning, I pass several school bus stops, with children, some in middle school, waiting in cars with a parent, usually one child per car. When I do see children mingling together at a bus stop, there is always at least one car, and usually several, with a watchful mom inside. This scene is replayed in the afternoon, as the yellow school bus unloads children to parents waiting in their cars.

In place of free play, many children today, beginning during the preschool years, take part in organized activities in the afternoons, usually with a parent nearby, from tumbling classes and dance lessons, to karate and tee-ball. Children keep plenty busy, but almost always at the direction of some adult, be it a parent, teacher, or coach. Free play or unorganized sports, with children making and enforcing the rules in the absence of an adult, is far less frequent than it was in decades past, but children are safe, with an adult always supervising the activities.

Lukianoff and Haidt see this emphasis on safety extending far beyond childhood into adolescence and young adulthood. They point out that in recent years colleges and universities have become overly concerned with the emotional safety of their young-adult students, who feel unsafe listening to speakers who espouse opinions different from their own and believe that the role of college is to provide them with a safe space rather than one that challenges them emotionally and intellectually. For example, in November 2019 a formal resolution of impeachment was brought against the University of Florida's student body president, primarily for using student fees to bring a speaker (Donald Trump, Jr.) to campus to promote a particular political party (which is against University rules), but also because having such a speaker "endangered students marginalized by the speaker's white nationalist supporters." Being exposed to the views of a speaker's supporters was not viewed as an expression of free speech but, rather, as something that would make some students uncomfortable ("endangered") and, thus, a reason for impeachment.

These attitudes seem to be more common of students at more elite universities, although I've witnessed occasional complaints about controversial speakers or lecture topics from students at the public university where I teach. The extent of the emphasis on "safety" on college campuses really hit home for me when I heard about the brouhaha at Yale over what constitutes an appropriate Halloween costume. College administrators had cautioned students about wearing costumes that may reflect cultural appropriation or may offend fellow students. An Anglo student wearing a sombrero, for example, may be viewed as offensive to some Latin-American students. In response to administrators' concerns, Erika Christakis, a lecturer and house master of one of the residential colleges at Yale, wrote an email urging students to think critically about the administrators' guidelines on costumes to avoid at Halloween:

> I don't wish to trivialize genuine concerns about cultural and personal representation . . . I know that many decent people have proposed guidelines

on Halloween costumes from a spirit of avoiding hurt and offense. I laud those goals, in theory, as most of us do. But in practice, I wonder if we should reflect more transparently, as a community, on the consequences of an institutional (which is to say: bureaucratic and administrative) exercise of implied control over college students.[7]

Christakis's call for what many would consider to be a reasonable request for dialogue, was met with fury and demands by many students, faculty, and deans that she be fired. Perhaps Christakis was wrong, and the societal climate requires greater sensitivity to people's feeling of cultural identity, but surely this can be an issue for discussion and not one so offensive that anyone who proposes it should be fired.

Lukianoff and Haidt view the oversensitivity of Yale and other college students as a result of the emphasis their parents and teachers have placed on the their physical and emotional safety in all aspects of their lives, and they believe that there are larger consequences to safetyism:

> When children are raised in a culture of safetyism, which teaches them to stay "emotionally safe" while protecting them from every imaginable danger, it may set up feedback loops; kids become more fragile and less resilient, which signals to adults that they need more protection, which then makes them even more fragile and less resilient.[8]

There are other consequences to safetyism, some of them positive. Consistent with life history theory, children who follow a slow strategy should be more apt to take a futuristic as opposed to an opportunistic perspective on life and thus engage in less risky behavior. In other words, parents' and teachers' emphasis on keeping children safe should result in the children themselves emphasizing their own safety, in essence continuing to practice safetyism in their own lives. This, indeed, seems to be the case, and this has been thoroughly documented by social psychologist Jean Twenge in her 2017 book *iGen: Why Today's Super-connected Kids Are Growing Up Less Rebellious, More Tolerant, Less Happy—and Completely Unprepared for Adulthood*. Twenge defines *iGen'ers* (referred to by others as Generation Z, or sometimes "zoomers") as being born between 1995 and 2012. Not only are they the generation that experienced perhaps the height of safetyism, but they are also "the first generation to enter adolescence with smartphones already in their hands."[9] (More on this later.)

Twenge presents data culled from several long-term surveys of American teenagers and young adults, documenting secular changes in important behaviors, in some cases over the last five decades. These surveys, asking participants in 2012 or 2015, for example, the same questions at the same age as participants in 1976 or 1991, provide a look at how adolescent and young-adult behavior has changed between members of different generations (iGen, 1995–2012; Millennials, 1980–1994; GenX, 1965–1979). Twenge includes in her book over one hundred graphs displaying age changes in important behaviors. Some behaviors show gradual change in frequency over the generations, whereas others show marked changes associated with iGen.

The consequences of safetyism on iGen'ers are seen in a broad range of behaviors. Compared with earlier generations, iGen'ers are less likely to get together with their friends, go to parties, or spend time out of the house without their parents; they are less likely to date, have sex, and have children out of wedlock; iGen'ers are less likely to have jobs or otherwise make their own money; they are less likely to drive, are safer drivers when they do, and are less likely to get in a car driven by someone who has been drinking; they are less likely to get into fights, be involved in sexual assaults, or fight with their parents; iGen'ers spend more time alone than teenagers in past generations; as teenagers, they are less likely to drink, especially binge-drink, although they use marijuana as much as Millennials did because they think it is safe. And many iGen'ers apparently feel the same about COVID-19, believing it is only a "flu on steroids" that will do them little harm, accounting for why many ignored social-distancing guidelines.

Consider, for example, changes in four behaviors (having a driver's license, having tried alcohol, ever dated, worked for pay during the school year) for 12th graders between the years 1976 and 2016. Twenge reported that there has been a steady decline in each of these behaviors, accelerating around the year 2000. For example, compared with high school seniors in the late 1970s, in which about 85% had ever dated and about 75% had worked for pay during the school year, these values were both around 55% for 12th graders in 2016. Similar declines were found for having tried alcohol (about 83% in 1994 and 62% in 2016) and having a driver's license (about 86% in 1976 and 77% in 2016). This downward trend did not begin with iGen but reflects a gradual change over the last 40 years, with the iGen'ers holding the current anchor points. Taken together, the picture is one that most parents of teenagers had hoped for: iGen teens are doing what their parents want them to do. The rebelliousness of earlier generations has receded. According to

Twenge, "iGen doesn't rebel against their parents' overprotection—instead they embrace it."[10]

At first blush, it may be hard to see any downside in this pattern: teenagers are more cautious and safety conscious than ever before, displaying more responsible and adult-like behavior than previous generations of adolescents. But this is only partly true. Their reduced risk-taking is accompanied by taking less responsibility for their lives than did previous generations of teenagers, not more. A driver's license and money of one's own represent new levels of freedom for many adolescents, but more and more teens are happy to have their parents chauffer them around and to ask mom or dad for cash or their credit card when they want something. Rather than becoming adult-like sooner, they are remaining children longer. According to Twenge, "Instead of resenting being treated like children, iGen'ers wish they could stay children for longer."[11]

Given what we know about life history theory, this may be expected and a good thing. Why take unnecessary risks and take on adult responsibilities when it's not necessary? The answer, of course, is that the risk-taking in adolescence, so prevalent in generations past, involves not simply making bad decisions, but also a preparation for independence and adulthood. Risk has gotten a bad name. Most of the time when we speak of risk with respect to adolescents we consider only the downside—the potential damage that unprotected sex or drinking can produce. But risk not only has costs but also potential benefits. Adolescents who take risks and succeed (or even fail) have gained valuable experience and sometimes increase their status in the peer group. Risk-taking can include a wide range of novelty-seeking behaviors, such as joining the military, traveling cross-country, leaving home to attend college, taking a gap year, or trying one's luck in the big city, each of which has potential benefits. Sociologist Howard Sercombe has proposed that developing a sense of *agency*—becoming an actor in one's life rather than a passive observer of it—is the primary drive of adolescence,[12] and this seems something that many contemporary teenagers appear to be postponing in their quest, supported by their parents, to prolong childhood.

I am not arguing that we should encourage teens to drink more, have more sex, and text while driving. Having been a parent and grandparent of teenagers, I see the increased safety that the current trends reflect as a good thing. But these need not be coupled with a delay of the development of agency and independence, as they seem to be for many adolescents and young adults in the United States and other countries today. Humans' long road to adulthood played a critical role in evolution, and children's sensitivity to early environmental conditions to modify their rate of development in anticipation of future environments continues to play an adaptive role in contemporary children. Although extending some aspects of immaturity well into traditional adulthood can have important benefits (for example, getting advanced education for some occupations), postponing the development of agency, thwarting novelty-seeking, and remaining dependent on parents and other "real" adults to make decisions is, I believe, deleterious. It is perhaps a bit ironic that evolutionary mechanisms, as reflected in the enhanced plasticity associated with childhood and adolescence, coupled with sensitivity to social and economic contexts, can serve to prolong immaturity to an extent that it can actually be maladaptive to individuals. This seems to be the case for many children in WEIRD cultures today; this tendency may be bolstered in large part due to children and adolescents being immersed in the truly evolutionarily novel phenomenon of social media.

Matches and Mismatches with Social Media

I doubt if it would come as a surprise to any reader of this book that we are currently in the midst of a cultural revolution. I'm referring not to any political revolt, but to the digital revolution, beginning with desktop computers and email in the 1980s and continuing through the first two decades of the 21st century with the Internet, Google, computer tablets, smartphones, and social media. Platforms such as Facebook, Twitter, Snapchat, and Instagram (which could be outdated by the time this book is published) consume the time and attention of literally billions of people each day, while having computers and access to speedy WiFi service have become necessities for a proper education and quality of life. Later in this chapter I will examine how young children's ways of learning may not match the formats used in modern technology. In this section I focus on how children's and adolescents' use of social media reflects both a match and mismatch from evolved adaptations.

Social Media Matches Adolescents' Drive for Social Interaction and Belonging

Perhaps I haven't said it enough throughout this book, but humans are a highly social species. The previous chapter focused on how humans' unique social-cognitive abilities evolved from those of our common ancestor with chimpanzees as a result of changes in great ape ontogeny. The emphasis in that chapter was on the evolved social capabilities of infants and young children. These same adaptations, developed in the first 5 or 6 years of life, are subsequently used to navigate the social worlds of childhood and adolescence. Author Judith Harris proposed that human social behavior is predicated on four evolved adaptations that humans share with other primates: group affiliation and in-group favoritism; fear of and hostility toward strangers; within-group status seeking; and the seeking and establishment of close dyadic relationships, or friendships.[13] We saw in Chapter 6 that in-group favoritism and out-group hostility are found early in childhood, and the importance of friends and one's place in a peer group during middle childhood and adolescence have been recognized for many years (perhaps millennia) and have been the topic of much psychological study.[14]

Once children start school (or to begin to play in peer groups in unschooled cultures), they spend more time with other children and are increasingly influenced by them, with such influence peaking in mid-adolescence.[15] This is illustrated in a study by developmental psychologist Lisa Knoll and her colleagues in which people ranging from 8 to 59 years of age were first asked to rate the riskiness of a variety of everyday situations, such as crossing a street while texting, driving without a seatbelt, or climbing on a roof. Following this, the participants were told how either teenagers or adults rated the riskiness of the same behaviors, and then the participants were asked to rate the situations again. Would people change their assessment of risk based on the opinion of others, and, if so, would they be more influenced by what the teenagers or adults had to say? The subsequent ratings of children (8–11 years) and younger (19–25 years) and older adults (36–59 years) were more influenced by the opinions of adults, whereas the ratings of young adolescents (12–15 years) were more influenced by the opinion of fellow teens. Older teenagers (15–18 years) were influenced equally by the opinions of teenagers and adults.[16]

Adolescence is a time when social interactions and social approval (and rejection) are paramount to adolescents' sense of self and self-worth. (In large part, it was adolescents' and young adults' need for social interaction that made social isolation during the COVID-19 pandemic so difficult for them, and why many young people ignored social-distancing guidelines when the economy reopened.) This is an evolved feature of adolescence, coupled with an increased tendency to engage in risky behavior. Much of that risky behavior is done in the presence of peers or meant to enhance social approval. This realization caused neuroscientist Sarah-Jayne Blakemore to propose that adolescents' greater propensity to take physical risks than either children or adults is driven in part by their *avoidance* of social risk.[17] Better to risk the consequences of underage drinking than the social approbation of one's peers. (I recall one teenager swallowing a live goldfish at a showing of the *Rocky Horror Picture Show*. When asked why he would do such a thing, his answer was that he didn't want to look stupid in front of his peers.) Similarly, developmental psychologist Lawrence Steinberg and his colleagues view adolescent risk-taking as reflecting a competition between two developing brain systems: the *socioemotional network*, located primarily in the limbic system, and the *cognitive-control network*, governed primarily by the frontal lobes.[18] In particular, the nucleus accumbens, the amygdala, and other areas of the limbic system, associated with reward and emotion, develop ahead of the prefrontal lobes, associated with higher-level cognition and the control of behavior (for example, planning, inhibiting some responses while activating others). This leads to what some researchers call a *mismatch in maturation* (see Figure 7.1), which may be responsible, in part, for the sensation-seeking and risk-taking behaviors and sometimes the poor decision-making typical of adolescence.[19]

This mismatch is illustrated in a study of risk-taking in adolescents (13 to 16 years old), young adults (average age = 19 years), and adults (average age = 37 years) during a video driving game.[20] Participants played the game once while alone and again when friends were in the "car" with them. Interestingly, the number of crashes during the game was essentially the same for the three groups of participants (a little over one per session) when driving alone. In contrast, the number of crashes nearly tripled for the adolescents when driving with friends, doubled for young adults, and remained essentially unchanged for the adults. This pattern is similar to actual driving statistics for vehicular deaths. Teenagers are involved in proportionally more vehicle deaths per miles driven than are older adults, and the death rate increases the more people (usually other teens) are in the car: the rate of vehicular deaths for 16- and 17-year-old drivers more than doubles when there are three or more passengers in the car relative to when teens drive alone. In contrast, there is no relationship between vehicular deaths and the number of passengers for older drivers.[21]

I must emphasize that although this mismatch in brain development may be responsible, in part, for some of the problematic risky behaviors

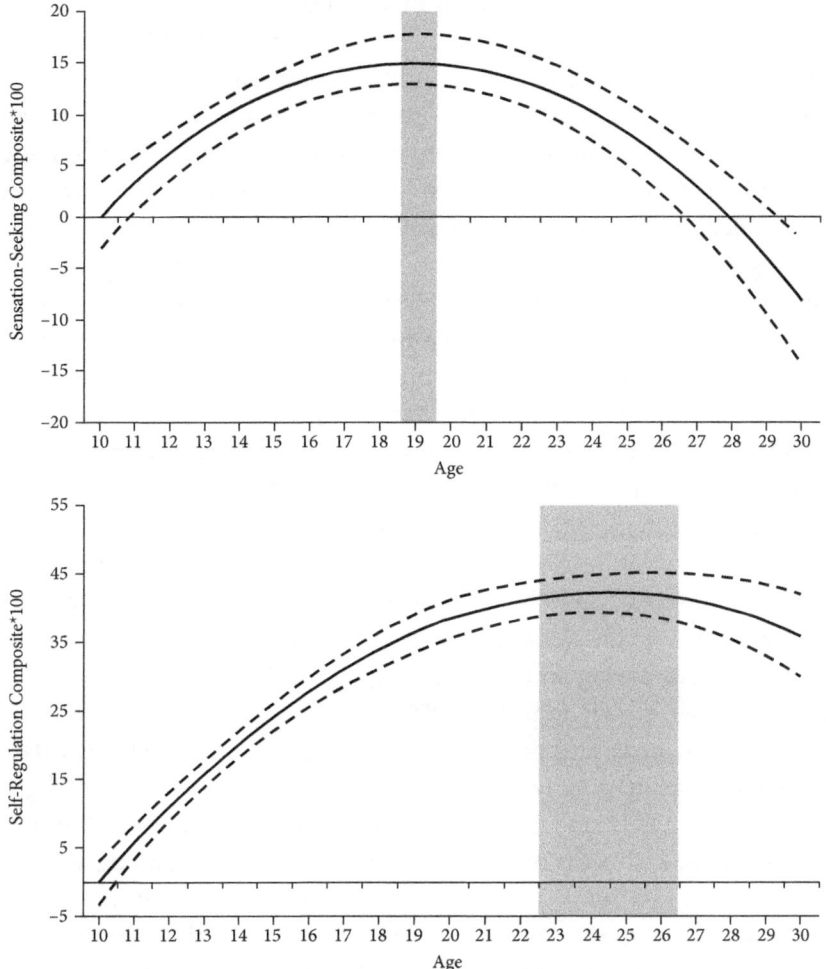

Figure 7.1. Average sensation seeking (top) and self-regulation (bottom) as a function of age across 11 different cultures. Gray shading denotes plateau or peak, and dashed lines indicate 95% confidence intervals.
Source: Steinberg et al., 2017, with permission.

of adolescence, it is not a reflection of a dysfunctional brain. Rather, it is a brain shaped by natural selection to be well suited to the tasks of adolescence. According to neuroscientist Jay Giedd, "the teen brain is not a broken or defective adult brain. It's been exquisitely forged by the forces of our evolutionary history to be a very good teen brain. It's different than children, and its different than adult, but it's not broken."[22]

Until relatively recently, children made friends and enemies and strove for recognition and status in person. Although friends could stay in touch through letters or phone calls, such forms of communication supplemented face-to-face interaction, where "real" social life was conducted. With the advent of social media, this swiftly changed. Although some social media sites were online in the late 1990s, the first "big" site launched in 2003 (MySpace, which still had 50.6 million unique monthly visitors in 2019), with Facebook opening to anyone over 13 years of age in 2006. As of June 2020, Facebook had over 2.6 billion monthly active users worldwide.[23] Add to these social media platforms like Twitter, WhatsApp, Instagram, YouTube, Messenger, and Snapchat, among many others, and one can get an idea of the immensity of social media's presence in people's lives today.

Use of social media skyrocketed, however, with the advent of smartphones. Smartphones had been around since the 1990s, first became widespread with the Blackberry, marketed for business use, and then exploded in 2007 with the introduction of the iPhone. Google's Android phones came out a year later, and now nearly 3 billion people across the globe have smartphones, including 81% of the American population, with approximately 95% of American teens having access to a smartphone. (South Korea is the nation with the highest smartphone use at 95%.)[24]

These social media are used by people of all ages. The current United States president, a man in his early 70s, makes daily use of Twitter, and even a digital dinosaur like myself has a Facebook account, frequently sends and receives text messages, and occasionally uses WhatsApp to communicate with my European friends. But it is adolescents and young adults, and increasingly preteens, who are the heaviest users of social media, and the ones whom social scientists are most concerned about. According to surveys reviewed by Twenge in her 2017 book, the average American teenager spends six or more hours a day interacting with some screen (texting, social media, Internet, video games); more than 80% of 10th- and 12th-grade children use social media daily, with adolescent girls being heavier users than boys.[25] Part of the reason why adolescents are often consumed by social media is because they grew up with it and use it intuitively. They are digital natives. I would guess that many older (40 years plus) readers of this book have more than once asked a teenager to help them use an app; configure a smartphone, computer, or television; or in some way assist them with operating digital technology.

Teenagers' special fascination with social media is no mystery. Although all humans have evolved to be social creatures, natural selection has shaped adolescents' brains to be especially sensitive to social cues. Teenagers stay in touch with friends on social media and can even make new friends. They can receive social approval, often in the form of "likes," the number of friends they have, or the number of visits their posts get. Social media can be a boon to shy or inhibited children and teens who find face-to-face interaction uncomfortable; adolescents can find other like-minded peers who share interests not found among their physically present friends. In short, social media match adolescents' evolved social tendencies exceptionally well, exciting some of the same brain regions and neurochemicals that in-person social interaction does.[26] However, these same matches between social media and adolescents' evolved tendencies also present potential for maladaptations.

Mismatches Between Social Media and Children's and Adolescents' Lives

The ethologist and Nobel Laurate Nikolaas Tinbergen noted how certain stimuli could automatically elicit stereotypic and survival-related behaviors in a variety of animals. For example, male stickleback fish will engage in aggressive behavior in response to the red spot on the underside of another male fish or to inanimate objects with a red lower half, and herring gull chicks will make a begging response to the markings on the head (white head, and yellow bill with a red spot) of an adult herring gull or to similar artificial stimuli. What is especially interesting in the latter case is that herring gull chicks respond even more strongly to a red knitting needle with three white bands painted on it than to a real herring gull face (see Figure 7.2). Tinbergen referred to an artificial stimulus that produces an exaggerated response relative to the natural stimulus as a *supernormal stimulus*, or a *superstimulus*.[27] Supernormal stimuli have been found for a variety of behaviors and for many different animals, and they are consistent with the idea that natural selection shaped an animal's responsiveness to perceptual features associated with a natural stimulus rather than to the natural stimulus itself. For example, herring gull chicks evolved not to recognize and make begging responses to the head of adult herring gulls, per se, but to make begging responses to perceptual features *associated* with adult herring gull faces. Thus, artificial stimuli that exaggerate those features can have an even stronger effect on behavior than the natural stimulus itself (see Figure 7.2). Humans' preference for junk food is a case in point. Our ancestors evolved to prefer foods that tasted sweet

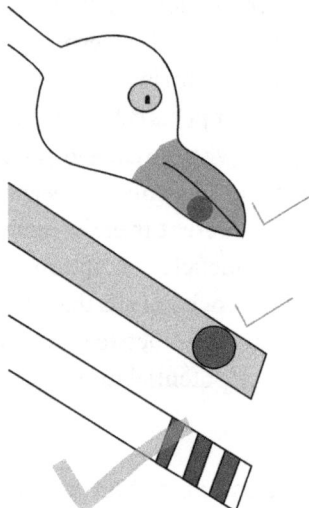

Figure 7.2. An adult herring gull's head, an artificial stimulus with a red dot, and supernormal stimulus that elicits an exaggerated begging response from herring gull chicks.
Source: With permission from Chelsea Schuyler, The Chelsea Scrolls, "Why Seagulls Have That Weird Red Spot: Push the Red Button." https://thechelseascrolls.com/2018/01/23/advice-of-the-seagull-push-the-red-button/ (Retrieved August 23, 2019).

or salty, with these tastes being honest signs of a nutritious meal. Today, junk food has higher sugar and salt content than is good for us, but we find them even more appealing, not because we evolved to love Ben & Jerry's Chunky Monkey ice cream, chocolate cream-filled doughnuts, or sea-salt-and-vinegar potato chips, but because these foods tickle our taste buds to an exaggerated degree. The same argument can be made for social media, especially for adolescents, who have evolved to be particularly sensitive to social cues of acceptance and rejection. Just as it's difficult for many of us to eat ice cream or potato chips in moderation ("I bet you can't each just one!"), so is it difficult for adolescents to limit their use of social media.

Unlike flesh-and-blood people, social media is always available to you. Adolescents can check it first thing in the morning and take it to bed with them at night. They can send and receive texts anytime during the day, create content ("Here's my pumpkin bagel with peanut butter and cream cheese"), view other people's posts, and count the likes and views they have on their own postings. They can post photos of themselves doing interesting things, or doing nothing at all. Because of cellphone cameras, people can take numerous selfies, run the photos through filters, and display the most flattering (or funniest) images of themselves. And they can check the postings of celebrities, seeing what wealthy, famous, or socially connected people are wearing or promoting, or how they are otherwise spending their time.

Mismatches of Social Media with Social Relations. But just as foods high in sugar and salt can be simultaneously attractive and maladaptive, so can social media. Social psychologist David Sbarra and his colleagues make this explicit, proposing an evolutionary mismatch between smartphone use and close relationships. Ancient humans lived in small groups of hunter-gatherers and evolved sensitivity to social cues and processes, including intimacy, necessary for forming and maintaining close relationships. Ready access to social media via smartphones may interfere with such relationships, in large part by causing people to be less attentive during in-person interactions.[28] For example, in a study of 143 married or cohabitating women, 70% reported that smartphone use interfered with face-to-face interactions with their partners. Sixty-two percent of the women said that their partner's attention to his phone or tablet during the couple's leisure time occurred at least once a day.[29] In other research by social psychologist Kostadin Kushlev and his colleagues, use of smartphones was found to distract people and to reduce enjoyment during social engagements, such as studying or eating a meal together, to result in reduced friendliness toward strangers, and in reduced likelihood of making casual contact with people during a wayfinding task.[30]

Constant use of social media not only serves to distract people when interacting with others, but for many adolescents it is also actually replacing in-person interaction. For example, although face-to-face interaction with friends is still popular, recent surveys find that many teens prefer texting than in-person interaction.[31] Although the benefits of smartphones are many in terms of social connectiveness, entertainment, and communication, their downside, especially for many teens and young adults, is that they can distract from and reduce the pleasure of ongoing face-to-face contacts, as well as replace to a large extent such in-person interactions.

Other downsides to the ubiquity of smartphones is sleep deprivation and its psychological consequences, and a reduction of exercise and the subsequent health effects. Regarding sleep, smartphones and tablets do not sit on a desk but are mobile, and a number of studies have found negative consequences for teenagers who have access to social media in their bedrooms. Adolescents who take their smartphones or tablets to bed with them report fewer hours of sleep, spend more time looking at screens, read less, have poorer school performance, have a greater tendency toward obesity, and report lower psychological well-being than adolescents who do not have bedroom media.[32]

With respect to exercise and Internet use, a number of studies have reported that heavy Internet use is associated with children and adolescents getting less exercise and being at an increased risk for obesity.[33] Relatedly, children and adolescents are also outdoors less often, which means they are spending less time in nature. Author Richard Louv calls this situation *nature-deficit disorder*[34] and points out that it has been increasing over the past few decades. Biologist and naturalist E. O Wilson coined the term *biophilia* to refer to people's love of and fascination with the biological world, which seems to be especially strong in childhood.[35] A number of studies have reported the positive effects on cognition or psychological well-being of spending time in natural versus in synthetic environments.[36] Louv contends that, in part because of parents' overprotectiveness and in part because of social-media use, children and adolescents today spend less time outdoors, which is resulting in increases in attention disorders and feelings of depression. Other research has suggested that there is a more direct route between social media use and mental health, and it is to this topic we now turn.

Social Media and Mental Health. A number of surveys have documented that levels of depression, anxiety, loneliness, and suicide among teenagers have increased over the past decade or so. The increase is especially sharp for girls beginning in 2012, which Jean Twenge notes corresponds with members of iGen—the first generation of native smartphone users—entering adolescence. These changes in mental health are correlated with an increase in smartphone adoption, but are smartphones and the access to the social media they provide the cause for the secular change in adolescent well-being? Many think so, viewing excessive use of social media as an addiction with the mental (and sometimes physical) consequences that addiction entails.

Although social media addiction has not been recognized as a disorder by the World Health Organization or the *Diagnostic and Statistical Manual of Mental Disorders* (*DSM-5*), a quick Google search brings up hundreds of references to the topic, with the first scholarly paper on Internet addiction being published in 1998.[37] Since then a number of researchers have documented associations between excessive use of social media (some would say addictive) and poor mental health, especially in adolescents and young adults, the most frequent users of social media.[38] For example, Jean Twenge and W. Keith Campbell surveyed a large sample of American children in 2016, examining the relation between amount of daily screen time and lifetime diagnoses of depression and anxiety, controlling for socioeconomic level, grade level, race/ethnicity, and sex (male of female). The results for 14- to 17-year-old children are shown in Figure 7.3. As you can see, adolescents who were "online" 1 to 4 hours a day were less likely to be diagnosed for depression or anxiety than teens with no screen time, illustrating a seeming benefit for youth who use social media versus those who have no access to social media or choose not to use it. The relation was reversed, however, for higher levels of screen time. Adolescents who were online an average of 7 hours a day were about three times as likely to be diagnosed with depression or anxiety than teens who spent just 1 hour a day online.[39]

Other research has shown relations between amount of screen time and measures of psychological well-being, including ratings of happiness,

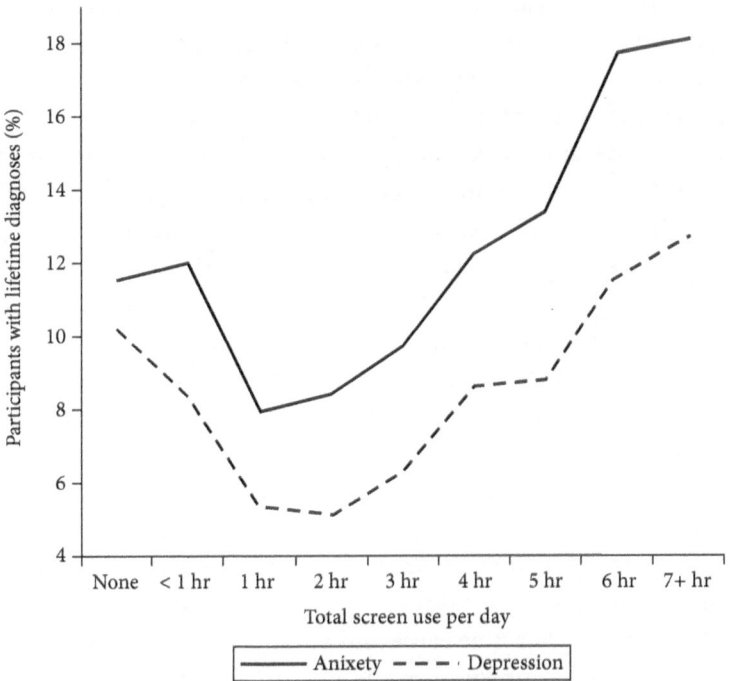

Figure 7.3. Percentage of 14- to 17-year-olds with lifetime diagnoses of anxiety and depression as a function of their hours of screen use, controlling for socioeconomic level, grade level, race/ethnicity, and sex (male of female).
Source: Data from Twenge & Campbell, 2018; figure from Twenge, 2019, p. 374, with permission.

aggression, social relations with significant others, and suicide and suicide-related cognitions.[40] For example, Jean Twenge, Gabrielle Martin, and W. Keith Campbell used data from a large national survey of adolescents to examine the relation between ratings of happiness and a variety of screen and non-screen behaviors for teenagers interviewed between 2013 and 2016. Although correlations in general were low, they were statistically significant and positive for engaging in non-screen activities such as sports or exercise, in-person social interaction, attending religious services, and reading print media (for example, the more one exercised, the happier one reported being); they were statistically significant and negative for engaging in screen activities such as video chats, social media, texting, playing video games, and Internet use in general. That is, the more time teens spent on social media, the less happy they reported being.[41] In other research, the more time adolescents spent on social media and text messaging during a day, the greater were their symptoms of attention deficit hyperactivity disorder (ADHD) and conduct disorder.[42] In a six-year longitudinal study examining texting starting at age 13, adolescents classified as "perpetual" users displayed higher levels of depression, anxiety, and aggression, and poorer relations with their fathers than adolescents who texted less often.[43]

Although most studies examining teenagers' social media use and measures of psychological well-being report negative findings, others find only small relations[44] or question the direction of causality. For example, psychologist Taylor Heffer and her colleagues followed a group of nearly 600 12-year-olds over two years and a group of undergraduate students over a six-year period, measuring social media use and depression. They reported that social media use did not predict later depression but, rather, that levels of depression predicted subsequent social media use among adolescent girls. That is, teenage girls showing signs of depression were more likely to subsequently use higher amounts of social media.[45] Other studies report opposite results, however. For example, one study of college students reported that use of Facebook predicted future increased feelings of unhappiness, but that unhappiness did not predict subsequent increases in use of Facebook.[46]

The best way to determine cause and effect is to conduct experiments in which different levels of social media use are determined by researchers, and the effects on well-being measured. Such experiments are rare but several have been done. For example, a 2016 Danish study reported improved self-ratings of life satisfaction and emotional well-being for Facebook users who volunteered to stay off the platform for a week relative to people who used Facebook as usual (average age 34 years, 1,095 participants in total).[47] Another study instructed Facebook users either to passively scroll through Facebook or to actively post comments.[48] In both a laboratory and field (naturalistic) study, the authors reported that the passive-scrolling group reported lower levels of well-being and higher levels of envy than the more active users, indicating that *how* one uses Facebook has consequences for well-being. In the most recent experimental study, clinical psychologist Melissa Hunt and her colleagues assessed college students' baseline levels (time per day) on three social media platforms (Facebook, Snapchat, and Instagram), as well as measures of loneliness, depression, anxiety, and fear of missing out (FOMO).[49] One group of students was then asked to limit their use on each platform to 10 minutes a day for the next three weeks, whereas the control group was simply asked to keep track of how much time they spent on each platform. The group that limited its use to 10 minutes per platform showed reductions in loneliness and depression relative to baseline, and both groups showed reductions in anxiety and FOMO. The authors proposed that their results provided strong evidence that excessive social media use is detrimental to psychological well-being. They interpreted the reduction in anxiety and FOMO of the control group as a result of increased self-monitoring of social media use.

A large majority of teenagers and young adults in developed countries use social media daily, and most research indicates that too much use has negative consequences for their mental health. Social media push all the right buttons in the adolescent brain, which has evolved to be sensitive to social cues of acceptance and rejection. Facebook and Snapchat almost demand social comparison, and because everyone puts his or her best face forward on these platforms, it appears that everyone has a better life than you do. Support for this interpretation comes from psychologists Mai-Ly Steers, Robert Wickham, and Linda Acitelli, who asked college students to keep a diary over a two-week period of Internet use and to answer online questionnaires assessing social comparisons and depressive symptomology. They reported that feelings of depression were mediated by social comparison: college students felt depressed after spending time on Facebook because they felt bad when comparing themselves with others.[50]

* * *

The qualities of social media both match and mismatch adolescents' evolved adaptations. Some social media use seems to be beneficial for teenagers' psychological well-being, and how can it not, as "everyone is doing it," and this is how adolescents keep in touch with their peers today? But too much use is associated with reduced face-to-face interaction, less sleep and exercise, and feelings of anxiety, loneliness, unhappiness, and depression. The effects are sometimes small and not experienced by everyone, and the direction of causality is sometimes in question: does being on social media cause depression, or do feelings of depression cause adolescents to spend more time on social media? My guess is that the relation is bidirectional and cyclical. Social media is the fast food of the Internet. Like fast food, social media platforms are supernormal stimuli, signaling experiences that our ancestors found valuable and thus worthy of our attention. We're very much attracted to them and a little bit won't hurt us. It's overconsumption that can be maladaptive.

Hyper-Individualism

Author Sebastian Junger starts his 2016 book, *Tribe*, with a look at colonial America and relations between the newly arrived Europeans and the native Indians. It was not uncommon for Europeans, sometimes as a result of kidnapping or the spoils of war, to live among Indians, and likewise for Indians to live among Europeans. When opportunities arose for people to be reunited with their birth communities, Indians—often reared from childhood in European-style societies—quickly reverted to a native lifestyle. The reverse rarely happened. Europeans who had experienced life in an Indian community wanted to stay, and, when forcefully reunited with their kin, often escaped back to their adopted tribe. This was perplexing to the Euro-Americans, who viewed the Indians as savages and themselves as the epitome of civilized people. When given the choice, why would anyone choose the primitive and difficult life of an Indian over the more comfortable and civilized life of Europeans?[51]

It's not that the Indians were nicer. They were frequently at war among themselves, as well as with the settlers. They had slaves and could be brutal to their enemies. So could the Europeans, of course, but Junger argues that it wasn't any enhanced kindness of Indian lifestyle that appealed to people, but the greater sense of community. The greater material wealth of Western civilization had its appeal, but Indian life was intensely communal, with people embedded in a complex web of relationships and dependencies. Tribal life was more similar to the conditions in which our ancestors evolved. In

Chapter 6 I described humans as a *hypersocial species*, and deviations from a communal to a more individualistic lifestyle as found in many contemporary societies produces a mismatch. Although this mismatch likely affects people of all ages, it may be particularly large for teenagers from highly individualistic countries such as the United States.

New York Times columnist David Brooks is the latest in a long line of social commentators and scholars (for example, Gail Sheehy, *Passages*; Robert Putnam, *Bowling Alone*) who have noted American's march toward increasing individualism—*hyper-individualism* in Brooks's term—over the past 50 years.[52] Hyper-individualism, which typifies other WEIRD countries such as Great Britain and Australia, emphasizes personal freedom ("I'm free to be myself") as well as personal achievement. It has resulted in many positive outcomes over the last half-century, including reductions in sexism, racism, and homophobia, as well as producing remarkable economic accomplishments exemplified by Silicon Valley. However, hyper-individualism makes it more difficult to lead a bonded, communal life, and Brooks notes the decline in community involvement, stable marriages, trust in societal institutions, and close friendships in America over this same time period with a corresponding increase in loneliness, suicide, and depression, with the young being especially affected.

The connection between social support and depression has long been noted. In the late 1800s, the French sociologist Emile Durkheim showed that people embedded in social relations had lower suicide rates than people who were socially isolated.[53] At a global level, people living in collectivist cultures have lower rates of depression and other negative emotions than people living in more individualistic cultures.[54] One possible explanation for this is that people from individualistic cultures are genetically disposed to become depressed relative to people in collectivist cultures. For example, behavioral geneticists have identified an allele of a gene responsible for the processing of the neurotransmitter serotonin that is associated with a predisposition to negative emotions such as anxiety and depression. Neuroscientists Joan Chiao and Katherine Blizinsky found across a sample of 29 nations that people from collectivists cultures, including Japan, Singapore, and China, were *more,* not less, likely to have the specific allele associated with negative emotions, despite the fact that they were less apt to suffer from mood disorders. The authors attributed the lower levels of depression for people in collectivists countries to greater collectivist cultural values.[55]

Jean Twenge, in her 2017 book *iGen*, noted that iGen'ers, perhaps even more so than previous generations, are believers in individualism. Their delay in becoming adults affords them more time to develop an integrated sense of self. They believe ardently in the belief that people should be free to make their own decisions—to have choices—and thus, they are less likely than previous generations to value community involvement or to accept traditional social roles and rules. Adolescents' sense of individualism is associated with their online behavior. According to Twenge,

> teens who spend more time online on social media are more likely to value individualistic attitudes and less likely to value community involvement ... The good news is that they are supportive of equality of race and gender, one of the primary outcomes of individualism. But they are also less civically engaged and feel more entitled to things even if they don't work for them.[56]

So what's the mismatch, and especially for adolescents? As we discussed earlier, teenagers and young adults are highly focused on social relations, and, as we saw in Chapter 6, even preschool children are aware of and respond differently to in-group than to out-group members. Children's and adolescents' evolved tendencies to belong and identify with groups is in conflict with some of the values of hyper-individualism that characterize WEIRD cultures. This conflict can result in adolescents and young adults being reluctant to commit to romantic relationships and, because they eschew conventional community groups, when experiencing loneliness and a lack of belonging, they may be vulnerable to the lure of gangs or cults that provide the communal relationships humans have evolved to expect.

Adolescent Mismatches

Adolescence is both a biological and cultural phenomenon. It is also an evolved feature of our species. Many cultures have rites of passage sometime during the teen years, marking the transition from childhood to adulthood. Yet, few 13- or 14-year-olds in any culture are viewed as true adults after completing their rituals, and in most WEIRD cultures "adulting" for many is postponed well into the third decade of life. This is consistent with developmental psychologist Jeffrey Arnett's concept of *emerging adulthood*, describing people roughly between 18 and 25 years of age. Arnett coined the term in 2000 to describe a stage in life of many young people in WEIRD societies that is neither adolescence nor young adulthood, distinguished by independence from traditional social roles and normative expectations (for example, marriage, beginning a career). Emerging adults are able to explore their options for the future with respect to relationships, work, and worldviews.[57]

Despite cultural differences, the biology of adolescence is similar worldwide. The brains of teenagers and young adults emphasize risk, sensation seeking, social relations, and mating, while the parts of the brain responsible for regulation of behavior lag behind. In ancient and many modern environments, these features were adaptive, helping young people move away from their parents and form identifies and relations of their own. The sensation seeking and quest for social belonging may have been adaptive to young men in hunter-gatherer and other traditional cultures, making them valued warriors and hunters, as well as making them attractive to young women, who were experiencing their own quest for independence. Adolescents today have the same brains as their ancient ancestors at that age, but environmental conditions are greatly different. As a result, children grow up more slowly than in generations past—that is, they follow a very slow life history course—and this affects, sometimes positively and sometimes negatively, the adults they will become. The relative lack of community and social bonding characteristic of individualistic societies is associated with increases in loneliness and mental health problems, and this may be especially potent for young people and can sometimes be exaggerated by social media. The genies will not soon be put back into their digital and individualism bottles, but an understanding of adolescents' evolved features—adaptations shaped for dealing with very different environments—may help us better construct conditions for them and help them deal with problems when mismatches occur.

How Young Children Learn and the Mismatch with Formal Educational Practices

We, more than any other animal, live by our wits and acquired knowledge. Our ability to learn and to solve novel problems has permitted our kind to inhabit nearly all ecosystems of the earth, from the steamy tropics to the frigid Arctic; to adapt to any one of thousands of cultures; to invent writing, numerical, and musical systems; and to develop and use technologies from stone axes to smartphones. Humans possess and retain well into adulthood a high degree of neural, cognitive, and behavioral plasticity that affords such learning, although we are most plastic early in development, and learning in infancy and childhood sets the stage for future education.

Homo Sapiens Is the Most Educable of Animals

I use the term *education* to refer to the acquisition of abilities, values, beliefs, and knowledge valued by one's culture. Education is the process of becoming a functional member of one's society—of learning the ways of one's social group, as well as acquiring the technological skills of one's society. Education is not a modern phenomenon but is a core part of our species' natural history. Throughout that history, crucial skills and knowledge were acquired "in context" or "on the job," so to speak, while observing or interacting with other people or with things, many of which were cultural artifacts. Much of what was learned was of immediate survival value (for example, what is good to eat and what should be avoided, how to gather tubers), and others were related to established group practices (for example, how to greet one another, how to worship deities). Long after our ancestors left their hunter-gatherer lifestyles and settled down in agrarian communities, most important knowledge and skills continued to be learned in such a hands-on manner. It was not until centuries after the invention of writing that literacy and numeracy became important skills for a vast number of our species.

Humans may not have evolved to read, maneuver automobiles on busy highways, or live in metropolises, but we have learned to do so. To accomplish such evolutionarily novel feats has required major changes in how culture is inculcated in children and transmitted across generations—chiefly through the invention of formal schooling. Literacy and numeracy date back only about 6,000 years, and for most of this time, only elite members of society (priests, members of the ruling class, some merchants) were literate. With the invention of the printing press in the late 1400s, literacy became important for religion (the Protestant Reformation in Europe emphasizing that people should receive the word of God directly, not through priests) and politics (the indoctrination of its members by the state to promote nationalism and create patriots).[58] Subsequently, as a nation's economy became more dependent on literacy and numeracy, formal education became the norm in nearly all countries, such that today people in most developed nations believe that having an educated populace is the backbone of a successful society; around the world, nations vie to develop curricula that will produce intelligent and productive citizens.

These changes in the demands of culture required changes in how children acquired that culture. Critically, in most cultures today, the most basic technological skills, including reading, writing, and numeracy, are *context independent* (that is, children learn them in contexts independent of any immediate use), and they are typically taught to children by unfamiliar adults in unfamiliar settings. The result is that much of formal education is an evolutionary novelty. This is in contrast to the way that our forechildren learned, assuming that hunter-gatherer practices are an indication of how our ancestors lived and passed on information from one generation to the next. From an early age, hunter-gatherer children spend most of their day playing in mixed-aged groups, mostly unsupervised by adults. Children acquire most practical skills from their older peers and occasionally learn important skills by watching and interacting with their parents or other adults. Modern hunter-gatherer adults seldom directly instruct children in any skill, and it is likely that this was also true for our ancestors.[59]

Although what constitutes teaching can be subjective, with different academic disciplines having slightly different definitions,[60] there is general agreement that formal instruction, as typifies schooling in WEIRD societies, is rare in hunter-gatherer and traditional societies; rather, according to anthropologists David Lancy and M. Annette Grove, in hunter-gatherer cultures, the "entire community and its surroundings are seen as the 'classroom,' and the 'curriculum' is displayed as an 'open book.'"[61] To this point, a number of educators and scholars have proposed that educational environments that depart substantially from ancestral environments can create unintended consequences, and they suggest that modern educational practices can be made more effective by considering the evolutionary history of children and learning.[62]

As I mentioned earlier, one feature of ancient educational environments was learning "in context" from more knowledge people (adults and peers). This was central to Russian psychologist Lev Vygotsky's sociocultural theory and the concept of the *zone of proximal development*, defined as the difference between a child's "actual developmental level as determined by independent problem solving" and his or her level of "potential development as determined through problem solving under adult guidance or in collaboration with more capable peers."[63] Children become competent at a skill when they engage in collaboration with other people, such that a more-experienced individual can *scaffold* the performance of a less-experienced individual.[64] Scaffolding happens when the more-skilled person is sensitive to the abilities of a novice and responds contingently to the novice's responses in a learning situation. As a result, the novice gradually increases his or her understanding of a problem. Scaffolding is most effective when done within the zone of proximal development. Although scaffolding occurs quite naturally in the home and on the playground, it is more difficult to achieve in the classroom.[65] Strict adherence to a standardized curriculum and classroom size usually exceeding 20 children limit teachers' abilities to assess individual children's current skills and appropriately scaffold their learning. Another problem is that when students are arranged in same-age and same-skill groups, they miss the opportunity to learn from other more-skilled children and to serve as teachers to less-skilled children.

Learning Through Watching and Playing

Although formal instruction in a classroom may be the primary way in which most children in the world today are educated, in the distant past children mostly educated themselves via social learning and play in the context of mixed-aged peer groups.

Learning Through Watching. Children evolved remarkable abilities to acquire the skills and knowledge necessary to survive in hunter-gatherer communities through observation, without the need for formal instruction. I reviewed children's development of social-learning skills in Chapter 6, as well as how they differ from those of our simian relatives. As you may recall, one important difference between the social learning of apes and children is that children, beginning reliably around 3 years of age, but not apes, will engage in *overimitation*, copying even unnecessary actions displayed by a model. Although this sometimes results in a less efficient way to use a tool, for example, it more often results in children acquiring culturally important information (both technological, as in tool use, and symbolic, such as ritualistic behavior). Relatedly, Hungarian developmental psychologists György Gergely and Gergely Csibra proposed that overimitation is an adaptation that permits fast and accurate transmission of information between individuals, which they refer to as *natural pedagogy*.[66]

Learning Through Playing and the Mismatch with Contemporary Educational Practices. Most of the social learning of hunter-gatherer children is achieved in the context of play, defined as a "type of exploratory learning in which the young animal engages in a variety of behaviors in a low-risk, low-cost context."[67] In Chapter 5 I looked at the importance of play in child development as well as in the evolution of *Homo sapiens*. It is primarily through play that children acquire tool-using skills and, most critically, the people skills necessary for navigating the social environment. As educational psychologist Anthony Pellegrini and I wrote, "play seems to have been especially adapted for the period of childhood and is what children are 'intended' to do."[68] Children still learn through play today, although modern school curricula tend to minimize the role of play in learning, replacing free play with formal instruction. To some extent this is necessary. It is rare that children learn to read or do long division solely by playing. Instruction is usually necessary. But a curriculum without play is deviating substantially from the way children have evolved to learn, and incorporating play into formal education may have substantial benefits.

As I noted earlier in this chapter, the amount time American children engage in free play has been declining steadily over the past five or six decades, being replaced by adult-supervised play at home and formal instruction in school. Psychologist Peter Gray argues that the increase seen in mental health problems of children and teens over this same time period is due, in part, to children's loss of freedom to choose the activities they partake in (that is, the loss of free play). Gray also argues that the near absence of play in contemporary schools has negative consequences for learning.[69] I am sympathetic to this viewpoint, but what evidence do we have that play actually supports learning, as opposed to being merely a distraction from "real" education?

A number of studies have found beneficial effects of play on various aspects of children's cognition. In one study, the amount of time 3-year-olds spent talking with peers during fantasy play was positively associated with the size of their vocabularies at age 5;[70] other studies found that the more children engaged in spontaneous sociodramatic play, the better they were at remembering and comprehending stories.[71]

Perhaps the area of research that has garnered the most attention recently is the relation between play and children's *executive function*. Executive function refers to processes involved in regulating one's attention and behavior and is critical in planning and behaving flexibly. Executive function consists of a related set of basic information-processing abilities, including *working memory* (or *updating*), involved in storing and manipulating information; inhibiting responding and resisting interference; and cognitive flexibility, as reflected by how easily individuals can switch between different sets of rules or different tasks.[72] Scientists sometimes refer to "cold" executive functions used to regulate basic cognition related to learning, and "hot" executive functions used to regulate emotions.[73] We've encountered aspects of executive function earlier in this book, for example, when discussing the evolution of inhibition being necessary for self-regulation and enhanced sociality in Chapter 4. Research over the last decade has clearly shown that both developmental and individual differences in executive function in childhood are predictive of IQ, academic performance, emotional competencies, and social cognition and behavior in adolescence and adulthood.[74] And other research suggests that individual and developmental differences in executive function are influenced by children's fantasy play.

The connection between play and executive function actually predates the modern era and can be found in the work of Vygotsky. Vygotsky argued that during fantasy play children use language to regulate their behavior—to stay in character—and this, in turn, enhances self-control. According to Vygotsky, "in play, the child always behaves above his average age, above his daily behavior; in play it is as though he were a head taller than himself."[75] More contemporary research seems to back Vygotsky's contention. For example, in one study, parents reported on 6- to 7-year-old children's daily activities, which neuroscientist Jane Barker and her colleagues classified as more- or less-structured. Tests of children's executive function were then correlated with how children spent their leisure time. The researchers reported that the more time children spent in less-structured activities (such as free play), the greater their executive function tended to be.[76] Other research has reported: significant relations between measures of executive function and pretending in preschool children,[77] that impulsive preschoolers who engaged in a high frequency of sociodramatic play showed enhancement in self-regulatory behaviors over the course of the school year,[78] and programs that encouraged children to use self-regulatory speech and to engage in dramatic play produced improvements in children's executive-function abilities.[79]

Why should pretend play and executive function be related? Developmental psychologists Clancy Blair and Adele Diamond write: "During social pretend play, children must hold their own role and those of others in mind (working memory), inhibit acting out of character (inhibitory control), and flexibly adjust to twists and turns in the evolving plot (mental flexibility); all three of the core executive functions thus get exercise."[80] Although most of these studies are correlational, making it difficult to infer that fantasy play *causes* improvements in executive function, a number of researchers have argued that the relation is bidirectional, so that not only does executive functioning play a role in children's ability to immerse themselves in pretend play, but pretend play, in turn, also facilitates the development of executive functions.[81]

Free, unstructured, fantasy play has been touted as having many benefits for child development, including cognitive development of children growing up in WEIRD societies. Play was how our forechildren spent most of their time and learned the ways of their culture in the process. Today's children spend much less time in pretend play, both in and out of school, in part because of recent changes in media-centered activities and school curricula that emphasize more formal learning, even during the preschool years. The result is a departure from developmentally (and species-) appropriate activities, which may have consequences not only for children's learning, but also for their emotional development.[82] According to Peter Gray,

> We are pushing the limits of children's adaptability. We have pushed children into an abnormal environment, where they are expected to spend ever greater portions of their day under adult direction, sitting at desks, listening to and reading about things that don't interest them, and answering questions that are not their own and are not, to them, real questions. We leave them ever less time and freedom to play, explore, and pursue their own interests.[83]

Incorporating Play into Preschool Curricula. It was not long ago that preschool and kindergarten children spent most of their schooldays developing social and intellectual skills mainly by playing with other children, with the rigors of learning to read or to calculate being left to first grade. This is still true in many parts of the world, but many preschools, particularly in the United States, emphasize using direct instruction, more typical of techniques used in elementary school, rather than more developmentally appropriate approaches that take children's "natural" propensities for play and activity into consideration. Do children perform any better (or worse) in developmentally appropriate programs than in direct-instructional programs? Results of research contrasting these two types of programs have provided mixed results: Concerning academic abilities following a year in these programs, some studies report better performance for children attending direct-instruction programs, some for developmentally appropriate programs, and others find no differences. When looking at longer-term effects (that is, greater than one year), a majority of studies find more benefits for developmentally appropriate programs. Results are more consistent when motivational and psychosocial factors are considered, with most studies reporting that children who attend developmentally appropriate programs experience less stress, like school better, are more creative, and have less test anxiety than children attending direct-instructional programs.[84] Although most of the differences reported in these studies are small in magnitude, the research indicates that there are no long-term benefits of academically oriented preschool programs for middle-class children, and some evidence that such programs might actually be detrimental. This caused educational researcher Marion Hyson and her colleagues to conclude that there seems to be no defensible reason for encouraging formal academic instruction during the preschool years. Hyson and her colleagues write: "it may be developmentally prudent to let children explore the world at their own pace rather than to impose our adult timetables and anxieties on them."[85]

All but the most unstructured preschool programs will involve some direct instruction, or teaching, of course. Whether children learn more effectively through teaching or play will depend on what is being learned. Developmental psychologist Elizabeth Bonawitz and her colleagues proposed that teaching is beneficial when children need to learn specific skills or information, but, on the downside, it also limits the range of hypotheses that children are able to consider. Bonawitz and colleagues contrasted direct instruction with *discovery learning*, or learning through play. The researchers either taught children a specific set of behaviors with a novel apparatus (pushing a button to make a squeaking sound) or just let children explore the apparatus freely without giving them any specific instructions on what the apparatus does. Children taught how to make the apparatus make a sound spent more time with the squeaker but spent less time overall playing with the apparatus and discovered fewer of the other things that the apparatus could do than children given no specific instructions. Thus, discovery learning may facilitate children learning new properties of items or events, although it may slow the learning of specific skills or information. Young children's social-learning abilities permit them to learn new skills rapidly through direct teaching, but direct teaching tends to limit exploration and the discovery of novel properties of artifacts. As Bonawitz and her colleagues write, "the decision about how to balance direct instruction and discovery learning largely depends on the lesson to be learned."[86]

One technique that takes advantage of young children's evolved social-learning skills *and* playful approach to life is *guided play*, which is a compromise, of sorts, between free play and direct instruction. Like free play, guided play involves the autonomy and discovery of free play in addition to the adult guidance of direct instruction. Developmental psychologist Deena Skolnick Weisberg and her colleagues define guided play as "learning experiences that combine the child-directed nature of free play with the focus on learning outcomes and adult mentorship."[87]

One form of guided play involves adults constructing situations to emphasize specific learning goals, making sure children have the freedom to explore freely within that setting. Several studies have set up exhibits in science museums, constructed to increase the chance that children will discover certain facts or principles while playing with the materials (that is, discovery learning), and have reported that children, indeed, learn from these exhibits and can transfer their newly acquired knowledge to new learning situations.[88]

A second form of guided play involves adults watching children play and making comments or encouraging them to learn more in the setting. For example, in one study, 4- and 5-year-old children were shown an array of geometric shapes (triangles, rectangles, pentagons, and hexagons) in one of three conditions: *Free-Play*, in which children could play with the materials in any way they wished; *Didactic Instruction*, in which an adult described each of the shapes and explored the shapes (discovering the shapes' "secret," for instance, that triangles have three sides) while the child watched; and *Guided-Play*, in which an adult described the shapes in the same way as in the Didactic Instruction condition but encouraged the child to explore and discover the shapes' secret. When later asked to sort shapes (for example, sort the triangles together), children in the Guided-Play condition performed best, and children the Free-Play condition performed worst, with performance of children in the Didactic-Instruction in between the two.[89]

Why might guided play work better than direct instruction or free play for many contents? The active nature of guided play and the act of discovery are intrinsically rewarding to children and may help foster children's love of learning and persistence on a task. The social-interactive nature of the task is also reinforcing for children, and, as we've seen earlier in this section and in Chapter 6, children evolved highly efficient social-learning abilities, increasing the chance that they will learn from instruction.[90] Guided play also takes advantage of working within Vygotsky's zone of proximal development, which, according to theory and research, is the level of difficulty in which most improvements in skills occur.

Most educators and theorists recognize the need for direct instruction for higher-level concepts and skills, such as mathematics,[91] which would seemingly make free or guided play less useful at older ages. However, a meta-analysis of studies examining the effectiveness of different pedagogical methods in children, adolescents, and adults reported better outcomes, on average, of enhanced discovery learning (much like guided play) when compared with other forms of instruction for people of all ages.[92] Similarly, the theory behind a Montessori curriculum has much in common with guided play (children are free to engage in a carefully prepared environment), and research has found that children attending Montessori programs frequently outperform children attending conventional schools in terms of academic achievement.[93]

Peter Gray, a proponent for educational settings mimicking as much as possible hunter-gatherer conditions, argues that a free-play orientation should be implemented at all levels of education, not just for preschoolers. If children want to learn to read or do calculus they can do so by watching others or ask for instruction if some is needed. Gray believes that each child is solely responsible for his or her own education, and as evidence he describes a successful preschool-to-high-school program that follows this philosophy (Sudbury Valley School in Framingham, Massachusetts).[94] Gray's perspective is consistent with Jean Piaget's view of the role of teachers in modern education, who wrote:

> It is despite adult authority, and not because of it, that the child learns. And also it is to the extent that the intelligent teacher has known to efface him or herself, to become an equal and not a superior, to discuss and examine, rather than to agree and constrain morally, that the traditional school has been able to render service.[95]

Both Gray's and Piaget's views on education are out of the mainstream, and many scholars, although touting the benefits of discovery learning in some contexts, argue that what children need to learn today and what our ancestors needed to learn to succeed are so different that eschewing direct instruction is unwise. For example, evolutionary developmental psychologist

David Geary makes a distinction between biologically primary and biologically secondary abilities. *Biologically primary abilities* were selected over the course of evolution, such as language and a rudimentary sense of quantities. In contrast, *biologically secondary abilities* are built upon primary abilities but are cultural inventions, such as reading and mathematics beyond simple addition. Many biologically secondary abilities that people must master today are vastly different from what our ancestors needed to master and increasingly discrepant from the biologically primary abilities from which they derive. To this point Geary writes,

> The gist is that the cognitive and motivational complexities of the processes involved in the generation of secondary knowledge and the ever widening gap between this knowledge and folk knowledge leads me to conclude that most children will not be sufficiently motivated nor cognitively able to learn all of secondary knowledge needed for functioning in modern societies without well organized, explicit and direct teacher instruction [italics in the original].[96]

Although much of modern schooling reflects a mismatch from the way our ancestors became educated, modern *environments* are also highly different from those of our forechildren, making it necessary to modify ancient forms of pedagogy. I believe that evolutionary theory tells us that children usually learn best when they are motivated to explore their surroundings and free to discover new knowledge. However, humans, especially children, have also evolved a high degree of plasticity and the ability to learn from instruction, and these abilities need also be considered when applying evolutionary ideas to education.

Visual Media for Infants and Toddlers: A Mismatch with How Young Children Learn

Infants and toddlers don't have smartphones (at least, most don't), but they nonetheless have extensive exposure to screens. A 2017 surveys of American parents found that children 2 years of age and younger had, on average, 42 minutes of screen time per day, most of it (29 minutes) from television.[97] The rest of this time (13 minutes per day) was with DVDs, tablets, or smartphones, presumably watching videos. And a 2015 study sampling 350 U.S. children

6 months to 4 years of age who visited a pediatric clinic in an urban, low-income minority community reported that 97% of the children used mobile devices, with most starting to use them before their first birthdays.[98]

Videos, whether presented on tablets, televisions, or smartphones, present two-dimensional representations of people and objects. Although ancient humans were known to make two-dimensional drawings on cave walls as far back as 40,000 years ago, most of what children encountered until relatively recently was 3D in nature, not 2D. Can infants and young children process two-dimensional information? Can they learn from 2D screens? And might exposure to 2D screens be a mismatch for the way children have evolved to make sense of their surroundings?

The answer to the first question is, yes, infants and toddlers can process 2D displays, but they seem not to treat them as symbolic representations of "real" objects but, rather, as worthy entities in their own rights, often attempting, for example, to pick pictures off the page of a book.[99] To answer the second question, infants and toddlers can, indeed, learn from 2D representations, just not as readily as they can from 3D models. For example, 12- to 21-month-old infants who watched a televised model perform some novel actions on objects later imitated those actions significantly better than expected by chance; however, they required twice the exposure to perform as well as when they witnessed a live model perform the same activity.[100] This finding is typical of much research with children 2 years of age and younger and is the answer to our third question: although infants and children can learn from pictures and videos, researchers report a *video deficit*, with performance based on viewing 2D representations consistently being worse than when real people or objects are involved. For instance, toddlers who watch a video of a model performing some novel behaviors remember about half as many actions as children who observe a live model.[101] Developmental psychologist Rachel Barr notes that this deficit is not limited to videos but is found for other 2D displays as well, including touchscreens and picture books.[102]

Despite this well-documented deficit, parents wishing to enhance their infants' cognitive development have bought educational software purporting to do just that. Perhaps not surprisingly, there is little evidence that digital media aimed at infants and toddlers has any benefit to children's cognitive development, and several companies have been forced out of business for making false claims (Your Baby Can Read®), or offered refunds in response to questions about the legitimacy of their educational claims (Baby Einstein®).

For example, in one study, developmental psychologist Judy DeLoache and her colleagues taught 12- and 18-month-old infants new words by either watching a video without parental interaction, watching a video where parents were encouraged to interact with their children, or direct parent teaching. Only the infants who had direct parent teaching learned words better than infants in a control condition who had not had any instruction.[103] Perhaps it should not be surprising that infants do not learn much content from digital media. Developmental psychologists Mary Courage and Alissa Setliff note that although infants are often highly attentive to videos, including television, it is not until about 18 months that the *content* of the video, rather than the physical stimulus qualities of the display, will hold children's attention.[104]

Why might infants and toddlers not benefit from exposure to video and other 2D displays? Some have suggested that early exposure to visual media impairs executive function.[105] For instance, in one study 3-year-old children who had been exposed to high levels of visual media in the home at 9 months of age displayed increased irritability, distractibility, failure to delay gratification, and difficulty shifting focus from one task to another, all reflections of poor self-regulation.[106] However, the negative effect of too much screen time may be related to the type of programs children watch. Several studies have found impairments in executive function only for preschoolers who watch fast-paced cartoon shows,[107] and that watching high-quality educational preschool programs has positive effects on academic performance.[108]

Humans evolved in environments with little if any two-dimensional stimuli. With the advent of painting, followed by printing, and now visual digital media, the 2D world is as "real" and as ubiquitous as everyday 3D stimuli. Human adults and older children seem to have little trouble dealing with 2D representations, but this seems not to be the case for infants and toddlers. The American Academy of Pediatrics recently reiterated its original 1999 recommendation that children under 2 years of age should have no digital-media time (excepting occasional video chats, presumably with grandparents; Figure 7.4), and that children between the ages of 2 and 5 years limit their digital-media time to one hour a day.[109] The principal reason the American Academy of Pediatrics recommends limiting screen time for infants and toddlers is that the nervous systems of young children are immature and that they learn best from physical and social interaction. In other words, extensive exposure to visual media is a mismatch with young children's evolved adaptations for learning and making sense of their world.

Figure 7.4. The American Academy of Pediatrics recommends that children under 2 years of age have no screen time, other than occasional FaceTime.
Source: Shutterstock, with permission.

Evidence for this contention comes from a recent study in which the amount of time 3- to 5-year-old children spent looking at a screens per day was associated with the amount of white matter (myelin) in certain areas of the brain. White matter is associated with speed and efficiency of neural processing. The more time preschool children spent looking at screens, the less white matter they had in areas associated with language and emerging literacy skills.[110] Although the research is far from conclusive at this point, what evidence we do have is consistent, once again, with the position that stimulation in excess of the species norm early in life can have negative consequences on subsequent development.[111]

* * *

Children have been educated (some would say they've been educating themselves) for millennia. They have evolved remarkable social-learning abilities, which, along with substantial neural plasticity, have permitted them to master the technological and social skills to function in any culture. Much of this education occurred during play with peers. Children today have the same impressive social-learning skills as their forechildren and still learn through play, but the rapid changes in material and cognitive culture have put a strain on children's evolved adaptations for learning. The fact that children can acquire skills such as reading and mathematics in settings that would be foreign to our ancestors attests to the substantial neural and cognitive plasticity characteristic of our species. Modern education takes advantage of children's evolved learning abilities on the one hand, but presents a mismatch with their evolved adaptations on the other. Formal education and direct instruction seem necessary for children from WEIRD cultures to attain the skills and knowledge needed for success, and it is nearly impossible to escape the lure of digital media, even for infants and toddlers. Yet, the mismatches cause problems: some children lack the motivation to learn the modern curriculum, and the stress of formal schooling has consequences for social and emotional functioning. Being aware of the mismatches between how children have evolved to learn and how we teach them can help us develop curricula that provide children with the socially important skills they need while minimizing the problems such mismatches cause.

Dealing with Mismatches

As a species' environment changes, adaptations that had evolved over generations in earlier, stable ecologies will sometimes be at odds with current conditions. Such mismatches could result in subsequent evolution, species extinction, or, if animals have enough plasticity, adjustments to the new contexts. Humans are the poster child for evolutionary mismatches. This is because *Homo sapiens*, more than any other animal, is a cultural species, and cultural changes occur at a much faster pace than biological changes. Humans' neural, cognitive, and behavioral plasticity has permitted us to (1) create cultural change and transmit it across generations and (2) adjust our evolved adaptations to deal with cultural novelty. This doesn't mean we make adjustments easily or without costs, but mismatches between evolved adaptations and cultural innovations have not meant extinction for us, at least not so far.

Evolutionary mismatches can have different consequences for people at different stages of the lifespan. Children are not simply incomplete or immature versions of adults. Natural selection has honed the nervous systems of infants, children, and adolescents to the particular niche in which they live and their ancestors evolved. The significance of this is that new material or cognitive artifacts can be especially disruptive for younger members of the species, and this has consequences for development into adulthood. We are not about to turn back the cultural-innovation clock. For most of human existence we lived as hunter-gatherers, and children made their way in life the same way, with pretty much the same set of artifacts, as their parents and grandparents did. With the advent of agriculture and cities and a more sedentary way of life, new lifestyles were invented, but even then, technology changed slowly, and the lives of children continued to be much like those of their parents. Technological change accelerated over the past several hundred years and is moving at supersonic speed today.

What's a Parent to Do?

What can parents do to minimize the problems caused by evolutionary mismatches? First, simply being mindful of the increasing mismatches between modern culture and the evolved adaptations of our species' youngest members may help us make it easier for children to use the new technologies and also to be happier and less stressed as they do. Beginning in infancy, parents can follow the recommendations of the American Academy of Pediatrics and limit screen times of infants and toddlers. Given the prevalence of visual media today and young children's fascination with video (they may not learn much from it, but they do pay attention to it), it is nearly impossible to follow the Academy's recommendation for children under 2 of having no exposure to visual media and no more than one hour a day for children 2 to 5 years of age. Although it seems unlikely that occasionally watching videos on television or on a tablet will have dire consequences for children's cognitive or social development, excessive exposure may.

Avoiding screen time is nearly impossible once children start school, as computers or tablets are a central part of the curriculum in many classrooms. Children in WEIRD cultures need to be computer literate. But this does not mean that they need to be glued to smartphones and active on social media. Many parents (including those who are Silicon Valley executives) have recognized the downside of having their children constantly online, and one parent group is advocating waiting until 8th grade before children have their own smartphones (Wait Until 8th).[112] In place of spending their time on social media—interacting with age-mates virtually—parents can encourage their children to get exercise outside, playing face to face with flesh-and-blood children. While outdoors, children can be encouraged to walk, bicycle, skateboard, hike, canoe, or kayak through natural areas, activities that have been shown to reduce stress and risk of mood disorders.[113] And once children do have smartphones and tablets, they should not be allowed to take them to bed with them at night or use them at family mealtimes. Dinner-time conversations with teenagers can often be difficult, but they are almost impossible when one is staring at a smartphone. This goes for adults as well. This not only sets a good model for smartphone etiquette but also will enhance parent–child interactions, even with infants and toddlers.[114]

Children can get exercise in many ways, including adult-directed activities such as dance or martial-arts lessons, or playing in organized sports such as basketball or soccer. But they would be better off if some of this time were unstructured and unsupervised free play with other children. Children and teens do not need adults to make up rules for a game, determine when a rule has been broken, or adjudicate disputes. Generations of children have made up their own rules to games, have resolved arguments when they arise, and have learned much in the process. Given the emphasis on safety in many communities, it may be difficult to find times and places for children to congregate freely. Consider establishing a "free-play" space in your backyard or basement. If something comes up that children can't handle, adult intervention is not far away, but children need the space and freedom to exert some control over their lives. This increase of freedom and choice for children and teens should foster the development of a sense of agency, becoming an actor in one's life rather than a passive observer of it. Greater agency may result in some increased risk-taking, such as earning one's own money or traveling alone by bus or train to visit friends or family in another city, but it need not result in an increase in unsafe behavior such as binge drinking, unsafe sex, or texting while driving. Children following a slow life history strategy can still remain cautious with an eye to the future, but success in the future also favors the bold, and children and teens can be adventurous without being foolhardy if given the chance.

What's an Educator to Do?

Children's natural way of learning is through play. They learn important skills and social behaviors "in context," mostly through observation and by doing. Hunter-gatherers do not need to learn how to write or do calculus, so it should not be surprising that different pedagogical techniques are needed to learn evolutionarily novel skills, such as reading and mathematics, and few children acquire such skills spontaneously without the need for direct instruction. But even if direct instruction is the best way to learn many of the technological skills of WEIRD cultures, it does not mean that this is how all children should be educated all the time, especially young children. Studies with monkeys by the primatologist Harry Harlow and with human infants by the developmental psychologist Hanus Papousek, showed that starting a learning task too early (for Harlow's monkeys, beginning a discriminating-learning task at 60 days; for Papousek's infants, starting an operant-conditioning task at birth), actually slows down learning compared with monkeys and infants who start the task at a later age.[115] In a similar vein, preschool children who are given direct instruction, similar to that used in elementary schools, rarely learn more than children encouraged to discover new facts and skills through play, and they are more stressed and like school less than children who attend developmentally appropriate preschools. Preschool educators may be pressured by parents to have their children reading and knowing their math facts by the time they start kindergarten, but they risk long-term costs in exchange for questionable short-term benefits.

And discovery learning need not end with preschool. Children of all ages learn best through exploration and discovery, even when some instruction is required. When instruction is necessary, it should be compatible with children's intuitive learning biases related to folk psychology, folk biology, and folk physics (see discussion in Chapter 1), which are well suited to the niche of early childhood.[116]

Other scholars contend that discovery learning should be the principal means of education for children through high school. For example, in one retrospective study, evolutionary psychologists Kathryne Gruskin and Glenn Geher[117] interviewed 361 college students about aspects of their elementary school experiences that were consistent with evolutionary theory (for example, academic, playful, and collaborative interactions with different-age peers; free play; hands-on learning; explicit real-world applications for learning) as well as those that were not (for example, teacher lecturing; learning from textbooks and workbooks; assessment based on testing) and related them to subsequent academic performance (for example, grade point average in middle and high school; enjoyment of middle and high school). They reported statistically significant positive correlations (ranging from .20

to .37) between evolutionarily relevant elementary education practices and subsequent middle- and high-school grade point averages and enjoyment of middle school and high school, supporting the contention that evolutionarily relevant early education may lead to subsequent success in secondary education.

Peter Gray, a staunch advocate for education at all ages being based on hunter-gatherer lifestyles, describes the success of students from 4 years old through high-school age at the Sudbury Valley School, which is modeled after hunter-gatherer childhoods. Like hunter-gatherers, Sudbury Valley School children are solely responsible for their own education. Children are provided with a mixed-age, supportive, and opportunity-rich environment that they can explore as they wish, with adult staff members (they are not called teachers) available to children who request assistance. These practices reflect the way children have learned for thousands of years, consistent with the evolved neurocognitive architecture that allows such incredible amounts of learning during childhood.[118]

Another program, the Regents Academy, used cooperative small groups, also characteristic of ancient human environments, as the basis for a high-school intervention program for academically at-risk 9th and 10th graders in Binghamton, New York.[119] The program encouraged group cohesion through consensus decision-making and appropriate individual and group autonomy and accountability. Teenagers who participated in this program performed better than matched control children in regular school, were no different academically from not-at-risk children enrolled in the same school, and scored just as well as the average high-school student on state-mandated exams of algebra and English.

Bullying is a common problem in WEIRD schools across nations. Although bullying is also found in traditional and hunter-gatherer cultures,[120] the structure of modern schools reflects a substantial mismatch from traditional environments, making bullying especially common: approximately half of U.S. adolescents reported being involved as a victim or perpetrator of bullying within a two-month period.[121] Antibullying programs have had mixed success in reducing bullying, with most programs that involved zero-tolerance or empathy training having little or no success, especially for adolescents. One possible reason for the failure of many of these programs is that they fail to recognize that bullying provides some benefits for the bully in terms of reputation and status, particularly for the social-conscious adolescent. An evolutionary perspective views bullying as being based on evolved mechanisms in which some individuals are motivated to engage in aggressive goal-directed behavior when benefits outweigh costs.[122] Consistent with evolutionary theorizing, programs that increase the costs or reduce the benefits of bullying are more apt to report reductions in bullying.[123] One pilot program with 7th- and 8th-grade students in the United States that was explicitly designed following evolutionary principles is the Meaningful Roles Intervention, in which bullies are given high-visibility, meaningful roles and responsibilities as part of a school jobs program. In this program, bullies were initially paired with highly competent and socially accepted students and given high-status jobs to perform, such as being a door greeter, parliamentarian (looks up and interprets the rules), or photographer. Students wrote "praise" notes, recognizing their peers' prosocial behavior. Over the course of a year, the incidence of fighting, injuries/illness, absences, and detentions all decreased significantly in the school compared with the previous year as a result of the program. Bullies were now gaining status and praise through prosocial behavior, which was associated with a reduction in aggressive behavior.[124]

Mismatched Youth

Evolutionary mismatches are abundant for modern humans. According to physician and nutritionist Brandon Hidaka, "In effect, humans have dragged a body with a long hominid history into an overfed, malnourished, sedentary, sunlight-deficient, sleep-deprived, competitive, inequitable, and socially-isolating environment with dire consequences."[125] Not all the stress, mood disorders, and loneliness associated with modern culture can be attributed to evolutionary mismatches, but many can, and some are associated with specific periods of development. Children and adolescents evolved age-appropriate adaptations that did a good-enough job of getting them through their particular time in life and preparing them for adulthood. The rate of cultural change has outstripped the rate of biological change since *Homo sapiens* became a sedentary species about 10,000 years ago, and both childhood and adulthood have changed, most would say for the overall benefit of the species, substantially in the ensuing millennia. Neural and behavioral plasticity is greatest early in life, and children and adolescents have been able to make adjustments to the many mismatches from their evolved adaptations. There have been costs associated with these mismatches, however, with children and adolescents increasingly suffering from mood disorders and, recently, being unprepared for adulthood. As parents, educators, and policy-makers, we can recognize the problems associated with evolutionary mismatches in development and perhaps make the life of children and the adults they will become a bit happier.

8
Epilogue

How Children Invented Humanity

> My heart leaps up when I behold
> A rainbow in the sky: So was it when my life began;
> So is it now I am a man;
> So be it when I shall grow old,
> Or let me die!
> The Child is the father of the Man;
> And I could wish my days to be
> Bound each to each by natural piety.
> William Wordsworth, "My Heart Leaps Up" (1807)

According to the poet William Wordsworth, the child is the father of the man (and, may I add, the mother of the woman). This homily conveys the common-sense idea that experiences in childhood shape the adults we become, and at one level it must be true. Even the most ardent believer in genetic determinism (the belief that all of our behaviors, thoughts, and emotions are determined by our genes) has to admit that childhood experiences influence the men and women we grow into. As adults, identical twins—one growing up in poverty and the other in affluence—may share many characteristics, but they will no longer be identical in behavior and thought. Thus, in a sense, Wordsworth's statement is a poetic expression of an obvious and perhaps trivial fact. But there is a second way of interpreting this statement, and that is not at the level of the individual (that is, the experiences you and I have during childhood that shaped our man- or womanhood), but at the level of the species: over the course of human evolution, changes during infancy and childhood affected not only the adults our forefathers and foremothers became, but also species-typical features that characterize all *Homo sapiens* today and differentiate us from our ancient ancestors.

The central theme of this book is that, despite the differences in timescales, development, or *ontogeny*, and evolution, or *phylogeny*, are intimately related. All of our ancestors developed, grew into adults, and had children of their own. This again may be a self-evident truth. *Of course* our ancestors developed. How else could they have become adults? But there is something special about the early stages of development in many species, including humans, and that is a high level of *plasticity*, or the ability to change. Despite the fact that most members of a species grow up to be pretty much alike, development is not a predetermined series of steps, dictated by genes we inherited from our parents (and they from their parents, ad infinitum) but, rather, a series of dynamical events, each affected by earlier events and influencing future ones. Changes early in development can cause a cascade of effects producing very different outcomes from what is "expected." From this perspective, evolution can be seen as a series of ontogenies, with changes in development over generations producing adults who themselves procreated and eventually produced a species capable of writing and reading books like this one. Counter to the claims of some evolutionary theorists, *development matters*, not only in influencing who we become as adults but also in who we became as a species.

In the sections to follow, I summarize the major ideas of this book, loosely following the contents of Chapters 1 through 7.*

Development Matters

Central to the theme of this book is the contention that natural selection operated just as powerfully, or more so, on preborn, infant, and juvenile members of a species as on adults. Some adaptations are particular to specific times in development. These *ontogenetic adaptations* help young organisms adapt to their immediate environment and not necessarily to a future one; they are inherited but only develop properly through interaction within a supportive context.

Children are not born as blank slates, equally able to acquire any information that impinges on their senses. Rather, infants are prepared by natural selection with a set of skeletal competencies, which are fleshed out over development through exploration, play, and social engagement. Animals, including humans, inherit not only a species-typical genome (the set of genes one gets from one's parents), but also a species-typical environment. A species-typical environment is one that is similar to the environment

---

* I have not included research citations for the phenomena I describe here and refer readers to the earlier chapters for documentation.

experienced by one's ancestors. Genes and environments coevolved, and development can be viewed as the product of gene expression correlated with local ecologies.

Humans evolved most of their unique psychological features over the last 2 million years or so, living in small groups of hunter-gatherers on the savannahs of Africa. Psychological evolution continued after members of our species emigrated out of Africa into Europe and Asia around 100,000 years ago. These are the environments in which human nature evolved, and many scholars contend that hunter-gatherer childhoods are the models upon which we should judge the practices we use in raising children today.

Plasticity Is an Evolved Characteristic of *Homo sapiens* and Is Greatest in the Young

Central to an evolutionary developmental perspective is that neural, cognitive, and behavioral *plasticity* is an evolved feature of *Homo sapiens* and is greatest early in development. This can be seen from the diverse types of rearing environments found in different cultures around the world, from the child-adoring and tolerant hunter-gatherers and many WEIRD societies, to those that view children as drains on resources and place infants on ant nests to motivate walking. Despite the great differences in how infants and children are treated in different societies, most grow up to be functioning adults of their group.

Plasticity is not infinite, however, but declines with age. Children who experience species-*atypical* environments, such as institutionalized infants deprived of adequate social stimulation, often display severe social, emotional, and cognitive deficits within months of life. Yet, children are highly resilient during their first 2 years, and these deleterious effects can be reversed if children subsequently experience more positive environments. If children continue to be deprived of species-typical social stimulation much past the age of 2, however, negative effects can persist for a lifetime.

Natural selection has used children's substantial plasticity to help them prepare for the future. This begins prenatally, with the diets or stress levels of pregnant women affecting the metabolism or endocrine systems of fetuses in anticipation of environments they will likely face after birth. More generally, natural selection has provided children with sensitivity to early postnatal environments and the plasticity to entrain their development in adaptive ways. This is reflected in children adopting different *life history strategies*, using their early environments as predictors for what their future environments will be like, if imperfectly.

Recent advances in the biological sciences have provided important evidence for the proximal causes of changes in behavior as a result of experience—*epigenetics*, or how genes are expressed in different contexts. We can now begin to understand plasticity not only at the level of behavior and the nervous system, but also at the level of the gene, and this has substantial implications for understanding all forms of human functioning.

The high level of plasticity shown by children today was also a feature of our forechildren, and it was through changes in development that changes in species occurred. Development has sometimes been viewed as an *epiphenomenon* with respect to phylogeny—important to the individual but irrelevant to the evolution of the species. From this perspective, development is little more than an interesting distraction. Yet there have always been maverick scientists who recognized that, because of the plasticity early in development, experiences can modify the morphology or behavior of an animal and result in new selection pressures that can be the focus of natural selection. Behavior, in fact, takes the lead in evolution, because it is more susceptible to change (that is, more plastic) than morphology or genes. Highly plastic organisms (that presumably have genes associated with high levels of plasticity) can develop new forms or behaviors, and, over many generations, features that were once evoked only in response to specific stimuli are now expressed without the need of a provoking environment. One need not invoke concepts of Lamarckism to explain the influence of development on evolution; they can be explained within the Darwinian tradition.

Although changes in early development may have been the origin of changes in the species, most of these changes, especially for mammals, were accomplished in the presence of mothers. To a significant extent, mothers *are* the environment for young mammals. Because infants are highly plastic, they can be responsive to actions of their mothers, making mothers the environment for evolutionary change. If ancient children had the plasticity of modern children, they would be prime targets for mothers who reared their children just a little bit differently from regular mothers, prompting social-cognitive changes that could have profound effects on the species. Such changes are most likely to occur in large-brained animals, who are better able to deal with novel environments through innovation and social transmission of information than smaller-brained animals.

Many people think of the evolution of behavior as involving "instincts," or hardwired mechanisms. In truth, the foundation of evolutionary theory is plasticity and change; humans are the most behaviorally plastic of animals, with plasticity being greatest in infancy and childhood.

Timing Is Everything

As any comedian will tell you, timing is everything, and this is especially true when considering the effect of development on evolution. Changes in gene expression will have different consequences on the developing organism depending on when in ontogeny they occur. This is demonstrated by the field of *evolutionary developmental biology*, or *Evo Devo*. Regulatory genes turn on and off coding (or protein-producing) genes, and it is differences in regulatory genes between closely related species, such as chimpanzees and humans, that are directly responsible for many of the physical and behavioral differences we see between species. Animals are made of relatively independent units, or *modules*, and one important way that regulatory genes can affect evolution is by modifying the timing of gene expression for different organ systems/modules. Development of different systems may be retarded or accelerated relative to the developmental rates experienced by a species' ancestors. Genetic-based differences in developmental timing are referred to as *heterochrony*, and, because of modularity, heterochrony can be a powerful mechanism of evolutionary change.

Humans Are a Neotenous Species

Although evolution in *Homo sapiens* shows evidence of both acceleration and retardation relative to our ancestors, many aspects of what makes humans unique are related to developmental retardation, or *neoteny*, causing several theorists to propose that humans are a neotenous species. This can be seen in a number of physical characteristics, such as: infants' features of "babyness," which promote attention, affection, and caring from adults; adult facial features that are more like those of infants than those seen in other primates; and the way the spine connects to the skull making upright walking possible. Humans also show signs of *behavioral neoteny*, specifically, a reduction of *reactive aggression*, which occurs in response to a real or perceived threat. This may have been brought about through increased inhibition abilities, which in turn facilitated increased cooperation among group members. From this perspective, humans can be considered a *self-domesticated* species, evolving a more docile orientation to deal with members of their own species, which was favored by natural selection mainly for its enhanced social benefits.

Of equal importance is the role of neoteny in brain evolution and development. Although humans have substantially larger brains relative to body size than our closest genetic relatives, we achieved this by extending the primate prenatal brain-growth rate well past birth. As a result, much development that in great apes would have occurred in the protective environment of the womb is done postnatally in human infants. Such experiences transformed the brains of infants relative to those of our primate cousins and ancestors, leading to many of the extraordinary intellectual and social abilities of our species.

Homo sapiens extended the time it takes to reach adulthood relative to other primates, in part, by inventing new life stages—*childhood* and *adolescence*. Childhood follows weaning (and, thus, infancy) and is characterized by substantial cognitive accomplishments, including *language, imitation,* and *counterfactual reasoning* as displayed during pretend play. The stage of adolescence follows the juvenile period and is characterized by changes in brain organization, maturation of the body and reproductive system, and cognitive/behavioral changes involving increased concern about self- and social awareness, emotional instability, and increased risk-taking and novelty seeking. The social and cognitive abilities of *Homo sapiens'* youth may be well suited to the childhood and adolescent stages and to the attainment of skills necessary for developing into functional adults.

There are also many aspects of young children's thinking that are immature on the surface but have adaptive value for the young learner, a form of *cognitive neoteny*. These include young children's self-centered, or egocentric, perspective; inefficient aspects of memory; tendencies to copy all relevant and irrelevant actions of adult models (*overimitation*); tendencies to overestimate their abilities; and strong propensity to play. Although each of these forms of immaturity is typical of children, they persist in reduced form past childhood and continue to yield adaptive advantages in adulthood.

Although there is much debate about how language develops and how it evolved, all agree that young children are especially prepared to learn any human language they are exposed to. There is evidence that children are responsible for the invention of true language, based on research showing that children create *creoles* (a true language) from exposure to *pidgins* (a protolanguage) in a single generation, and that children at a school for the deaf created Nicaraguan Sign Language over several generations of school children. Other research suggests that young children's proficiency at language acquisition is accomplished to some extent because their limited cognitive skills simplify the body of language they process, making the complicated syntactical system of any human language easier to learn.

It was during early development that the roots of many of humans' most important psychological adaptions arose. Ancient human adults retained many youthful characteristics including behavioral plasticity, curiosity, play, imagination, and optimism, which, coupled with enhanced reasoning and executive function, led to advances in material and cognitive culture far surpassing anything achieved by other species and to the evolution of the modern human mind.

Humans Are a Hypersocial Species

Humans are a hypersocial species, comparable in many ways to the eusocial insects, but with much greater flexibility. The evolution of *hypersociality* required that natural selection operate both at the level of the individual (or gene) and the level of the group, as described by *multilevel selection theory*, which proposes that groups of individuals that function more efficiently than other groups, chiefly through cooperation, are more apt to survive and thrive.

According to the *social brain hypothesis,* increased social cognition was the driving force in human social-cognitive evolution. The interaction of a big brain, living in socially complex groups, and an extended period of immaturity (and plasticity) were the ingredients necessary to produce an animal with high levels of intelligence, with these three factors becoming entwined in feedback loops, producing increased social intelligence.

Hypersociality has its origins in infancy. Infants have evolved "psychological weapons" designed by natural selection to obtain attention and caregiving from adults. These include the *baby schema*, which adults find endearing, and *jealousy protest*, in which infants as young as 9 months of age respond negatively to their mothers' attention to another infant, a potential rival.

To understand social-cognitive evolution it is necessary to examine how great ape ontogeny was transformed into human ontogeny. Michael Tomasello's *shared intentionality theory* is a neo-Vygotskian approach that emphasizes that human infants and children are biologically prepared to develop a suite of social skills that, in interaction with their environment, produce a unique type of human sociality. Central to his theory is that early in life infants begin to view others as *intentional agents*, people who do things "on purpose," appealing to the mental states of others when attempting to explain what they do. This is reflected in *shared attention* beginning around 9 months, and later, between the ages of 3 and 5 years, in *collective intentionality*, in which children establish a *group-minded "we"* with other people, which improves their perspective-taking ability and results in children being attentive to social conventions and norms. The development and evolution of hypersociality and how it is similar and different from the sociality displayed in great apes is reflected in perspective taking, empathy, normativity, social learning, prosociality (helping, sharing, a sense of fairness), and collaboration. Each of these and other social-cognitive abilities were necessary for the evolution of a highly cooperative, hypersocial species. These abilities have their origins in infancy and evolved as a result of changes in great ape ontogeny.

Evolutionary Mismatches Occur at Certain Times in Development

Differences between modern and ancient environments sometimes cause *evolutionary mismatches*, and these can be specific, or especially potent, during certain times in development.

Many of today's children and adolescents follow an especially slow life history strategy, taking a futuristic perspective, which is reinforced by their parents. As a result, many adolescents and young adults today are safer and engage in less risky behavior than in the past (*safetyism*). The slow pace to maturity has also resulted in adolescents and young adults being more psychologically fragile and less resilient and to a delay of the development of agency and independence.

Today's adolescents (iGen'ers to use Jean Twenge's term) are the first generation to enter their teen years with smartphones in their hands and instant access to social media. Social media is a *supernormal stimulus* for social relations, which has both benefits and deficits. Excessive use of social media is associated with poorer physical and mental health, including reduced amounts of sleep and increases in depression, anxiety, loneliness, and suicide and suicide-related cognitions.

Today's adolescents display a high degree of *hyper-individualism* that emphasizes personal freedom and achievement, and this can produce a mismatch with human's evolved tendency toward a more communal lifestyle. The relative lack of social bonding in individualistic societies is associated with increases in loneliness and mental health problems, and this may be especially strong for young people and can sometimes be exaggerated by social-media use.

Modern schools represent a mismatch with the environments in which our forechildren learned, developed, and evolved. Throughout history and prehistory children acquired crucial skills and knowledge "in context," mainly through observing competent others and via play with peers. Many modern technological skills, such as literacy and numeracy, are now learned in contexts independent of any immediate use, mainly through formal schooling, making much of formal education an evolutionary novelty. Formal, direct-instruction methods of teaching may be especially maladaptive for preschool children, who learn best and with less stress in more developmentally appropriate (play-oriented) educational situations. Similarly, young children's exposure to digital (two-dimensional) representations, such as television, DVDs, tablets, and computer screens, may have detrimental effects on subsequent learning and psychological development. Although young children can learn from pictures and videos, they experience a *video deficit*, with their learning of 2D representations consistently being worse than when real people or objects are involved. Excessive exposure to fast-paced visual media for preschool children may impair their executive function.

Although modern education takes advantage of children's evolved learning abilities on the one hand, it presents a mismatch with their evolved adaptations on the other. Parents, educators, and policy makers can identify problems associated with evolutionary mismatches in development and design environments that make the lives of children a bit happier.

Phylogeny Happens via Ontogeny

Plasticity is an evolved feature of *Homo sapiens* and is greatest early in development. Development is the creative force in evolution, producing the variation upon which natural selection works. Such variation and selection have been particularly substantial for behavior, which is more susceptible to change than morphology or genes. Much of human evolution has been the result of a retardation of development relative to our ancestors and an extension of youthful features into later life stages, some of which (childhood and adolescence) are unique to our species. Such neoteny has contributed to our upright stance, reduced reactive aggression, large brain, and generally youthful cognitive and behavioral features associated with our unique forms of social cognition.

Infants and children are the often-ignored heroes when it comes to understanding human evolution. If we want to understand what it means to be human and perhaps improve the human condition, we need to understand human development and its evolution. In the words of anthropologist Melvin Konner, "life is development, and modifications of development are of the essence of evolution."[1] Ontogeny is not an epiphenomenon with respect to evolution, nor does ontogeny recapitulate phylogeny. To echo the early 20th-century biologist Walter Garstang,[2] ontogeny *creates* phylogeny.

Notes

Preface

1. de Beer, 1958, p. 1.
2. Bjorklund, 1997a, 2018a, 2018b.

Chapter 1

1. Lorenz, 1943
2. Nielsen, 2012
3. Caspi et al., 2002
4. Laboratory of Comparative Human Cognition, 1983
5. Hart & Risely, 2003
6. Darwin, *On the Origins of the Species*, 1859, p. 488; Darwin, *The Descent of Man, and Selection in Relation to Sex*, 1871
7. Founders of evolutionary psychology, Barkow, Cosmides, & Tooby, 1992; Buss, 1989; Daly & Wilson, 1988
8. Geary, 2005, 2021
9. Spelke & Kinzler, 2007
10. Buss et al.,1998, p. 535
11. Fessler, 1992; Flaxman & Sherman, 2000; Pepper & Roberts, 2006; Profet, 1992
12. Blakemore & Jennett, 2003
13. Gould & Lewontion, 1979, p. 584
14. Bering, 2006, p. 29
15. Kukekova et al., 2008
16. Hara, Iminishi, & Satto, 2012
17. Tattersall, 2013; Antón, Potts, & Aiello, 2014. This, at least, is one of the most popular scenarios for human evolution, although alternatives to this description exist, and a clearer picture of human evolution will be obtained as new fossil discoveries are made.
18. Austad, 1997; Bjorklund & Pellegrini, 2002; Kaplan et al., 2000.
19. Dunbar's number: Dunbar, 1998, 2010
20. Hrdy, 2007
21. Li, van Vugt, & Colarelli, 2018
22. Dawkins, 1976
23. Lickliter & Honeycutt, 2003; Overton, 2015; Witherington & Lickliter, 2016; but see Bjorklund, 2016

24. Gopnik, 2016, p. 208
25. Bateson, 2002, p. 2212
26. Gottlieb, 1992, 2007; Witherington & Lickliter, 2016
27. Hubel & Wiesel 1962; Lickliter 1990
28. Le Grand et al., 2001; Maurer, Mondloch, & Lewis, 2007; see Maurer & Lewis, 2013, for a review.
29. Miller, 1998, p. 105
30. Gottlieb, 1992
31. Waddington, 1975
32. Piaget, 1967, p. 149
33. Gottlieb, 2007
34. Volk & Atkinson, 2013
35. Bjorklund, Ellis, & Rosenberg, 2007, p. 22; see also Bjorklund, 2015
36. Öhman, Flykt, & Esteves, 2001
37. Rakison, 2018; LoBue & DeLoache, 2010; Hoehl & Pauen, 2017
38. DeLoache & LoBue, 2009; LoBue & Adolph, 2019
39. Batki et al., 2000; Farroni et al., 2002
40. Di Giorgio et al., 2012; Pascalis, de Haan, & Nelson, 2002; Kelly et al., 2007, 2009
41. Anzures et al., 2012; Kobayashi et al., 2018
42. Hernández Blasi & Bjorklund, 2003
43. Bjorklund, 1997b
44. Meltzoff & Moore, 1977; Oostenbroek et al., 2016
45. Boyce & Ellis, 2005, p. 290
46. Ellis et al., 2009
47. Alexander, 1989; Dunbar, 2003; Kappeler & Silk, 2010
48. Bjorklund, 1997b
49. See Gray 2016; Konner 2010

Chapter 2

1. Bull, 1980
2. Black & Grober, 2003; Munday, White, & Warner, 2006
3. Pen et al., 2010; Refsnider & Janzen, 2015; Santidrián Tomillo et al., 2015
4. Lorenz, 1952
5. Gottlieb, 1976, 1997
6. Lickliter, 1990
7. Gottlieb, 1971; Turkewitz & Kenny, 1982
8. Spear, 1984, p. 335
9. Als, 1995, p. 462
10. Caspi et al., 2002; Similar findings have been reported by Guo, Roettger, & Cai, 2008, and Fergusson et al., 2011.
11. Ursini et al., 2018
12. Caspi et al., 2007; failure to replicate, Steer et al., 2010

13. Black et al. 1998; Greenough, Black, & Wallace, 1987; see also Johnson, 2007; Nelson, 2001
14. Lillard & Erisir, 2011; Nelson, Thomas, and de Haan, 2006; Shore, 2014
15. Singh & Zingg, 1966
16. Mail and Guardian, 1997
17. Kuo, 1967
18. John Locke, 1993, p. 53
19. Curtiss, 1977
20. Hrdy, 1999
21. Blum, 2002
22. Nelson et al., 2009
23. Pinheiro, 2006
24. Feeling "something like sawdust dolls . . .," Provence & Lipton, 1962, p. 56; emotional behavior as "increasingly impoverished and predominantly bland . . .," Provence & Lipton, 1962, p. 145
25. For example, Beckett et al., 2010; Bick et al., 2018; Dennis, 1973; Nelson et al., 2007; Provence & Lipton, 1962; Merz et al., 2016; Rutter et al., 2007; Troller-Renferee et al., 2018
26. Bjorklund, 2007a, p. 76
27. Nelson, 2007; both quotes, p. 16
28. New York Post, April 9, 2010. https://nypost.com/2010/04/09/us-woman-put-adopted-russian-son-on-one-way-flight-alone-back-to-homeland/. Downloaded June 16, 2018.
29. REBRN. https://www.dailydot.com/unclick/mother-adopted-russian-girls-reddit/. Downloaded June 23, 2020.
30. Merz & McCall, 2010, p. 468
31. Beckett et al., 2006; see also Nelson et al., 2007
32. Clark & Hanisee, 1982; see also Winick, Meyer, & Harris, 1975
33. McCall, 1981, p. 5
34. For a concise statement of the effects, see the statement by the Society for Research in Child Development, Bouza et al., 2018, in References.
35. Henrich, Heine, & Norenzayan, 2010; Nielsen et al., 2017
36. Konner, 2010; see also Bjorklund & Pellegrini, 2002; Bowlby, 1980; Gray, 2013
37. Lancy, 2015, p. 72
38. Scarr, 1992, p. 15
39. Baumrind, 1993; Jackson, 1993; "In response, Scarr concurred that . . .," Scarr, 1993
40. Breier et al., 2001
41. Glover, 2011; Pluess & Belsky, 2011; see also Sandman, Davis, & Glynn, 2013, for fetuses' adaptive response to maternal depression
42. Rice et al., 2010
43. Del Giudice, Gangestad, & Kaplan, 2016; Ellis et al., 2009, 2012; Hill & Kaplan, 1999; Stearns, 1992
44. Belsky, Steinberg, & Draper, 1991, p. 650

45. For some examples, see Chang & Jing Liu, 2018; Ellis et al., 2009; Hentges & Wang, 2018; Chang et al., 2019; Nettle & Cockerill, 2010; Simpson et al., 2012; Szepsenwol et al., 2018; for evidence that early-life adversity accelerates child and adolescent development generally, see Belsky, 2019.
46. Simpson et al., 2012
47. Mittal et al., 2015
48. Frankenhuis et al., 2019; Frankenhuis et al., 2016
49. Ellis et al., 2012
50. Ellis et al., 2017
51. Boyce & Ellis 2005; Ellis & Boyce, 2008; Ellis, Essex, & Boyce, 2005
52. Boyce & Ellis, 2005
53. Obradović et al., 2010
54. Gilissen et al., 2008; Kochanska, 1993; Stright, Gallagher, & Kelly, 2008; see Belsky, 2005
55. Slagt et al., 2016
56. Belsky, 2000, 2005; Belsky et al., 2007
57. Genes associated with individual differences in "children's sensitivity to context . . .," Bakermans-Kranenburg et al., 2008; Sumner et al., 2015; "and there is evidence that prenatal stress may increase children's sensitivity to parenting effects . . .," Hartman et al., 2018
58. For a book length treatment of orchid and dandelion children written for a general audience by the scientist who first used the terms, read W. Thomas Boyce's (2019) book, *The Orchid and the Dandelion: Why Some Children Struggle and How All Can Thrive*, New York: Knopf.
59. Moore, 2015, p. 14
60. van IJzendoorn, Bakermans-Kranenburg, & Ebstein, 2011, p. 305
61. Beach et al., 2016; see also Naumova et al., 2016
62. Bosmans, Young, & Hankin, 2018; Conradt et al., 2016; Parade et al., 2016; Kertes et al., 2016; Romens et al., 2015; Stroud et al., 2016; see Conradt, 2017, for a review
63. Romens et al., 2015
64. Cao-Lei et al., 2014
65. Conradt, 2017, p. 111

Chapter 3

1. Flynn, 2007, 2012
2. Ritchie & Tucker-Drob, 2018
3. Scott, 1968
4. Flynn et al., 2013; Stotz, 2017
5. West-Eberhard, 2003, p. 139
6. Baldwin, 1896, 1902; see Depew, 2003, for overview
7. Mayr, 1982; Mayr & Provine, 1980
8. Youngson & Whitelaw, 2008

NOTES   281

9. Schmalhausen, 1949; see Gottlieb, 1992, for a brief summary of Schmalhausen's theory
10. All results of Waddington's experiments from Waddington, 1975
11. For other examples and replications of Waddington's work, see Waddington, 1975, and Gibson & Hogness, 1996.
12. Waddington, 1975, p. 61
13. For reviews, see Jablonka, 2017; Jablonka & Lamb, 1995; Moore, 2015; West-Eberhard, 2003
14. Agrawal, Laforsch, & Tollrian, 1999
15. Gottlieb, 1987, 1992, 2002; West-Eberhard, 2003
16. Denenberg & Rosenberg, 1967
17. Ressler, 1966, p. 267
18. Francis et al., 1999; Meaney, 2010, 2013
19. Meaney, 2001, pp. 1170–1171
20. See Morgan & Whitelaw, 2008, for a discussion of possible epigenetic inheritance of diseases in humans.
21. Tobi et al., 2015
22. Lumey, 1992; Painter et al., 2008
23. Kaati, Byrgen, & Edvinsson, 2002
24. Konner, 2010, p. 343
25. See Geary, 2021
26. Konner, 2010
27. Clutton-Brock, 1991
28. Campbell, 1999, 2013
29. Allman, 1999
30. See, e.g., papers in Maestripieri & Mateo, 2009
31. Whiten, 2017; Whiten et al., 1999
32. Bering, Bjorklund, & Ragan, 2000; Bjorklund et al., 2002; Tomasello, Savage-Rumbaugh, & Kruger, 1993
33. Moore, 2003
34. Bjorklund, 2006, p. 233
35. Wyles, Kunkel, & Wilson, 1983
36. Sol et al., 2015
37. Deacon, 1997, pp. 345 and 349

Chapter 4

1. See Gottlieb, 1992; Gould, 1977; Hall, 2000; Mayr, 1982, for historical reviews; Garstang, 1922, p. 81
2. Chimpanzee Sequencing and Analysis Consortium, 2005
3. International Human Genome Sequencing Consortium, 2004
4. The ENCODE Project Consortium, 2012; Rands et al., 2014
5. Raff, 1996, p. 325
6. Carroll, 2005, p. 71

7. Raff, 1996, p. 27
8. Halder, Callaerts, & Gehring, 1995; Quiring et al., 1994
9. Raff, 1996, p. 384
10. Carroll, 2005, p. 111
11. Carroll, 2003; Noonan, 2003; Wray, 2007
12. Arbiza et al., 2013; Gilad et al., 2006; Prabhakar et al., 2006; McClean et al., 2011
13. de Beer, 1958; Gould, 1977; McKinney, 1998, 2000; Shea, 1989, 2000
14. Carroll, 2005, p. 267
15. de Beer, 1958
16. Gould, 1977; Hattori, 1998; Montagu, 1989; Schwartz, 1999; Thomson, 1988; Wesson, 1991
17. Montagu, 1989, p. 246
18. Gould, 1977, p. 375
19. See Gould, 1977
20. For examples, see Gould, 1977, Raff, 1996; West-Eberhard, 2003
21. Trut, 1999
22. Trut, Oskina, & Kharlamova, 2009, p. 354
23. Carroll, 2005, p. 283
24. Bolk, 1926, p. 470.
25. McKinney, 1998, 2000; Shea, 1989
26. See Gould, 1977; Montagu, 1989
27. See Allman, 1999; Crook, 1980; Gould, 1977; Hattori, 1998; Wesson 1991
28. For example, see Hare, 2017; Hood, 2014; Wrangham, 2019
29. See, for example, Buss, 2005; Daly & Wilson, 1988
30. Hrdy, 2009; Wrangham, 2018
31. Hrdy, 2009
32. For example, Bjorklund & Harnishfeger, 1995; Chance, 1962; Stenhouse, 1974
33. Dewey, 1933/1964, p. 212; pp. 258, 259
34. see Bjorklund & Harnishfeger, 1995; Bjorklund & Kipp, 1996
35. Jerrison, 2000; Rilling & Insel, 1999
36. Azevedo et al., 2009
37. Finlay & Darlington, 1995; Finlay, Darlington, & Nicastro, 2001; Herculano-Houzel, 2012
38. DeSilva, 2016; Trevathan & Rosenberg, 2016
39. Bogin, 2006
40. Bogin, 2006; Gould, 1977; Tanner, 1978
41. Trevanthan, 1987
42. Portmann, 1990; Montagu, 1989; Konner, 2010
43. Portmann, 1990, p. 93 (originally published in 1944)
44. See Bufill, Agustí, & Blesa, 2011; Charrier et al., 2012; Goyal et al., 2014; Liu et al., 2012; Petanjek et al., 2011; Somel et al., 2009
45. Miller et al., 2012
46. Bufill et al., 2011, p. 735
47. Poirier & Smith, 1974

48. Hill & Hurtado, 1996; Kaplan et al., 2000
49. Gurven & Kaplan, 2007
50. Bogin, 1999, 2001, 2003, 2006
51. Piaget, 1983
52. See Bjorklund, 2013; Bjorklund & Causey 2018; Siegler & Alibali, 2004
53. Hill, Barton, & Hurtado, 2009
54. Brookes, 1991; Thomas de Benitez, 2009
55. See Dennis et al., 2013; Giedd et al., 1999, 2015; Luna et al., 2001; Spear, 2000, 2007
56. Giedd, 2015; Mills et al., 2014
57. See Bogin, 1999
58. Bogin, 1999, 2003; see also Gibbons, 2008
59. Tomasello, 2019; Nielsen, 2012
60. Locke & Bogin, 2006; Locke, 2009
61. Del Giudice, Angeleri, & Manera, 2009; Del Giudice, 2014
62. Sercombe, 2014

Chapter 5

1. Trivers, 1974, p. 249
2. Volk & Atkinson, 2013
3. Daly & Wilson, 1988; Hrdy, 1999
4. Bowlby, 1969
5. Lorenz, 1943
6. E.g., Brosch et al., 2007; see Kringelbach et al., 2016, and Lucion et al., 2017, for reviews
7. E.g., Alley, 1981; Leibenluft et al., 2004; Senese et al., 2013; Sprengelmyer et al., 2009
8. Langlois et al., 1995; Glocker et al., 2009a; Machluf & Bjorklund, 2016; Waller, Volk, & Quinsey, 2004; see Franklin & Volk, 2018, for a review
9. Volk, Lukjanczuk, & Quinsey, 2007
10. Esposito et al., 2014; Golle et al., 2015
11. Glocker et al., 2009a
12. Cárdenas et al., 2013; Lobmaier et al., 2010; Maestripieri & Pelka, 2002; Parsons et al., 2010; Sprengelmeyer et al., 2009; Yamamoto et al., 2009
13. Sprengelmeyer et al., 2009
14. Lobmaier et al., 2015
15. e.g., Borgi et al., 2014; Fullard & Reiling, 1976; Goldberg, Blumberg, & Kriger, 1982; Gross, 1997
16. Goldberg et al., 1982
17. Borgi et al., 2014; Van Duuren, Kendal-Scott, & Start, 2003
18. E.g., Glocker et al., 2009b; Hahn & Perrett, 2014; Leibenluft et al., 2004
19. E.g., Baeken et al., 2010; Glocker et al., 2009b; Nitschke et al., 2004; Luo et al., 2015, p. 10
20. Empathy, Glocker et al., 2009b; Leibenluft et al., 2004; reward and attachment, Leibenluft et al., 2004; Nitschke et al., 2004; and motor areas, Glocker et al., 2009b

21. Sherman et al., 2009, 2013
22. E.g., Nitschke et al., 2004; see Rigo et al., 2019 for a review
23. Luo et al., 2015
24. Franklin & Volk, 2018
25. Franklin et al., 2018
26. See Zebrowitz & Montepare, 1992, for a review
27. Luo, Li, & Lee, 2011
28. Proverbio et al., 2011
29. Hernández Blasi et al., 2018
30. Bjorklund, Hernández Blasi, & Periss, 2010; Hernández Blasi, Bjorklund, & Ruiz Soler, 2015
31. Hernandez Blasi & Bjorklund, 2018; Hernández Blasi, Bjorklund, & Ruiz Soler, 2017; Periss, Hernández Blasi, & Bjorklund, 2012
32. Guthrie, 1993; Woolley, 1997; Casler & Kelemen, 2008; see Brainerd, 1978
33. Lyons, 2005
34. Goldberg & Thompson-Schill, 2009
35. Periss et al., 2012, pp. 1205, 1212
36. Montagu, 1989, pp. 61, 94, 95
37. Bjorklund, 1997b; Bjorklund & Green, 1992; Gopnik et al., 2017
38. Piaget, 1955, 1983
39. Borke, 1975; Flavell et al., 1981
40. Rubin, Watson, & Jambor, 1978; Piaget, 1955
41. Bakeman & Brownlee, 1980; Bjorklund & Green, 1992
42. Vygotsky, 1962
43. Alderson-Day & Fernyhough, 2015; Duncan & Tarulli, 2009
44. Berk, 1986, 1992; Berk & Landau, 1993; Kohlberg et al., 1968; Rittle-Johnson, 2006; see Winsler, 2009, for a review
45. Lord, 1980; see also Pratkanis & Greenwald, 1985
46. Ross et al., 2011; see also Mood, 1979
47. Elkind, 1967; Elkind & Bowen, 1979; Vartanian, 2000
48. See Banerjee et al., 2015; Lapsley & Hill, 2010; Hill, Duggan, & Lapsley, 2012; Potard et al., 2018
49. Klaczynski, 2017; Lapsley & Hill, 2010
50. Bjorklund & Green, 1992; Hill & Lapsley, 2011; Sercombe, 2014
51. Hill, Duggan, & Lapsley, 2012
52. Brooks, 2011
53. Nations Treaty Collection, 1990
54. Donald, 1991; Suddendorf & Corballis, 2007; Tulving, 1985
55. Nelson, 2005, p. 369
56. Bauer, 2007; Howe, Courage, & Rooksby, 2009; Rovee-Collier & Giles, 2010
57. Bjorklund & Green, 1992, pp. 49, 50
58. See Brainerd & Reyna, 2005; Bruck, Ceci, & Principle, 2006; Ceci & Bruck, 1993, for reviews
59. Bjorklund & Sellers, 2014; Sellers & Bjorklund, 2014

60. See Hoehl et al., 2019; Horner & Whiten, 2005; Lyons, Young, & Kiel, 2007; Nielsen, 2012; Tomasello, 2019
61. Kenward, 2012; Nielsen, 2012
62. Lucas et al., 2017
63. Dennett, 1990
64. Duncker, 1945
65. Bloom & Markson, 1998; German & Johnson, 2002
66. Casler & Kelemen, 2005, p. 479
67. Buttelmann et al., 2008; Cummin-Sebree & Fragaszy, 2005; Ruiz & Santos, 2013
68. Quoted from Bjorklund, 2007a, p. 111
69. See Boulton & Smith, 1990; Humphreys & Smith, 1987; Lipko, Dunlosky, & Merriman, 2009; Muenks, Wigfield, & Eccles, 2018; Mills & Keil, 2004; Plumert & Schwebel, 1997; Schneider, 1998; Spinath & Spinath, 2005; Stipek, 1981; Thomaes, Brummelman, & Sedikides, 2017
70. Stipek & Daniels, 1988
71. Bjorklund, 1997b; Bjorklund et al., 2009; Seligman, 1998
72. Bandura, 1997
73. Seligman, 1998, p. 126
74. Bjorklund, Gaultney, & Green, 1993, pp. 87, 88
75. van Loon et al., 2017; Schneider, 1985
76. Shin, Bjorklund, & Beck, 2007
77. Lockhart, Chang, & Tyler, 2002; Lockhart, Goddu, & Keil, 2017
78. Stipek, 1984, p. 52
79. Rheingold, 1985
80. Plumert, 1995, p. 875
81. Loftus & Pickrell, 1995; McGuigan, Makinson, & Whiten, 2011
82. Carstensen & Mikels, 2005
83. Bickerton, 2014, p. 187
84. Tomasello, 2019, p. 132
85. E.g., Pinker, 1994; Tomasello, 2005, 2019
86. See Hauser, Chomsky, & Fitch, 2002; Számadó & Sazthmáry, 2006
87. Crystal, 2010
88. See Kuhl et al., 2006
89. Chomsky, 1957; Bickerton, 2014; Evans & Levinson, 2009; Tomasello, 2005, 2019
90. Bickerton, 1981, 1990, 2014
91. Bonefant, 2011; Klinger, & Neuman-Holzschuh, 2013; Bickerton, 2014
92. Senghas & Coppola, 2001; Senghas, Kita, & Ozyürek, 2004
93. Bohn, Kachel, & Tomasello, 2019
94. Locke & Bogin, 2006; see also Locke, 2009
95. Newport, 1990, 1991
96. Newport, 1991, p. 127
97. Elman, 1994
98. Kersten & Earles, 2001
99. Fernald, 1992; Kuhl et al., 1997

100. Cooper & Aslin, 1990, 1994; Karzon, 1985; Moore, Spence, & Katz, 1997; Vouloumanis & Waxman, 2014
101. Golinkoff et al., 2015
102. Fernald, 1992
103. Whitham et al., 2007
104. Bruner, 1983; Fernald, 1992; Bjorklund & Schwartz, 1996
105. Locke, 1693
106. Groos, 1898/1975, p. 75
107. Fagen, 1981
108. Huizinga, 1950
109. Harris, 1989, p. 256
110. Parten, 1932
111. Bjorklund, 2007a, p. 139
112. McGrew, 1972; Smith & Connolly, 1980
113. Konner, 2010; Pellegrini & Smith, 1998
114. See Bjorklund & Pellegrini, 2002, and Pellegrini & Smith, 1998, for reviews
115. Biben, 1998
116. Smith, 1982, p. 151
117. Lockman, 2000, p. 137
118. See Bjorklund & Gardiner, 2011; Pellegrini, 2013, for a reviews
119. See Bjorklund & Gardiner, 2011; Pellegrini, 2013
120. Gredlein & Bjorklund, 2005
121. Geary, 2021
122. Gómez & Beatriz Martín-Andrade, 2005
123. Deloach, 2010; DeLoache & Marzolf, 1992; see also Flavell, Green, & Flavell, 1986; Jowker-Baniani & Schmuckler, 2013
124. Ganea et al., 2009
125. Cemore & Herwig, 2005; Lillard et al., 2013
126. Nielsen, 2012, p. 176
127. Berk et al., 2006; Pierucci et al., 2014
128. Greve & Thomsen, 2016; Greve, Thomsen, & Dehio, 2014
129. Cited in Montagu, 1989, p. 103
130. Cited in Clark, 1971, p. 10

Chapter 6

1. Kohlberg, 1969, 1966
2. Dodge, 1986; Bandura, 1986
3. Bjorklund, 1989, p. 174
4. Hamilton, 1964
5. Trivers, 1971
6. Wilkinson, 1984
7. Nowak, 2006; Tomasello, 2014, 2019; E. O. Wilson, 2013

8. E. O. Wilson, 2013, 2019
9. D. S. Wilson, 2015, 2019; D. S. Wilson & E. O. Wilson, 2007
10. Wilson & Wilson, 2007, p. 335
11. D. S. Wilson, 2019, p. 86
12. Alexander, 1989; Dunbar, 2003; Hare, 2011; Whiten & Erdal, 2014
13. Byrne & Whiten, 1988
14. Alexander, 1989
15. Horner et al., 2006; Whiten & Flynn, 2010
16. Humphrey, 1976
17. Bjorklund & Bering, 2003; Bjorklund, Cormier, & Rosenberg, 2005; Dunbar, 1995
18. Joffe, 1997
19. Antón, Potts, & Aiello, 2014; Wrangham, 2009
20. Dunbar, 2014
21. Wiessner, 2014
22. Kinard et al., 2017; Sameroff & Chandler, 1975
23. Bardi, Regolin, & Simion, 2011, 2014; Bertenthal, Proffitt, & Cutting, 1984; see also Di Giorgio et al., 2017, for newborns' attention to self-propelled motion
24. Bertenthal, 1996
25. Easterbrook et al., 1999; Gava, Valenza, Turati, & de Schonen, 2008; Mondloch et al., 1999
26. Haith, 1966; Salapatek & Kessen, 1966; Ruff & Birch, 1974; Macchi Cassia et al., 2004; Turati et al., 2002
27. Quinn et al., 2002; Kelly et al., 2009
28. May et al., 2018
29. Mehler et al., 1988; Moon, Cooper, & Fifer, 1993; May et al., 2011
30. Melzoff & Moore, 1977
31. Oostenbroek et al., 2016; see Bjorklund, 2018b; Redshaw et al., 2019
32. Bjorklund, 1987, 2018a; Byrne, 2005; Legerstee, 1991; Nagy, 2006
33. Dubowitz, Mushon, DeVries, & Arden, 1986
34. Heimann, 1989; Simpson et al., 2016
35. Bowlby, 1969; Del Giudice, 2009; Schore, 2013
36. Trevarthen et al., 1978; Yoo et al., 2018
37. Tronick, 1989
38. Ainsworth et al., 1978; Kirkpatrick, 2005
39. Fraley, 2002; Mikulincer & Shaver, 2007
40. Bowlby, 1980; Fraley & Brumbaugh, 2004
41. Groh et al. 2016
42. Buss, 2011; Symons, 1979
43. Hart & Carrington, 2002; Hart et al., 2004; Mize et al., 2014
44. Hart, 2018; Myers & Bjorklund, 2018
45. Nielsen & Haun, 2016; Whiten, 2017
46. Tomasello, 2019, p. 6
47. Nielsen & Haun, 2016; Tomasello, 2019; Whiten, 2017, 2018
48. Tomasello, 2019

49. Hunt, 2012
50. Vygotsky, 1962, 1978
51. Tomasello, 2019, p. 305
52. Meltzoff, 2007
53. Harari, 2017
54. Herrmann et al., 2007
55. Wobber et al., 2014
56. Carpenter, Nagell, & Tomasello, 1998; Tomasello & Carpenter, 2007
57. Dennett, 1987
58. Liszkowski, Carpenter, & Tomasello, 2007; Liszkowski et al., 2006; Brooks & Meltzoff, 2002
59. Hornik, Risenhoover, & Gunnar, 1987; Vaish & Striano, 2004
60. Carpenter et al., 1998
61. Callaghan et al., 2011
62. Carpenter et al., 1995; Tomasello & Carpenter, 2005; Tomonaga et al., 2004
63. See Carlson, Koenig, & Harms, 2013; Ruffman, 2014; Wellman, Cross, & Watson, 2001, for reviews
64. Mayer & Träuble, 2013; Slaughter & Perez-Zapata, 2014
65. Sabbagh et al., 2006; Tardif & Wellman, 2000; Avis & Harris, 1991
66. Repacholi & Gopnik, 1997
67. Rackozy et al., 2007
68. Clements & Perner, 1994
69. See Baillargeon et al., 2016, for a review
70. Onishi & Baillargeon, 2005; Scott, 2017
71. Ruffman, 2014; Kulke et al., 2018
72. Wiessman et al., 2017
73. Hare et al., 2000; Hare, Call, & Tomasello, 2001; see also Melis, Call, & Tomasello, 2006
74. Povinelli & Eddy, 1996
75. Hermann et al., 2007; Krachun et al., 2009
76. Buttelmann et al., 2017; Krupenye et al., 2016
77. Sagi & Hoffman, 1976; Martin & Clark, 1982; but see Ruffman, Lorimer, & Scarf, 2017, for an alternate interpretation
78. Hoffman, 2000; Zhan-Waxler et al., 1992
79. de Waal, 1997, 2005; Preston & de Waal, 2002
80. de Waal, 2005, 1997
81. Silk et al., 2005; see also Jensen et al., 2006
82. Hrdy, 1999, p. 392
83. de Waal, 1982
84. Xiao et al., 2018
85. Bauer, 1993; Martin, Ruble, & Szkrybala, 2002
86. Buttelmann et al., 2013; de Klerk et al., 2019
87. Ingram & Bering, 2010; Ingram, 2014
88. Riedl et al., 2015; Robbins & Rochat, 2011; Yang et al., 2018
89. Jordan, McAuliffe, & Warneken, 2014

90. McLoughlin et al., 2018
91. Tafel et al., 1971
92. Dunham, Baron, & Carey, 2011
93. Engelmann et al., 2013; Englemann et al., 2018; Haun & Over, 2014; Patterson & Bigler, 2006; Plötner et al., 2015
94. Wörle & Paulus, 2018
95. Schmidt, Rakoczy, & Tomasello, 2016
96. Kenward, 2012; see also Keupp, Behne, & Rakoczy, 2013
97. Tomasello, 2019, p. 250
98. Riedl et al., 2012
99. Quoted from Bjorklund & Hernández Blasi, 2012, p. 290
100. Tomasello, 1999; Tennie, Call, & Tomasello, & 2009
101. Legare, 2019
102. Nielsen, 2012; Tomasello, 2000; Want & Harris, 2001
103. Nagy & Molnar, 2004
104. Piaget, 1962, p. 10
105. Field, Guy, & Umbel, 1985
106. Sclafani et al., 2015
107. Barr & Hayne, 2003
108. McGuigan & Whiten, 2009; Nielsen, 2006
109. Gergely et al., 2002
110. Carpenter, Akhtar, & Tomasello, 1998; Meltzoff, 1995
111. Lyons et al., 2007
112. Gellén & Buttelmann, 2019; see Hoehl et al., 2019; Whiten, 2019, for reviews
113. Gardiner, Grief, & Bjorklund, 2011; McGuigan, 2013; Buttelmann et al., 2013; Whiten et al., 2009; Schleifauf et al., 2018
114. Nielsen & Tomaselli, 2010; Nielsen et al., 2014, 2016; Corriveau et al., 2017; Stengelin et al., 2020
115. McGuigan, Makinson, & Whiten, 2011; Hewlett, Berl, & Roulette, 2016
116. Kenward, 2012
117. Nielsen, 2018; Nielsen et al., 2014
118. Keupp, Behne, & Rakoczy, 2013; Nielsen, 2012
119. Nielsen, 2018, p. 266; see also Legare & Nielsen, 2015; Watson-Jones & Legare, 2016
120. Gruber et al., 2019
121. Chudek, Baron, & Birch, 2016; Nielsen, 2012; Whiten et al., 2009
122. Whiten et al., 2009
123. Gergely & Csibra, 2005; Csibra & Gergely, 2011
124. Tomasello, Kruger, & Ratner, 1993, p. 500
125. Tomasello, 2019, p. 135
126. Herrmann et al., 2007; Wobber et al., 2014
127. Whiten, 2010; Whiten et al., 1999; Bender, Herzing, & Bjorklund, 2009; Rendell & Whitehead, 2001
128. Nagell, Olguin, & Tomasello, 1993; Horner & Whiten, 2005
129. Clay & Tennie, 2018; Nielsen, 2012

130. Boesch, 1991; Greenfield et al., 2000; Musgrave et al., 2019
131. Tomasello, Savage-Rumbaugh, & Kruger, 1993, p. 1689
132. Bjorklund & Rosenberg, 2005; Call & Tomasello, 1996
133. Tomasello et al., 1993
134. Bering, Bjorklund, & Ragan, 2000; Bjorklund et al. 2002; Buttelmann et al., 2008
135. Fouts, 1997
136. Hawley, 1999, 2003
137. Hamlin, Wynn, & Bloom, 2007
138. Scarf et al., 2012
139. Hamlin, 2013; Wynn et al., 2018
140. Rheingold, 1982
141. Warneken & Tomasello, 2006
142. Allen, Perry, & Kaufman, 2018; Dahl et al., 2016; Warneken & Tomasello, 2013; Hepach, Vaish, & Tomasello, 2017; Hepach, 2016
143. Warneken & Tomasello, 2008; Fabes et al., 1989
144. Callahghan et al., 2011
145. For reviews, see Köster & Kärtner, 2019; Warneken, 2015
146. Brownell and The Early Social Development Research Lab, 2016; Dahl & Brownell, 2019; Dahl & Paulus, 2019
147. Warenken, 2015
148. Hay & Ross, 1982
149. Ulber, Hamann, & Tomasello, 2015
150. Green & Schneider, 1974; Rochat et al., 2009
151. Benenson, Pascoe, & Radmore, 2007; Blake & Rand, 2010
152. Vaish, Hepach, & Tomasello, 2018
153. Olson & Spelke, 2008
154. House & Tomasello, 2018
155. Ulber, Hamann, & Tomasello, 2016
156. Callaghan et al., 2011; Rochat et al., 2009
157. House et al., 2013; Rochat et al., 2009
158. Brownell, Svetlova, & Nichols, 2009
159. Silk et al., 2005; Jensen et al., 2006
160. Gilby, 2006
161. Silk et al., 2013
162. Damon, 1994; Lane & Coon, 1972
163. McAuliffe et al., 2017
164. Schmidt & Sommerville, 2011; Sommerville et al., 2013; Wang & Henderson, 2018
165. Burns & Sommerville, 2014; see Sommerville, 2018, for a review
166. Hamann et al., 2011
167. Falk et al., 2003; Sutter, 2007
168. Wittig et al., 2013
169. Jensen, Call, & Tomasello, 2007; Kaiser et al., 2012
170. Tomasello, 2019, p. 234
171. Brosnan & de Waal, 2014

172. Brosnan & de Waal, 2003
173. Muller & Mitani, 2005, p. 320, p. 278
174. Melis, Hare, & Tomasello, 2006
175. Greenberg et al., 2010
176. Hamann et al., 2011
177. Tomasello, 2019, p. 167
178. Kachel, Svetlova, & Tomasello, 2018, 2019; Kachel & Tomasello, 2019
179. Grueneisen & Tomasello, 2017
180. Warneken, Chen, & Tomasello, 2006
181. Warneken, Gräfenhain, & Tomasello, 2012
182. Callaghan et al., 2011
183. Warneken, Chen, & Tomasello, 2006
184. Endedijk et al., 2015; Nielsen et al., 2016
185. Curry, Mullins, & Whitehouse, 2019
186. Tomasello, 2019, p. 192

Chapter 7

1. Skenazy. (2008, April 8). "Why I Let My 9-Year-Old Ride the Subway Alone." *The New York Sun*. Retrieved August 13, 2019. https://www.nysun.com/news/why-i-let-my-9-year-old-ride-subway-alone
2. Lukianoff & Haidt, 2018
3. Schön, 2007
4. Blankenstein et al., 2019
5. Bogin, 2006; see Chapter 4
6. Roser, M. Fertility rate, Our World in Data. Retrieved August 16, 2019. https://ourworldindata.org/fertility-rate
7. Cristakis, E. (2016, October 28). My Halloween email led to a campus firestorm—and a troubling lesson about self-censorship. *The Washington Post*. Retrieved August 16, 2019. https://www.washingtonpost.com/opinions/my-halloween-email-led-to-a-campus-firestorm--and-a-troubling-lesson-about-self-censorship/2016/10/28/70e55732-9b97-11e6-a0ed-ab0774c1eaa5_story.html
8. Lukianoff and Haidt, 2018, p. 30
9. Twenge, 2017, p. 4
10. Twenge, 2017, p. 47
11. Twenge, 2017, p. 45
12. Sercombe, 2014
13. Harris, 1995
14. See, for example, chapters in Rubin, Bukowski, & Laursen, 2018
15. Lam et al., 2014
16. Knoll et al., 2015
17. Blakemore, 2018
18. Steinberg, 2007, 2008; Steinberg et al., 2017

19. Giedd, 2015; Mills et al., 2014; Steinberg et al., 2017
20. Gardner & Steinberg, 2005
21. Chen et al., 2000
22. Geidd, in Sercombe, 2014, p. 62
23. Statista, https://www.statista.com/statistics/264810/number-of-monthly-active-facebook-users-worldwide/
24. Taylor, K., & Silver, L. (2019). Anderson & Jiang (2018).
25. Twenge, 2017, Chapter 2
26. Kanai et al., 2012
27. Tinbergem, 1951; Tinbergen & Perdeck, 1950
28. Sbarra, Biskin, & Slatcher, 2019
29. McDaniel & Coyne, 2016
30. Dwyer, Kushlev, & Dunn, 2018; Kushlev, Hunter, Proulux, Pressman, & Dunn, 2019; Kushlev, Proulux, & Dunn, 2017; see Kushlev, Dwyer, & Dunn, 2019
31. Rideout & Robb, 2018
32. Gentile et al., 2017; Twenge & Campbell, 2018; Twenge, Krizan, & Hisler, 2017; Vernon, Modecki, & Barber, 2018
33. Anderson & Whitaker, 2010; de Jong et al., 2013; Rosen et al., 2014
34. Louv, 2005, 2016; Charles & Louv, 2009
35. Wilson, 1984
36. See meta-analysis by Bowler et al., 2010, and brief review by Schertz & Berman, 2019; see also Harper, 2017, for a discussion of Western parents' aversion to children's risky play.
37. Young, 1998.
38. See Dickson et al., 2019; Twenge, 2017; Twenge, Joiner, Rogers, & Martin, 2018
39. Data from Twenge & Campbell, 2018; figure from Twenge, 2019
40. See, for example, George et al., 2018; Twenge, 2017; Twenge, Martin, & Campbell, 2018; Twenge, Joiner, Rogers, & Martin, 2018
41. Twenge, Martin, & Campbell, 2018
42. George et al., 2018
43. Coyne et al., 2018
44. Daly, 2018; Orben & Przybylski, 2019
45. Heffer et al., 2019
46. Kross et al., 2013
47. Tromholt, 2016
48. Verduyn et al., 2015
49. Hunt et al., 2018
50. Steers, Wickham, & Acitelli, 2014
51. Junger, 2016
52. Brooks, 2019
53. From Jones, 1986. See also Baumeister & Leary, 1995.
54. Kessler, Üstün, & World Health Organization, 2008; Weissman et al., 1996
55. Chiao & Blizinsky, 2010
56. Twenge, 2017, p. 176

57. Arnett, 2000
58. Postman, 1982
59. Konner, 2010; Lancy, 2016; Lancy & Grove, 2010
60. Kline, 2015
61. Lancy & Grove, 2010, pp. 164–165
62. Bjorklund, 2007b; Bjorklund & Bering, 2002; Bjorklund & Beers, 2016; Geary & Berch, 2016; Gray, 2013, 2016; Grushin & Geher, 2018; Sellers, Machluf, & Bjorklund, 2016; Wilson et al., 2009
63. Vygotsky, 1978, p. 8
64. Wood, Bruner, & Ross, 1976
65. Blank & White, 1999
66. Gergely & Csibra, 2005; Csibra & Gergely, 2011
67. Gopnik & Walker, 2013, p. 15
68. Pellegrini & Bjorklund, 2004, p. 38
69. Gray, 2013, 2016
70. Elias & Berk, 2002
71. Pellegrini & Galda, 1982; Smilansky, 1968
72. See Garon, Bryson, & Smith, 2008; McAuley & White, 2011; Zelazo et al., 2008
73. Barker et al., 2014; Rueda & Posner, 2013
74. For example, see Berk & Meyers, 2013; Carlson & White, 2013; Zelazo & Carlson, 2012
75. Vygotsky, 1933, p. 102, as cited in Elias & Berk, 2002, p. 219
76. Barker et al., 2014
77. Carlson, White, & Davis-Unger, 2014
78. Elias & Berk, 2002
79. Diamond et al., 2007
80. Blair & Diamond, 2008, p. 907
81. Carlson et al., 2014; Gopnik & Walker, 2013; Kelly et al., 2011
82. Berk & Myers, 2013
83. Gray, 2013, p. 5
84. See Bjorklund, 2007b, for a discussion of the effects of direct-instruction preschools versus developmentally appropriate preschools on children, social, emotional, and cognitive.
85. Hyson et al., 1990, p. 421
86. Bonawitz et al., 2011, p. 329
87. Weisberg et al., 2016, p. 177
88. Haden et al., 2016
89. Fisher et al., 2013
90. Toub et al., 2016; Weisberg, Hirsh-Pasek, & Golinkoff, 2013
91. Geary & Berch, 2016
92. Alfieri et al., 2011
93. See Lillard, 2018
94. Gray, 2013, 2016
95. Piaget, 1977, cited in Rogoff, 1998, p. 38
96. Geary, 2007, p. 43, italics in the original

97. The Common Sense Census, 2017
98. Kabali et al., 2015
99. DeLoache et al., 1998
100. Barr et al., 2007
101. See Barr, 2010
102. Barr, 2013; Zack et al., 2009; Strouse & Ganea, 2017
103. DeLoache et al., 2010; see also Richert et al., 2010
104. Courage and Setliff, 2010
105. Lillard, Li, & Boguszewski, 2015
106. Radesky et al., 2014
107. Nathanson et al., 2014; Lillard & Peterson, 2011; Lillard, Drell, et al., 2015; Huber et al., 2018
108. See Kostyrka-Allchorne, Cooper, & Simpson, 2017, for a review
109. American Academy of Pediatrics, 2016
110. Hutton et al., 2019
111. Turkewitz & Kenny, 1982
112. Wait Until 8th, https://www.waituntil8th.org
113. Engemann et al., 2019
114. Reed et al., 2017
115. Harlow, 1959; Papousek, 1969
116. Geary, 2007; Geary & Berch, 2016
117. Gruskin & Geher, 2018
118. Gray, 2013
119. Wilson, Kauffman, & Purdy, 2011
120. Briggs, 1970
121. Wang et al., 2009
122. Ellis et al., 2012; Volk et al., 2014
123. See Ellis et al., 2016; Yaeger, Dahl, & Dweck, 2018
124. Ellis et al., 2016
125. Hidaka, 2012, p. 211

Chapter 8

1. Konner, 2010, p. 741
2. Garstang, 1922

References

Agrawal, A. A., Laforsch, C., & Tollrian, R. (1999). Transgenerational induction of defences in animals and plants. *Nature, 401*, 60–63.

Ainsworth, M. D. S., Blehar, M. C., Waters, E., & Wall, S. (1978). *Patterns of attachment: A psychological study of the strange situation.* Hillsdale, NJ: Erlbaum.

Alderson-Day, B., & Fernyhough, C. (2015). Inner speech: Development, cognitive functions, phenomenology, and neurobiology. *Psychological Bulletin, 141*, 931–965.

Alexander, R. D. (1989). Evolution of the human psyche. In P. Mellers & C. Stringer (Eds.), *The human revolution: Behavioural and biological perspectives on the origins of modern humans* (pp. 455–513). Princeton, NJ: Princeton University Press.

Alfieri, L., Brooks, P. J., Aldrich, N. J., & Tenenbaum, H. R. (2011). Does discovery-based instruction enhance learning? *Journal of Educational Psychology, 103*, 1–18.

Allen, M., Perry, C., & Kaufman, J. (2018). Toddlers prefer to help familiar people. *Journal of Experimental Child Psychology, 174*, 90–102.

Alley, T. R. (1981). Head shape and the perception of cuteness. *Developmental Psychology, 17*, 650–654.

Allman, J. M. (1999). *Evolving brains.* New York, NY: Scientific American Library.

Als, H. (1995). The preterm infant: A model for the study of fetal brain expectation. In J-P. Lecanuet, W. P. Fifer, N. A. Krasnegor, & W. Smotherman (Eds.), *Fetal brain development: A psychobiological perspective* (pp. 439–471). Hillsdale, NJ: Erlbaum.

American Academy of Pediatrics. (2016). Media and young minds. *Pediatrics, 138*(5), e20162591. doi: 10.1542/peds.2016-2591

Anderson, S. E., Whitaker, R. C. (2010). Household routines and obesity in US preschool-aged children. *Pediatrics, 125*, 420–428.

Anderson, M., & Jiang, J. (2018, May). Teens, social media & technology 2018, Pew Research Center: Internet & Technology. Retrieved August 20, 2019. https://www.pewinternet.org/2018/05/31/teens-social-media-technology-2018/

Antón, S. C., Potts, R., & Aiello, L. C. (2014). Evolution of early *Homo*: An integrated biological perspective. *Science, 345*, 45–59.

Anzures, G., Wheeler, A., Quinn, P. C., Pascalis, O., Slater, A. M., Heron-Delaney, M., et al. (2012). Brief daily exposure to Asian females reverses perceptual narrowing for Asian faces in Caucasian infants. *Journal of Experimental Child Psychology, 112*, 484–495.

Arbiza, L., Gronau, I., Aksoy, B. A., Hubisz, M. J., Gulko, B., Keinan, A., & Siepel, A. (2013). Genome-wide inference of natural selection on human transcription factor binding sites. *Nature Genetics, 45*, 723–729.

Arnett, J. J. (2000). Emerging adulthood: A theory of development from the late teens to the early twenties. *American Psychologist, 55*, 469–480.

Austad, S. N. (1997). *Why we age: What science is discovering about the body's journey through life.* New York, NY: Wiley.

Avis, J., & Harris, P. L. (1991). Belief-desire reasoning among Baka children: Evidence for a universal conception of mind. *Child Development, 62*, 460–467.

Azevedo, F. A., Carvalho, L. R., Grinberg, L. T., Farfel, J. M., Ferretti, R. E., Leite, R. E., et al. (2009). Equal numbers of neuronal and nonneuronal cells make the human brain an isometrically scaled-up primate brain. *Journal of Comparative Neurology, 513,* 532–541.

Baeken, C., Van Schuerbeek, P., DeRaedt, R., DeMey, J., Vanderhasselt, M. A., Bossuyt, A., et al. (2010). The effect of one left-sided dorsolateral prefrontal cortical HF-rTMS session on emotional brain processes in women. *Psychiatria Danubina, 22*(Suppl. 1), S163.

Baillargeon, R., Scott, R., & Bian, L. (2016). Psychological reasoning in infancy. *Annual Review of Psychology, 67,* 159–186.

Bakeman, R., & Brownlee, J. R. (1980). The strategic use of parallel play: A sequential analysis. *Child Development, 51,* 873–878.

Bakermans-Kranenburg, M. J., van IJzendoorn, M. H., Pijlman, F. T., Mesman, J., & Juffer, F. (2008). Experimental evidence for differential susceptibility: Dopamine D4 receptor polymorphism (DRD4 VNTR) moderates intervention effects on toddlers' externalizing behavior in a randomized controlled trial. *Developmental Psychology, 44,* 293–300.

Baldwin, J. M. (1896). A new factor in evolution. *American Naturalist, 30*(354), 441–451, 536–553.

Baldwin, J. M. (1902). *Development and evolution.* New York, NY: McMillan.

Bandura, A. (1986). *Social foundations of thought and action: A social cognitive theory.* Englewood Cliffs, NJ: Prentice Hall.

Bandura, A. (1997). *Self-efficacy: The exercise of control.* New York, NY: Freeman.

Banerjee S. C., Greene, K., Yanovitzky, I., Bagdasarov, Z., Choi, S. Y., & Magsamem-Conrad, K. (2015). Adolescent egocentrism and indoor tanning: Is the relationship direct or mediated? *Journal of Youth Study, 18,* 357–375.

Bardi, L., Regolin, L., & Simion, F. (2011). Biological motion preference in humans at birth: Role of dynamic and configural properties. *Developmental Science, 14,* 353–359.

Bardi, L., Regolin, L., & Simion, F. (2014). The first time ever I saw your feet: Inversion effect in newborns' sensitivity to biological motion. *Developmental Psychology, 50,* 986–993.

Barker, J. E., Semenov, A. D., Michaelson, L., Provan, L. S., Snyder, H. R., & Munakata, Y. (2014). Less-structured time in children's daily lives predicts self-directed executive functioning. *Frontiers in Psychology, 5,* 1–16.

Barkow, J. H., Cosmides, L., & Tooby, J. (Eds.). (1992). *The adapted mind: Evolutionary psychology and the generation of culture.* New York, NY: Oxford University Press.

Barr, R. (2010). Transfer of learning between 2D and 3D sources during infancy: Informing theory and practice. *Developmental Review, 30,* 128–154.

Barr, R. (2013). Memory constraints on infant learning from picture books, television, and touchscreens. *Child Development Perspectives, 4,* 205–210.

Barr, R., & Hayne, H. (2003). It's not what you know, it's who you know: Older siblings facilitate imitation during infancy. *International Journal of Early Years Education, 11,* 7–21.

Barr, R., Muentener, P., & Garcia, A. (2007). Age-related changes in deferred imitation from television by 6- to 18-month-olds. *Developmental Science, 10,* 910–921.

Bateson, P. (2002). The corpse of a wearisome debate. *Science, 297,* 2212–2213.

Batki, A., Baron-Cohen, S., Wheelwright, S., Connellan, J., & Ahluwalia, J. (2000). Is there an innate gaze module? Evidence from human neonates. *Infant Behavior and Development, 23,* 223–229.

Bauer, P. J. (1993). Memory for gender-consistent and gender-inconsistent event sequences by twenty-five-month-old children. *Child Development, 64*, 285–297.

Bauer, P. J. (2007). *Remembering the times of our lives: Memory in infancy and beyond.* Mahwah, NJ: Erlbaum.

Baumeister, R. F., & Leary, M. R. (1995). The need to belong: Desire for interpersonal attachments as a fundamental human motivation. Psychological Bulletin, 117, 497–529.

Baumrind, D. (1993). The average expectable environment is not good enough: A response to Scarr. *Child Development, 64*, 1299–1317.

Beach, S. R. H., Lei, M-K., Brody, G. H., Kim, S., Barton, A. W., Dogan, M. V., et al. (2016). Parenting, socioeconomic status risk, and later young adult health: Exploration of opposing indirect effects via DNA methylation. *Child Development, 87*, 111–121.

Beckett, C., Castle, J., Rutter, M., & Sonuga-Barke, E. J. (2010). Institutional deprivation, specific cognitive functions, and scholastic achievement: English and Romanian adoptees (ERA) study findings. In M. Rutter, E. J. Sonuga-Barke, C. Beckett, J. Castle, J. Kreppner, R. Kumsta, et al. (Eds.), Deprivation-specific psychological patterns: Effects of institutional deprivation (pp. 125–142). In *Monographs of the Society for Research in Child Development, 75*(1, Serial No. 295).

Beckett, C., Maughan, B., Rutter, M., Castle, J., Colvert, E., Groothues, C., et al. (2006). Do the effects of early severe deprivation on cognition persist into early adolescence? Findings from the English and Romanian Adoptee Study. *Child Development, 77*, 696–711.

Belsky, J. (2000). Conditional and alternative reproductive strategies: Individual differences in susceptibility to rearing experiences. In J. L. Rodgers, D. C. Rowe, & W. B. Miller (Eds.), *Genetic influences on human fertility and sexuality* (pp. 127–146). New York, NY: Springer.

Belsky, J. (2005). Differential susceptibility to rearing influence. In B. J. Ellis & D. F. Bjorklund, (Eds.), *Origins of the social mind: Evolutionary psychology and child development* (pp. 139–163). New York, NY: Guilford.

Belsky, J. (2019). Early-life adversity accelerates child and adolescent development. *Current Directions in Psychological Science, 28*, 241–246.

Belsky, J., Steinberg, L., & Draper, P. (1991). Childhood experience, interpersonal development, and reproductive strategy: An evolutionary theory of socialization. *Child Development, 62*, 647–670.

Belsky, J., Steinberg, L. D., Houts, R. M., Friedman, S. L., DeHart, G., Cauffman, E., et al. (2007). Family rearing antecedents of pubertal timing. *Child Development, 78*, 1302–1321.

Bender, C. E., Herzing, D. L., & Bjorklund, D. F. (2009). Evidence of teaching in Atlantic Spotted Dolphins (*Stenella frontalis*) by mother dolphins foraging in the presence of their calves. *Animal Cognition, 12*, 43–53.

Benenson, J. F., Pascoe, J., & Radmore, N. (2007). Children's altruistic behavior in the dictator game. *Evolution and Human Behavior, 28*, 168–173.

Bering, J. M. (2006). The folk psychology of souls. *Behavioral and Brain Sciences, 29*(5), 2–26.

Bering, J. M., Bjorklund, D. F., & Ragan, P. (2000). Deferred imitation of object-related actions in human-reared juvenile chimpanzees and orangutans. *Developmental Psychobiology, 36*, 218–232.

Berk, L. E. (1986). Relationship of elementary school children's private speech to behavioral accompaniment to task, attention, and task performance. *Developmental Psychology, 22*, 671–680.

Berk, L. E. (1992). Children's private speech: An overview of theory and the status of research. In R. M. Diaz & L. E. Berk (Eds.), *Private speech: From social interaction to self-regulation* (pp. 17–53). Hillsdale, NJ: Erlbaum.

Berk, L. E., & Landau, S. (1993). Private speech of learning disabled and normally achieving children in classroom academic and laboratory contexts. *Child Development, 64*, 556–571.

Berk, L. E., Mann, T., & Ogan, A. (2006). Make-believe play: Wellspring for development of self-regulation. In D. G. Singer, R. M. Golinkoff, & K. Hirsh-Pasek (Eds.), *Play = learning: How play motivates and enhances children's cognitive and social-emotional growth* (pp. 74–100). New York, NY: Oxford University Press.

Berk, L. E., & Meyers, A. B. (2013). The role of make-believe and the development of executive functions: Status of research and future directions. *American Journal of Play, 6*, 98–110.

Bertenthal, B. I. (1996). Origins and early development of perception, action, and representation. *Annual Review of Psychology, 47*, 431–435.

Bertenthal, B. I., Proffitt, D. R., & Cutting, J. E. (1984). Infant sensitivity to figural coherence in biomechanical motions. *Journal of Experimental Child Psychology, 37*, 213–230.

Bertenthal, B. I., Proffitt, D. R., & Kramer, S. J. (1987). Perception of biomechanical motions by infants: Implementation of various processing constraints. *Journal of Experimental Psychology: Human Perception & Performance, 13*, 577–585.

Biben, M. (1989). Individual- and sex-related strategies in wrestling play in captive squirrel monkeys. *Ethology, 71*, 229–241.

Bick, J., Zeanah, C. H., Fox, N. A., & Nelson, C. A. (2018). Memory and executive functioning in 12-year-old children with a history of institutional rearing. *Child Development, 89*, 495–508.

Bickerton, D. (1981). *Roots of language*. Ann Arbor, MI: Karoma.

Bickerton, D. (1990). *Language and species*. Chicago, IL: University of Chicago Press.

Bickerton, D. (2014). *More than nature needs: Language, mind, and evolution*. Cambridge, MA: Harvard University Press.

Bjorklund, D. F. (1987). A note on neonatal imitation. *Developmental Review, 7*, 86–92.

Bjorklund, D. F. (1989). *Children's thinking: Developmental function and individual differences* (1st edition). Pacific Grove, CA: Brooks/Cole.

Bjorklund, D. F. (1997a). In search of a metatheory for cognitive development (or, Piaget is dead and I don't feel so good myself). *Child Development, 68*, 144–148.

Bjorklund, D. F. (1997b). The role of immaturity in human development. *Psychological Bulletin, 122*, 153–169.

Bjorklund, D. F. (2006). Mother knows best: Epigenetic inheritance, maternal effects, and the evolution of human intelligence. *Developmental Review, 26*, 213–242.

Bjorklund, D. F. (2007a). *Why youth is not wasted on the young*. Malden, MA: Wiley.

Bjorklund, D. F. (2007b). The most educable of species. In J. S. Carlson & J. R. Levin (Eds.), *Psychological perspectives on contemporary educational issues* (pp. 119–129). Greenwich, CT: Information Age Publishing.

Bjorklund, D. F. (2012). *Children's thinking: Cognitive development and individual differences* (5th edition). Belmont, CA: Wadsworth.

Bjorklund, D. F. (2013). Cognitive development: An overview. In P. D. Zelazo (Ed.), *Oxford handbook of developmental psychology* (Vol. 1, pp. 447–476). Oxford, UK: Oxford University Press.

Bjorklund, D. F. (2015). Developing adaptations. *Developmental Review, 38*, 13–35.

Bjorklund, D. F. (2016). Prepared is not preformed: Comment on Witherington and Lickliter. *Human Development, 59,* 235–241.

Bjorklund, D. F. (2018a) A metatheory for cognitive development (or "Piaget is dead" revisited). *Child Development, 89,* 2288–2302.

Bjorklund, D. F. (2018b). How children invented humanity. *Child Development, 89,* 1462–1466.

Bjorklund, D. F., & Beers, C. (2016). The adaptive value of cognitive immaturity: Applications of evolutionary developmental psychology to early education. In D. C. Geary & D. B. Berch (Eds.), *Evolutionary perspectives on education and child development* (pp. 3–32). New York, NY: Springer.

Bjorklund, D. F., & Bering, J. M. (2002). The evolved child: Applying evolutionary developmental psychology to modern schooling. *Learning and Individual Differences, 12,* 1–27.

Bjorklund, D. F., & Bering, J. M. (2003). Big brains, slow development, and social complexity: The developmental and evolutionary origins of social cognition. In M. Brüne, H. Ribbert, & W. Schiefenhövel (Eds.), *The social brain: Evolutionary aspects of development and pathology* (pp. 133–151). New York, NY: Wiley.

Bjorklund, D. F., & Causey, K. (2018). *Children's thinking: Cognitive development and individual differences* (6th edition). Los Angeles, CA: Sage.

Bjorklund, D. F., Cormier, C., & Rosenberg, J. S. (2005). The evolution of theory of mind: Big brains, social complexity, and inhibition. In W. Schneider, R. Schumann-Hengsteler, & B. Sodian (Eds.), *Young children's cognitive development: Interrelationships among executive functioning, working memory, verbal ability and theory of mind* (pp. 147–174). Mahwah, NJ: Erlbaum.

Bjorklund, D. F., & Ellis, B. J. (2014). Children, childhood, and development in evolutionary perspective. *Developmental Review, 34,* 225–264.

Bjorklund, D. F., Ellis, B. J., & Rosenberg, J. S. (2007). Evolved probabilistic cognitive mechanisms: An evolutionary approach to gene × environment × development. In R. V. Kail (Ed.), *Advances in child development and behavior* (Vol. 35, pp. 1–39). Oxford, UK: Elsevier.

Bjorklund, D. F., & Gardiner, A. K. (2011). Object play and tool use: Developmental and evolutionary perspectives. In A. D. Pellegrini (Ed.), *Oxford handbook of play* (pp. 153–171). Oxford, UK: Oxford University Press.

Bjorklund, D. F., Gaultney, J. F., & Green, B. L. (1993). "I watch, therefore I can do": The development of meta-imitation over the preschool years and the advantage of optimism in one's imitative skills. In R. Pasnak & M. L. Howe (Eds.), *Emerging themes in cognitive development* (Vol. 1, pp. 79–102). New York, NY: Springer-Verlag.

Bjorklund, D. F., & Green, B. L. (1992). The adaptive nature of cognitive immaturity. *American Psychologist, 47,* 46–54.

Bjorklund, D. F., & Harnishfeger, K. K. (1995). The role of inhibition mechanisms in the evolution of human cognition and behavior. In F. N. Dempster & C. J. Brainerd (Eds.), *New perspectives on interference and inhibition in cognition* (pp. 141–173). New York, NY: Academic Press.

Bjorklund, D. F., & Hernández Blasi, C. (2012). *Child and adolescent development: An integrative approach*. Belmont, CA: Wadsworth.

Bjorklund, D. F., Hernández Blasi, C., & Ellis, B. J. (2016). Evolutionary developmental psychology. In D. M. Buss (Ed.), *Evolutionary psychology handbook* (2nd edition, Vol. 2, pp. 904–925). New York, NY: Wiley.

Bjorklund, D. F., Hernández Blasi, C., & Periss, V. (2010). Lorenz revisited: The adaptive nature of children's supernatural thinking. *Human Nature, 21*, 371–392.
Bjorklund, D. F., & Kipp, K. (1996). Parental investment theory and gender differences in the evolution of inhibition mechanisms. *Psychological Bulletin, 120*, 163–188.
Bjorklund, D. F., & Pellegrini, A. D. (2002). *The origins of human nature: Evolutionary developmental psychology*. Washington, DC: American Psychological Association.
Bjorklund, D. F., Periss, V., & Causey, K. (2009). The benefits of youth. *European Journal of Developmental Psychology, 6*, 120–137.
Bjorklund, D. F., & Rosenberg, J. S. (2005). The role of developmental plasticity in the evolution of human cognition: Evidence from enculturated, juvenile great apes. In B. J. Ellis & D. F. Bjorklund (Eds.), *Origins of the social mind: Evolutionary psychology and child development* (pp. 45–75). New York, NY: Guilford.
Bjorklund, D. F., & Schwartz, R. (1996). The adaptive nature of developmental immaturity: Implications for language acquisition and language disabilities. In M. Smith & J. Damico (Eds.), *Childhood language disorders* (pp. 17–40). New York, NY: Thieme Medical.
Bjorklund, D. F., & Sellers, P. D. II. (2014). Memory development in evolutionary perspective. In P. Bauer & R. Fivush (Eds.), *Wiley-Blackwell-handbook on the development of children's memory* (pp. 126–150). New York, NY: Wiley-Blackwell.
Bjorklund, D. F., Yunger, J. L., Bering, J. M., & Ragan, P. (2002). The generalization of deferred imitation in enculturated chimpanzees (*Pan troglodytes*). *Animal Cognition, 5*, 49–58.
Black, J. E., Jones, T. A., Nelson, C. A., & Greenough, W. T. (1998). Neuronal plasticity and the developing brain. In N. E. Alessi, J. T. Coyle, S. I. Harrison, & S. Eth (Eds.), *Handbook of child and adolescent psychiatry. Vol. 6: Basic psychiatric science and treatment* (pp. 31–53). New York, NY: Wiley.
Black, M. P., & Grober, M. S. (2003). Group sex, sex change, and parasitic males: Sexual strategies among the fishes and their neurobiological correlates. *Annual Review of Sex Research, 14*, 160–184.
Blair, C., & Diamond, A. (2008). Biological processes in prevention and intervention: The promotion of self-regulation as a means of preventing school failure. *Development and Psychopathology, 20*, 899–911.
Blake, P. R., & Rand, D. G. (2010). Currency value moderates equity preference among young children. *Evolution and Human Behavior, 31*, 210–218.
Blakemore, C., & Jennett, S. (2003) *The Oxford companion to the body*. Oxford, UK: Oxford University Press.
Blakemore, S-J. (2018). Avoiding social risk in adolescence. *Current Directions in Psychological Science, 27*, 116–122.
Blank, M., & White, S. (1999). Activating the zone of proximal development in school: Obstacles and solutions. In P. Lloyd and C. Fernyhough (Eds.), *Lev Vygotsky: Critical Assessments. Vol. 3: The zone of proximal development* (pp. 331–350). London: Routledge.
Blankenstein, N. E., Telzer, E. H., Do, K. T., van Duijvenvoorde, A. C. K., & Crone, E. A. (2019). Behavioral and neural pathways supporting the development of prosocial and risk-taking behavior across adolescence. *Child Development*. [Early view. Online version of record before inclusion in an issue. August 27, 2019.] doi: 10.1111/cdev.13292
Bloom, P., & Markson, L. (1998). Capacities underlying word learning. *Trends in Cognitive Science, 2*, 67–73.

Blum, D. (2002). *Love at Goon Park: Harry Harlow and the science of affection*. New York, NY: Basic Books.
Boesch, C. (1991). Teaching among wild chimpanzees. *Animal Behavior, 41*, 530–532.
Bogin, B. (1999). *Patterns of human growth* (2nd edition). Cambridge, UK: Cambridge University Press.
Bogin, B. (2001). *The growth of humanity*. New York, NY: Wiley-Liss.
Bogin, B. (2003). The human pattern of growth and development in paleontological perspective. In J. L. Thompson, G. E. Krovitz, & A. J. Nelson (Eds.), *Patterns of growth and development in the genus Homo* (pp. 15–44). Cambridge, UK: Cambridge University Press.
Bogin, B. (2006). Modern human life history: The evolution of human childhood and fertility. In K. Hawkes & R. R. Paine (Eds.), *The evolution of human life history* (pp. 197–230). Oxford, UK: Curry.
Bohn, M., Kachel, G., & Tomasello, M. (2019). Young children spontaneously recreate core properties of language in a new modality. *PNAS, 116*, 26072–26077.
Bolk, L. (1926). On the problem of anthropogenesis. *Proceedings of the Section of Sciences Koninklijke gevestigd te Akademie van Wetenschappen Amsterdam, 29*, 465–475.
Bonawitz, E., Shafto, P., Gweon, H., Goodman, N. D., Spelke, E., & Schulz, L. (2011). The double-edged sword of pedagogy: Instruction limits spontaneous exploration and discovery. *Cognition, 120*, 322–330.
Bonenfant, J. L. (2011). History of Haitian-Creole: From pidgin to Lingua Franca and English influence on the language. *Review of Higher Education and Self Learning, 3*(11), 27–34.
Borgi, M., Cogliati-Dezza, I., Brelsford, V., Meints, K., & Cirulli, F. (2014). Baby schema in human and animal faces induces cuteness perception and gaze allocation in children. *Frontiers in Psychology, 5*, 411.
Borke, H. (1975). Piaget's mountains revisited: Changes in the egocentric landscape. *Developmental Psychology, 11*, 240–243.
Bosmans, G., Young, J. F., & Hankin, B. L. (2018). *NR3C1* methylation as a moderator of the effects of maternal support and stress on insecure attachment development. *Developmental Psychology, 54*, 29–38.
Boulton, M. J., & Smith, P. K. (1990). Affective bias in children's perceptions of dominance relations. *Child Development, 61*, 221–229.
Bouza, J., Camacho-Thompson, D. E., Carlo, G., Franco, X., Garcia Coll, C., Halgunseth, L. C., et al. (2018). The science is clear: Separating families has long-term damaging psychological and health consequences for children, families, and communities. Society for Research in Child Development: Statement of evidence. Retrieved June 21, 2018. https://www.srcd.org/policy-media/statements-evidence/separating-families?utm_source=June+2018+Member+List&utm_campaign=eb9540be79-EMAIL_CAMPAIGN_2018_06_16_06_32_COPY_01&utm_medium=email&utm_term=0_b7bfa993bb-eb9540be79-293898645
Bowlby, J. (1969). *Attachment and loss. Vol. 1: Attachment*. London, UK: Hogarth.
Bowlby, J. (1980). *Attachment and loss. Vol. 3: Loss: Sadness and depression*. London, UK: Hogarth Press and Institute of Psycho-Analysis.
Bowler, D. E., Buyung-Ali, L. M., Knight, T. M., & Pullin, A. S. (2010). A systematic review of evidence for the added benefits to health of exposure to natural environments. *BMC Public Health, 10*, 456. [Published online August 4, 2010.]

Boyce, W. T. (2019). *The orchid and the dandelion: Why some children struggle and how all can thrive*. New York, NY: Knopf.

Boyce, W. T., & Ellis, B. J. (2005). Biological sensitivity to context: I. An evolutionary-developmental theory of the origins and functions of stress reactivity. *Development and Psychopathology, 17*, 271–301.

Brainerd, C. J. (1978). *Piaget's theory of intelligence*. Englewood Cliffs, NJ: Prentice Hall.

Brainerd, C. J., & Reyna, V. F. (2005). *The science of false memory*. Oxford, UK: Oxford University Press.

Brakefield, P. M., Gates, J., Keys, D., Kesbeke, F., Wijngaarden, P. J., Montelro, A., et al. (1996). Development, plasticity and evolution of butterfly eyespot patterns. *Nature, 384*, 236–242.

Breier, B. H., Vickers, M. H., Ikenasio, B. A., Chan, K. Y., & Wong, W. P. S. (2001). Fetal programming of appetite and obesity. *Molecular and Cellular Endocrinology, 185*, 73–79.

Briggs, J. L. (1970). *Never in anger*. Cambridge, MA: Harvard University Press.

Brooks, D. (2019). *The second mountain: The quest for a moral life*. New York, NY: Random House.

Brooks, R. B. (2011). Child soldiers in the Civil War. Civil War Saga. Retrieved June 17, 2019. http://civilwarsaga.com/child-soldiers-in-the-civil-war/

Brooks, R., & Meltzoff, A. N. (2002). The importance of eyes: How infants interpret adult looking behavior. *Developmental Psychology, 38*, 958–966.

Brookes, S. (1991). Life on Rio's mean streets. *Insight, 5*(August 5), 12–19.

Brosch, T., Sander, D., & Scherer, K. R. (2007). That baby caught my eye... attention capture by infant faces. *Emotion, 7*, 685–689.

Brosnan, S. F., & de Waal, F. B. M. (2003). Monkeys reject unequal pay. *Nature, 425*, 297–299.

Brosnan, S. F., & De Waal, F. B. M. (2014). Evolution of responses to (un)fairness. *Science, 346*, 314–318.

Brownell, C. A., and The Early Social Development Research Lab. (2016). Prosocial behavior in infancy: The role of socialization. *Child Development Perspectives, 10*, 222–227.

Brownell, C. A., Svetlova, M., & Ni, S. (2009). To share or not to share: When do toddlers respond to another's needs? *Infancy, 14*, 117–130.

Bruck, M., Ceci, S. J., & Principe, G. F. (2006). The child and the law. In K. A. Renninger & I. E. Sigel (Vol. Eds.), *Vol. 4: Child psychology in practice* (pp. 776–816), in W. Damon & R. M. Lerner (Gen. Eds.), *Handbook of child psychology* (6th edition). New York, NY: Wiley.

Bruner, J. S. (1983). *Child's talk: Learning to use language*. New York, NY: Norton.

Bufill, E., Agustí, J., & Blesa, R. (2011). Human neoteny revisited: The case of synaptic plasticity. *American Journal of Human Biology, 23*, 729–739.

Bukowski, W. M., Rubin, K. H., & Laursen, B. (Eds.). (2018). *Handbook of peer interactions, relationships, and groups*. New York, NY: Guilford.

Bull, J. J. (1980). Sex determination in reptiles. *Quarterly Review of Biology, 55*, 3–21.

Burns, M. P., & Sommerville, J. A. (2014). "I pick you": The impact of fairness and race on infants' selection of social partners. *Frontiers in Psychology, 5*, 93.

Buss, D. M. (1989). Sex differences in human mate preferences: Evolutionary hypotheses testing in 37 cultures. *Behavioral and Brain Sciences, 12*, 1–49.

Buss, D. M. (2005). *The murderer next door: Why the mind is designed to kill*. New York, NY: The Penguin Press.

Buss, D. M. (2011). *The dangerous passion: Why jealousy is as necessary as love and sex* (2nd edition) New York, NY: The Free Press.

Buss, D. M., Haselton, M. G., Shackelford, T. K., Bleske, A. L., & Wakefield, J. C. (1998). Adaptations, exaptations, and spandrels. *American Psychologist, 53,* 533–548.

Buttelmann, D., Buttelmann, F., Carpenter, M., Call, J., & Tomasello, M. (2017). Great apes distinguish true from false beliefs in an interactive helping task. *PLoS One, 12,* e0173793. doi: 101371/journal.pone.0173793

Buttelmann, D., Carpenter, M., Call, J., & Tomasello, M. (2008). Rational tool use and tool choice in human infants and great apes. *Child Development, 79,* 609–626.

Buttelmann, D., Zmyj, N., Daum, M. M., & Carpenter, M. (2013). Selective imitation of in-group over out-group members in 14-month-olds. *Child Development, 84,* 422–428.

Byrne, R. W. (2005). Social cognition: Imitation, imitation, imitation. *Current Biology, 15,* R489–R500.

Byrne, R., & Whiten, A. (Eds.). (1988). *Machiavellian intelligence: Social expertise and the evolution of intellect in monkeys, apes, and humans.* Oxford, UK: Clarendon.

Call, J., & Tomasello, M. (1996). The effects of humans on the cognitive development of apes. In A. E. Russon, K. A. Bard, & S. T. Parker (Eds.), *Reaching into thought: The minds of the great apes* (pp. 371–403). New York, NY: Cambridge University Press.

Callaghan, T. C., Moll, H., Rakoczy, H., Warneken, F. L. U., Behne, T., & Tomasello, M. (2011). Early social cognition in three cultural contexts. *Monographs of the Society of Research in Child Development, 76*(2, Serial No. 299).

Campbell, A. (1999). Staying alive: Evolution, culture, and women's intrasexual aggression. *Behavioral and Brain Sciences, 22,* 203–252.

Campbell, A. (2013). The evolutionary psychology of women's aggression. *Philosophical Transaction of the Royal Society B, 368*(1631).

Cao-Lei, L., Massart, R., Suderman, M. J., Machnes, Z., Elgbeli, G., Laplante, D. P., et al. (2014). DNA methylation signatures triggered by prenatal maternal stress exposure to a natural disaster: Project Ice Storm. *PLoS One, 9*(9), e107653. doi: 101371/journal.pone.0107653

Cárdenas, R. A., Harris, L. J., & Becker, M. W. (2013). Sex differences in visual attention toward infant faces. *Evolution and Human Behavior, 34,* 280–287.

Carlson, S. M., Koenig, M. A., & Harms, M. B. (2013). Theory of mind. *WIREs Cognitive Science, 4,* 391–402.

Carlson, S. M., & White, R. E. (2013). Executive function, pretend play, and imagination. In M. Taylor (Ed.), *The Oxford handbook of the development of imagination* (pp. 161–174). New York, NY: Oxford University Press.

Carlson, S. M., White, R. E., & Davis-Unger, A. C. (2014). Evidence for a relationship between executive function and pretense representation in preschool children. *Cognitive Development 29*(January–March), 1–16.

Carpenter, M., Akhtar, N., & Tomasello, M. (1998). 14- through 18-month-old infants differentially imitate intentional and accidental actions. *Infant Behavior & Development, 21,* 315–330.

Carpenter, M., Nagell, K., & Tomasello, M. (1998). Social cognition, joint attention, and communicative competence from 9 to 15 months of age. *Monographs of the Society for Research in Child Development, 63*(4, Serial No. 255), i–vi, 1–143.

Carpenter, M., Tomasello, M., & Striano, T. (1995). Joint attention and imitative learning in children, chimpanzees, and enculturated chimpanzees. *Social Development, 4,* 217–237.

Carroll, S. B. (2003). Genetics and the making of *Homo sapiens*. *Nature, 422*, 849–857.
Carroll, S. B. (2005). *Endless forms most beautiful: The new science of Evo Devo*. New York, NY: Norton.
Carstensen, L. L., & Mikels, J. A. (2005). At the intersection of emotion and cognition: Aging and the positivity effect. *Current Directions in Psychological Science, 14*, 117–121.
Casler, K., & Kelemen, D. (2005). Young children's rapid learning about artifacts. *Developmental Science, 8*, 472–480.
Casler, K., and Kelemen, D. (2008). Developmental continuity in teleo-functional explanation: Reasoning about nature among Romanian Romani adults. *Journal of Cognition and Development, 9*, 340–362.
Caspi, A., McClay, J., Moffitt, T. E., Mill, J., Martin, J., Craig, I. W., et al. (2002). Role of genotype in the cycle of violence in maltreated children. *Science, 297*, 851–854.
Caspi, A., Williams, B., Kim-Cohen, J., Craig, I. W., Milne, B. J., Poulton, R., et al. (2007). Moderation of breastfeeding effects on the IQ by genetic variation in fatty acid metabolism. *Proceeding of the National Academy of Sciences of the United States of America, 104*, 18860–18865.
Ceci, S. J., & Bruck, M. (1993). Suggestibility of the child witness: A historical review and synthesis. *Psychological Bulletin, 113*, 403–439.
Cemore, J. J., & Herwig, J. E. (2005). Delay of gratification and make-believe play of preschoolers. *Journal of Research in Early Childhood Education, 19*, 251–266.
Chance, M. R. A. (1962). Social behaviour and primate evolution. In M. F. A. Montagu (Ed.), *Culture and the evolution of man* (pp. 84–130). New York, NY: Oxford University Press.
Chang, L., & Jing Lu, H. (2018). Resource and extrinsic risk in defining fast life histories of rural Chinese left-behind children. *Evolution and Human Behavior, 39*, 59–66.
Chang, L., Jing Lu, H., Lansford, J. E., Skinner, A. T., Bornstein, M. H., Steinberg, L., Dodge, K., et al. (2019). Environmental harshness and unpredictability, life history, and social and academic behavior of adolescents in nine countries. *Developmental Psychology, 55*, 890–903.
Charles, C., & Louv, R. (September, 2009). Children's nature deficit: What we know—and don't know. Children and Nature Network. Retrieved September 4, 2019. https://www.childrenandnature.org/wp-content/uploads/2015/04/CNNEvidenceoftheDeficit.pdf
Charrier, C., Joshi, K., Coutinho-Budd, J., Kim, J-E., Lambert, N., Jacqueline de Marchena, J., et al. (2012). Inhibition of SRGAP2 function by its human-specific paralogs induces neoteny during spine maturation. *Cell, 149*, 923–935.
Chen, L-H., Baker, S. P., Braver, E. R., & Li, G. (2000). Carrying passengers as a risk factor for crashes fatal to 16- and 17-year-old drivers. *Journal of the American Medical Association, 283*, 1578–1582.
Chiao, J. Y., & Blizinsky, K. D. (2010). Culture-gene coevolution of individualism-collectivism and the serotonin transporter gene. *Proceedings of the Royal Society B, 277*, 529–537.
Chimpanzee Sequencing and Analysis Consortium. (2005). Initial sequence of the chimpanzee genome and comparison with the human genome. *Nature, 437*, 69–87.
Chomsky, N. (1957). *Syntactic structures*. The Hague, the Netherlands: Mouton.
Chudek, M., Baron, A. S., & Birch, S. (2016). Unselective overimitators: The evolutionary implications of children's indiscriminate copying of successful and prestigious models. *Child Development, 87*, 782–794.

Clark, E. A., & Hanisee, J. (1982). Intellectual and adaptive performance of Asian children in adoptive American settings. *Developmental Psychology, 18*, 595–599.

Clark, R. W. (1971). *Einstein: The life and times*. New York, NY: William Morrow.

Clay, Z., & Tennie, C. (2018). Is overimitation a uniquely human phenomenon? Insight from human children as compared to bonobos. *Child Development, 89*, 1535–1544.

Clements, W. A., & Perner, J. (1994). Implicit understanding of belief. *Cognitive Development, 9*, 377–395.

Clutton-Brock, T. H. 1991. *The evolution of parental care*. Princeton, NJ: Princeton University Press.

The Common Sense Census. (2017). Media use by kids zero to eight. Retrieved September 13, 2019. https://philanthropynewsdigest.org/connections/the-common-sense-census-media-use-by-kids-age-zero-to-eight

Conradt, E. (2017). Using principles of behavioral epigenetics to advance research on early-life stress. *Child Development Perspective, 11*, 107–112.

Conradt, E., Hawes, K., Guerin, D., Armstrong, D. A., Marsit, C. J., Tronick, E., & Lester, B. M. (2016). The contributions of maternal sensitivity and maternal depressive symptoms to epigenetic processes and neuroendocrine functioning. *Child Development, 87*, 73–85.

Cooper, R. P., & Aslin, R. N. (1990). Preference for infant-directed speech in the first month after birth. *Child Development, 61*, 1584–1595.

Cooper, R. P., & Aslin, R. N. (1994). Developmental differences in infant attention to the spectral properties of infant-directed speech. *Child Development, 65*, 1663–1677.

Corriveau, K. H., DiYanni, C. J., Clegg, J. M., Min, G., Chin, J., & Nasrini, J. (2017). Cultural differences in the imitation and transmission of inefficient actions. *Journal of Experimental Child Psychology, 161*, 1–18.

Courage, M. L., & Setliff, A. E. (2010). When babies watch television: Attention-getting, attention holding, and the implications for learning from video material. *Developmental Review, 30*, 220–238.

Coyne, S. M., Padilla-Walker, L. M., & Holmgren, H. G. (2018). A six-year longitudinal study of texting trajectories during adolescence. *Child Development, 89*, 58–65.

Cristakis, E. (2016, October 28). My Halloween email led to a campus firestorm—and a troubling lesson about self-censorship. *The Washington Post*. Retrieved August 16, 2019. https://www.washingtonpost.com/opinions/my-halloween-email-led-to-a-campus-firestorm--and-a-troubling-lesson-about-self-censorship/2016/10/28/70e55732-9b97-11e6-a0ed-ab0774c1eaa5_story.html

Crook, J. M. (1980). *The evolution of human consciousness*. Oxford, UK: Clarendon Press.

Crystal, D. (2010). *The Cambridge encyclopedia of language* (3rd edition). Cambridge, UK: Cambridge University Press.

Csibra, G., & Gergely, G. (2011). Natural pedagogy as evolutionary adaptation. *Philosophical Transactions of the Royal Society of London, Biological Sciences, 366*, 1149–1157.

Cummins-Sebree, S. W., & Fragaszy, D. M. (2005). Choosing and using tools: Capuchins *(Cebus apella)* use a different metric than tamarins *(Saguinus oedipus)*. *Journal of Comparative Psychology, 119*, 210–219.

Curry, O. S., Mullins, D. A., & Whitehouse, H. (2019). Is it good to cooperate? Testing the theory of morality-as-cooperation in 60 societies. *Current Anthropology, 60*, 47–69.

Curtiss, S. (1977). *Genie: A psycholinguistic study of a modern day "wild child."* New York, NY: Academic Press.

Dahl, A., & Brownell, C. A. (2019). The social origins of human prosociality. *Current Directions in Psychological Science, 28*, 274–279.

Dahl, A., & Paulus, M. (2019). From interest to obligation: The gradual development of human altruism. *Child Development Perspective, 13*, 10–14.

Dahl, A., Satlof-Bedrick, E. S., Hammond, S. I., Drummond, J. K., Waugh, W. E., & Brownell, C. A. (2016). Explicit scaffolding increases simple helping in younger infants. *Developmental Psychology, 53*, 407–416.

Daly, M. (2018). Social media use may explain little of the recent rise in depressive symptoms among adolescent girls. *Clinical Psychological Science, 6*, 295.

Daly, M., & Wilson, M. (1988). *Homicide*. New York, NY: Aldine.

Damon, W. (1994). *Moral child: Nurturing children's natural moral growth*. New York, NY: Simon & Schuster.

Darwin, C. (1859). *On the origin of species*. New York, NY: Modern Library.

Darwin, C. (1871). *The descent of man, and selection in relation to sex*. New York, NY: D. Appleton and Company.

Dawkins, R. (1976). *The selfish gene*. New York, NY: Oxford University Press.

Deacon, T. (1997). *The symbolic species: The co-evolution of language and the brain*. New York, NY: W.W. Norton & Company.

de Beer, G. (1958). *Embryos and ancestors* (3rd edition). Oxford, UK: Clarendon Press.

Del Giudice, M. (2009). Sex, attachment, and the development of reproductive strategies. *Behavioral and Brain Sciences, 32*, 1–21.

Del Giudice, M. (2014). Middle childhood: An evolutionary-developmental synthesis. *Child Development Perspectives, 8*, 193–200.

Del Giudice, M., Angeleri, R., & Manera, V. (2009). The juvenile transition: A developmental switch point in human life history. *Developmental Review, 29*, 1–31.

Del Giudice, M., & Ellis, E. J. (2016). Evolutionary foundations of developmental psychopathology. In D. Cicchetti (Ed.), *Developmental psychopathology. Vol. 2: Developmental neuroscience* (3rd edition, pp. 1–58). New York, NY: Wiley.

Del Giudice, M., Gangestad, S. W., & Kaplan, H. S. (2016). Life history theory and evolutionary psychology. In D. Buss (Ed.), *Evolutionary psychology handbook* (Vol. 2, pp. 88–114). New York, NY: Wiley.

de Klerk, C. C., Bulgarelli, C., & Hamilton, A., & Southgate, V. (2019). Selective facial mimicry of native over foreign speakers in preverbal infants. *Journal of Experimental Child Psychology, 183*, 33–47.

DeLoache, J. S. (2010). Early development of the understanding and use of symbolic artifacts. In U. Goswami (Ed.), *The Wiley-Blackwell handbook of childhood cognitive development* (2nd edition, pp. 312–336). West Sussex, UK: Blackwell.

DeLoache, J. S., Chiong, C., Sherman, K., Islam, N., Vanderborght, M., Troseth, G. L., et al. (2010). Do babies learn from baby media? *Psychological Science, 21*, 1570–1574.

DeLoache, J. S., & LoBue, V. (2009). The narrow fellow in the grass: Human infants associate snakes and fear. *Developmental Science, 12*, 201–207.

DeLoache, J. S., & Marzolf, D. P. (1992). When a picture is not worth a thousand words: Young children's understanding of pictures and models. *Cognitive Development, 7*, 317–329.

DeLoache, J. S., Miller, K. F., & Pierroutsakos, S. L. (1998). Reasoning and problem solving. In D. Kuhn & R. S. Siegler (Vol. Eds.), *Vol. 2: Cognitive, language, and perceptual developmentt* (pp. 947–978), in W. Damon (Gen. Ed.), *Handbook of child psychology* (5th edition). New York, NY: Wiley.

Denenberg, V. H., & Rosenberg, K. M. (1967). Non-genetic transmission of information. *Nature, 216*, 549–550.

Dennett, D. (1987). *The intentional stance.* Cambridge, MA: The MIT Press.

Dennett, D. (1990). The interpretation of texts, people, and other artifacts. *Philosophy and Phenomenological Quarterly, 1*(Suppl.), 177–194.

Dennis, E. L., Jahanshad, N., McMahon, K. L., de Zubicaray, G. I., Martin, N. G., Hickie, I. B., et al. (2013). Development of brain structural connectivity between ages 12 and 30: A 4-Tesla diffusion imaging study in 439 adolescents and adults. *NeuroImage, 64*, 671–684.

Dennis, W. (1973). *Children of the Creche.* New York, NY: Appleton-Century-Crofts.

Depew, D. J. (2003). Baldwin and his many effects. In B. G. Weber & D. J. Depew (Eds.), *Evolution and learning: The Baldwin effect reconsidered* (pp. 3–31). Cambridge, MA: MIT Press.

DeSilva, J. M. (2016). Brains, birth, bipedalism, and the mosaic evolution of the helpless infant. In W. R. Trevathan & K. R. Rosenberg (Eds.), *Costly and cute: Helpless infants and human evolution* (pp. 67–86). Santa Fe, NM: School for Advanced Research Press.

de Waal, F. (1982). *Chimpanzee politics: Power and sex among apes.* Baltimore, MD: Johns Hopkins Press.

de Waal, F. B. M. (1997). *Bonobo the forgotten ape.* Los Angeles, CA: University of California Press.

de Waal, F. B. M. (2005). *Our inner ape.* New York, NY: Riverhead Books.

Dewey, J. (1964). How we think: A restatement of the relation of reflective thinking ro the education process. In R. D. Archambault (Ed.), *John Dewey on education.* (pp. 212–228). New York, NY: Modern Library. (Original work published 1933.)

Diamond, A., Barnett, W. S., Thomas, J., & Munro, S. (2007). Preschool program improves cognitive control. *Science, 318*(30 Nov), 1387–1388.

Dickson K., Richardson, M., Kwan, I., MacDonald, W., Burchett, H., Stansfield, C., Brunton, G., Sutcliffe, K., & Thomas, J. (January 1, 2019). *"Screen-based activities and children and young people's mental health: A Systematic Map of Reviews"* (PDF). EPPI-Centre, Social Science Research Unit, UCL Institute of Education, University College London, UK. Retrieved August 26, 2019.

Di Giorgio, E., Leo, I., Pascalis, O., & Simion, F. (2012). Is the face-perception system human-specific at birth? *Developmental Psychology, 48*, 1083–1090.

Di Giorgio, E., Lunghi, M., Simion, F., & Vallortigara, G. (2017). Visual cues of motion that trigger animacy perception at birth: The case of self-propulsion. *Developmental Science, 20*: e12394. doi: 10.1111/desc.12394

Dodge, K. A. (1986). A social information processing model of social competence in children. In M. Perlmutter (Ed.), *Minnesota symposium on child psychology* (Vol. 18, pp. 1–67). Hillsdale, NJ: Erlbaum.

Donald, M. (1991). *Origins of the modern mind: Three stages in the evolution of culture and cognition.* Cambridge, MA: Harvard University Press.

Dubowitz, L. M., Mushin, J., De-Vries, L., & Arden, G. B. (1986). Visual function in the newborn infant: Is it cortically mediated. *Lancet, 8490*, 1139–1141.

Dunbar, R. I. M. (1995). Neocortex size and group size in primates: A test of the hypothesis. *Journal of Human Evolution, 28*, 287–296.

Dunbar, R. (1998). *Grooming, gossip, and the evolution of language.* Cambridge, MA: Harvard University Press.

Dunbar, R. I. M. (2003). The social brain: Mind, language, and society in evolutionary perspective. *Annual Review of Anthropology, 32,* 163–181.

Dunbar, R. I. M. (2010). *How many friends does one person need? Dunbar's number and other evolutionary quirks.* London, UK: Faber & Faber.

Dunbar, R. I. M. (2014). How conversations around campfires came to be. *PNAS, 111,* 14013–14014.

Duncan, R., & Tarulli, D. (2009). On the persistence of private speech: Empirical and theoretical considerations. In A. Winsler, C. Fernyhough, & I. Montero (Eds.), *Private speech, executive functioning, and the development of verbal self-regulation* (pp. 176–187). Cambridge, UK: Cambridge University Press.

Duncker, K. (1945). On problem-solving. *Psychological Monographs, 58*(5), i–113.

Dunham, Y., Baron, A. S., & Carey, S. (2011). Consequences of "minimal" group affiliations in children. *Child Development, 82,* 793–811.

Dwyer, R., Kushlev, K., & Dunn, E. (2018). Smartphone use undermines enjoyment of face-to-face social interactions. *Journal of Experimental Social Psychology, 78,* 233–239.

Easterbrook, M. A., Kisilevsky, B. S., Hains, S. M. J., & Muir, D. W. (1999). Faceness or complexity: Evidence from newborn visual tracking of facelike stimuli. *Infant Behavior and Development, 22,* 17–35.

Elias, C. L., & Berk, L. E. (2002). Self-regulation in young children: Is there a role for executive function and pretense representation in preschool children. *Cognitive Development, 29,* 216–238.

Elkind, D. (1967). Egocentrism in adolescence. *Child Development, 38,* 1025–1033.

Elkind, D., & Bowen, R. (1979). Imaginary audience behavior in children and adolescents. *Developmental Psychology, 15,* 38–44.

Ellis, B. J., Bianchi, J., Griskevicius, V., & Frankenhuis, W. E. (2017). Beyond risk and protective factors: An adaptation-based approach to resilience. *Perspectives on Psychological Science, 12,* 561–587.

Ellis, B. J., & Boyce, W. T. (2008). Biological sensitivity to context. *Current Directions in Psychological Science, 17,* 183–187.

Ellis, B. J., Del Giudice, M., Dishion, T. J., Figueredo, A. J., Gray, P., Griskevicius, V., et al. (2012). The evolutionary basis of risky adolescent behavior: Implications for science, policy, and practice. *Developmental Psychology, 48,* 598–623.

Ellis, B. J., Essex, M. J., & Boyce, W. T. (2005). Biological sensitivity to context: II. Empirical explorations of an evolutionary-developmental theory. *Development and Psychopathology, 17,* 303–328.

Ellis, B. J., Figueredo, A. J., Brumbach, B. H., & Schlomer, G. L. (2009). Fundamental dimensions of environmental risk: The impact of harsh versus unpredictable environments on the evolution and development of life history strategies. *Human Nature, 20,* 204–268.

Ellis, B. J., Volk, A. A., Gonzalez, J-M., & Embry, D. D. (2016). The meaningful roles intervention: An evolutionary approach to reducing bullying and increasing prosocial behavior. *Journal of Research on Adolescence, 26,* 622–637.

Elman, J. (1994). Implicit learning in neural networks: The importance of starting small. In C. Umilta & M. Moscovitch (Eds.), *Attention and performance XV: Conscious and nonconscious information processing* (pp. 861–888). Cambridge, MA: MIT Press.

The ENCODE Project Consortium. (2012). An integrated encyclopedia of DNA elements in the human genome. *Nature, 489*, 57–74.

Endedijk, H., Ramenzoni, V. C. O., Cox, R. F. A., Cillessen, A. H. N., Bekkering, H., & Hunnis, S. (2015). Development of interpersonal coordination between peers during a drumming task. *Developmental Psychology, 51*, 714–721.

Engelmann, J. M., Over, H., Herrmann, E., & Tomasello, M. (2013). Young children care more about their reputation with ingroup members and potential reciprocators. *Developmental Science, 16*, 952–958.

Engelmann, J., Rapp, D., Herrmann, E., & Tomasello, M. (2018). Concern for group reputation increases prosociality in young children. *Psychological Science, 29*, 181–190.

Engemann, K., Pedersen, C. B., Arge, L., Tsirogiannis, C., Mortensen, P. B., & Svenning, J-C. (2019). Residential green space in childhood is associated with lower risk of psychiatric disorders from adolescence into adulthood. *PNAS, 116*, 5188–5193.

Esposito, G., Nakazawa, J., Ogawa, S., Stival, R., Kawashima, A., Putnick, D. L., et al. (2014). Baby, you light-up my face: Culture-general physiological responses to infants and culture-specific cognitive judgements of adults. *PLoS One, 9*(10), e106705. doi: 10371/journal/pone.0106705

Evans, N., & Levinson, S. (2009). The myth of language universals: Language diversity and its importance for cognitive science. *Behavioral and Brain Science, 32*, 429–492.

Fabes, R. A., Fultz, J., Eisenberg, N., May-Plumlee, T., & Christopher, F. S. (1989). Effects of rewards on children's prosocial motivation: A socialization study. *Developmental Psychology, 25*, 509–515.

Fagen, R. (1981). *Animal play behavior.* New York, NY: Oxford University Press.

Falk, A., Fehr, E., & Fischbacher, U. (2003). On the nature of fair behavior. *Economic Inquiry, 41*, 20–26.

Farroni, T., Csibra, G., Simion, F., & Johnson, M. H. (2002). Eye contact detection in humans from birth. *PNAS, 99*, 9602–9605.

Fergusson, D. M., Boden, J. M., Horwood, L. J., Miller, A. L., & Kennedy, M. A. (2011). MAOA, abuse exposure and antisocial behaviour: 30-year longitudinal study. *British Journal of Psychiatry, 198*, 457–463.

Fernald, A. (1992). Human maternal vocalizations to infants as biologically relevant signals: An evolutionary perspective. In J. H. Barkow, L. Cosmides, & J. Tooby (Eds.), *The adaptive mind: Evolutionary psychology and the generation of culture* (pp. 391–428). New York, NY: Oxford University Press.

Fessler, D. M. T. (2002). Reproductive immunosuppression and diet: An evolutionary perspective on pregnancy sickness and meat consumption. *Current Anthropology, 43*, 19–61.

Field, T., Guy, L., & Umbel, V. (1985). Infants' responses to mothers' imitative behaviors. *Infant Mental Health Journal, 6*, 40–44.

Finaly, B. L., & Darlington, R. D. (1995). Linked regularities in the development and evolution of mammalian brains. *Science, 268*(June 16), 1579–1584.

Finlay, B., L., Darlington, R. B., & Nicastro, N. (2001). Developmental structure in brain evolution. *Behavioral and Brain Sciences, 24*, 263–308.

Fisher, K. R., Hirsh-Pasek, K., Newcombe, N. S., Golinkoff, R. M. (2013). Taking shape: Supporting preschoolers' acquisition of geometric knowledge through guided play. *Child Development, 84*, 1972–1978.

Flavell, J. H., Everett, B. A., Croft, K., & Flavell, E. R. (1981). Young children's knowledge about visual perception: Further evidence for the Level 1–Level 2 distinction. *Developmental Psychology, 17*, 99–103.

Flavell, J. H., Green, F. L., & Flavell, E. R. (1986). Development of knowledge about the appearance-reality distinction. *Monographs of the Society for Research in Child Development*, 51(1), i–v, 1–87.

Flaxman, S. M., & Sherman, P. W. (2000). Morning sickness: A mechanism for protecting mother and embryo. *Quarterly Review of Biology*, 75, 113–147.

Flynn, E. G., Laland, K. N., Kendal, R. L., & Kendal, J. R. (2013). Developmental niche construction. *Developmental Science*, 16, 296–313.

Flynn, J. R. (2007). *What is intelligence? Beyond the Flynn Effect*. New York, NY: Cambridge University Press.

Flynn, J. R. (2012). *Are we getting smarter?: Rising IQ in the twenty-first century*. New York, NY: Cambridge University Press.

Fouts, R. (1997). *Next of kin: My conversations with chimpanzees*. New York, NY: William Morrow.

Fraley, R. C. (2002). Attachment stability from infancy to adulthood: Meta-analysis and dynamic modeling of developmental mechanisms. *Personality and Social Psychology Review*, 6, 123–151.

Fraley, R. C., & Brumbaugh, C. C. (2004). A dynamical systems approach to conceptualizing and studying stability and change in attachment security. In W. S. Rholes & J. A. Simpson (Eds.), *Adult attachment: Theory, research, and clinical implications* (pp. 86–132). New York, NY: Guilford.

Francis, D. D., Diori, J., Liu, D., & Meaney, M. J. (1999). Nongenomic transmission across generations in maternal behavior and stress response in the rat. *Science*, 286, 1155–1158.

Frankenhuis, W. E., de Vries, S. A., Bianchi, J. M., & Bruce J., & Ellis, B. J. (2019). Hidden talents in harsh conditions? A preregistered study of memory and reasoning about social dominance. *Developmental Science*, 23, e12835.

Frankenhuis, W. E., Panchanathan, K., & Barrett, H. C. (2013). Bridging developmental systems theory and evolutionary psychology using dynamic optimization. *Developmental Science*, 16, 584–598.

Frankenhuis, W. E., Panchanathan, K., & Nettle, D. (2016). Cognition in harsh and unpredictable environments. *Current Opinion in Psychology*, 7, 76–80.

Franklin, P., & Volk, A. A. (2018). A review of infants' and children's facial cues' influence on adults' perceptions and behaviors. *Evolutionary Behavioral Sciences*, 12, 296–321.

Franklin, P., Volk, A. A., & Wong, I. (2018). Are newborns' faces less appealing? *Evolution and Human Behavior*, 39, 269–276.

Fullard, W., & Reiling, A. M. (1976). An investigation of Lorenz's "babyness." *Child Development*, 47, 1191–1193.

Ganea, P. A., Allen, M. L., Butler, L., Carey, S., & DeLoache, J. S. (2009). Toddler's referential understanding of pictures. *Journal of Experimental Child Psychology*, 104, 283–295.

Gardiner, A., Greif, M., & Bjorklund, D. F. (2011). Guided by intention: Preschoolers' imitation reflects inferences of causation. *Journal of Cognition and Development*, 12, 355–373.

Gardner, M., & Steinberg, L. (2005). Peer influence on risk taking, risk preference, and risky decision making in adolescence and adulthood: An experimental study. *Developmental Psychology*, 41, 625–635.

Garon, N., Bryson, S. E., & Smith, I. M. (2008). Executive function in preschoolers: A review using an integrative framework. *Psychological Bulletin*, 134, 31–60.

Garstang, W. (1922). The theory of recapitulation: A critical restatement of the Biogenetic Law. *Proceedings of the Linnean Society of London: Zoology*, 35, 81–101.

Gava, L., Valenza, E., Turati, C., & de Schonen, S. (2008). Effect of partial occlusion on newborns' face preference and recognition. *Developmental Science, 11*, 563–574.

Geary, D. C. (2005). *The origin of mind: Evolution of brain, cognition, and general intelligence.* Washington, DC: American Psychological Association.

Geary, D. C. (2007). Educating the evolved mind: Conceptual foundations for an evolutionary educational psychology. In J. S. Carlson, & J. R. Levin (Eds.), *Educating the evolved mind: Conceptual foundations for an evolutionary educational psychology* (pp. 1–99). Charlotte, NC: IAP.

Geary, D. C. (2021). *Male, female: The evolution of human sex differences* (3rd edition). Washington, DC: American Psychological Association.

Geary, D. C., & Berch, D. B. (2016). Evolution and children's cognitive and academic development. In D. C. Geary & D. B. Berch (Eds.), *Evolutionary perspectives on education and child development* (pp. 217–250). New York, NY: Springer.

Gellén, K., & Buttelmann, D. (2019). Rational imitation declines within the second year of life: Changes in the function of imitation. *Journal of Experimental Child Psychology, 185*, 148–163.

Gentile, D. A., Berch, O. N., Choo, H., Khoo, A., & Walsh, D. A. (2017). Bedroom media: One risk factor for development. *Developmental Psychology, 53*, 2340–2355.

George, M. J., Russell, M. A., Piontak, J. R., & Odgers, C. L. (2018). Concurrent and subsequent associations between daily digital technology use and high-risk adolescent' mental health symptoms. *Child Development, 89*, 78–88.

Gergely, G., Bekkering, H., & Kiraly, I. (2002). Rational imitation in preverbal infants. *Nature, 41*(February 14), 755.

Gergely, G., & Csibra, G. (2005). The social construction of the cultural mind: Imitative learning as a mechanism of human pedagogy. *Interaction Studies, 6*, 463–481.

German, T., & Johnson, S. (2002). Function and the origins of the design stance. *Journal of Cognition and Development, 3*, 279–300.

Gibbons, A. (2008). The birth of childhood. *Science, 322*(November 14), 1040–1043.

Gibson, G., & Hogness, D. S. (1996). Effect of polymorphism in the *Drosophila* regulatory gene Ultrabithorax on homeotic stability. *Science, 271*, 200–203.

Giedd, J. N. (2015). Risky teen behavior is driven by an imbalance in brain development. *Scientific American, 312*(6), 33–37.

Giedd, J. N., Blumenthal, J., Jeffries, N. O., Castellanos, F. X., Liu, H., Zijdenbos, A., Paus, T., Evans, A. C, & Rapoport, J. L. (1999). Brain development during childhood and adolescence: A longitudinal MRI study. *Nature Neuroscience, 2*, 861–863.

Gilad, Y., Oshlack, A., Smyth, G. K., Speed, T. P., & White, K. P. (2006). Expression profiling in primates reveals a rapid evolution of human transcription factors. *Nature, 440*, 242–245.

Gilby, I. C. (2006). Meat sharing among the Gombe chimpanzees: Harassment and reciprocal exchange. *Animal Behaviour, 71*, 953–963.

Gilissen, R., Bakermans-Kranenburg, M. J., van IJzendoorn, M. H., & Linting, M. (2008). Electrodermal reactivity during the Trier Social Stress Test for children: Interaction between the serotonin transporter polymorphism and children's attachment representation. *Developmental Psychobiology, 50*, 615–625.

Glocker, M. L., Langleben, D. D., Ruparel, K., Loughead, J. W., Gur, R. C., & Sachser, N. (2009a). Baby schema in infant faces induces cuteness perception and motivation for caretaking in adults. *Ethology, 115*, 257–263.

Glocker, M. L., Langleben, D. D., Ruparel, K., Loughead, J. W., Valdez, J. N., Griffin, M. D., et al. (2009b). Baby schema modulates the brain reward system in nulliparous women. *PNAS, 106,* 9115–9119.

Glover, V. (2011). Prenatal stress and the origins of psychopathology: An evolutionary perspective. *Journal of Child Psychology and Psychiatry, 52,* 356–367.

Goldberg, R. F., & Thompson-Schill, S. L. (2009). Developmental "roots" in mature biological knowledge. *Psychological Science, 20,* 480–487.

Goldberg, S., Blumberg, S. L., & Kriger, A. (1982). Menarche and interest in infants: Biological and social influences. *Child Development, 53,* 1544–1550.

Golinkoff, R. M., Can, D. D., Soderstrom, M., & Hirsh-Pasek, K. (2015). (Baby) talk to me: The social context of infant-directed speech and its effects on early language acquisition. *Current Directions in Psychological Science, 24,* 339–344.

Golle, J., Lisibach, S., Mast, F. W., & Lobmaier, J. S. (2013). Sweet puppies and cute babies: Perceptual adaptation to baby facedness transfers across species. *PLoS One, 8*(3), e58248. doi: 101371/journal.pone.0058248

Gómez, J-C., & Martín-Andrade, B. (2005). Fantasy play in apes. In A. D. Pellegrini & P. K. Smith (Eds.), *The nature of play: Great apes and humans* (pp. 139–172). New York, NY: Guilford Press.

Gopnik, A. (2016). *The gardener and the carpenter: What the new science of child development tells us about the relationship between parents and children.* New York, NY: Farrar, Straus, and Giroux.

Gopnik, A., & Walker, C. M. (2013). Considering counterfactuals: The relationship between causal learning and pretend play. *Journal of Play, 6,* 15–28.

Gottlieb, G. (1971). Ontogenesis of sensory function in birds and mammals. In E. Tobach, L. R. Aronson, & E. Shaw (Eds.), *The biopsychology of development* (pp. 67–128). New York, NY: Academic Press.

Gottlieb, G. (1975). Development of species identification in ducklings: I. Nature of perceptual deficit caused by embryonic auditory deprivation. *Journal of Comparative and Physiological Psychology, 89,* 387–399.

Gottlieb, G. (1976). The roles of experience in the development of behavior and the nervous system. In G. Gottlieb (Ed.), *Neural and behavioral plasticity* (pp. 25–54). New York, NY: Academic Press.

Gottlieb, G. (1987). The developmental basis of evolutionary change. *Journal of Comparative Psychology, 101,* 262–271.

Gottlieb, G. (1992). *Individual development and evolution: The genesis of novel behavior.* New York, NY: Oxford University Press.

Gottlieb, G. (1997). *Synthesizing nature-nurture: Prenatal roots of instinctive behavior.* Mahwah, NJ: Erlbaum.

Gottlieb, G. (2002). Developmental-behavioral initiation of evolutionary change. *Psychological Review, 109,* 211–218.

Gottlieb, G. (2007). Probabilistic epigenesis. *Developmental Science, 10,* 1–11.

Gould, S. J. (1977). *Ontogeny and phylogeny.* Cambridge, MA: Harvard University Press.

Gould, S. J., & Lewontin, R. C. (1979). The spandrels of San Marco and the Panglossian Paradigm: A critique of the adaptationist programme. *Proceedings of the Royal Society of London. Series B, Biological Sciences, 205,* 581–598.

Goyal, M. S., Hawrylycz, M., Millwre, J. A., Snyder, A. Z., & Raichle, M. E. (2014). Aerobic glycolysis in the human brain is associated with development and neotenous gene expression. *Cell Metabolism, 19,* 49–57.

Gray, P. (2013). *Free to learn: Why unleashing the instinct to play will make our children happier, more self-reliant, and better students for life*. New York, NY: Basic Books.

Gray, P. (2016). Children's natural ways of educating themselves still works: Even for the three Rs. In D. C. Geary & D. B. Berch (Eds.), *Evolutionary perspectives on education and child development* (pp. 66–94). New York, NY: Springer.

Gredlein, J. M., & Bjorklund, D. F. (2005). Sex differences in young children's use of tools in a problem-solving task: The role of object-oriented play. *Human Nature, 16*, 211–232.

Green, F. P., & Schneider, F. W. (1974). Age differences in the behavior of boys on three measures of altruism. *Child Development, 45*, 248–251.

Greenberg, J. R., Hamann, K., Warneken, F., & Tomasello, M. (2010). Chimpanzee helping in collaborative and noncollaborative contexts. *Animal Behaviour, 80*, 873e880.

Greene, E. (1996). Effect of light quality and larval diet on morph induction in the polymorphic caterpillar *Nemoria arizonaria* (Lepidoptera: Geometridae). *Biological Journal of the Linnean Society, 58*, 277–285.

Greenfield, P., Maynard, A., Boehm, C., & Schmidtling, E. Y. (2000). Cultural apprenticeship and cultural change: Tool learning and imitation in chimpanzees and humans. In S. T. Parker, J. Langer, & M. L. McKinney (Eds.), *Biology, brains, and behavior: The evolution of human development* (pp. 237–277). Santa Fe, NM: School of American Research Press.

Greenough, W. T., Black, J. E., & Wallace, C. S. (1987). Experience and brain development. *Child Development, 58*, 539–559.

Greve, W., & Thomsen, T. (2016). Evolutionary advantages of free play during childhood. *Evolutionary Psychology*, October–December, 1–9.

Greve, W., Thomsen, T., & Dehio, C. (2014). Does playing pay? The fitness-effect of free play during childhood. *Evolutionary Psychology, 12*, 434–447.

Groh, A. M., Pasco Fearon, R. M., van IJzendoorn, M. H., Bakermans-Kranenburg, M. J., & Roisman, G. I. (2016). Attachment in the early life course: Meta-analytic evidence for its role in socioemotional development. *Child Development Perspective, 11*, 70–76.

Groos, K. (1898). *The play of animals*. New York, NY: Appleton.

Gross, Th. F. (1997). Children's perception of faces of varied immaturity. *Journal of Experimental Child Psychology, 66*, 42–63.

Grueneisen, S., & Tomasello, M. (2017). Children coordinate in a recurrent social dilemma by taking turns and along dominance asymmetries. *Developmental Psychology, 53*, 265–273.

Gruber, T., Deschenaux, A., Frick, A., & Clément, F. (2019). Group membership influences more social identification than social learning or overimitation in children. *Child Development, 90*, 728–745.

Gruskin, K., & Geher, G. (2018). The evolved classroom: Using evolutionary theory to inform elementary pedagogy. *Evolutionary Behavioral Sciences, 12*, 336–347.

Guo, G., Roettger, M. E., & Cai, T. (2008). The integration of genetic propensities into social-control models of delinquency and violence among male youths. *American Sociological Review, 73*, 543–556.

Gurven, M., & Kaplan, H. (2007). Longevity among hunter-gatherers: A cross-cultural examination. *Population and Development Review, 33*, 321–365.

Guthrie, S. (1993). *Faces in the clouds*. New York, NY: Oxford University Press.

Haden, C. A., Cohen, T., Uttal, D. H., & Marcus, M. (2016). Building learning: Narrating experiences in a children's museum. In D. M. Sobel & J. L. Jipson (Eds.), *Cognitive development in museum settings: Relating research and practice* (pp. 84–103). New York, NY: Routledge/Taylor & Francis Group.

Hahn, A. C., & Perrett, D. I. (2014). Neural and behavioral responses to attractiveness in adult and infant faces. *Neuroscience and Behavioral Reviews, 46,* 591–603.

Haith, M. M. (1966). The response of the human newborn to visual movement. *Journal of Experimental Child Psychology, 3,* 235–243.

Halder, F., Callaerts, P., & Gehring, W. J. (1995). Induction of ectopic eyes by targeted expression of the eyeless gene on *Drosophila. Science, 267,* 1788–1792.

Hall, B. K. (2000). Balfour, Garstang and de Beer: The first century of evolutionary embryology. *American Zoologist, 40,* 718–728.

Hamann, K., Warneken, F., Greenberg, J. R., & Tomasello, M. (2011). Collaboration encourages equal sharing in children but not in chimpanzees. *Nature, 476,* 328–331.

Hamilton, W. D. (1964). The genetical theory of social behavior. *Journal of Theoretical Biology, 7,* 1–52.

Hamlin, J. K. (2013). Moral judgment and action in preverbal infants and toddlers: Evidence for an innate moral code. *Current Directions in Psychological Science, 22,* 186–193.

Hamlin, J. K., Wynn, K., & Bloom, P. (2007). Social evaluation by preverbal infants. *Nature, 450,* 557–559.

Hara, Y., Imanishi, T., & Satto, Y. (2012). Reconstructing the demographic history of the human lineage using whole-genome sequences from human and three great apes. *Genome and Biological Evolution, 4,* 1133–1145.

Harari, Y. N. (2017). *Homo Deus: A brief history of tomorrow.* New York, NY: HarperCollins.

Hare, B. (2017). Survival of the friendliest: *Homo sapiens* evolved via selection for prosociality. *Annual Review Psychology, 68,* 155–186.

Hare, B., Call, J., Agnetta, B., & Tomasello, M. (2000). Chimpanzees know what conspecifics do and do not see. *Animal Behaviour, 59,* 771–785.

Hare, B., Call, J., & Tomasello, M. (2001). Do chimpanzees know what conspecifics know? *Animal Behaviour, 61,* 139–151.

Harlow, H. (1959). The development of learning in the Rhesus monkey. *American Scientist, 47*(December), 459–479.

Harper, N. J. (2017). Outdoor risky play and healthy child development in the shadow of the "risk society": A forest and nature school perspective. *Child and Youth Services, 38,* 318–334.

Harris, J. R. (1995). Where is the child's environment? A group socialization theory of development. *Psychological Review, 102,* 458–489.

Harris, P. (1989). *Children and emotion: The development of psychological understanding.* Oxford, UK: Blackwell.

Hart, B., & Risley, T. R. (2003). The early catastrophe: The 30 million word gap by age 3. *American Educator, 27*(1), pp. 4–9.

Hart, S. L. (2015). *Infant jealousy: Responses to differential treatment.* Cham, Switzerland: Springer.

Hart, S. L. (2018). Jealousy *and* attachment: Adaptations to threat posed by the birth of a sibling. *Evolutionary Behavioral Sciences, 12,* 263–275.

Hart, S. L., & Carrington, H. (2002). Jealousy in 6-month-old infants. *Infancy, 3,* 395–402.

Hart, S. L., Carrington, H. A, Tronick, E. Z., & Carroll, S. R. (2004). When infants lose exclusive maternal attention: Is it jealousy? *Infancy, 6,* 57–78.

Hartman, S., Freeman, S. M., Bales, K. L., & Belsky, J. (2018). Prenatal stress as a risk—and an opportunity—factor. *Psychological Science, 29*, 572–580.

Hattori, K. (1998). Drivers of intelligence evolution in Homo: Sexual behavior, food acquisition and infant neoteny. *The Mankind Quarterly, 39*, 127–146.

Haun, D. B., & Over, H. (2014). Like me: A homophily-based account of human culture. In P. J. Richardson & M. Christiansen (Eds.), *Cultural evolution* (pp. 75–85). Cambridge, MA: MIT Press.

Hauser, M. D., Chomsky, N., & Fitch, T. (2002). The faculty of language: What is it, who has it, and how did it evolve? *Science, 298*, 1569–1579.

Hawley, P. H. (1999). The ontogenesis of social dominance: A strategy-based evolutionary perspective. *Developmental Review, 19*, 97–132.

Hawley, P. H. (2003). Strategies of control, aggression, and morality in preschoolers: An evolutionary perspective. *Journal of Experimental Child Psychology, 85*, 213–235.

Hay, D. F., & Ross, H. S. (1982). The social nature of early conflict. *Child Development, 53*, 105–113.

Heffer, T., Good, M., Daly, O., MacDonell, E., & Willoughby, T. (2019). The longitudinal association between social-media use and depressive symptoms among American adolescents and young adults: An empirical reply to Twenge et al. (2018). *Clinical Psychological Science, 7*, 462–470.

Heimann, M. (1989). Neonatal imitation gaze aversion and mother-infant interaction. *Infant Behavior & Development, 12*, 495–505.

Henrich, J., Heine, S. J., & Norenzayan, A. (2010). The weirdest people in the world. *Behavioral and Brain Sciences, 33*, 61–135.

Hentges, R. F., & Wang, M-T. (2018). Gender differences in the developmental cascade from harsh parenting to educational attainment: An evolutionary perspective. *Child Development, 89*, 397–413.

Hepach, R. (2016). Prosocial arousal in children. *Child Development Perspectives, 11*, 50–55.

Hepach, R., Vaish, A., & Tomasello, M. (2017). The fulfillment of others' needs elevates children's body posture. *Developmental Psychology, 53*, 100–113.

Herculano-Houzel, S. (2012). The remarkable, yet not extraordinary, human brain as a scaled-up primate brain and its associated cost. *PNAS, 109*, 10661–10668.

Hernández Blasi, C., & Bjorklund, D. F. (2003). Evolutionary developmental psychology: A new tool for better understanding human ontogeny. *Human Development, 46*, 259–281.

Hernández Blasi, C., & Bjorklund, D. F. (2018). Adolescents' sensitivity to children's supernatural thinking: A preparation for parenthood? *Psicothema, 30*, 201–206.

Hernández Blasi, C., Bjorklund, D. F., Agut, S, Lozano, F., & Martínez, M. A. (2018, July). *Vocal cues as signaling behavior in early childhood*. 30th Annual Meeting of the Human Behavior and Evolution Society, Amsterdam, The Netherlands.

Hernández-Blasi, C., Bjorklund, D. F., & Ruiz Soler, M. (2015). Cognitive cues are more compelling than facial cues in determining adults' reactions towards young children. *Evolutionary Psychology, 13*, 511–530.

Hernández Blasi, C., Bjorklund, D. F., & Ruiz Soler, M. (2017). Children's supernatural thinking as a signaling behavior in early childhood, *British Journal of Psychology, 108*, 467–485.

Herrmann, E., Call, J., Hernandez-Lloreda, M., Hare, B., & Tomasello, M. (2007). Humans have evolved specialized skills of social cognition: The cultural intelligence hypothesis. *Science, 317*, 1360–1366.

Hewlett, B. S., Berl, R. E. W., & Roulette, C. J. (2016). Teaching and overimitation among Aka hunter-gatherers. In H. Terashima & B. S. Hewlett (Eds.), *Social learning and innovation in contemporary hunter-gatherers, Replacement of Neanderthals by Modern Humans Series* (pp. 35–45). New York, NY: Springer.

Hidaka, B. (2012). Depression as a disease of modernity. *Journal of Affective Disorders, 140,* 205–214.

Hill, K., Barton, M., & Hurtado, A. M. (2009). The emergence of human uniqueness: Characters underlying behavioral modernity. *Evolutionary Anthropology, 18,* 187–200.

Hill, K., & Hurtado, A. M. (1996). *Ache life history: The ecology and demography of a foraging people.* New York, NY: Aldine de Gruyter.

Hill, K., & Kaplan, H. (1999). Life history traits in humans: Theory and empirical studies. *Annual Review of Anthropology, 28,* 397–430.

Hill, P., Duggan, P., & Lapsley, D. (2012). Subjective invulnerability, risk behavior, and adjustment in early adolescence. *The Journal of Early Adolescence, 32,* 489–501.

Hill, P., & Lapsley, D. (2011). Adaptive and maladaptive narcissism in adolescent development. In C. T. Barry, P. K. Kerig, K. K. Stellwagen, & B. D. Tammy (Eds.), *Narcissism and Machiavellianism in youth: Implications for the development of adaptive and maladaptive behavior* (pp. 89–105). Washington, DC: American Psychological Association.

Hoehl, S., Keupp, S., Schleihauf, H., McGuigan, N., Buttelmann, D., & Whiten, A. (2019). "Overimitation": A review and appraisal of a decade of research. *Developmental Review, 51,* 90–108.

Hoehl, S., & Pauen, S. (2017). Do infants associate spiders and snakes with fearful facial expressions? *Evolution and Human Behavior, 38,* 404–413.

Hoffman, M. L. (2000). *Empathy and moral development: Implications for caring and justice.* New York, NY: Cambridge University Press.

Hood, B. (2014). *The domesticated brain.* London, UK: Pelican.

Horner, V., & Whiten, A. (2005). Causal knowledge and imitation/emulation switching in chimpanzees (*Pan troglodytes*) and children (*Homo Sapiens*). *Animal Cognition, 8,* 164–181.

Horner, V., Whiten, A., Flynn, E., & de Waal, F. B. M. (2006). Faithful replication of foraging techniques along cultural transmission chains by chimpanzees and children. *PNAS, 103,* 13878–13883.

Hornik, R., Risenhoover, N., & Gunnar, M. (1987). The effects of maternal positive, neutral, and negative affective communications on infant responses to new toys. *Child Development, 58,* 937–944.

House, B. R., Silk, J. B., Henrich, J., Barrett, H. C., Scelza, B. A., Boyette, A. H., Hewlett, B. S., & Laurence, S. (2013). Ontogeny of prosocial behavior across diverse societies. *PNAS, USA, 110,* 14586–14591.

House, B. R., & Tomasello, M. (2018). Modeling social norms increasingly influences costly sharing in middle childhood. *Journal of Experimental Child Psychology, 171,* 84–98.

Howe, M. L., Courage, M. L., & Rooksby, M. (2009). The genesis and development of autobiographical memory. In M. L. Courage & N. Cowan (Eds.), *The development of memory in infancy and childhood* (pp. 178–196). New York, NY: Psychology Press.

Hrdy, S. B. (1999) *Mother nature: A history of mothers, infants and natural selection.* New York, NY: Pantheon.

Hrdy, S. (2007). Evolutionary context of human development: The cooperative breeding model. In C. Solomon & T. K. Shackelford (Eds.), *Family relationships: Evolutionary perspectives* (pp. 39–68). New York, NY: Oxford University Press.

Hrdy, S. B. (2009). *Mothers and others: The evolutionary origins of mutual understanding.* Cambridge, MA: Belnap Press.

Hubel, D. H., & Wiesel, T. N. (1962). Receptive fields, binocular interaction and functional architecture in the cat's visual cortex. *Journal of Physiology, 160,* 106–154.

Huber, B., Yeates, M., Meyer, D., Fleckhammer, L., & Kaufman, J. (2018). The effects of screen media content on young children's executive function. *Journal of Experimental Child Psychology, 170,* 72–85.

Huizinga, J. (1950). *Homo ludens: A study of the play-element in culture.* Boston, MA: Beacon Press.

Humphreys, A. P., & Smith, P. K. (1987). Rough and tumble, friendship, and dominance in schoolchildren: Evidence for continuity and change with age. *Child Development, 58,* 201–212.

Humphrey, N. K. (1976). The social function of intellect. In P. P. G. Bateson & R. A. Hinde (Eds.), *Growing points in ethology* (pp. 303–317). Cambridge, UK: Cambridge University Press.

Hunt, E. (2012). What makes nations intelligent? *Perspectives on Psychological Science, 7,* 284–306.

Hunt, M. G., Marx, R., Lipson, C., & Young, J. (2018). No more FOMO: Limiting social media decreases loneliness and depression. *Journal of Social and Clinical Psychology, 37,* 761–768.

Hutton, J. S., Dudley, J., Horowitz-Kraus, T., DeWitt, T., & Holland, S. K. (2019). Associations between screen-based media use and brain white matter integrity in preschool-aged children. *JAMA Pediatrics, 174*(1), e193869. Published online November 4, 2019. doi: 10.1001/jamapediatrics.2019.3869

Hyson M. C, Hirsh-Pasek, K., & Rescorla, L. (1990). Academic environments in preschool: Challenge or pressure? *Early Education and Development, 1,* 401–423.

Ingram, G. (2014). From hitting to tattling to gossip: An evolutionary rationale for the development of indirect aggression. *Evolutionary Psychology, 12,* 343–363.

Ingram, G., & Bering, J. M. (2010). Children's tattling: A developmental precursor to gossip? *Child Development, 81,* 945–957.

International Human Genome Sequencing Consortium. (2004). Finishing the euchromatic sequence of the human genome. *Nature, 431,* 931–945.

Jablonka, E. (2017). New trends in evolutionary biology: Biological, philosophical and social science perspectives. *Interface Focus, 7*(5), 20160135. doi: 10.1098.rsfs.2017.0051

Jablonka, E., & Lamb, M. (1995). *Epigenetic inheritance and evolution: The Lamarckian dimension.* New York, NY: Oxford University Press.

Jackson, J. F. (1993). Human behavioral genetics: Scarr's theory, and her views on intervention: A critical review and commentary of their implications for African American children. *Child Development, 64,* 1318–1332.

Jensen, K., Call, J., & Tomasello, M. (2007). Chimpanzees are rational maximizers in an ultimatum game. *Science, 318,* 107–109.

Jensen, K., Hare, B., Call, J., & Tomasello, M. (2006). What's in it for me? Self-regard precludes altruism and spite in chimpanzees. *Proceedings of the Royal Society of London, 273,* 1013–1021.

Jerison H. (2000). The evolution of intelligence. In R. Sternberg (Ed.), *Handbook of intelligence* (pp. 216–244), Cambridge, UK: Cambridge University Press.

Joffe, T. H. (1997). Social pressures have selected for an extended juvenile period in primates. *Journal of Human Evolution, 32*, 593–605.

Johnson, M., Stokes, R. G., & Arndt, T. (2018). *The Thalidomide Catastrophe: How it happened, who was responsible and why the search for justice continues after more than six decades.* Exeter, UK: Onwards and Upwards.

Johnson, M. H. (2007). The social brain in infancy: A developmental cognitive neuroscience approach. In D. Coch, K. W. Fischer, & G. Dawson (Eds.), *Human behavior, learning, and the developing brain: Typical development* (pp. 115–137). New York, NY: Guilford.

Jones, R. A. (1986). *Emile Durkheim: An introduction to four major works.* Beverly Hills, CA: Sage.

Jong, E., Visscher, T. L. S., HiraSing, R. A., Heymans, M. W., Seidell, J. C., & Renders, C. M. (2013). Association between TV viewing, computer use and overweight, determinants and competing activities of screen time in 4- to 13-year-old children. *International Journal of Obesity, 37*, 47–53.

Jordan, J. J., McAuliffe, K., & Warneken, F. (2014). Development of in-group favoritism in children's third-party punishment of selfishness. *PNAS, 111*, 12710–12715.

Jowkar-Baniani, G., & Schmuckler, M. (2013). The role of perceptual similarity of the task environments in children's perseverative responding. *Journal of Experimental Child Psychology, 116*, 640–658.

Junger, S. (2016). *Tribe: On homecoming and belonging.* New York, NY: Twelve.

Kaati, G., Bygren, L. O., & Edvinsson, S. (2002). Cardiovascular and diabetes mortality determined by nutrition during parents' and grandparents' slow growth period. *European Journal of Human Genetics, 10*, 682–688.

Kabali, H. K., Irigoyen, M. M., Nunez-Davis, R., Budacki, J. G., Mohanty, S. H., Leister, K. P., & Bonner, R. L. (2015). Exposure and use of mobile media devices by young children. *Pediatrics, 136*, 1044–1050.

Kachel, U., Svetlova, M., & Tomasello, M. (2018). Three-year-olds' reactions to a partner's failure to perform her role in a joint commitment. *Child Development, 89*, 1691–1703.

Kachel, U., Svetlova, M., & Tomasello, M. (2019). Three- and 5-year-old children's understanding of how to dissolve a joint commitment. *Journal of Experimental Child Psychology, 184*, 34–47.

Kaiser, I., Jensen, K., Call, J., & Tomasello, M. (2012). Theft in the ultimatum game: Chimpanzees and bonobos are insensitive to unfairness. *Biology Letters, 8*, 942–945.

Kanai, R., Bahrami, B., Roylance, R., & Rees, G. (2012). Online social network size is reflected in human brain structures. *Proceedings of the Royal Society, B, 279*, 1327–1334.

Kaplan, H., Hill, K., Lancaster, J., & Hurtado, A. M. (2000). A theory of human life history evolution: Diet intelligence, and longevity. *Evolutionary Anthropology, 9*, 156–185.

Kappeler, P. M., & Silk, J. B. (Eds.). (2010). *Mind the gap: Tracing the origins of human universals.* New York, NY: Springer.

Karzon, R. G. (1985). Discrimination of polysyllabic sequences by one- to four-month-old infants. *Journal of Experimental Child Psychology, 39*, 326–342.

Kelly, D. J., Liu, S., Lee, K., Quinn, P. C., Pascalis, O., Slater, A. M., et al. (2009). Development of the other-race effect in infancy: Evidence toward universality? *Journal of Experimental Child Psychology, 104*, 105–114.

Kelly, D. J., Quinn, P. C, Slater, A. M., Lee, K., Ge, L., & Pascalis, O. (2007). The other-race effect develops during infancy. *Psychological Science, 18*, 1084–1089.

Kelly, R., Hammond, S., Dissanayaka, C., & Ihsen, E. (2011). The relationship between symbolic play and executive function in young children. *Australian Journal of Early Childhood, 36*, 21–27.

Kenny, P., & Turkewitz, G. (1986). Effects of unusually early visual stimulation on the development of homing behavior in the rat pup. *Developmental Psychobiology, 19*, 57–66.

Kenward, B. (2012). Over-imitating preschoolers believe unnecessary actions are normative and enforce their performance by a third party. *Journal of Experimental Child Psychology, 112*, 195–207.

Kersten A. W., & Earles, J. L. (2001). Less really is more for adults learning a miniature artificial language. *Journal of Memory and Language, 44*, 250–273.

Kertes, D. A., Kamin, H. S., Hughes, D. A., Rodney, N. C., Bhatt, S., & Mulligan, C. J. (2016). Prenatal maternal stress predicts methylation of genes regulating the hypothalamic-pituitary-adrenocortical system in mothers and newborns in the Democratic Republic of Congo. *Child Development, 87*, 61–72.

Kessler, R. C., Üstün, T. B., & World Health Organization. (2008). *The WHO world mental health surveys: Global perspectives on the epidemiology of mental disorders*. Cambridge, UK: Cambridge University Press.

Keupp, S., Behne, T., & Rakoczy, H. (2013). Why do children overimitate? Normativity is crucial. *Journal of Experimental Child Psychology, 116*, 392–406.

Kinard, J. L., Sideris, J., Watson, L. R., Baranek, G. T., Crais, E. R., Wakeford, L., et al. (2017). Predictors of parent responsiveness to 1-year-olds at-risk for autism spectrum disorder. *Journal of Autism and Developmental Disorders, 47*, 172–186.

Kirkpatrick, L. A. (2005). *Attachment, evolution, and the psychology of religion*. New York, NY: Guilford.

Klaczynski, P. (2017). Age differences in optimism bias are mediated by reliance on intuition and religiosity. *Journal of Experimental Child Psychology, 163*, 126–139.

Kline, M. A. (2015). How to learn about teaching: An evolutionary framework for the study of teaching behavior in humans and other animals. *Behavioral and Brain Sciences, 38*, e31. doi: 10.1017/S0140525X14000090

Klinger, T. A., Neumann-Holzschuh, I. (2013). Louisiana Creole. In S. M. Michaelis, P. Maurer, M. Haspelmath, & M. Huber (Eds.), *The survey of pidgin and creole languages. Volume II: Portuguese-based, Spanish-based, and French-based Languages* (pp. 229–240). Oxford, UK: Oxford University Press.

Knoll, L. J., Magis-Weinberg, L., Speekenbrink, M., & Blakemore, S-J. (2015). Social influence on risk perception during adolescence. *Psychological Science, 26*, 583–592.

Kobayashi, M., Macchi Cassia, B., Kanazawa, S., Yamaguchi, M. K., & Kakigi, R. (2018). Perceptual narrowing towards adult faces is a cross-cultural phenomenon in infancy. A behavioral and near-infrared spectroscopy study in Japanese infants. *Developmental Science, 21*, e12498. doi: 10.1111/desc.12498

Kochanska, G. (1993). Toward a synthesis of parental socialization and child temperament in early development of conscience. *Child Development, 64*, 325–347.

Kohlberg, L. (1966). A cognitive-developmental analysis of children's sex-role concepts and attitudes. In E. E. Maccoby (Ed.), *The development of sex differences* (pp. 82–173). Stanford, CA: Stanford University Press.

Kohlberg, L. (1969). Stage and sequence: The cognitive-developmental approach to socialization. In D. A. Goslin (Ed.), *Handbook of socialization theory and research* (pp. 347–480). Chicago, IL: Rand McNally.

Kohlberg, L., Yaeger, J., & Hjertholm, E. (1968). Private speech: Four studies and a review of theories. *Child Development, 39*, 691–736.

Konner, M. (2010). *The evolution of childhood: Relationships, emotions, mind*. Cambridge, MA: Belknap Press.

Köster, M., & Kärtner, J. (2019). Why do infants help? A simple action reveals a complex phenomenon. *Developmental Review, 51*, 175–187.

Kostyrka-Allchorne, K., Cooper, N. R., & Simpson, A. (2017). The relationship between television exposure and children's cognition and behavior: A systematic review. *Developmental Review, 44*, 19–58.

Krachun, C., Carpenter, M., Call, J., & Tomasello, M. (2009). A competitive nonverbal false belief task for children and apes. *Developmental Science, 12*, 521–535.

Kringelbach, M. L., Stark, E. A., Alexander, C., Bornstein, M. H., & Stein, A. (2016). On cuteness: Unlocking the parental brain and beyond. *Trends in Cognitive Science, 20*, 545–558.

Kross, E., Verduyn, P., Demiralp, E., Park, J., Lee, D. S., Lin, N., Shablack, H., Jonides, J., & Ybarra, O. (2013). Facebook use predicts declines in subjective well-being in young adults. *PLoS One, 8*, e69841. doi: 10.1371/desc.pone.0069841

Krupenye, C., Kano, F., Hirata, S., Call, J., & Tomasello, M. (2016). Great apes anticipate that other individuals will act according to false beliefs. *Science* (07 Oct), *354*(6308), 110–114.

Kuhl P. K., Andruski, J. E., Christovich, I. A., Christovich, L. A., Kozhevnikova, E. V., Ryskfna, V. L., et al. (1997). Cross-language analysis of phonetic units in language addressed to infants. *Science, 277*, 684–686.

Kuhl, P. K., Stevens, E., Hayashi, A., Deguchi, T., Kiritani, S., & Iverson, P. (2006). Infants show a facilitation effect for native language phonetic perception between 6 and 12 months. *Developmental Science, 9*, F13–F21.

Kukekova, A., Trut, L. N., Chase, K., Shepeleva, D. V., Vladimirova, A. V., Kharlamova, A. V., et al. (2008). Measurement of segregating behaviors in experimental silver fox pedigrees. *Behavior Genetics, 38*, 185–194.

Kulke, L., von Duhn, B., Schneider, D., & Rakoczy, H. (2018). Is implicit theory of mind a real and robust phenomenon? Results from a systematic replication study. *Psychological Science, 29*, 888–900.

Kuo, Z-Y. (1967). *The dynamics of behavior development*. New York, NY: Random House.

Kushlev, K., Dwyer, R., & Dunn, E. W. (2019). The social price of constant connectivity: Smartphones impose subtle costs on well-being. *Current Directions in Psychological Science, 28*, 347–352.

Kushlev, K., Hunter, J. F., Proulux, J., Pressman, S. D., & Dunn, E. (2019). Smartphones reduce smiles between strangers. *Computers in Human Behavior, 91*, 12–16.

Kushlev, K., Proulux, J., & Dunn, E. (2017). Digitally connected, socially disconnected: The effects of relying on technology rather than other people. *Computers in Human Behavior, 76*, 68–74.

Laboratory of Comparative Human Cognition. (1983). Culture and cognitive development. In W. Kessen (Vol. Ed.), *Vol. 1: History, theory, and methods*, in P. H. Mussen (Gen. Ed.), *Handbook of child psychology* (4th edition, pp. 295–356). New York, NY: Wiley.

Lam, C. B., McHale, S. M., & Couter, A. C. (2014). Time with peers from middle school to late adolescence: Developmental course and adjustment correlates. *Child Development, 85*, 1677–1693.

Lancy, D. (2015). *The anthropology of childhood* (2nd edition). Cambridge, UK: Cambridge University Press.

Lancy, D. F. (2016). Teaching: Natural or cultural? In D. C. Geary & D. B. Berch (Eds.), *Evolutionary perspectives on education and child development* (pp. 33–66). New York, NY: Springer.

Lancy, D., & Grove, M. A. (2010). The role of adults in children's learning. In D. F. Lancy, J. Bock, & S. Gaskins (Eds.), *The anthropology of childhood* (pp. 145–179). New York, NY: AltaMira Press.

Lane, I. M., & Coon, R. C. (1972). Reward allocation in preschool children. *Child Development, 43*, 1382–1389.

Langlois, J., Ritter, J., Casey, R., & Sawin, D. (1995). Infant attractiveness predicts maternal behavior and attitudes. *Developmental Psychology, 31*, 464–472.

Lapsley, D. K., & Hill, P. L. (2010). Subjective invulnerability, optimism bias and adjustment in emerging adulthood. *Journal of Youth and Adolescence, 39*, 847–857.

Legare, C. H. (2019). The development of cumulative cultural learning. *Annual Review of Developmental Psychology, 1*, 119–145.

Legare, C. H., & Nielsen, M. (2015). Imitation and innovation: The dual engines of cultural learning. *Trends in Cognitive Sciences, 19*, 688–699.

Legerstee, M. (1991). The role of person and object in eliciting early imitation. *Journal of Experimental Child Psychology, 51*, 423–433.

Le Grand, R., Mondloch, C. J., Maurer, D., & Brent, H. P. (2001). Early visual experience and face processing. *Nature, 410*, 890.

Leibenluft, E., Gobbini, M. I., Harrison, T., & Haxby, J. V. (2004). Mothers' neural activation in response to pictures of their children and other children. *Biological Psychiatry, 56*, 225–232.

Li, N. P., van Vugt, M., & Colarelli, S. M. (2018). The evolutionary mismatch hypothesis: Implications for psychological science. *Current Perspectives in Psychological Science, 27*, 38–44.

Lickliter, R. (1990). Premature visual stimulation accelerates intersensory functioning in bobwhite quail neonates. *Developmental Psychobiology, 23*, 15–27.

Lickliter, R., & Honeycutt, H. (2003). Developmental dynamics: Towards a biologically plausible evolutionary psychology. *Psychological Bulletin, 129*, 819–835.

Lillard, A. S. (2018). Rethinking education: Montessori's approach. *Current Directions in Psychological Science, 27*, 395–400.

Lillard, A. S., Drell, M. B., Richey, E., Boguszewski, K., & Smith. E. D. (2015). Further examination of the immediate impact of television on children's executive function. *Developmental Psychology, 51*, 92–805.

Lillard, A. S., & Erisir, A. (2011). Old dogs learning new tricks: Neuroplasticity beyond the juvenile period. *Developmental Review, 31*, 207–239.

Lillard, A. S., Lerner, M. D., Hopkins, E. J., Dore, R. A., Smith, E. D., & Palmquist, C. M. (2013). The impact of pretend play on children's development: A review of the evidence. *Psychological Bulletin, 139*, 1–34.

Lillard, A. S., Li, H., & Boguszewski, K. (2015). Television and children's executive function. In J. B. Benson (Ed.), *Advances in Child Development and Behavior* (Vol. 48, pp. 219–247). New York, NY: Academic Press.

Lillard, A. S., & Peterson, J. (2011). The immediate impact of different types of television on young children's executive function. *Pediatrics, 128*, 644–649.

Lipko, A. R., Dunlosky, J., & Merriman, W. E. (2009). Persistent overconfidence despite practice: The roles of task experience in preschooler's recall predications. *Journal of Experimental Child Psychology, 103*, 152–166.

Liszkowski, U., Carpenter, M., Striano, T., & Tomasello, M. (2006). 12- and 18-month-olds point to provide information for others. *Journal of Cognition and Development, 7*, 173–187.

Liszkowski, U., Carpenter, M., & Tomasello, M. (2007). Pointing out new news, old news, and absent referents at 12 months of age. *Developmental Science, 10*, F1–F7.

Liu, X., Somel, M., Tang, L., Yan, Z., Jiang, X., Guo, S., et al. (2012). Extension of cortical synaptic development distinguishes humans from chimpanzees and macaques. *Genome Research, 22*, 611–622.

Lobmaier, J. S., Probst, F., Perrett, D. I., & Heinrichs, M. (2015). Menstrual cycle phase affects discrimination of infant cuteness. *Hormones and Behavior, 70*, 1–6.

Lobmaier, J. S., Sprengelmeyer, R., Wiffen, B., & Perrett, D. I. (2010). Female and male responses to cuteness, age and emotion in infant faces. *Evolution and Human Behavior, 31*, 6–21.

LoBue, V., & Adolph, K. E. (2019). Fear in infancy: Lessons from snakes, spiders, heights, and strangers. *Psychological Bulletin, 55*, 1889–1907.

LoBue, V., & DeLoache, J. S. (2010). Superior detection of threat-relevant stimuli in infancy. *Developmental Science, 13*, 221–228.

Locke, J. (1693). *Some thoughts concerning education* (1st edition). London: A. and J. Churchill at the Black Swan in Paternoster-row. Retrieved July 28, 2016—via Google Books.

Locke, J. L. (1993). *The child's path to spoken language.* Cambridge, MA: Harvard University Press.

Locke, J. L. (2009). Evolutionary developmental linguistics: Naturalization of the faculty of language. *Language Sciences, 31*, 33–59.

Locke, J. L., & Bogin, B. (2006). Language and life history: A new perspective on the development and evolution of human language. *Behavioral and Brain Sciences, 29*, 259–280.

Lockhart, K. L., Chang, B., & Tyler, S. (2002). Young children's belief about the stability of traits: Protective optimism. *Child Development, 73*, 1408–1430.

Lockhart, K. L., Goddu, M. K., & Keil, F. C. (2017). Overoptimism about future knowledge: Early arrogance? *Journal of Positive Psychology, 12*, 36–46.

Lockman, J. J. (2000). A perception-action perspective on tool use development. *Child Development, 71*, 137–144.

Loftus, E. F., & Pickrell, J. E. (1995). The formation of false memories. *Psychiatric Annals, 25*, 720–725.

Lord, C. G. (1980). Schemas and images as memory aids: Two modes of processing social information. *Journal of Personality and Social Psychology, 38*, 257–269.

Lorenz, K. (1952). *King Solomon's rings.* New York, NY: Crowell.

Lorenz, K. Z. (1943). Die angeboren Formen moglicher Erfahrung [The innate forms of possible experience]. *Zeitschrift fur Tierpsychologie, 5*, 233–409.

Louv, R. (2005). *Last child in the woods: Saving our children from nature-deficit disorder.* Chapel Hill, NC: Algonquin Books of Chapel Hill.

Louv, R. (2016). *Vitamin N: The essential guide to a nature-rich life.* Chapel Hill, NC: Algonquin Books of Chapel Hill.

Lu, J. G., Martin, A. E., Usova, A., & Galinsky, A. D. (2019). Creativity and humor across cultures: Where Aha meets Haha. In S. R. Luria, J. Baer, & J. C. Kaufman (Eds.), *Creativity and humor* (pp. 183–203). San Diego, CA: Academic Press.

Lucas, A. J., Burdett E. R. R., Burgess, V., Wood L. A., McGuigan, N., Harris, P. L., et al. (2017). The development of selective copying: Children's learning from an expert versus their mother. *Child Development, 88*, 2026–2042.

Lucion, M. K., Oliveira, V., Bizarro, L., Rahde Bischoff, A., Pelufo Silveria, P., & Kauer-Sant'Anna, M. (2017). Attentional bias toward infant faces—Review of the adaptive and clinical relevance. *International Journal of Psychology, 114*, 1–8.

Lukianoff, G., & Haidt, J. (2018). *The coddling of the American mind: How good intentions and bad ideas are setting up a generation for failure.* New York, NY: Penguin Press.

Lumey, L. H. (1992). Decreased birthweights in infants after maternal in utero exposure to the Dutch famine of 1944–45. *Paediatric and Perinatal Epidemiology, 6*, 240–253.

Luna, B., Thulborn, K. R., Monoz, D. P., Merriam, E. P., Garver, K. E., Minshew, N. J., et al. (2001). Maturation of widely distributed brain function subserves cognitive development. *NeuroImage, 13*, 786–793.

Luo, L. Z., Li, H., & Lee, K. (2011). Are children's faces really more appealing than those of adults? Testing the baby schema hypothesis beyond infancy. *Journal of Experimental Child Psychology, 110*, 115–124.

Luo, L., Ma, X., Zheng, X., Zhao, W., Xu, L., Becker, B., et al. (2015). Neural systems and hormones mediating attraction to infant and child faces. *Frontiers in Psychology, 6*, 970.

Lyons, D. E., Young, A. G., & Keil, F. C. (2007). The hidden structure of overimitation. *PNAS, 104*, 19751–19756.

Lyons, L. (2005). One-third of Americans believe dearly may not have departed: Belief declines with age. Gallup. Retrieved from http://www.gallup.com/poll/17275/OneThird-Americans-Believe-Dearly-May-Departed.aspx

Macchi Cassia, V., Turati, C., & Simion, F. (2004). Can a nonspecific bias toward top-heavy patterns explain newborns' face preference? *Psychological Science, 15*, 379–383.

Machluf, K., & Bjorklund, D. F. (2016, May). *Physical immaturity in infants triggers greater empathy in adults.* Paper presented at meeting of the Association of Psychological Science, Chicago, IL.

Maestripieri, D., & Mateo J. (Eds.) (2009). *Maternal effects in mammals.* Chicago, IL: University of Chicago Press.

Maestripieri, D., & Pelka, S. (2002). Sex differences in interest in infants across the lifespan: A biological adaptation for parenting. *Human Nature, 13*, 327–344.

Mail and Guardian. (1997, November 21). "Child of the wild still spurns life as a human." Retrieved June 11, 2018.

Martin, C. L., Ruble, D. N., & Szkrybalo, J. (2002). Cognitive theories of early gender development. *Psychological Bulletin, 128*, 903–933.

Martin, G. B., & Clark, R. D., III. (1982). Distress crying in neonates: Species and peer specificity. *Developmental Psychology, 38*, 3–9.

Maurer, D., & Lewis, T. L. (2013). Sensitive periods in visual development. In P. D. Zelazo (Ed.), *Oxford handbook of developmental psychology, Vol. 1* (pp. 202–234). Oxford, UK: Oxford University Press.

Maurer, D., Mondloch, C. J., & Lewis, T. L. (2007). Effects of early visual deprivation on perceptual and cognitive development. *Progress in Brain Research, 164*, 87–104.

May, L., Byers-Heilein, K., Gervain, J., & Werker, J. F. (2011). Language and the newborn brain: Does prenatal language experience shape the neonate neural response to speech? *Frontiers in Psychology, 2,* 222.

May, L., Gervain, J., Carreiras, M., & Werker, J. F. (2018). The specificity of the neural response to speech at birth. *Developmental Science, 21*(3), e12564.

Mayer, A., & Träuble, B. (2013). The weird world of cross-cultural false-belief research: A true- and false-belief study among Samoan children based on commands. *Journal of Cognition and Development, 16,* 650–665.

Mayr, E. (1982) *The growth of biological thought: Diversity, evolution, and inheritance.* Cambridge, MA: Belknap Press.

Mayr, E., & Provine, W. B. (1980). *The evolutionary synthesis: Perspectives on the unification of biology.* Cambridge, MA: Harvard University Press.

McAuley, T., & White, D. A. (2011). A latent variables examination of processing speed, response inhibition, and working memory during typical development. *Journal of Experimental Child Psychology, 108,* 152–166.

McAuliffe, K., Blake, P. R., Steinbeis, N., & Warneken, F. (2017). The developmental foundation of human fairness. *Nature Human Behavior, 1,* article no. 0042. doi: 10.1038/s41562-016-0042

McBride, T., & Lickliter, R. (1994). Specific postnatal auditory stimulation interferes with species-typical responsiveness to maternal visual cues in bobwhite quail chicks. *Journal of Comparative Psychology, 107,* 320–327.

McCall, R. B. (1981). Nature-nurture and the two realms of development: A proposed integration with respect to mental development. *Child Development, 52,* 1–12.

McClean, C. Y., Reno, P. L., Pollen, A. A., Bassan, A. I., Capellini, T. D., Guenther, C., et al. (2011). Human-specific loss of regulatory DNA and the evolution of human-specific traits. *Nature, 471,* 216–219.

McDaniel, B. T., & Coyne, S. M. (2016). "Technointerference": The interference of technology in couple relationships and implications for women's personal and relational well-being. *Psychology of Popular Media Culture, 5,* 85–98.

McGrew, W. C. (1972). *An ethological study of children's behaviour.* London, UK: Metheun.

McGuigan, N. (2013). The influence of model status on the tendency of young children to over-imitate. *Journal of Experimental Child Psychology, 116,* 962–969.

McGuigan, N., Makinson, J., & Whiten, A. (2011). From over-imitation to super-copying: Adults imitate causally irrelevant aspects of tool use with higher fidelity than young children. *British Journal of Psychology, 102,* 1–18.

McGuigan, N., & Whiten, A. (2009). Emulation and "over-emulation" in the social learning of causally opaque versus causally transparent tool use by 23- and 30-month-old children. *Journal of Experimental Child Psychology, 104,* 367–381.

McKinney, M. L. (1998). Cognitive evolution by extending brain development: On recapitulation, progress, and other heresies. In J. Langer & M. Killen (Eds.), *Piaget, evolution, and development* (pp. 9–31). Mahwah, NJ: Erlbaum.

McKinney, M. L. (2000). Evolving behavioral complexity by extending development. In S. T. Parker, J. Langer, & M. L. McKinney (Eds.), *Biology, brains, and behavior: The evolution of human development* (pp. 25–40). Santa Fe, NM: School of American Research Press.

McKinney, M. L., & McNamara, K. (1991). *Heterochrony: The evolution of ontogeny.* New York, NY: Plenum.

McLoughlin, N., Tipper, S. P., & Over, H. (2018). Young children perceive less humanness in outgroup faces. *Developmental Science, 21*(2), e12539. doi: 101111/desc.12539

Meaney, M. J. (2001). Maternal care, gene expression, and the transmission of individual differences in stress reactivity across generations. *Annual Review of Neuroscience, 24*, 1161–1192

Meaney, M. J. (2010). Epigenetics and the biological definition of gene environment interactions. *Child Development, 81*, 41–79.

Meaney, M. J. (2013). Epigenetics and the environmental regulation of the genome and its function. In D. Narvaez, J. Panksepp, A. N. Schore, & T. R. Gleason (Eds.), *Evolution, early experience and human development: From research to practice and policy* (pp. 99–128). Oxford, UK: Oxford University Press.

Mehler, J., Jusczyk, P., Lambertz, G., Halsted, N., Bertoncini, J., & Amiel-Tison, C. (1988). A precursor of language acquisition in young infants. *Cognition, 29*, 143–178.

Melis, A. P., Call, J., & Tomasello, M. (2006). Chimpanzees conceal visual and auditory information from others. *Journal of Comparative Psychology, 120*, 154–162.

Meltzoff, A. N. (1995). Understanding the intentions of others: Re-enactment of intended acts by 18-month-old children. *Developmental Psychology, 31*, 838–850.

Meltzoff, A. (2007). "Like me": A foundation for social cognition. *Developmental Science, 10*, 126–134.

Meltzoff, A. N., & Moore, M. K. (1977). Imitation of facial and manual gestures by human neonates. *Science, 198*, 75–78.

Merz, E. C., Harlé, K. M., Noble, K. G., & McCall, R. B. (2016). Executive function in previously institutionalized children. *Child Development Perspectives, 10*, 105–110.

Merz, E. C., & McCall, R. B. (2010). Behavior problems in children adopted from psychosocially depriving institutions. *Journal of Abnormal Child Psychology, 38*, 459–470.

Mikulincer, M., & Shaver, P. R. (2007). *Attachment in adulthood: Structure, dynamics, and change*. New York, NY: Guilford.

Mill, C. M., & Keil, F. C. (2004). Knowing the limits of one's understanding: The development of an awareness of an illusion of explanatory depth. *Journal of Experimental Child Psychology, 87*, 1–32.

Miller, D. B. (1998). Epigenesis. In G. Greenberg & M. M. Haraway (Eds.), *Comparative psychology: A handbook* (pp. 105–106). New York, NY: Garland.

Miller, D. J., Duka, T., Stimpson, C. D., Schapiro, S. J., Baze, W. B., McArthur, M. J., et al. (2012). Prolonged myelination in human neocortical evolution. *PNAS, 109*, 16480–16485.

Mills, K. L., Goddings, A. L., Clasen, L. S., Giedd, J. N., & Blakemore, S. J. (2014). The developmental mismatch in structural brain maturation during adolescence. *Developmental Neuroscience, 36*, 147–160.

Mittal, C., Griskevicius, V., Simpson, J. A., Sung, S., & Young, E. S. (2015). Cognitive adaptations to stressful environments: When childhood adversity enhances adult executive function. *Journal of Personality and Social Psychology, 109*, 604–621.

Mize, K. D., Pineda, M., Blau, A. K., Marsh, K., & Jones, N. A. (2014). Infant physiological and behavioral responses to a jealousy provoking condition. *Infancy, 19*, 338–348.

Mondloch, C. J., Lewis, T. M., Budreau, D. R., Maurer, D., Dannemiller, J. L., Stephens, B. R., et al. (1999). Face perception during early infancy. *Psychological Science, 10*, 419–422.

Montagu, A. (1989). *Growing young* (2nd edition). Granby, MA: Bergin & Garvey.

Mood, D. W. (1979). Sentence comprehension in preschool children: Testing an adaptive egocentrism hypothesis. *Child Development, 50,* 247–250.

Moon, C., Cooper, R. P., & Fifer, W. R. (1993). Two-day-olds prefer their native language. *Infant Behavior and Development, 16,* 495–500.

Moore, C. L. (2003). Evolution, development, and the individual acquisition of traits: What we've learned since Baldwin. In B. H. Weber & D. J. Depew (Eds.), *Evolution and learning: The Baldwin effect reconsidered* (pp. 115–139). Cambridge, MA: MIT Press.

Moore, D. D. (2015). *The developing genome: An introduction of behavioral epigenetics.* New York, NY: Oxford University Press.

Moore, D. S., Spence, M. J., & Katz, G. S. (1997). Six-month-olds' categorization of natural infant-directed utterances. *Developmental Psychology, 33,* 980–989.

Morgan, D. K., & Whitelaw, E. (2008). The case for transgenerational epigenetic inheritance in humans, *Mammalian Genome, 19,* 394–397.

Muenks, K., Wigfield, A., & Eccles, J. S. (2018). I can do this! The development and calibration of children's expectation for success and competence beliefs. *Developmental Review, 48,* 24–39.

Muller, M. N., & Mitani, J. C. (2005). Conflict and cooperation in wild chimpanzees. *Advances in the Study of Behavior, 35,* 275–331.

Munday, P. L., White, J. W., & Warner, R. R. (2006). A social basis for the development of primary males in a sex-changing fish. *Proceedings of the Royal Society of London B: Biological Sciences, 273,* 2845–2851.

Musgrace, S., Lonsdorf, E., Morgan, D., Prestipino, M., Bernstein-Kurtycz, L., Mundry, R., & Sanz, C. (2019). Teaching varies with task complexity in wild chimpanzees. *PNAS, 117*(2), 969–976. doi: 10.1073/pnas.1907476116

Myers, A. J., & Bjorklund, D. F. (2018). An evolutionary perspective of rivalry in the family. In N. A. Jones & S. Hart (Eds.), *The psychology of rivalry* (pp. 1–33). Hauppauge, NY: Nova Science Publishers.

Naef, A. (1926). Über die Urformen der Anthropomorphen und die Stammesgeschichte des Menschenschädels. *Naturwissenschaften, 14,* 445–452.

Nagell, K., Olguin, K., & Tomasello, M. (1993). Processes of social learning in the tool use of chimpanzees (*Pan troglodytes*) and human children (*Homo sapiens*). *Journal of Comparative Psychology, 107,* 174–186.

Nagy, E. (2006). From imitation to conversation: The first dialogues with human neonates. *Infant and Child Development, 15,* 223–232.

Nagy, E., & Molnar, P. (2004). Homo imitans or homo provocans? Human imprinting model of neonatal imitation. *Infant Behavior and Development, 27,* 54–63.

Nathanson, A. I., Aladé, F., Sharp, M. L., Rasmusse, E. E., & Christy, K. (2014). The relation between television exposure and executive function among preschoolers. *Developmental Psychology, 50,* 1497–1506.

Naumova, O. Y., Hein, S., Suderman, M., Barbot, B., Lee, M., Raefski, A., et al. (2016). Epigenetic patterns modulate the connection between developmental dynamics and parenting offspring psychosocial adjustment. *Child Development, 87,* 98–110.

Neisser, U. (1967). *Cognitive psychology.* Englewood Cliffs, NJ: Prentice-Hall.

Nelson, C. A. (2001), Neural plasticity and human development: The role of experience in sculpting memory systems. *Developmental Science, 3,* 115–130.

Nelson, C. A. (2007). A neurobiological perspective on early human deprivation. *Child Development Perspectives, 1,* 13–18.

Nelson, C. A., Furtado, E. A., Fox, N. A., & Zeanah, Jr., C. H. (2009). The deprived human brain. *American Scientist, 97*, 222–229.

Nelson, C. A., Thomas, K. M., & de Haan, M. (2006). Neural bases of cognitive development. In D. Kuhn & R. S. Siegler (Vol. Eds.), *Vol. 2: Cognition, perception, and language* (pp. 3–57), in W. Damon & R. M. Lerner (Gen. Eds.), *Handbook of child psychology* (6th edition). New York, NY: Wiley.

Nelson, C. A., Ill, Zeanah, C. H., Fox, N. A., Marshall, P. J., Smuke, A. T., & Guthrie, D. (2007). Cognitive recovery in socially deprived young children: The Bucharest Early Intervention Program. *Science, 318*, 1937–1940.

Nelson, K. (2005). Evolution and development of human memory systems. In B. J. Ellis & D. F. Bjorklund (Eds.), *Origins of the social mind: Evolutionary psychology and child development* (pp. 354–382). New York, NY: Guilford.

Nettle, D., & Cockerill, M. (2010). Development of social variation in reproductive schedules: A study from an English urban area. *PLoS One, 5*, e12690. doi: 10.1371/journal.pone.0012690

Newport, E. L. (1990). Maturational constraints on language learning. *Cognitive Science, 14*, 11–28.

Newport, E. L. (1991). Contrasting concepts of the critical period for language. In S. Carey & R. Gelman (Eds.), *Epigenesis of mind: Essays in biology and knowledge* (pp. 111–130). Hillsdale, NJ: Erlbaum.

New York Post (April 9, 2010). US woman put adopted Russian son on one-way flight alone back to homeland. *New York Post*. Retrieved June 16, 2018. https://nypost.com/2010/04/09/us-woman-put-adopted-russian-son-on-one-way-flight-alone-back-to-homeland/

Nielsen, M. (2006). Copying actions and copying outcomes: Social learning through the second year. *Developmental Psychology, 42*, 555–565.

Nielsen, M. (2012). Imitation, pretend play, and childhood: Essential elements in the evolution of human culture? *Journal of Comparative Psychology, 126*, 170–181.

Nielsen, M. (2018). The social glue of cumulative culture and ritual behavior. *Child Development Perspectives, 12*, 264–268.

Nielsen, M., & Haun, D. (2016). Why developmental psychology is incomplete without comparative and cross-cultural perspectives. *Philosophical Transactions of the Royal Society of London B: Biological Sciences, 371*(1686), 20150071. doi: 10.1098/rstb.2015.0071

Nielsen, M., Haun, D., Kärtner, J., & Legar, C. H. (2017). The persistent sampling bias in developmental psychology: A call to action. *Journal of Experimental Child Psychology, 162*, 31–38.

Nielsen, M., Mushin, I., Tomaselli, K., & Whiten, A. (2014). Where culture takes hold: "Overimitation" and its flexible deployment in Western, Aboriginal, and Bushmen children. *Child Development, 85*, 2169–2184.

Nielsen, M., Mushin, B., Tomaselli, K., & Whiten, A. (2016). Imitation, collaboration, and their interaction among Western and indigenous Australian preschool children. *Child Development, 87*, 755–806.

Nielsen, M., & Tomaselli, K. (2010). Overimitation in Kalahari Bushman children and the origins of human cultural cognition. *Psychological Science, 21*, 729–736.

Nitschke, J. B., Nelson, E. E., Rusch, B. D., Fox, A. S., Oakes, T. R., & Davidson, R. J. (2004). Orbitofrontal cortex tracks positive mood in mothers viewing pictures of their newborn infants. *Neuroimage, 21*(2), 583–592.

Noonan, J. P. (2003). Regulatory DNAs and the evolution of human development. *Current Opinion in Genetics & Development, 19*, 557–564.

Nowak, M. A. (2006). Five rules for the evolution of cooperation. *Science, 314*, 1560–1563.

Nussey, D. H., Postma, E., Gienapp, P., & Visser, M. E. (2005). Selection on heritable phenotypic plasticity in a wild bird population. *Science, 310*(Oct. 14), 304–306.

Obradović, J., Bush, N. R., Stamperdahl, J., Adler, N. E., & Boyce, W. T. (2010). Biological sensitivity to context: The interactive effects of stress reactivity and family adversity on socioemotional behavior and school readiness. *Child Development, 81*, 270–289.

Öhman, A., Flykt, A., & Esteves, F. (2001). Emotion drives attention: Detecting the snake in the grass. *Journal of Experimental Psychology: General, 130*, 466–478.

Olson, K. R., & Spelke, E. S. (2008). Foundations of cooperation in young children. *Cognition, 108*, 222–231.

Onishi, K. H., & Baillargeon, R. (2005). Do 15-month-old infants understand false belief? *Science, 308*, 255–258.

Oostenbroek, J., Suddendorf, T., Nielsen, M., Redshaw, J., Kennedy-Costantini, S., Davis, J., et al. (2016). Comprehensive longitudinal study challenges the existence of neonatal imitation in humans. *Current Biology, 26*, 1334–1338.

Orben, A., & Przybylski, A. K. (2019). Screens, teens, and psychological well-being: Evidence from three time-use-diary studies. *Psychological Science, 30*, 682–696.

Overton, W. F. (2015). Processes, relations, and relational-developmental-systems. In W. F. Overton & P. C. M. Molenaar (Eds.), *Handbook of child psychology and developmental science. Vol. 1: Theory & method* (7th edition, pp. 9–62). Hoboken, NJ: Wiley.

Painter, R. C., Osmond, C., Gluckman, P., Hanson, M., Philips, D. I. W., & Roseboom, T. J. (2008). Transgenerational effects on prenatal exposure to the Dutch famine on neonatal adiposity and health in later life. *BJOG, 115*, 1243–1249.

Papousek, H. (1969). Individual variability in learned responses in human infants. In R. J. Robinson (Ed.), *Brain and early behavior* (pp. 229–252). New York, NY: Academic Press.

Parade, S. H., Ridoput, K. K., Seifer, R., Armstrong, D. A., Marsit, C. J., McWilliams, M. A., et al. (2016). Methylation of the glucocorticoid receptor gene promoter in preschoolers: Links with internalizing behavior problems. *Child Development, 87*, 86–97.

Parsons, C. E., Young, K. S., Murray, L., Stein, A., & Kringelbach, M. L. (2010). The functional neuroanatomy of the evolving parent–infant relationship. *Progress in Neurobiology, 91*, 220–241.

Parten, M. (1932). Social participation among preschool children. *Journal of Abnormal and Social Psychology, 27*, 243–269.

Pascalis, O., de Haan, M., & Nelson, C. A. (2002). Is face processing species-specific during the first year of life? *Science, 296*(5571), 1321–1323.

Patterson, M. M., & Bigler, R. S. (2006). Preschool children's attention to environmental messages about groups: Social categorization and the origins of intergroup bias. *Child Development, 77*, 847–860.

Pellegrini, A. D. (2013). Object use in childhood: Development and possible functions. *Behaviour, 150*, 813–843.

Pellegrini, A. D., & Bjorklund, D. F. (2004). The ontogeny and phylogeny of children's object and fantasy play. *Human Nature, 15*, 23–43.

Pellegrini, A. D., & Galda, L. (1982). The effects of thematic-fantasy play training on the development of children's story comprehension. *American Educational Research Journal, 19*, 443–452.

Pellegrini, A. D., & Smith, P. K. (1998). Physical activity play: The nature and function of a neglected aspect of playing. *Child Development, 69*, 577–598.

Pen, I., Uller, T., Feldmeyer, B., Harts, A., While, G. M., & Wapstra, E. (2010). Climate-driven population divergence in sex-determining systems. *Nature, 468*, 436–439.

Pepper, G. V., & Roberts, S. C. (2006). Rates of nausea and vomiting in pregnancy and dietary characteristics across populations. *Proceeding of the Royal Society, B, 273*, 2675–2679.

Periss, V., Hernández Blasi, C., & Bjorklund, D. F. (2012). Cognitive "babyness": Developmental differences in the power of young children's supernatural thinking to influence positive and negative affect. *Developmental Psychology, 48*, 1203–1214.

Petanjek, Z., Judaš, M., Šimić, G., Roko Rašin, M., Uylings, H. B. M., Rakic, P., et al. (2011). Extraordinary neoteny of synaptic spines in the human prefrontal cortex. *PNAS, 108*, 13281–13286.

Piaget, J. (1955). *The language and thought of the child.* New York, NY: World.

Piaget, J. (1962). *Play, dreams, and imitation in childhood.* New York, NY: Norton.

Piaget, J. (1967). Genesis and structure in the psychology of intelligence. In D. Elkind (Ed.), *Six psychological studies* (pp. 143–158). New York, NY: Vintage Books.

Piaget, J. (1983). Piaget's theory. In P. Mussen (Ed.), *Handbook of child psychology* (Vol. 1, 4th edition, pp. 167–231). New York, NY: Wiley.

Pierucci, J. M., O'Brien, C. T., McInnis, M. A., Gilpin, A. T., & Barber, A. B. (2014). Fantasy orientation constructs and related executive function development in preschool: Developmental benefits to executive functions by being a fantasy-oriented child. *International Journal of Behavioral Development, 38*, 62–69.

Pinheiro, P. S. (2006). *United Nations Secretary-General's study on violence against children.* Geneva, Switzerland: ATAR Roto Presse SA.

Pinker, S. (1994). *The language instinct: How the mind creates language.* New York, NY: Morrow.

Plötner, M., Over, H., Carpenter, M., & Tomasello, M. (2015). The effects of collaboration and minimal-group membership on children's prosocial behavior, liking, affiliation, and trust. *Journal of Experimental Child Psychology, 139*, 161–173.

Pluess, M., & Belsky, J. (2011). Prenatal programming of postnatal plasticity? *Development and Psychopathology, 23*, 29–38.

Plumert, J. M. (1995). Relation between children's overestimation of their physical abilities and accident proneness. *Developmental Psychology, 31*, 866–876.

Plumert, J. M., & Schwebel, D. C. (1997). Social and temperamental influences on children's overestimation of their physical abilities: Links to accidental injuries. *Journal of Experimental Child Psychology, 67*, 317–337.

Poirier, F. E., & Smith, E. O. (1974). Socializing functions of primate play. *American Zoologist, 14*, 275–287.

Portmann, A. (1990). *A zoologist looks at humankind.* Judith Schaefer, Translator. New York, NY: Columbia University Press. (Originally published in 1944.)

Postman, N. (1982). *The disappearance of childhood.* New York, NY: Vintage Books.

Potard, C., Kubiszewski, V., Camus, G., Courtois, R., & Gaymard, S. (2018). Driving under the influence of alcohol and perceived invulnerability among young adults: An extension of the theory of planned behavior. *Transportation Research Part F: Traffic Psychology and Behaviour, 55*, 38–46.

Povinelli, D. J., & Eddy, T. J. (1996). What young chimpanzees know about seeing. *Monograph of the Society for Research in Child Development, 61*(3, Serial No. 247), i–vi, 1–152; discussion 153–191.

Prabhakar, S., Noonan, J. P., Pääbo, S., & Rubin, E. M. (2006). Accelerated evolution of conserved noncoding sequences in humans. *Science, 314,* 786.

Pratkanis, A. R., & Greenwald, A. B. (1985). How shall the self be conceived? *Journal for the Theory of Social Behavior, 15,* 311–328.

Preston, S. D., & de Waal, F. B. M. (2002). Empathy: Its ultimate and proximate bases. *Behavioral & Brain Sciences, 25,* 1–72.

Profet, M. (1992). Pregnancy sickness as an adaptation: A deterrent to maternal ingestion of teratogens. In J. Barkow, L. Cosmides, & J. Tooby (Eds.), *The adapted mind: Evolutionary psychology and the generation of culture* (pp. 327–366). New York, NY: Oxford University Press.

Provence, S., & Lipton, R. C. (1962). *Infants in institutions: A comparison of their development with family-reared infants during the first year of life.* New York, NY: International Universities Press.

Proverbio, A. M., Riva, F., Zani, A., & Martin, E. (2011). Is it a baby? Perceived age affects brain processing of faces differently in women and men. *Journal of Cognitive Neuroscience, 23,* 3197–3208.

Putnam, R. D. (2000). *Bowling alone: The collapse and revival of American community.* New York, NY: Simon & Schuster.

Quinn, P. C., Yahr, J., Kuhn, A., Slater, A. M., & Pascalis, O. (2002). Representation of the gender of human faces by infants: A preference for female. *Perception, 31,* 1109–1121.

Quiring, R. U., Walldorf, U., Kloter, U., & Gehring, W. J. (1994). Homology of the *eyeless* gene of *Drosophila* to the *Small eye* gene in mice and the *Aniridia* in humans. *Science, 265,* 785–789.

Radesky, J. S., Silverstein, M., Zuckerman, B., & Christakis, D. A. (2014). Infant self-regulation and early childhood media exposure. *Pediatrics, 133,* e1172–e1178. doi: 10.1542/peds.2013-2367

Raff, R. A. (1996). *The shape of life: Genes, development, and the evolution of animal form.* Chicago, IL: University of Chicago Press.

Rakison, D. (2018). Do 5-month-old infants possess an evolved detection mechanism for snakes, sharks, and rodents? *Journal of Cognition and Development, 19,* 456–476.

Rakoczy, H., Warneken, F., & Tomasello, M. (2007) "This way!", "No! That way!"—3-year-olds know that two people can have mutually incompatible desires. *Cognitive Development, 22,* 47–68.

Rands, C. M., Meader, S., Ponting, C. P., & Lunter, G. (2014). 8.2% of the human genome is constrained: Variation in rates of turnover across functional element classes in the human lineage. *PLoS Genetics, 10*(7), e1004525. doi: 10.1371/journal.pgen.1004525

REBRN. (2018). Retrieved June 16, 2018. https://rebrn.com/re/-years-ago-we-adopted-girls-from-eastern-europe-if-i-had-known-t-1500336/

Redshaw, J., Nielsen, M., Slaughter, V., Kennedy-Costantini, S., Oostenbroek, J., Crimston, J., & Suddendorf, T. (2019). Individual differences in neonatal "imitation" fail to predict early social cognitive behavior. *Developmental Science, 23*(2), e12892. doi: 10.1111/desc.12892. [Epub ahead of print]

Reed, J., Hirsh-Pasek, K., & Golinkoff, R. M. (2017). Learning on hold: Cell phones sidetrack parent-child interactions. *Developmental Psychology, 53,* 1428–1436.

Refsnider, J. M., & Janzen, F. J. (2015). Temperature-dependent sex determination under rapid anthropogenic environmental change: Evolution at a turtle's pace? *Journal of Heredity, 107,* 61–70.

Rendell, L., & Whitehead, H. (2001). Culture in whales and dolphins. *Behavioral and Brain Science, 24,* 309–382.

Repacholi, B. M., & Gopnik, A. (1997). Early reasoning about desires: Evidence from 14- and 18-month-olds. *Developmental Psychology, 33,* 12–21.

Ressler, R. H. (1966). Inherited environmental influences on the operant behavior of mice. *Journal of Comparative and Physiological Psychology, 61,* 264–267.

Rheingold, H. L. (1982). Little children's participation in the work of adults: A nascent prosocial behavior. *Child Development, 53,* 114–125.

Rheingold, H. L. (1985). Development as the acquisition of familiarity. *Annual Review of Psychology, 36,* 1–17.

Rice, F., Harold, G. T., Boivin, J., van den Bree, M., Hay, D. F., & Thapar, A. (2010). The links between prenatal stress and offspring development and psychopathology: Disentangling environmental and inherited influences. *Psychological Medicine, 40,* 335–345.

Richert, R., Robb, M. B., Fender, J. G., & Wartella, E. (2010). Word learning from baby videos. *Archives of Pediatric and Adolescent Medicine, 164,* 432–437.

Rideout, V., & Robb, M. B. (2018). *Social media, social life: Teens reveal their experiences.* San Francisco, CA: Common Sense Media.

Riedl, K., Jensen, K., Call, J. M., & Tomasello, M. (2012). No third-party punishment in chimpanzees. *PNAS, 109,* 14824–14829.

Riedl, K., Jensen, K., Call, J. M., & Tomasello, M. (2015). Restorative justice in children. *Current Biology, 25,* 1731–1735.

Rigo, P., Kim, P., Esposito, G., Putnick, D. L., Venuti, P., & Bornstein, M. H. (2019). Specific maternal brain responses to their own child's face: An fMRI meta-analysis. *Developmental Review, 51,* 58–69.

Rilling, J. K., & Insel, T. R. (1999). The primate neocortex in comparative perspective using magnetic resonance imaging. *Journal of Human Evolution, 37,* 191–223.

Ritchie, S. J., & Tucker-Drob, E. M. (2018). How much does education improve intelligence? A meta-analysis. *Psychological Science, 29,* 1358–1369.

Rittle-Johnson, B. (2006). Promoting transfer: Effects of self-explanation and direct instruction. *Child Development, 77,* 1–29.

Robbins, E., & Rochat, P. (2011). Emerging signs of strong reciprocity in human ontogeny. *Frontiers in Psychology, 353,* 1–14.

Rochat, P. M., Dias, D. G., Guo, L., Broesch, T., Passos-Ferreira, C., Winning, A., et al. (2009). Fairness in distributive justice by 3- and 5-year-olds across seven cultures. *Journal of Cross-Cultural Psychology, 40,* 416–442.

Rogoff, B. (1998). Cognition as a collaborative process. In W. Damon (Gen. Ed.), *Handbook of child psychology* (5th ed.). In D. Kuhn & R. S. Siegler (Vol. Eds.), Vol. 2: *Cognition language, and perceptual development* (pp. 679–744). New York, NY: Wiley.

Romens, S. E., McDonald, J., Svaren, J., & Pollak, S. D. (2015). Associations between early life stress and gene methylation in children. *Child Development, 86,* 303–309.

Rosen, L. D., Lim, A. F., Felt, J., Carrier, L. M., Cheever, N. A., Lara-Ruis, J. M., et al. (2014). Media and technology use predicts ill-being among children, preteens and teenagers independent of the negative health impacts of exercise and eating habits. *Computers and Human Behavior, 35,* 364–375.

Roser, M. Fertility rate. Our World in Data. Retrieved August 16, 2019. https://ourworldindata.org/fertility-rate

Ross, J., Anderson, J. R., & Campbell, R. N. (2011). I remember me: Mnemonic self-reference effects in preschool children. *Monographs of the Society for Research in Child Development, 76*(3, Serial No. 300), i–vii, 1–102.

Rovee-Collier, C., & Giles, A. (2010). Why a neuromaturational model of memory fails: Exuberant learning in early infancy. *Behavioural Processes, 83*, 197–206.

Rubin, K. H., Watson, K. S., & Jambor, T. W. (1978) Free-play behaviors in preschool and kindergarten children. *Child Development, 49*, 534–536.

Rueda, M. R., & Posner, M. I. (2013). Development of attention networks. In P. D. Zelazo (Ed.), *Oxford handbook of developmental psychology* (pp. 683–705). Oxford, UK: Oxford University Press.

Ruff, H. A., & Birch, H. G. (1974). Infant visual fixation: The effect of concentricity, curvilinearity, and number of directions. *Journal of Experimental Child Psychology, 17*, 460–473.

Ruffman, T. (2014). To belief or not belief: Children's theory of mind. *Developmental Review, 34*, 265–293.

Ruffman, T., Lorimer, B., & Scarf, D. (2017). Do infants really experience emotional contagion? *Child Development Perspective, 11*, 270–274.

Ruiz, A. M., & Santos, L. R. (2013). Understanding differences in the way human and non-human primates represent tools: The role of teleological-intentional information. In C. M. Sanz, J. Call, & C. Boesch (Eds.), *Tool use in animals: Cognition and ecology* (pp. 119–133). Cambridge, UK: Cambridge University Press.

Rutter, M., Beckett, C., Castle, J., Colvert, E., Kreppner, J., Mehta, M., et al. (2007). Effects of profound early institutional deprivation: An overview of findings from a UK longitudinal study of Romanian adoptees. *European Journal of Developmental Psychology, 4*, 332–350.

Sabbagh, M. A., Xu, F., Carlson, S. M., Moses, L. J., & Lee, K. (2006). The development of executive functioning and theory of mind. *Psychological Science, 17*, 74–81.

Sagi, A., & Hoffman, M. L. (1976). Empathic distress in the newborn. *Developmental Psychology, 12*, 175–176.

Salapatek, P., & Kessen, W. (1966). Visual scanning of triangles by the human newborn. *Journal of Experimental Child Psychology, 3*, 155–167.

Sameroff, A. J., & Chandler, M. J. (1975). Reproductive risk and the continuum of caretaking causality. In F. D. Horowitz, M. Hetherington, S. Scarr-Salapatek, & G. Siegal (Eds.), *Review of child development research* (Vol. 4, pp. 187–244). Chicago, IL: University of Chicago Press.

Sandman, C. A., Davis, E. P., & Glynn, L. M. (2013). Prescient human fetuses thrive. *Psychological Science, 23*, 93–100.

Santidrián Tomillo, P., Genovart, M., Paladino, F. V., Spotila, J. R., & Oro, D. (2015). Climate change overruns resilience conferred by temperature-dependent sex determination in sea turtles and threatens their survival. *Global Change Biology, 21*, 2980–2988.

Sbarra, D. A., Briskin, J. L., & Slatcher, R. B. (2019). Smartphones and close relationships: The case for an evolutionary mismatch. *Perspectives on Psychological Science, 14*, 596–618.

Scarf, D., Imuta, K., Colombo, M., & Hayne, H. (2012). Social evaluation or simple association? Simple association may explain moral reasoning in infants. *PLoS One, 7*(8), e42698. doi: 10.1371/journal.pone.0042698

Scarr, S. (1992). Developmental theories for the 1990s: Development and individual differences. *Child Development, 63*, 1–19.

Scarr, S. (1993). Biological and cultural diversity: The legacy of Darwin. *Child Development, 64*, 1333–1353.

Schertz, K. E., & Berman, M. G. (2019). Understanding nature and its cognitive benefits. *Current Directions in Psychological Science, 28*, 496–502.

Schleihauf, H., Graetz, S., Pauen, S., & Hoehl, S. (2018). Contrasting social and cognitive accounts on overimitation: The role of causal transparency and prior experience. *Child Development, 89*, 1039–1055.

Schmalhausen, I. I. (1949). *Factors of evolution: The theory of stabilizing selection*. Philadelphia, PA: Blakiston.

Schmidt, M. F., Rakoczy, H., & Tomasello, M. (2016). Young children understand and defend the role of agreement in establishing arbitrary norms—but unanimity is key. *Child Development, 87*, 612–626.

Schmidt, M. F., & Sommerville, J. A. (2011). Fairness expectations and altruistic sharing in 15-month-old human infants. *PLoS One, 6*(10), e23223. doi: 10.1371/pone.0023223

Schneider, W. (1985). Developmental trends in the metamemory-memory behavior relationship: An integrative review. In D. L. Forrest-Pressley, G. E. MacKinnon, & T. G. Waller (Eds.), *Cognition, metacognition, and human performance* (Vol. 1, pp. 57–109). New York, NY: Academic Press.

Schneider, W. (1998). Performance prediction in young children: Effects of skill, metacognition and wishful thinking. *Developmental Science, 1*(2), 291–297.

Schön, R. A. (2007). Natural parenting—Back to basics in infant care. *Evolutionary Psychology, 5*, 102–183.

Schore, A. N. (2013). Bowlby's "environment of evolutionary adaptedness": Recent studies on the interpersonal neurobiology of attachment and emotional development. In D. Narvaez, J. Panksepp, A. N. Schore, & T. R. Gleason (Eds.), *Evolution, early experience and human development: From research to practice and policy* (pp. 31–67). New York, NY: Oxford University Press.

Schwartz, J. H. (1999). *Sudden origins: Fossils, genes, and the emergence of species*. New York, NY: Wiley.

Sclafani, V., Paukner, A., Suomi, S. J., & Ferrari, P. F. (2015). Imitation promotes affiliation in infant macaques at risk for impaired social behaviors. *Developmental Science, 18*, 614–621.

Scott, J. P. (1968). *Early experience and the organization of behavior*. Belmont, CA: Brooks/Cole.

Scott, R. M. (2017). The developmental origins of false-belief understanding. *Current Directions in Psychological Science, 26*, 68–74.

Seligman, M. E. P. (1998). *Learned optimism: How to change your mind and your life* (2nd edition). New York, NY: Free Press.

Sellers, P. D., II, & Bjorklund, D. F. (2014). The development of adaptive memory. In B. L. Schwartz, M. L. Howe, M. P. Toglia, & H. Otgaar (Eds.), *What's adaptive about adaptive memory?* (pp. 286–307). New York, NY: Oxford University Press.

Sellers, P. D., II, Machluf, K., & Bjorklund, D. F. (2016). How do hunter-gatherers learn calculus? Applying an evolutionary perspective to modern education practice. In A. Alvergne, C. Jenkinson, & C. Faurie, (Eds.), *Evolutionary medicine: A guide for researchers, practitioners and policy-makers* (pp. 89–102). Oxford, UK: Springer.

Senese, V. P., De Falco, S., Bornstein, M. H., Caria, A., Buffolino, S., & Venutti, P. (2013). Human infant faces provoke implicit positive affective responses in parents and non-parents alike. *PLoS One, 8*(11), e80379. doi: 10.1371/journal.pone.0080379

Senghas, A., & Coppola, M. (2001). Children creating language: How Nicaraguan Sign Language acquired a spatial grammar. *Psychological Science, 12*, 323–326.

Senghas, A., Kita, S., & Ozyurek, A. (2004). Children creating core properties of language: Evidence from an emerging sign language in Nicaragua. *Science, 305*, 1179–1782.

Sercombe, H. (2014). Risk, adaptation and the functional teenage brain. *Brain and Cognition, 89*, 61–69.

Shea, B. T. (1989). Heterochrony in human evolution: The case for neoteny revisited. *Yearbook of Physical Anthropology, 32*, 69–101.

Shea, B. T. (2000). Current issues in the investigation of evolution by heterochrony, with emphasis on the debate over human neoteny. In S. T. Parker, J. Langer, & M. L. McKinney (Eds.), *Biology, brains, and behavior: The evolution of human development* (pp. 181–213). Santa Fe, NM: School of American Research Press.

Sheehy, G. (1976). *Passages: Predictable crises of adult life*. New York, NY: Ballantine.

Sherman, G. D., Haidt, J., & Coan, J. A. (2009). Viewing cute images increases behavioral carefulness. *Emotion, 9*, 282–286.

Sherman, G. D., Haidt, J., Iyer, R., & Coan, J. A. (2013). Individual differences in the physical embodiment of care: Prosocially oriented women respond to cuteness by becoming more physically careful. *Emotion, 13*, 151–158.

Shin, H-E., Bjorklund, D. F., & Beck, E. F. (2007). The adaptive nature of children's overestimation in a strategic memory task. *Cognitive Development, 22*, 197–212.

Shore, T. J. (2014). The adult brain makes new neurons, and effortful learning keeps them alive. *Current Directions in Psychological Science, 23*, 311–318.

Siegler, R. S., & Alibali, M. W. (2004). *Children's thinking* (4th edition). Upper Saddle River, NJ: Prentice Hall.

Silk, J. B., Brosnan, S. F., Henrich, J., Lambeth, S. P., & Shapiro, S. J. (2013). Chimpanzees share food for many reasons: The role of kinship, reciprocity, social bonds and harassment on food transfers. *Animal Behavior, 85*, 941–947.

Silk, J. B., Brosnan, S. F., Vonk, J., Henrich, J., Povinelli, D. J., Richardson, A. S., et al. (2005). Chimpanzees are indifferent to the welfare of unrelated group members. *Nature, 347*, 1357–1359.

Simpson, E. A., Miller, G. M., Ferrari, P. F., Suomi, S. J., & Paukner, A. (2016). Neonatal imitation and early social experience predict gaze following abilities in infant monkeys. *Scientific Reports, 6*, article no. 20233. doi: 10.1038/srep20233

Simpson, J. A., Griskevicius, V., Kuo, S., Sung, S., & Collins, W. A. (2012). Evolution, stress, and sensitive periods: The influence of unpredictability in early versus late childhood on sex and risky behavior. *Developmental Psychology, 48*, 674–686.

Singh, J. A. L., & Zingg, R. M. (1966). *Wolf-children and feral man* (English and German edition). Brooklyn, NY: Shoe String Press.

Skenazy, L. (2008, April 8). "Why I Let My 9-Year-Old Ride the Subway Alone." *New York Sun*. Retrieved August 13, 2019. https://www.nysun.com/news/why-i-let-my-9-year-old-ride-subway-alone

Skulachev, V. P., Holtze, S., Vyssokikh, M. Y., Bakeeva, L. E., Skulachev, M. V., Markov, A. V., et al. (2017). Neoteny, prolongation of youth: From naked mole rats to "naked ape" (humans). *Physiological Review, 97*, 699–720.

Slagt, M., Dubas, J. S., Deković, M., & van Aken, M. A. G. (2016). Differences in sensitivity to parenting depending on child temperament: A meta-analysis. *Psychological Bulletin, 142*(10), 1068–1110.

Slaughter, V., & Perez-Zapata, D. (2014). Cultural variations in the development of mind reading. *Child Development Perspectives, 8*, 237–241.

Smilansky, S. (1968). *The effects of sociodramatic play on disadvantaged preschool children.* New York, NY: Wiley.

Smith, P. K. (1982). Does play matter? Functional and evolutionary aspects of animal and human play. *Behavioral and Brain Sciences, 5*, 139–184.

Smith, P. K., & Connolly, K. (1980). *The ecology of preschool behaviour.* London, UK: Cambridge University Press.

Sol, D., Bacher, S., Reader, S. M., & Lefebvre, L. (2015). Brain size predicts the success of mammal species introduced into novel environments. *The American Naturalist, 172*, S63–S71.

Somel, M., Franz, H., Yan, Z., Lorenc, A., Guo, S., Giger, T., et al. (2009). Transcriptional neoteny in the human brain. *PNAS, 106*, 5743–5748.

Somel, M., Rohlfs, R., & Liu, X. (2014). Transcriptomic insights into human brain evolution: Acceleration, neutrality, heterochrony. *Genetics & Development, 29*, 110–119.

Sommerville, J. A. (2018). Infants' understanding of distributive fairness as a test case for identifying the extents and limits of infants' sociomoral cognition and behavior. *Child Development Perspectives, 12*, 141–145.

Sommerville, J. A., Schmidt, M. F., Yun, J. E., & Burns, M. (2013). The development of expectations of fairness and prosocial behavior in the second year of life. *Infancy, 18*, 40–66.

Spear, L. P. (2000). Neurobehavioral changes in adolescence. *Current Directions in Psychological Science, 9*, 111–114.

Spear, L. P. (2007). Brain development and adolescent behavior. In D. Coch, K. W. Fischer, & G. Dawson (Eds.), *Human behavior, learning, and the developing brain: Typical development* (pp. 362–396). New York, NY: Guilford.

Spear, N. E. (1984). Ecologically determined dispositions control the ontogeny of learning and memory. In R. Kail & N. E. Spear (Eds.), *Memory development: Comparative perspectives* (pp. 325–358). Hillsdale, NJ: Erlbaum.

Spelke, E. S., & Kinzler, K. D. (2007). Core knowledge. *Developmental Science, 10*, 89–96.

Spinath, B., & Spinath, F. M. (2005). Development of self-perceived ability in elementary school: The role of parents' perceptions, teacher evaluations, and intelligence. *Cognitive Development, 20*, 190–204.

Sprengelmeyer, R., Perrett, D. I., Fagan, E. C., Cornwell, R. E., Lobmaier, J. S., Sprengelmeyer, A., et al. (2009). The cutest little baby face: A hormonal link to sensitivity to cuteness in infant faces. *Psychological Science, 20*, 149–154.

Statista, https://www.statista.com/statistics/264810/number-of-monthly-active-facebook-users-worldwide/. Downloaded June 27, 2020.

Stearns, S. (1992). *The evolution of life histories.* Oxford, UK: Oxford University Press.

Steer, C. D., Davey Smith G., Emmett P. M., Hibbel, J. R., & Golding J. (2010). FADS2 polymorphisms modify the effect of breastfeeding on child IQ. *PLoS One*, 5(7), e11570. doi: 10.1371/journal.pone.0011570

Steers, M. N., Wickham, R. E., & Acitelli, L. K. (2014). Seeing everyone else's highlight reels: How Facebook usage is linked to depressive symptoms. *Journal of Social and Clinical Psychology, 33*, 701–731.

Steinberg, L. (2007). Risk taking in adolescence: New perspectives from brain and behavioral science. *Current Directions in Psychological Science, 16*, 55–59.

Steinberg, L. (2008). A social neuroscience perspective on adolescent risk-taking. *Developmental Review, 28*, 78–106.

Steinberg, L., Icenogle, G., Shulman, E. P., Breiner, K., Chein, J., Bacchini, D., et al. (2017). Around the world, adolescence is a time of heightened sensation seeking and immature self-regulation. *Developmental Science, 21*, e12532. doi: 10.111.desc.12532

Stengelin, R., Hepach, R., & Haun, D. (2020). Cross-cultural variation in how much, but not whether, children overimitate. *Journal of Experimental Child Psychology, 193*, 104796.

Stenhouse, D. (1974). *The evolution of intelligence: A general theory and some of its implications.* London, UK: Allen & Unwin.

Stipek, D. (1981). Children's perceptions of their own and their classmates' ability. *Journal of Experimental Child Psychology, 73*, 404–410.

Stipek, D. (1984). Young children's performance expectations: Logical analysis or wishful thinking? In J. G. Nicholls (Ed.), *Advances in motivation and achievement: Vol. 3. The development of achievement motivation* (pp. 33–56). Greenwich, CT: JAI.

Stipek, D., & Daniels, D. (1988). Declining perceptions of competence: A consequence of changes in the child or the educational environment? *Journal of Educational Psychology, 80*, 352–356.

Stotz, K. (2017). Why developmental niche construction is not selective niche construction: And why it matters. *Interface Focus, 7*(5), 20160157. doi: 10.1098/rsfs.2016.0157

Stright, A. D., Gallagher, K. C., & Kelley, K. (2008). Infant temperament moderates relations between maternal parenting in early childhood and children's adjustment in first grade. *Child Development, 79*, 186–200.

Stroud, L. R., Papandonatos, G. D., Salisbury, A. L., Phipps, M. G., Huestis, M. A., Niaura, R., et al. (2016). Epigenetic regulation of placental NR3C1: Mechanisms underlying prenatal programming of infant neurobehavior by maternal smoking? *Child Development, 87*, 49–60.

Strouse, G. A., & Ganea, P. A. (2017). Toddlers' word learning and transfer from electronic and print books. *Journal of Experimental Child Psychology, 156*, 129–142.

Suddendorf, T., & Corballis, M. C. (2007). The evolution of foresight: What is mental time travel, and is it unique to humans? *Behavioral and Brain Sciences, 30*, 299–313.

Sumner, J. A., McLaughlin, K. A., Walsh, K., Sheridan, M. A., & Koenen, K. C. (2015). Caregiving and 5-HTTLPR genotype predict adolescent physiological stress reactivity: Confirmatory tests of gene × environment interactions. *Child Development, 86*, 985–994.

Sutter, M. (2007). Outcome versus intention: On the nature of fair behavior and its development with age. *Journal of Economic Psychology, 28*, 69–78.

Symons, D. (1979). *The evolution of human sexuality.* Oxford, UK: Oxford University Press.

Számadó, S., & Sazthmáry, E. (2006). Selective scenarios for the emergence of natural language. *Trends in Ecology and Evolution, 21*, 555–561.

Szepsenwol, O., Griskevicius, V., Simpson, J. A., Young, E. S., Fleck, C., & Jones, R. E. (2018). The effect of predictable early childhood environments on sociosexuality in early adulthood. *Evolutionary Behavioral Sciences, 11*, 131–145.

Tajfel, H., Billig, M. G., Bundy, R. P., & Flament, C. (1971). Social categorization and intergroup behaviour. *European Journal of Social Psychology, 1*, 149–178.

Tanner, J. M. (1978). *From fetus into man: Physical growth from conception to maturity.* Cambridge, MA: Harvard University Press.

Tardif, T., & Wellman, H. M. (2000). Acquisition of mental state language in Mandarin- and Cantonese-speaking children. *Developmental Psychology, 36,* 25–43.

Tattersall, I. (2013). *Masters of the planet: The search for our human origins.* New York, NY: St. Martin's Griffin.

Taylor, K., & Silver, L. (February, 2019). Smartphone ownership is growing rapidly around the world, but not always equally. Pew Research Center, Global Attitudes & Trends. Retrieved August 20, 2019, https://www.pewresearch.org/global/2019/02/05/smartphone-ownership-is-growing-rapidly-around-the-world-but-not-always-equally/

Tennie, C., Call, J., & Tomasello, M. (2009). Ratcheting up the ratchet: On the evolution of cumulative culture. *Philosophical Transactions of the Royal Society B, 364,* 2405–2415.

Thomaes, S., Brummelman, E., & Sedikides, C. (2017). Why most children think well of themselves. *Child Development, 88,* 1873–1884.

Thomas de Benitez, S. (February 23, 2009). "State of the World's Street Children: Violence Report." SlideShare. SlideShare Inc. Retrieved January, 28, 2019.

Thomson, K. W. (1988). *Morphogenesis and evolution.* New York, UK: Oxford University Press.

Tinbergen, N. (1951). *The study of instinct.* Oxford, UK: Clarendon Press.

Tinbergen, N., & Perdeck, A. C. (1950). On the stimulus situation releasing the begging response in the newly hatched Herring Gull chick (Larus argentatus Pont.). *Behaviour, 3,* 1–39.

Tobi, E. W., Slieker, R. C., Stein, A. D., Suchiman, H. E. D., Slagboo, P. E., van Zwet, E. W., et al. (2015). Early gestation as the critical time-window for changes in the prenatal environment to affect the adult human blood methylome. *International Journal of Epidemiology, 44,* 1211–1223.

Tomasello, M. (1999). *The cultural origins of human cognition.* Cambridge, MA: Harvard University Press.

Tomasello, M. (2000). Culture and cognitive development. *Current Directions in Psychological Science, 9,* 37–40.

Tomasello, M. (2005). *Constructing a language: A usage-based theory of language acquisition.* Cambridge, MA: Harvard University Press.

Tomasello, M. (2014). The ultra-social animal. *European Journal of Social Psychology, 44,* 187–194.

Tomasello, M. (2019). *Becoming human: A theory of ontogeny.* Cambridge, MA: Belknap Press.

Tomasello, M., & Carpenter, M. (2005). The emergence of social cognition in three young chimpanzees. *Monographs of the Society for Research in Child Development, 70*(1, Serial No. 279), vii–132.

Tomasello, M., & Carpenter, M. (2007). Shared intentionality. *Developmental Science, 10,* 121–125.

Tomasello, M., & Herrmann, E. (2010). Ape and human cognition: What's the difference? *Current Directions in Psychological Science, 19,* 3–8.

Tomasello, M., Kruger, A. C., & Ratner, H. H. (1993). Cultural learning. *Behavioral and Brain Sciences, 16,* 495–552.

Tomasello, M., Savage-Rumbaugh, S., & Kruger, A. C. (1993). Imitative learning of actions on objects by children, chimpanzees, and enculturated chimpanzees. *Child Development, 64,* 1688–1705.

Tomonaga, M., Tankak, M., Matsuzawa, T., Myowa-Yamakoshi, M., Kosugi, D., Mizuno, Y., et al. (2004). Development of social cognition in infant chimpanzees (*Pan troglodytes*): Face recognition, smiling, gaze, and the lack of triadic interactions. *Japanese Psychological Research, 46,* 227–235.

Toub, T. S., Rajan, V., Golinkoff, R. M., & Hirsh-Pasek, K. (2016). Guided play: A solution to the play versus discovery learning dichotomy. In D. C. Geary & D. B. Berch (Eds.), *Evolutionary perspectives on education and child development* (pp. 117–141). New York, NY: Springer.

Trevanthan, W. R. (1987). *Human birth: An evolutionary perspective.* Hawthorne, NY: Aldine de Gruyter.

Trevathan, W. R., & Rosenberg, K. R. (2016). Human evolution and the helpless infant. In W. R. Trevathan & K. R. Rosenberg (Eds.), *Costly and cute: Helpless infants and human evolution* (pp. 1–28). Santa Fe, NM: School for advanced Research Press.

Trivers, R. L. (1971). The evolution of reciprocal altruism. *The Quarterly Review of Biology, 46,* 35–57.

Trivers, R. L. (1974). Parent-offspring conflict. *American Zoologist, 14,* 249–264.

Troller-Renferee, S., Zeanah, C. H., Nelson, C. A., & Fox, N. A. (2018). Neural and cognitive factors influencing the emergence of psychopathology: Insights from the Bucharest Early Intervention Project. *Child Development Perspectives, 12,* 28–33.

Tromholt, M. (2016). The Facebook experiment. Quitting Facebook leads to higher levels of well-being: *Cyberpsychology, Behavior, and Social Networking, 19,* 661–666.

Tronick, E. Z. (1989). Emotions and emotional communication in infants. *American Psychologist, 44,* 112–119.

Tronick, E., Als, H., Adamson, L., Wise, S., & Brazelton, T. B. (1978). The infant's response to entrapment between contradictory messages in face-to-face interaction. *Journal of the American Academy of Child Psychiatry, 17,* 1–13.

Trut, L. (1999). Early canid domestication: The Farm-Fox Experiment. *American Scientist, 87*(2), 160.

Trut, L., Oskina, I., & Kharlamova, A. (2009) Animal evolution during domestication: The domesticated fox as a model. *BioEssays, 31,* 349–360.

Tulving, E. (1985). How many memory systems are there? *American Psychologist, 40,* 385–398.

Turati, C., Simion, F., Milani, I., & Umiltà, C. (2002). Newborns' preference for faces: What is crucial? *Developmental Psychology, 38,* 875–882.

Turkewitz, G., & Kenny, P. (1982). Limitations on input as a basis for neural organization and perceptual development: A preliminary theoretical statement. *Developmental Psychobiology, 15,* 357–368.

Twenge, J. M. (2017). *iGen: Why today's super-connected kids are growing up less rebellious, more tolerant, less happy—and completely unprepared for adulthood.* New York, NY: Atria Books.

Twenge, J. M. (2019). More time on technology, less happiness? Association between digital media use and psychological well-being. *Current Directions in Psychological Science, 28,* 372–379.

Twenge, J. M., & Campbell, W. K. (2018). Associations between screen time and lower psychological well-being among children and adolescents: Evidence from a population-based study. *Preventive Medicine Report, 12,* 271–283.

Twenge, J., Joiner, T. E., Rogers, M. L., & Martin, G. N. (2018). Increases in depressive symptoms, suicide-related outcomes, and suicide rates among U.S. adolescents after

2010 and links to increased new media screen time. *Clinical Psychological Science, 6*, 3–17.

Twenge, J. M., Krizan, Z., & Hisler, G. (2017). Decreases in self-reported sleep duration among U.S. adolescents 2009–2015 and links to new media screen time. *Sleep Medicine, 39*, 47–53.

Twenge, J., Martin, G. N., & Campbell, W. K. (2018). Decreases in psychological well-being among American adolescents after 2012 and links to screen time during the rise of smartphone technology. *Emotion, 18*, 765–780.

Ulber, J., Hamann, K., & Tomasello, M. (2015). How 18- and 24-month-old peers divide resources among themselves. *Journal of Experimental Child Psychology, 140*, 228–244.

Ulber, J., Hamann, K., & Tomasello, M. (2016). Extrinsic rewards diminish costly sharing in 3-year-olds. *Child Development, 87*, 1192–1203.

United Nations Treaty Collection. (1990). Convention on the Rights of the Child. Retrieved June 17, 2019. https://treaties.un.org/Pages/ViewDetails.aspx?src=TREATY&mtdsg_no=IV-11&chapter=4&lang=en

Ursini, G., Punzi, G., Chen, Q., Marenco, S., Robinson, J. F., Porcelli, A., et al. (2018). Convergence of placenta biology and genetic risk for schizophrenia. *Nature Medicine, 24*(6), 792–801. doi: 10.1038/s41591-018-0021-y

Vaish, A., Hepach, R., & Tomasello, M. (2018). The specificity of reciprocity: Young children reciprocate more generously to those who *intentionally* benefit *them*. *Journal of Experimental Child Psychology, 167*, 336–353.

Vaish, A., & Striano, T. (2004). Is visual reference necessary? Contributions of facial versus vocal cues in 12-month-olds' social referencing behavior. *Developmental Science, 7*, 261–269.

Van Duuren, M., Kendell-Scott, L., & Stark, N. (2003). Early aesthetic choices: Infant preferences for attractive premature infant faces. *International Journal of Behavioral Development, 27*, 212–219.

van IJzendoorn, M. H., Bakermans-Kranenburg, M. J., & Ebstein, R. P. (2011). Methylation matters in child development: Toward developmental behavioral epigenetics. *Child Development Perspectives, 5*, 305–310.

van Loon, M., de Bruin, A., Leppink, J., & Roebers, C. (2017). Why are children overconfident? Developmental differences in the implantation of accessibility cues when judging concept learning. *Journal of Experimental Child Psychology, 158*, 77–94.

Vartanian, L. R. (2000). Revisiting the imaginary audience and personal fable constructs of adolescent egocentrism: A conceptual review. *Adolescence, 35*, 639–661.

Verduyn, P., Lee, D. S., Park, J., Shablack, H., Orvell, A., Bayer, J., et al. (2015). Passive Facebook usage undermines affective well-being: Experimental and longitudinal evidence. *Journal of Experimental Psychology: General, 144*, 480–488.

Vernon, L., Modecki, K. L., & Barber, B. L. (2018). Mobile phones in the bedroom: Trajectories of sleep habits and subsequent adolescent psychosocial development. *Child Development, 89*, 66–77.

Volk, A. A., & Atkinson, J. A. (2013). Infant and child death in the human environment of evolutionary adaptation. *Evolution and Human Behavior, 34*, 182–192.

Volk, A. A., Dane, A. V., & Marini, A. (2014). What is bullying? A theoretical definition. *Developmental Review, 34*, 327–343.

Volk, A. A., Lukjanczuk, J. L., & Quinsey, V. L. (2007). Perceptions of child facial cues as a function of child age. *Evolutionary Psychology, 5*, 801–814.

Vouloumanos, A., & Waxman, S. (2014). Listen up! Speech is for thinking during infancy. *Trends in Cognitive Sciences, 18*, 642–646.

Vygotsky, L. S. (1933). *Play and its role in the mental development of the child.* Source: Voprosy psikhologii, 1966, No. 6. (Translator, Catherine Mulholland) https://www.marxists.org/archive/vygotsky/works/1933/play.htm

Vygotsky, L. S. (1962). *Thought and language.* Cambridge, MA: MIT Press.

Vygotsky, L. S. (1978). *Mind in Society: The development of higher psychological processes.* Cambridge, MA: Harvard University Press.

Waddington, C. H. (1975). *The evolution of an evolutionist.* Ithaca, NY: Cornell University Press.

Wait Until 8th. (2019). https://www.waituntil8th.org. Retrieved October 1, 2019.

Waller, K. L., Volk, A., & Quinsey, V. L. (2004). The effect of infant fetal alcohol syndrome facial features on adoption preferences. *Human Nature, 15*, 101–117.

Wang, J., Iannotti, R. J., & Nansel, T. R. (2009). School bullying among adolescents in the United States: Physical, verbal, relational, and cyber. *Journal of Adolescent Health, 45*, 368–375.

Wang, Y., & Henderson, A. M. E. (2018). Just rewards: 17-month-old infants expect agents to take resources according to the principle of distributive justice. *Journal of Experimental Child Psychology, 172*, 25–40.

Want, S. C., & Harris, P. L. (2001). Learning from other peoples' mistakes: Causal understanding in learning to use a tool. *Child Development, 72*, 431–443.

Warneken, F. (2015). Precocious prosociality: Why do young children help? *Child Development Perspectives, 9*, 1–6.

Warneken, F., Chen, F., & Tomasello, M. (2006). Cooperative activities in young children and chimpanzees. *Child Development, 77*, 640–663.

Warneken, F., Gräfenhain, M., & Tomasello, M. (2012). Collaborative partner or social tool? New evidence for young children's understanding of joint intentions in collaborative activities. *Developmental Science, 15*, 54–61.

Warneken, F., & Tomasello, M. (2007). Helping and cooperation at 14 months of age. *Infancy, 11*, 271–294.

Warneken, F., & Tomasello, M. (2008). Extrinsic rewards undermine altruistic tendencies in 20-month-olds. *Developmental Psychology, 44*, 1785–1788.

Warneken, F., & Tomasello, M. (2013). Parental presence and encouragement do not influence helping in young children. *Infancy, 18*, 345–368.

Watson-Jones, R. E., & Legare, C. H. (2016). The social functions of group rituals. *Current Directions in Psychological Science, 25*, 42–46.

Weisberg, D. S., Hirsh-Pasek, K., & Golinkoff, R. M. (2013). Guide play: Where curricular goals meet a playful pedagogy. *Mind, Brain, and Education, 7*, 104–112.

Weisberg, D. S., Hirsh-Pasek, K., & Golinkoff, R. M., Kittredge, A. K., & Klahr, D. (2016). Guided play: Principles and practices. *Current Directions in Psychological Science, 25*, 177–182.

Weissman, M. M., Bland, R. C., Canino, G. J., Faravelli, C., Greenwald, S., Hwu, H. G., et al. (1996). Cross-national epidemiology of major depression and bipolar disorder. *JAMA, 31*, 293–299.

Wellman, H. M., Cross, D., & Watson, J. (2001). Meta-analysis of theory-of-mind development: The truth about false belief. *Child Development, 72*, 655–684.

Wesson, R. (1991). *Beyond natural selection.* Cambridge, MA: MIT Press.

West-Eberhard, M. J. (2003). *Developmental plasticity and evolution*. New York, NY: Oxford University Press.
Whiten, A. (2010). Ape behavior and the origins of human culture. In P. Kappeler & J. Silk (Eds.), *Mind the gap: Tracing the origins of human universals* (pp. 429–450). New York, NY: Springer.
Whiten, A. (2017). Social learning and culture in child and chimpanzee. *Annual Review of Psychology, 68*, 129–154.
Whiten, A. (2018). Social, Machiavellian and cultural cognition: A golden age of discovery in comparative and evolutionary psychology. *Journal of Comparative Psychology, 132*(4), 437–441.
Whiten, A. (2019). Conformity and over-imitation: An integrative review of variant forms of hyper-reliance on social learning. *Advances in the Study of Behavior, 51*, 31–75.
Whiten, A., & Erdal, D. (2014). The human socio-cognitive niche and its evolutionary origins. *Philosophical Transactions of the Royal Society B, 367*, 2119–2129.
Whiten, A., & Flynn, E. G. (2010). The transmission and evolution of experimental 'microcultures' in groups of young children. *Developmental Psychology, 46*, 1694–1709.
Whiten, A., Goodall, J., McGrew, W. C., Nishida, T., Reynolds, V., Sugiyama, Y., et al. (1999). Cultures in chimpanzees. *Nature, 399*, 682–685.
Whiten, A., McGuigan, N., Marshall-Pescini, S., & Hopper, L. M. (2009). Emulation, imitation, over-imitation and the scope of culture for child and chimpanzee. *Philosophical Transactions of the Royal Society of London: Biological Sciences, 364*, 2417–2428.
Whitham, J. C, Gerald, M. S., Santiago, C., & Maestripieri, D. (2007). Intended receivers and functional significance of grunt and girney vocalizations in free-ranging female rhesus macaques, *Ethology, 113*, 862–874.
Wiesmann, C. G., Friederici, A. D., Singer, T., & Steinbeis, N. (2017). Implicit and explicit false belief development in preschool children. *Developmental Science, 20*(5), e12445. doi: 10.1111/desc.12445
Wiessner, P. W. (2014). Embers of society: Firelight talk among the Ju/hoansi Bushmen. *PNAS, 111*, 14027–14035.
Wilkinson, G. W. (1984). Reciprocal food sharing in the vampire bat. *Nature, 308*, 181–184.
Wilson, D. S. (2015). *Does altruism exist? Culture, genes, and the welfare of others*. New Haven, CT: Yale University Press.
Wilson, D. S. (2019). *This view of life: Completing the Darwinian revolution*. New York, NY: Pantheon Books.
Wilson, D. S., Geher, G., & Waldo, J. (2009). EvoS: Completing the evolutionary synthesis in higher education. *The Journal of Evolutionary Studies Consortium, 1*, 3–10.
Wilson, D. S., Kauffman, Jr., R. A., & Purdy, M. S. (2011). A program for at-risk high school students informed by evolutionary science. *PLoS One, 6*, e27826.
Wilson, D. S., & Wilson, E. O. (2007). Rethinking the theoretical foundation of sociobiology. *Quarterly Review of Biology, 82*, 327–348.
Wilson, E. O. (1984). *Biophilia*. Cambridge, MA: Harvard University Press.
Wilson, E. O. (2013). *The social conquest of earth*. New York, NY: Liveright.
Wilson, E. O. (2019). *Genesis: The deep origin of societies*. New York, NY: Liveright.
Winick, M., Meyer, K. K., & Harris, R. C. (1975). Malnutrition and environmental enrichment by early adoption. *Science, 190*, 1173–1175.
Winsler, A. (2009). Still talking to ourselves after all these years: A review of current research on private speech. In A. Winsler, C. Fernyhough, & I. Montero (Eds.), *Private*

speech, executive functioning, and the development of verbal self-regulation (pp. 3–41). Cambridge, UK: Cambridge University Press.

Witherington, D. C., & Lickliter, R. (2016). Integrating development and evolution in psychological science: Evolutionary developmental psychology, developmental systems, and explanatory pluralism. *Human Development, 59*, 200–234.

Wittig, M., Jensen, K., & Tomasello, M. (2013). Five-year-olds understand fair as equal in a mini-ultimatum game. *Journal of Experimental Child Psychology, 116*, 324–337.

Wobber, V., Herrmann, E., Hare, B., Wrangham, R., & Tomasello, M. (2014). Differences in the early cognitive development of children and great apes. *Developmental Psychobiology, 56*, 547–573.

Wood, D., Bruner, J. S., & Ross, G. (1976). The role of tutoring in problem-solving. *Journal of Child Psychology and Psychiatry, 17*, 89–100.

Woolley, J. D. (1997). Thinking about fantasy: Are children fundamentally different thinkers and believers from adults? *Child Development, 68*, 991–1011.

Wörle, M., & Paulus, M. (2018). Normative expectations about fairness: The development of a charity norm in preschoolers. *Journal of Experimental Child Psychology, 165*, 66–84.

Wrangham, R. W. (2009). *Catching fire: How cooking made us human*. New York, NY: Basic Books.

Wrangham, R. W. (2018). Two types of aggression in human evolution. *PNAS, 115*, 245–253.

Wrangham, R. (2019). *Goodness paradox: The strange relationship between virtue and violence in human evolution*. New York, NY: Pantheon Books.

Wray, G. A. (2007). The evolutionary significance of *cis*-regulatory mutations. *Nature Review Genetics, 8*(3), 206–216.

Wyles, J. S., Kunkel, J. G., & Wilson, A. C. (1983). Birds, behavior, and anatomical evolution. *PNAS, 80*, 4394–4397.

Wynn, K., Bloom, P., Jordan, A., Marshall, J., & Sheskin, M. (2018). Not noble savages after all: Limits to early altruism. *Current Directions in Psychological Science, 27*, 3–8.

Xiao, N. G., Quinn, P. C., Liu, S., Ge, L., Pascalis, O., & Lee, K. (2018). Older but not younger infants associate own-race faces with happy music and other-race faces with sad music. *Developmental Science, 21*(2), e12537. doi: 10.1111/desc.12537

Yaeger, D. S., Dahl, R. E., & Dweck, C. S. (2018). Why interventions to influence adolescent behavior often fail but could succeed. *Perspectives on Psychological Science, 13*, 101–122.

Yamamoto, R., Ariely, D., Chi, W., Langleben, D. D., & Elman, I. (2009). Gender differences in the motivational processing of babies are determined by their facial attractiveness. *PLoS One, 4*(6), e6042. doi: 10.1371/journal.pone.0006042

Yang, F., Choi, Y-J., Misch, A., Yang, X., & Dunham, Y. (2018). In defense of the commons: Young children negatively evaluate and sanction free riders. *Psychological Science, 29*, 1598–1611.

Yoo, H., Bowman, D. A., & Oller, D. K. (2018). The origin of protoconversation: An examination of caregiver responses to cry and speech-like vocalizations. *Frontiers in Psychology, 9*, article no. 1510. doi: 10.3389/fpsyg.2018.01510

Young, K. S. (1998). Internet addiction: The emergence of a new clinical disorder. *CyberPsychology & Behavior, 1*, 237–244.

Youngson, N. A., & E. Whitelaw, E. (2008). Transgenerational epigenetic effects. *Annual Review of Genomics and Human Genetics, 9*, 233–257.

Zack, E., Barr, R., Gerhardstein, P., Dickerson, K., & Meltzoff, A. N. (2009). Infant imitation from television using novel touch-screen technology. *British Journal of Developmental Psychology, 27*, 13–16.

Zahn-Waxler, C., Radke-Yarrow, M., Wagner, E., & Chapman, M. (1992). Development of concern for others. *Developmental Psychology, 28*, 126–136.

Zebrowitz, L. A., & Montepare, J. M. (1992). Impressions of babyfaced individuals across the life span. *Developmental Psychology, 28*, 1143–1152.

Zelazo, P. D., & Carlson, S. M. (2012). Hot and cool executive function in childhood and adolescence: Development and plasticity. *Child Development Perspectives, 6*, 354–360.

Zelazo, P. D., Carlson, S. M., & Kesek, A. (2008). The development of executive function in childhood. In C. A. Nelson & M. Luciana (Eds.), *Handbook of cognitive developmental neuroscience* (2nd edition, pp. 553–574). Cambridge, MA: MIT Press.

Author Index

Page numbers followed by n indicate endnotes. Tables and figures are indicated by *t* and *f* following the page number.

For the benefit of digital users, indexed terms that span two pages (e.g., 52–53) may, on occasion, appear on only one of those pages.

Acitelli, Linda K., 241, 292n50
Adler, N. E., 280n53
Adolph, K. E., 278n38
Agnetta, B., 288n73
Agrawal, A. A., 281n14
Agustí, Jordi, 114, 282n44, 282n46
Ahluwalia, J., 278n39
Aiello, L. C., 277n17, 287n19
Ainsworth, Mary D. S., 183–84, 287n38
Akhtar, N., 288n56, 288n60, 289n110
Aksoy, B. A., 282n12
Aladé, F., 294n107
Alderson-Day, B., 284n43
Aldrich, N. J., 293n92
Alexander, C., 283n6
Alexander, Richard D., 176–77, 278n47, 287n12, 287n14
Alfieri, L., 293n92
Alibali, M. W., 283n52
Allen, M., 290n142
Allen, M. L., 286n124
Alley, T. R., 283n7
Allman, John Morgan, 83–85, 281n29, 282n27
Als, Heidelise, 38, 278n9
American Academy of Pediatrics, 257–58, 258*f*, 260, 294n109
Amiel-Tison, C., 287n29
Anderson, J. R., 284n46
Anderson, M., 292n24
Anderson, S. E., 292n33
Andruski, J. E., 285n99
Angeleri, R., 283n61, 287n35
Antón, S. C., 277n17, 287n19

Anzures, G., 278n41
Arbiza, L., 282n12
Arden, G. B., 287n33
Arge, L., 294n113
Ariely, D., 283n12
Armstrong, D. A., 280n62
Arnett, Jeffrey, 245, 293n57
Aslin, R. N., 286n100
Atkinson, J. A., 278n34, 283n2
Austad, S. N., 277n18
Avis, J., 288n65
Azevedo, F. A., 282n36

Bacchini, D., 231–32, 233*f*, 292n19
Bacher, S., 281n36
Baeken, C., 283n19
Bagdasarov, Z., 284n48
Bahrami, B., 292n26
Baillargeon, R., 288n70
Bakeeva, L. E., 105*t*
Bakeman, R., 284n41
Baker, S. P., 292n21
Bakermans-Kranenburg, M. J., 280n54, 280n57, 280n60, 287n41
Baldwin, James Mark, 75–76, 76*f*, 280n6
Bales, K. L., 280n57
Bandura, Albert, 145, 171, 285n72, 286n2
Banerjee, S. C., 284n48
Baranek, G. T., 287n22
Barber, A. B., 286n127
Barber, B. L., 292n32
Barbot, B., 280n61
Bardi, L., 287n23
Barker, J. E., 293n73, 293n76

Barkow, J. H., 277n7
Barnett, W. S., 293n79
Baron, A. S., 289n92, 289n121
Baron-Cohen, S., 278n39
Barr, Rachel, 256, 289n107, 294n102
Barrett, H. C., 22, 290n157
Barton, A. W., 280n61
Barton, M., 283n53
Bassan, A. I., 282n12
Bateson, Patrick, 20, 278n25
Batki, A., 278n39
Bauer, P. J., 284n56, 288n85
Baumeister, 292n53
Baumrind, D., 279n39
Bayer, J., 292n48
Baze, W. B., 282n45
Beach, S. R. H., 280n61
Beck, E. F., 285n76
Becker, B., 283n19, 284n23
Becker, M. W., 283n12
Beckett, C., 279n25, 279n31
Beers, C., 293n62
Behne, T., 288n61, 289n96, 289n118, 290n144, 290n156, 291n182
Bekkering, H., 201–2, 289n109
Belsky, Jay, 60–61, 279n41, 279–80n45, 280n54, 280n57
Belyayev, Dmitry, 102–3, 108
Bender, C. E., 289n127
Benenson, J. F., 290n151
Berch, D. B., 293n62, 293n91, 294n117
Berch, O. N., 292n32
Bering, Jesse M., 197–98, 277n14, 281n32, 287n17, 288n87, 290n134, 293n62
Berk, L. E., 284n44, 286n127, 293n70, 293n75, 293n78, 293n82
Berl, R. E. W., 289n115
Berman, M. G., 292n36
Bernstein-Kurtycz, L., 290n130
Bertenthal, B. I., 287n24
Bertoncini, J., 287n29
Bhatt, S., 280n62
Bian, L., 288n69
Bianchi, J., 280n50
Bianchi, J. M., 280n48
Biben, M., 286n115
Bick, 279n25
Bickerton, Derek, 150–51, 153–54, 285n83, 285n91

Bigler, R. S., 289n93
Billig, M. G., 289n91
Birch, H. G., 287n26
Birch, S., 289n121
Bizarro, L., 283n6
Bjorklund, David F., ix–xi, 22, 87, 101, 131–32, 141, 146, 147f, 162–63, 165, 171, 191f, 249, 277n18, 277n23, 277n2, 278n35, 278n43, 278n48, 279n26, 279n36, 281n32, 281n34, 282n32, 282n34, 283n52, 283n8, 284n31, 284n37, 284n41, 284n50, 284n57, 284n59, 285n68, 285n71, 285n74, 285n76, 286n104, 286n111, 286n114, 286n118, 286n120, 286n3, 287n17, 287n32, 287n44, 289n99, 289n113, 289n127, 290n132, 290n134, 293n62, 293n68, 293n84
Black, J. E., 279n13
Black, M. P., 278n2
Blair, Clancy, 250–51, 293n80
Blake, P. R., 290n151, 290n163
Blakemore, C., 277n12
Blakemore, Sarah-Jayne, 231–32, 291n17, 292n19
Bland, R. C., 292n54
Blank, M., 293n65
Blankenstein, N. E., 291n4
Blau, A. K., 287n43
Blehar, M. C., 183–84, 287n38
Blesa, Rafael, 114, 282n44, 282n46
Bleske, A. L., 277
Blizinsky, Katherine D., 243, 292n55
Bloom, P., 208, 285n65, 290n137, 290n139
Blum, D., 279n21
Blumberg, S. L., 283n15
Blumenthal, J., 283n55
Boden, J. M., 278n10
Boehm, C., 290n130
Boesch, Christophe, 205, 290n130
Bogin, Barry, 116, 117–19, 119f, 156, 223, 282n39, 283n50, 283n57, 283n60, 285n94, 291n5
Boguszewski, K., 294n105, 294n107
Bohn, Manuel, 155, 285n93
Boivin, J., 279n42
Bolk, Louis, 104–6, 105t, 282n24
Bonawitz, Elizabeth, 252–53, 293n86
Bonenfant, J. L., 285n91

Bonner, R. L., 294n98
Borgi, M., 283n15, 283n17
Borke, H., 284n39
Bornstein, M. H., 280n45, 283n7, 284n22
Bosmans, G., 280n62
Bossuyt, A., 283n19
Boulton, M. J., 285n69
Bouza, J., 279n34
Bowen, R., 284n47
Bowlby, John, 125–26, 183–84, 279n36, 283n4, 287n35, 287n40
Bowler, D. E., 292n36
Bowman, D. A., 287n36
Boyce, W. Thomas, 29, 278n45, 280n53, 280n58
Boyette, A. H., 290n157
Brainerd, C. J., 284n32, 284n58
Braver, E. R., 292n21
Breier, B. H., 279n40
Breiner, K., 231–32, 233f, 292n19
Brelsford, V., 283n15, 283n17
Brent, H. P., 278n28
Briggs, J. L., 294n120
Briskin, J. L., 237, 292n28
Brody, G. H., 280n61
Broesch, T., 290n150, 290n157
Brookes, S., 283n54
Brooks, David, 292n52
Brooks, P. J., 293n92
Brooks, R., 288n58
Brooks, R. B., 284n52
Brosch, T., 283n6
Brosnan, Sarah F., 213–14, 288n81, 290n159, 290n161, 291n172
Brownell, C. A., 290n142, 290n146, 290n158
Brownlee, J. R., 284n41
Bruce J., 280n48
Bruck, M., 284n58
Brumbach, B. H., 278n46, 279n43, 280n45
Brumbaugh, C. C., 287n40
Brummelman, E., 285n69
Bruner, Jerome S., 160, 286n104, 293n64
Brunton, G., 292n38
Bryson, S. E., 293n72
Budacki, J. G., 294n98
Budreau, D. R., 287n25
Buffolino, S., 283n7
Bufill, Enric, 114, 282n44, 282n46

Bukowski, 291n14
Bulgarelli, C., 288n86
Bull, J. J., 278n1
Bundy, R. P., 289n91
Burchett, H., 292n38
Burdett, E. R. R., 285n62
Burgess, V., 285n62
Burns, M., 290n164
Burns, M. P., 290n165
Bush, N. R., 280n53
Buss, David M., 11, 12–13, 277, 282n29, 287n42
Butler, L., 286n124
Buttelmann, D., 285n60, 285n67, 288n76, 288n86, 289n113, 290n134
Buttelmann, F., 288n76
Buyung-Ali, L. M., 292n36
Byers-Heilein, K., 287n29
Bygren, L. O., 281n23
Byrne, Richard W., 176–77, 287n13, 287n32

Cai, T., 278n10
Call, J., 188–89, 285n67, 288n54, 288n73, 288n76, 288n81, 289n100, 290n134, 290n159, 290n169, 291n174
Call, J. M., 288n88, 289n98
Callaerts, P., 282n8
Callaghan, T. C., 288n61, 290n144, 290n156, 291n182
Camacho-Thompson, D. E., 279n34
Campbell, Anne, 83, 281n28
Campbell, R. N., 284n46
Campbell, W. Keith, 238–40, 292n32, 292n40
Camus, G., 284n48
Can, D. D., 286n101
Canino, G. J., 292n54
Cao-Lei, L., 280n64
Capellini, T. D., 282n12
Cárdenas, R. A., 283n12
Carey, S., 286n124, 289n92
Caria, A., 283n7
Carlo, G., 279n34
Carlson, S. M., 288n63, 288n65, 293n72, 293n74, 293n77, 293n81
Carpenter, M., 285n67, 288n56, 288n58, 288n60, 288n62, 288n76, 288n86, 289n93, 289n110, 289n113, 290n134

Carrier, L. M., 292n33
Carrington, H. A., 184, 287n43
Carroll, S. R., 184, 287n43
Carroll, Sean B., 97–98, 99–100, 101, 104, 281n6, 282n11, 282n14, 282n23
Carstensen, L. L., 285n82
Carvalho, L. R., 282n36
Casey, R., 283n8
Casler, Krista, 144, 284n32, 285n66
Caspi, Avshalom, 39–40, 41, 277n3, 278n10, 278n12
Castellanos, F. X., 283n55
Castle, J., 279n25, 279n31
Cauffman, E., 280n56
Causey, K., 283n52, 285n71
Ceci, S. J., 284n58
Cemore, J. J., 286n125
Chan, K. Y., 279n40
Chance, M. R. A., 282n32
Chandler, M. J., 287n22
Chang, B., 148, 285n77
Chang, L., 280n45
Chapman, M., 288n78
Charles, C., 292n34
Charrier, C., 282n44
Chase, K., 277n15
Cheever, N. A., 292n33
Chein, J., 231–32, 233f, 292n19
Chen, 291n180, 291n183
Chen, L-H., 292n21
Chen, Q., 278n11
Chi, W., 283n12
Chiao, Joan Y., 243, 292n55
Chimpanzee Sequencing and Analysis Consortium, 281n2
Chin, J., 289n114
Chiong, C., 256–57, 294n103
Choi, S. Y., 284n48
Choi, Y-J., 288n88
Chomsky, N., 285n86, 285n89
Choo, H., 292n32
Christakis, D. A., 294n106
Christakis, Erika, 226–27
Christopher, F. S., 290n143
Christovich, I. A., 285n99
Christovich, L. A., 285n99
Christy, K., 294n107
Chudek, M., 289n121
Churchill, Winston, 130

Cirulli, F., 283n15, 283n17
Clark, E. A., 279n32
Clark, R. D., III., 288n77
Clark, R. W., 286n130
Clasen, L. S., 292n19
Clay, Z., 289n129
Clegg, J. M., 289n114
Clément, F., 289n120
Clements, W. A., 288n68
Clutton-Brock, T. H., 281n27
Coan, J. A., 284n21
Cockerill, M., 280n45
Cogliati-Dezza, I., 283n15, 283n17
Cohen, T., 293n88
Colarelli, S. M., 277n21
Collins, W. A., 280n46
Colombo, M., 290n138
Colvert, E., 279n25, 279n31
The Common Sense Census, 294n97
Connellan, J., 278n39
Connolly, K., 286n112
Conradt, Elisabeth, 69–70, 280n62, 280n65
Coon, R. C., 290n162
Cooper, N. R., 294n108
Cooper, R. P., 286n100, 287n29
Coppola, M., 154, 285n92
Corballis, M. C., 284n54
Cormier, C., 287n17, 290n132
Cornwell, R. E., 283n7, 283n12
Corriveau, K. H., 289n114
Cosmides, L., 277n7
Courage, Mary L., 256–57, 284n56, 294n104
Courtois, R., 284n48
Couter, A. C., 291n15
Coutinho-Budd, J., 282n44
Coyne, S. M., 292n29, 292n43
Craig, I. W., 277n3, 278n10, 278n12
Crais, E. R., 287n22
Crimston, J., 287n31
Cristakis, E., 291n7
Croft, K., 284n39
Crone, E. A., 291n4
Crook, J. M., 282n27
Cross, D., 288n63
Crystal, D., 285n87
Csibra, G., 203–4, 248, 278n39, 289n123, 293n66

Cummins-Sebree, S. W., 285n67
Curry, Oliver S., 218–19, 291n185
Curtiss, S., 279n19
Cutting, J. E., 287n23

Dahl, A., 290n142, 290n146
Dahl, R. E., 294n123
Daly, M., 282n29, 283n3, 292n44
Daly, O., 240, 292n45
Damon, W., 290n162
Dane, A. V., 294n122
Daniels, D., 285n70
Dannemiller, J. L., 287n25
Darlington, R. D., 282n37
Darwin, Chales, 8, 19–20, 74–75, 76f, 102–3, 172, 174–75, 186, 277n6
Daum, M. M., 288n86, 289n113
Davey Smith, G., 278n12
Davidson, R. J., 283n20, 284n22
Davis, E. P., 279n41
Davis, J., 278n44, 287n31
Davis-Unger, A. C., 293n77, 293n81
Dawkins, Richard, 7, 19–20, 277n22
Deacon, Terrance, 89–90, 281n37
de Beer, Gavin, ix, 94–95, 277n1, 282n13, 282n15
de Bruin, A., 285n75
De Falco, S., 283n7
Deguchi, T., 285n88
de Haan, M., 278n40, 279n14
DeHart, G., 280n56
Dehio, C., 167–68, 286n128
de Jong, 292n33
de Klerk, C. C., 288n86
Deković, M., 280n55
Del Giudice, Marco, 22, 121, 279n43, 280n49, 283n61, 287n35, 294n122
DeLoache, Judy S., 26–27, 167, 256–57, 278n38, 286n124, 294n99, 294n103
de Marchena, Jacqueline, 282n44
DeMey, J., 283n19
Demiralp, E., 292n46
Denenberg, V. H., 281n16
Dennett, Daniel, 143–44, 190, 191–92, 285n63, 288n57
Dennis, E. L., 283n55
Dennis, W., 279n25
Depew, D. J., 280n6
DeRaedt, R., 283n19

Deschenaux, A., 289n120
de Schonen, S., 287n25
DeSilva, J. M., 282n38
De-Vries, L., 287n33
de Vries, S. A., 280n48
de Waal, Franz B. M., 195, 213–14, 288n79, 288n83, 291n172
Dewey, John, 109, 282n33
DeWitt, T., 294n110
de Zubicaray, G. I., 283n55
Diamond, Adele, 250–51, 293n80
Dias, D. G., 290n150, 290n157
Dickerson, K., 294n102
Dickson K., 292n38
Di Giorgio, E., 278n40, 287n23
Diori, J., 281n18
Dishion, T. J., 280n49, 294n122
Dissanayaka, C., 293n81
DiYanni, C. J., 289n114
Do, K. T., 291n4
Dodge, Kenneth A., 171, 280n45, 286n2
Dogan, M. V., 280n61
Donald, M., 284n54
Dore, R. A., 286n125
Draper, Patricia, 60–61, 279n44
Drell, M. B., 294n107
Dubas, J. S., 280n55
Dubowitz, L. M., 287n33
Dudley, J., 294n110
Duggan, P., 284n48, 284n51
Duka, T., 282n45
Dunbar, Robin I. M., 17, 178, 277n19, 278n47, 287n12, 287n17, 287n20
Duncan, R., 284n43
Duncker, Karl, 143f, 143–44, 285n64
Dunham, Y., 288n88, 289n92
Dunlosky, J., 285n69
Dunn, E., 292n30
Dunn, E. W., 237, 292n30
Durkheim, Emile, 243
Dweck, C. S., 294n123
Dwyer, R., 237, 292n30

Earles, J. L., 285n98
The Early Social Development Research Lab, 290n146
Easterbrook, M. A., 287n25
Ebstein, R. P., 280n60
Eccles, J. S., 285n69

Eddy, T. J., 288n74
Edvinsson, S., 281n23
Eisenberg, N., 290n143
Elgbeli, G., 280n64
Elias, C. L., 293n70, 293n75, 293n78
Elkind, David, 138–39, 284n47
Ellis, B. J., 22, 278n35, 278n46, 279n43, 280n45, 280n52, 294n123
Ellis, E. J., 22
Elman, I., 283n12
Elman, Jeffrey, 157–58, 285n97
Embry, D. D., 294n123
Emmett, P. M., 278n12
ENCODE Project Consortium, 281n4
Endedijk, 291n184
Engelmann, J., 289n93, 289n126
Engemann, K., 294n113
Erdal, D., 287n12
Erisir, A., 279n14
Esposito, G., 283n10, 284n22
Essex, M. J., 280n51
Esteves, F., 278n36
Evans, A. C., 283n55
Evans, N., 285n89
Everett, B. A., 284n39

Fabes, R. A., 290n143
Fagan, E. C., 283n7, 283n12
Fagen, R., 286n107
Falk, A., 290n167
Faravelli, C., 292n54
Farfel, J. M., 282n36
Farroni, T., 278n39
Fehr, E., 290n167
Feldmeyer, B., 278n3
Felt, J., 292n33
Fender, J. G., 294n103
Fergusson, D. M., 278n10
Fernald, Ann, 159, 285n99, 286n102, 286n104
Fernyhough, C., 284n43
Ferrari, P. F., 287n34, 289n106
Ferretti, R. E., 282n36
Fessler, D. M. T., 277n11
Field, T., 289n105
Fifer, W. R., 287n29
Figueredo, A. J., 278n46, 279n43, 280n45, 280n49, 294n122

Finlay, B. L., 282n37
Fischbacher, U., 290n167
Fisher, K. R., 293n89
Fitch, T., 285n86
Flament, C., 289n91
Flavell, E. R., 286n123
Flavell, J. H., 286n123
Flaxman, S. M., 277n11
Fleck, C., 280n45
Fleckhammer, L., 294n107
Flykt, A., 278n36
Flynn, 287n15
Flynn, E. G., 280n4
Flynn, James R., 71, 73, 280n1
Fouts, Roger, 206, 290n135
Fox, A. S., 283n20, 284n22
Fox, N. A., 279n22, 279n25, 279n31
Fragaszy, D. M., 285n67
Fraley, R. C., 287n40
Francis, D. D., 281n18
Franco, X., 279n34
Frankenhuis, Willem E., 22, 62–63, 280n48, 280n50
Franklin, Benjamin, 87–88
Franklin, Prarthana, 130–31, 283n8, 284n25
Franz, H., 282n44
Freeman, S. M., 280n57
Frick, A., 289n120
Friederici, A. D., 288n72
Friedman, S. L., 280n56
Fröbel, Frederick, 159–60
Fullard, W., 283n15
Fultz, J., 290n143
Furtado, E. A., 279n22

Galda, L., 293n71
Gallagher, K. C., 280n54
Ganea, P. A., 286n124, 294n102
Gangestad, S. W., 279n43
Garcia, A., 294n100
Garcia Coll, C., 279n34
Gardiner, A., 289n113
Gardiner, A. K., 286n118
Gardner, M., 292n20
Garon, N., 293n72
Garstang, Walter, 94–95, 275, 281n1, 294n2

Garver, K. E., 283n55
Gaultney, Jane F., 146, 147f, 285n74
Gava, L., 287n25
Gaymard, S., 284n48
Ge, L., 278n40, 288n84
Geary, David C., 9, 10f, 165–66, 254–55, 277n8, 281n25, 286n121, 293n62, 293n91, 293n96, 294n117
Geher, G., 293n62, 294n117
Gehring, Walter J., 99, 282n8
Gellén, K., 289n112
Genovart, M., 278n3
Gentile, D. A., 292n32
George, M. J., 292n40, 292n42
Gerald, M. S., 286n103
Gergely, György, 201–2, 203–4, 248, 289n109, 289n123, 293n66
Gerhardstein, P., 294n102
German, T., 285n65
Gervain, J., 287n29
Gesell, Arnold, 45–46
Gibbons, A., 283n58
Gibson, 281n11
Giedd, Jay N., 232–33, 283n56, 292n19, 292n22
Giger, T., 282n44
Gilad, Y., 282n12
Gilby, I. C., 290n160
Giles, A., 284n56
Gilissen, R., 280n54
Gilpin, A. T., 286n127
Glocker, Melanie L., 126–28, 127f, 283n8, 283n11, 283n20
Glover, V., 279n41
Gluckman, P., 281n22
Glynn, L. M., 279n41
Gobbini, M. I., 283n7, 283n18, 283n20
Goddings, A. L., 292n19
Goddu, M. K., 148, 285n77
Goldberg, R. F., 284n34
Goldberg, S., 283n15
Golding, J., 278n12
Golinkoff, R. M., 253, 286n101, 293n87, 293n90, 294n114
Golle, J., 283n10
Gómez, Juan-Carlos, 166–67, 286n122
Gonzalez, J-M., 294n123
Good, M., 240, 292n45

Goodall, J., 281n31, 289n127
Goodman, N. D., 252–53, 293n86
Gopnik, Alison, 20, 278n24, 284n37, 288n66, 293n67, 293n81
Gottlieb, Gilbert, 7, 25, 34–36, 35f, 39, 278n26, 278n30, 278n33, 278n5, 278n7, 281n9, 281n15, 281n1
Gould, Stephen Jay, 7, 12–13, 102, 104, 134, 277n13, 281n1, 282n13, 282n16, 282n18, 282n27, 282n40
Goyal, M. S., 282n44
Graetz, S., 289n113
Gräfenhain, 291n181
Gray, Peter, 249, 251, 254–55, 263, 278n49, 279n36, 280n49, 293n62, 293n69, 293n83, 293n94, 294n118, 294n122
Gredlein, Jeffrey M., 165, 286n120
Green, Brandi L., 141, 146, 147f, 284n36, 284n41, 284n50, 284n57, 285n74
Green, F. L., 286n123
Green, F. P., 290n150
Greenberg, J. R., 212–13, 215–16, 290n166, 291n176
Greene, K., 284n48
Greenfield, P., 290n130
Greenough, William T., 43–44, 279n13
Greenwald, A. B., 284n45
Greenwald, S., 292n54
Greif, M., 289n113
Greve, Werner, 167–68, 286n128
Griffin, M. D., 283n20
Grinberg, L. T., 282n36
Griskevicius, V., 280n47, 280n50, 294n122
Grober, M. S., 278n2
Groh, A. M., 287n41
Gronau, I., 282n12
Groos, Karl, 160, 286n106
Groothues, C., 279n31
Gross, Th. F., 283n15
Grove, M. Annette, 247, 293n59, 293n61
Gruber, T., 289n120
Grueneisen, 291n179
Gruskin, K., 293n62, 294n117
Guenther, C., 282n12
Guerin, D., 280n62
Gulko, B., 282n12
Gunnar, M., 288n59
Guo, G., 278n10

Guo, L., 290n150, 290n157
Guo, S., 282n44
Gur, R. C., 126–28, 127f, 283n8, 283n11
Gurven, M., 283n49
Guthrie, D., 279n25, 279n31
Guthrie, S., 284n32
Guy, L., 289n105
Gweon, H., 252–53, 293n86

Haden, C. A., 293n88
Haeckel, Ernst, 94–95, 101, 104–5
Hahn, A. C., 283n18
Haidt, Jonathan, 220–21, 226, 227, 284n21, 291n2, 291n8
Hains, S. M. J., 287n25
Haith, M. M., 287n26
Halder, F., 282n8
Halgunseth, L. C., 279n34
Hall, B. K., 281n1
Halsted, N., 287n29
Hamann, Katharina, 212–13, 215–16, 290n149, 290n155, 290n166, 291n176
Hamilton, A., 288n86
Hamilton, Alexander, 87–88
Hamilton, William D., 173, 286n4
Hamlin, J. Kiley, 208, 290n137, 290n139
Hammond, S., 293n81
Hanisee, J., 279n32
Hankin, B. L., 280n62
Hanson, M., 281n22
Hara, Y., 277n16
Harari, Yuval Noah, 188, 288n53
Hare, Brian, 108, 188–89, 189f, 287n12, 288n55, 288n73, 288n75, 288n81, 289n126, 290n159
Harlé, K. M., 279n25
Harlow, Harry, 261–62, 294n115
Harms, M. B., 288n63
Harnishfeger, K. K., 282n32, 282n34
Harold, G. T., 279n42
Harper, N. J., 292n36
Harris, Judith R., 230–31, 291n13
Harris, L. J., 283n12
Harris, Paul L., 161, 285n62, 286n109, 288n65, 289n102
Harris, R. C., 279n32
Harrison, T., 283n7, 283n18, 283n20
Hart, B., Risley, T. R., 277n5

Hart, Sybil L., 184–85, 185f, 287n44
Hartman, S., 280n57
Harts, A., 278n3
Hartsoeker, Nicolaas, 24f
Haselton, M. G., 277
Hattori, K., 282n16, 282n27
Haun, D., 279n35, 287n45, 287n47, 289n114, 291n184
Haun, D. B., 289n93
Hauser, M. D., 285n86
Hawes, K., 280n62
Hawley, Patricia H., 208, 290n136
Hawrylycz, M., 282n44
Haxby, J. V., 283n7, 283n18, 283n20
Hay, D. F., 279n42, 290n148
Hayashi, A., 285n88
Hayne, H., 289n107, 290n138
Heffer, Taylor, 240, 292n45
Heimann, Mikael, 181–82, 287n34
Hein, S., 280n61
Heine, S. J., 279n35
Heinrichs, M., 283n12, 283n14
Henderson, A. M. E., 290n164
Henrich, J., 279n35, 288n81, 290n157, 290n159, 290n161
Hentges, R. F., 280n45
Hepach, R., 289n114, 290n142, 290n152
Herculano-Houzel, S., 282n37
Hernández Blasi, Carlos, 131–32, 191f, 278n42, 284n31, 284n35, 289n99
Hernandez-Lloreda, M., 188–89, 288n54, 288n75
Heron-Delaney, M., 278n41
Herrmann, Esther, 188–89, 189f, 288n55, 288n75, 289n93, 289n126
Herwig, J. E., 286n125
Herzing, D. L., 289n127
Hewlett, B. S., 289n115, 290n157
Hibbel, J. R., 278n12
Hickie, I. B., 283n55
Hidaka, Brandon, 264–65, 294n125
Hill, K., 277n18, 283n48, 283n53
Hill, P., 284n48, 284n51
Hill, P. L., 284n49
Hirsh-Pasek, K., 251–52, 253, 286n101, 293n85, 293n87, 293n90, 294n114
Hisler, G., 292n32
Hjertholm, E., 284n44
Hodges, 281n11

Hoehl, S., 278n37, 285n60, 289n113
Hoffman, M. L., 288n78
Holland, S. K., 294n110
Holmgren, H. G., 292n43
Holtze, S., 105*t*
Honeycutt, H., 277n23
Hood, B., 282n28
Hopkins, E. J., 286n125
Hopper, L. M., 203–4, 289n113, 289n122
Horner, V., 285n60, 287n15, 289n128
Hornik, R., 288n59
Horowitz-Kraus, T., 294n110
Horwood, L. J., 278n10
House, B. R., 290n154, 290n157
Houts, R. M., 280n56
Howe, M. L., 284n56
Hrdy, Sarah B., 17–18, 109, 196, 277n20, 279n20, 282n30, 283n3, 288n82
Hubel, D. H., 278n27
Huber, B., 294n107
Hubisz, M. J., 282n12
Huestis, M. A., 280n62
Hughes, D. A., 280n62
Huizinga, Johann, 160–61, 286n108
Humphrey, Nicholas, 177, 287n16
Humphreys, A. P., 285n69
Hunt, E., 288n49
Hunt, Melissa G., 240–41, 292n49
Hunter, J. F., 292n30
Hurtado, A. M., 277n18, 283n48, 283n53
Hutton, J. S., 294n110
Hwu, H. G., 292n54
Hyson Marion C., 251–52, 293n85

Iannotti, R. J., 294n121
Icenogle, G., 231–32, 233*f*, 292n19
Ihsen, E., 293n81
Ikenasio, B. A., 279n40
Imanishi, T., 277n16
Imuta, K., 290n138
Ingram, Gordon, 197–98, 288n87
Insel, T. R., 282n35
Irigoyen, M. M., 294n98
Islam, N., 256–57, 294n103
Iverson, P., 285n88

Jablonka, E., 281n13
Jackson, J. F., 279n39
Jahanshad, N., 283n55

Jambor, T. W., 284n40
Janzen, F. J., 278n3
Jefferson, Thomas, 87–88
Jeffries, N. O., 283n55
Jennett, S., 277n12
Jensen, K., 288n81, 288n88, 289n98, 290n159, 290n169
Jerison, H., 282n35
Jiang, J., 292n24
Jiang, X., 282n44
Jing Lu, H., 280n45
Joffe, Tracey H., 177–78, 287n18
Johnson, M. H., 278n39, 279n13
Johnson, S., 285n65
Joiner, T. E., 292n38, 292n40
Jones, N. A., 287n43
Jones, R. A., 292n53
Jones, R. E., 280n45
Jones, T. A., 279n13
Jonides, J., 292n46
Jordan, A., 290n139
Jordan, J. J., 288n89
Joshi, K., 282n44
Jowkar-Baniani, G., 286n123
Judaš, M., 282n44
Juffer, F., 280n57
Junger, Sebastian, 242, 292n51
Jusczyk, P., 287n29

Kaati, G., 281n23
Kabali, H. K., 294n98
Kachel, G., 155, 285n93, 291n178
Kakigi, R., 278n41
Kamin, H. S., 280n62
Kanai, R., 292n26
Kanazawa, S., 278n41
Kaplan, H., 277n18, 279n43, 283n49
Kaplan, H. S., 279n43
Kappeler, P. M., 278n47
Kärtner, J., 279n35, 290n145
Karzon, R. G., 286n100
Katz, G. S., 286n100
Kauer-Sant'Anna, M., 283n6
Kauffman, R. A., Jr., 294n119
Kaufman, J., 290n142, 294n107
Kawashima, A., 283n10
Keil, F. C., 148, 285n60, 285n69, 285n77, 289n111
Keinan, A., 282n12

Kelemen, Deborah, 144, 284n32, 285n66
Kelley, K., 280n54
Kelly, D. J., 278n40, 287n27
Kelly, R., 293n81
Kendal, J. R., 280n4
Kendal, R. L., 280n4
Kennedy, M. A., 278n10
Kennedy-Costantini, S., 278n44, 287n31
Kenny, P., 278n7, 294n111
Kenward, B., 285n61, 289n96, 289n116
Kersten A. W., 285n98
Kertes, D. A., 280n62
Kesek, A., 293n72
Kessen, W., 287n26
Kessler, R. C., 292n54
Keupp, S., 285n60, 289n96, 289n112, 289n118
Kharlamova, A. V., 277n15
Khoo, A., 292n32
Kim, J-E., 282n44
Kim, P., 284n22
Kim, S., 280n61
Kim-Cohen, J., 278n12
Kinard, J. L., 287n22
Kinzler, K. D., 277n9
Kipp, K., 282n34
Kiraly, I., 201–2, 289n109
Kiritani, S., 285n88
Kirkpatrick, Lee A., 183–84, 287n38
Kisilevsky, B. S., 287n25
Kita, S., 154, 285n92
Kittredge, A. K., 253, 293n87
Klaczynski, P., 284n49
Klahr, D., 253, 293n87
Kline, M. A., 293n60
Klinger, T. A., 285n91
Kloter, U., 282n8
Knight, T. M., 292n36
Knoll, Lisa J., 231, 291n16
Kobayashi, M., 278n41
Kochanska, G., 280n54
Koenen, K. C., 280n57
Koenig, M. A., 288n63
Kohlberg, Lawrence, 171, 284n44, 286n1
Konner, Melvin, 55, 58, 275, 278n49, 279n36, 281n24, 281n26, 282n42, 286n113, 293n59, 294n1
Köster, M., 290n145

Kostyrka-Allchorne, K., 294n108
Kosugi, D., 288n62
Kozhevnikova, E. V., 285n99
Krachun, C., 288n75
Kreppner, J., 279n25
Kriger, A., 283n15
Kringelbach, M. L., 283n6, 283n12
Krizan, Z., 292n32
Kross, E., 292n46
Kruger, Ann, 204, 205–6, 281n32, 289n124, 290n131
Krupenye, 288n76
Kubiszewski, V., 284n48
Kuhl, P. K., 285n88, 285n99
Kuhn, A., 287n27
Kukekova, A., 277n15
Kulke, L., 288n71
Kunkel, J. G., 89t, 281n35
Kuo, S., 280n46
Kuo, Zing-Yang, 46–47, 279n17
Kushlev, Kostadin, 237, 292n30
Kwan, I., 292n38

Laboratory of Comparative Human Cognition, 277n4
Laforsch, C., 281n14
Laland, K. N., 280n4
Lam, C. B., 291n15
Lamarck, Jean Baptiste, 74–75, 76f
Lamb, M., 281n13
Lambert, N., 282n44
Lambertz, G., 287n29
Lambeth, S. P., 290n161
Lancaster, J., 277n18, 283n48
Lancy, D. F., 293n59
Lancy, David, 55–56, 247, 279n37, 293n59, 293n61
Landau, S., 284n44
Lane, I. M., 290n162
Langleben, D. D., 126–28, 127f, 283n8, 283n12, 283n20
Langlois, J., 283n8
Lansford, J. E., 280n45
Laplante, D. P., 280n64
Lapsley, D., 284n48, 284n51
Lapsley, D. K., 284n49
Lara-Ruis, J. M., 292n33
Laurence, S., 290n157

Laursen, 291n14
Leary, 292n53
Lee, D. S., 292n46, 292n48
Lee, K., 278n40, 284n27, 287n27, 288n65, 288n84
Lee, M., 280n61
Lefebvre, L., 281n36
Legar, C. H., 279n35
Legare, C. H., 289n101, 289n119
Legerstee, M., 287n32
Le Grand, R., 278n28
Lei, M-K., 280n61
Leibenluft, E., 283n7, 283n18, 283n20
Leibniz, Gottfried Wilhelm, 87–88
Leister, K. P., 294n98
Leite, R. E., 282n36
Leo, I., 278n40
Leppink, J., 285n75
Lerner, M. D., 286n125
Lester, B. M., 280n62
Levinson, S., 285n89
Lewis, T. L., 278n28
Lewis, T. M., 287n25
Lewontin, Richard C., 12–13, 277n13
Li, G., 292n21
Li, H., 284n27, 294n105
Li, N. P., 277n21
Lickliter, Robert, 22, 36, 38, 113, 277n23, 278n27, 278n6
Lillard, A. S., 279n14, 286n125, 293n93, 294n105, 294n107
Lim, A. F., 292n33
Lin, N., 292n46
Linting, M., 280n54
Lipko, A. R., 285n69
Lipson, C., 240–41, 292n49
Lipton, Rose C., 48–49, 279n25
Lisibach, S., 283n10
Liszkowski, U., 288n58
Liu, D., 281n18
Liu, H., 283n55
Liu, S., 278n40, 287n27, 288n84
Liu, X., 282n44
Lobmaier, J. S., 283n7, 283n10, 283n14
LoBue, Vanessa, 26–27, 278n38
Lock, John L., 47, 120–21, 156, 279n18, 283n60, 285n94
Locke, John, 159–60, 286n105

Lockhart, Kristi L., 148, 285n77
Lockman, Jeffrey J., 164–65, 286n117
Loftus, E. F., 285n81
Lonsdorf, E., 290n130
Lord, Charles G., 137–38, 284n45
Lorenc, A., 282n44
Lorenz, Konrad, 1, 34, 125–26, 133–34, 277n1, 278n4, 283n5
Lorimer, B., 288n77
Loughead, J. W., 126–28, 127f, 283n8, 283n11, 283n20
Louv, Richard, 238, 292n34
Lu, H. J., 280n45
Lucas, A. J., 285n62
Lucion, M. K., 283n6
Lukianoff, Greg, 220–21, 226, 227, 291n2, 291n8
Lukjanczuk, J. L., 126, 283n9
Lumey, L. H., 281n22
Luna, B., 283n55
Lunghi, M., 287n23
Lunter, G., 281n4
Luo, L., 283n19, 284n23
Luo, L. Z., 284n27
Lyons, D. E., 285n60, 289n111
Lyons, L., 284n33

Ma, X., 283n19, 284n23
Macchi Cassia, B., 278n41
Macchi Cassia, V., 287n26
MacDonald, W., 292n38
MacDonell, E., 240, 292n45
Machluf, K., 283n8, 293n62
Machnes, Z., 280n64
Maestripieri, D., 281n30, 283n12, 286n103
Magis-Weinberg, L., 231, 291n16
Magsamem-Conrad, K., 284n48
Mail and Guardian, 279n16
Makinson, J., 285n81, 289n115
Manera, V., 283n61, 287n35
Mann, T., 286n127
Marcus, M., 293n88
Marenco, S., 278n11
Marini, A., 294n122
Markov, A. V., 105*t*
Markson, L., 285n65
Marsh, K., 287n43
Marshall, J., 290n139

Marshall, P. J., 279n25, 279n31
Marshall-Pescini, S., 203–4, 289n113, 289n122
Marsit, C. J., 280n62
Martin, C. L., 288n85
Martin, E., 284n28
Martin, G. B., 288n77
Martin, Gabrielle N., 239–40, 292n38, 292n40
Martin, J., 277n3, 278n10
Martin, N. G., 283n55
Martín-Andrade, Beatriz, 166–67, 286n122
Marx, R., 240–41, 292n49
Marzolf, D. P., 286n123
Massart, R., 280n64
Mast, F. W., 283n10
Mateo, 281n30
Matsuzawa, T., 288n62
Maughan, B., 279n31
Maurer, Daphne, 22, 278n28, 287n25
May, L., 287n29
Mayer, A., 288n64
Maynard, A., 290n130
May-Plumlee, T., 290n143
Mayr, E., 280n7, 281n1
McArthur, M. J., 282n45
McAuley, T., 293n72
McAuliffe, K., 288n89, 290n163
McCall, Robert B., 50–51, 279n25, 279n30, 279n33
McClay, J., 277n3, 278n10
McClean, C. Y., 282n12
McDaniel, B. T., 292n29
McDonald, J., 280n63
McGrew, W. C., 281n31, 286n112, 289n127
McGuigan, N., 203–4, 285n60, 285n62, 285n81, 289n108, 289n113, 289n115, 289n122
McHale, S. M., 291n15
McInnis, M. A., 286n127
McKinney, M. L., 101, 282n13, 282n25
McLaughlin, K. A., 280n57
McLoughlin, N., 289n90
McMahon, K. L., 283n55
McNamara, K., 101
McWilliams, M. A., 280n62

Meader, S., 281n4
Meaney, Michael J., 80, 85, 281n18
Mehler, J., 287n29
Mehta, M., 279n25
Meints, K., 283n15, 283n17
Melis, A. P., 288n73, 291n174
Meltzoff, A. N., 278n44, 287n30, 288n52, 288n58, 289n110, 294n102
Mendel, Gregor, 74–75
Merriam, E. P., 283n55
Merriman, W. E., 285n69
Merz, Emily C., 50–51, 279n25, 279n30
Mesman, J., 280n57
Meyer, D., 294n107
Meyer, K. K., 279n32
Meyers, A. B., 293n74, 293n82
Michaelson, L., 293n73, 293n76
Mikels, J. A., 285n82
Mikulincer, M., 287n39
Milani, I., 287n26
Mill, C. M., 285n69
Mill, J., 277n3, 278n10
Miller, A. L., 278n10
Miller, D. B., 278n29
Miller, D. J., 282n45
Miller, G. M., 287n34
Miller, K. F., 294n99
Mills, K. L., 292n19
Millwre, J. A., 282n44
Milne, B. J., 278n12
Min, G., 289n114
Minshew, N. J., 283n55
Misch, A., 288n88
Mitani, John, 215, 291n173
Mittal, C., 280n47
Mize, K. D., 287n43
Mizuno, Y., 288n62
Modecki, K. L., 292n32
Moffitt, T. E., 277n3, 278n10
Mohanty, S. H., 294n98
Moll, H., 288n61, 290n144, 290n156, 291n182
Molnar, P., 289n103
Mondloch, C. J., 278n28, 287n25
Monoz, D. P., 283n55
Montagu, Ashley, 102, 105t, 134–35, 170, 282n17, 282n26, 282n42, 284n36, 286n129

Montepare, J. M., 284n26
Montessori, Maria, 159–60
Mood, D. W., 284n46
Moon, C., 287n29
Moore, C. L., 281n33
Moore, D. S., 286n100
Moore, David D., 67, 280n59, 281n13
Moore, M. K., 278n44, 287n30
Morgan, Conway Lloyd, 75–76
Morgan, D., 290n130
Morgan, D. K., 281n20
Mortensen, P. B., 294n113
Moses, L. J., 288n65
Mozart, Wolfgang Amadeus, 87–88
Mthiyane, Saturday, 45–46
Mueller, Martine, 215, 291n173
Muenks, K., 285n69
Muentener, P., 294n100
Muir, D. W., 287n25
Mulligan, C. J., 280n62
Mullins, D. A., 218–19, 291n185
Munakata, Y., 293n73, 293n76
Munday, P. L., 278n2
Mundry, R., 290n130
Munro, S., 293n79
Murray, L., 283n12
Musgravce, S., 290n130
Mushin, I., 289n114, 289n117
Mushin, J., 287n33
Myers, A. J., 287n44
Myowa-Yamakoshi, M., 288n62

Nagell, K., 289n128
Nagy, E., 287n32, 289n103
Nakazawa, J., 283n10
Nansel, T. R., 294n121
Nasrini, J., 289n114
Nathanson, A. I., 294n107
Naumova, O. Y., 280n61
Neisser, Ulric, 171
Nelson, Charles A., 49–50, 278n40,
    279n14, 279n22, 279n25, 279n27
Nelson, Charles A., III, 279n25, 279n31
Nelson, E. E., 283n20, 284n22
Nelson, Katherine, 141, 284n55
Nettle, D., 280n45, 280n48
Neumann-Holzschuh, I., 285n91
Newcombe, N. S., 293n89

Newport, Elisa L., 157–58, 285n95
Newton, Isaac, 87–88, 170
New York Post, 279n28
Ni, S., 290n158
Niaura, R., 280n62
Nicastro, N., 282n37
Nielsen, Mark, 4, 167, 277n2, 278n44,
    279n35, 283n59, 285n61, 286n126,
    287n31, 287n45, 287n47, 289n102,
    289n108, 289n114, 289n119,
    289n121, 289n129, 291n184
Nishida, T., 281n31, 289n127
Nitschke, J. B., 283n20, 284n22
Noble, K. G., 279n25
Noonan, J. P., 100, 282n12
Norenzayan, A., 279n35
Nowak, M. A., 286n7
Nunez-Davis, R., 294n98

Oakes, T. R., 283n20, 284n22
Obradović, J., 280n53
O'Brien, C. T., 286n127
Odgers, C. L., 292n40, 292n42
Ogan, A., 286n127
Ogawa, S., 283n10
Öhman, A., 278n36
Olguin, K., 289n128
Oliveira, V., 283n6
Oller, D. K., 287n36
Olson, K. R., 290n153
Onishi, K. H., 288n70
Oostenbroek, J., 278n44, 287n31
Orben, A., 292n44
Oro, D., 278n3
Orvell, A., 292n48
Osborn, Henry Fairfield, 75–76
Oshlack, A., 282n12
Osmond, C., 281n22
Over, H., 289n90, 289n93
Overton, W. F., 22, 277n23
Ozyurek, A., 154, 285n92

Pääbo, S., 100, 282n12
Padilla-Walker, L. M., 292n43
Painter, R. C., 281n22
Paladino, F. V., 278n3
Palmquist, C. M., 286n125
Panchanathan, K., 22, 280n48

Papandonatos, G. D., 280n62
Papousek, Hanus, 261–62, 294n116
Parade, S. H., 280n62
Park, J., 292n46, 292n48
Parsons, C. E., 283n12
Parten, M., 286n110
Pascalis, O., 278n41, 287n27, 288n84
Pascoe, J., 290n151
Pasco Fearon, R. M., 287n41
Passos-Ferreira, C., 290n150, 290n157
Patterson, M. M., 289n93
Pauen, S., 278n37, 289n113
Paukner, A., 287n34, 289n106
Paulus, M., 289n94, 290n146
Paus, T., 283n55
Pedersen, C. B., 294n113
Pelka, S., 283n12
Pellegrini, Anthony D., 249, 277n18, 279n36, 286n114, 286n118, 293n68, 293n71
Pelufo Silveria, P., 283n6
Pen, I., 278n3
Pepper, G. V., 277n11
Perdeck, A. C., 292n27
Perez-Zapata, D., 288n64
Periss, V., 284n31, 284n35, 285n71
Perner, J., 288n68
Perrett, D. I., 283n7, 283n14, 283n18
Perry, C., 290n142
Petanjek, Z., 282n44
Peterson, J., 294n107
Philips, D. I. W., 281n22
Phipps, M. G., 280n62
Piaget, Jean, 23–24, 53, 117, 136, 138–39, 160, 184, 201, 254–55, 278n32, 283n51, 284n38, 284n40, 289n104, 293n95
Pickrell, J. E., 285n81
Pierroutsakos, S. L., 294n99
Pierucci, J. M., 286n127
Pijlman, F. T., 280n57
Pineda, M., 287n43
Pinheiro, P. S., 279n23
Pinker, S., 285n85
Piontak, J. R., 292n40, 292n42
Plötner, M., 289n93
Pluess, M., 279n41
Plumert, Jodi M., 149, 285n69, 285n80

Poirier, F. E., 282n47
Pollak, S. D., 280n63
Pollen, A. A., 282n12
Ponting, C. P., 281n4
Porcelli, A., 278n11
Portmann, Adolf, 113–14, 282n42
Posner, M. I., 293n73
Postman, N., 293n58
Potard, C., 284n48
Potts, R., 277n17, 287n19
Poulton, R., 278n12
Povinelli, D. J., 288n74, 288n81, 290n159
Prabhakar, Shyam, 100, 282n12
Pratkanis, A. R., 284n45
Pressman, S. D., 292n30
Prestipino, M., 290n130
Preston, Stephanie D., 195, 288n79
Principe, G. F., 284n58
Probst, F., 283n12, 283n14
Profet, M., 277n11
Proffitt, D. R., 287n23
Proulux, J., 292n30
Provan, L. S., 293n73, 293n76
Provence, Sally, 48–49, 279n25
Proverbio, A. M., 284n28
Provine, W. B., 280n7
Przybylski, A. K., 292n44
Pullin, A. S., 292n36
Punzi, G., 278n11
Purdy, M. S., 294n119
Putnam, Robert D., 243
Putnick, D. L., 283n10, 284n22

Quinn, P. C., 278n41, 287n27, 288n84
Quinsey, V. L., 126, 283n9
Quiring, R. U., 282n8

Radesky, J. S., 294n106
Radke-Yarrow, M., 288n78
Radmore, N., 290n151
Raefski, A., 280n61
Raff, Rudolf A., 97, 98, 99, 101, 281n5, 282n7, 282n9, 282n20
Ragan, P., 281n32, 290n134
Rahde Bischoff, A., 283n6
Raichle, M. E., 282n44
Rajan, V., 293n90
Rakic, P., 282n44

Rakison, D., 278n37
Rakoczy, H., 288n61, 288n67, 288n71, 289n96, 289n118, 290n144, 290n156, 291n182
Rand, D. G., 290n151
Rands, C. M., 281n4
Rapoport, J. L., 283n55
Rapp, D., 289n93
Rasmusse, E. E., 294n107
Ratner, 204, 289n124
Reader, S. M., 281n36
REBRN, 279n29
Redshaw, J., 278n44, 287n31
Reed, J., 294n114
Rees, G., 292n26
Refsnider, J. M., 278n3
Regolin, L., 287n23
Reiling, A. M., 283n15
Rendell, L., 289n127
Reno, P. L., 282n12
Repacholi, B. M., 288n66
Rescorla, L., 251–52, 293n85
Ressler, R. H., 281n17
Reyna, V. F., 284n58
Reynolds, V., 281n31, 289n127
Rheingold, Harriet L., 149, 208–9, 285n79, 290n140
Rice, F., 279n42
Richardson, A. S., 288n81, 290n159
Richardson, M., 292n38
Richert, R., 294n103
Richey, E., 294n107
Rideout, V., 292n31
Ridoput, K. K., 280n62
Riedl, K., 288n88, 289n98
Rigo, P., 284n22
Rilling, J. K., 282n35
Risenhoover, N., 288n59
Ritchie, S. J., 280n2
Ritter, J., 283n8
Rittle-Johnson, B., 284n44
Riva, F., 284n28
Robb, M. B., 292n31, 294n103
Robbins, E., 288n88
Roberts, S. C., 277n11
Robinson, J. F., 278n11
Rochat, P., 288n88
Rochat, P. M., 290n150, 290n157
Rodney, N. C., 280n62
Roebers, C., 285n75
Roettger, M. E., 278n10
Rogers, M. L., 292n38, 292n40
Rogoff, 293n95
Roisman, G. I., 287n41
Roko Rašin, M., 282n44
Romens, S. E., 280n63
Rooksby, M., 284n56
Roseboom, T. J., 281n22
Rosen, L. D., 292n33
Rosenberg, J. S., 278n35, 287n17, 290n132
Rosenberg, K. M., 281n16
Rosenberg, K. R., 282n38
Roser, M., 291n6
Ross, 293n64
Ross, H. S., 290n148
Ross, J., 284n46
Roulette, C. J., 289n115
Rousseau, Jean Jacques, 159–60, 218
Rovee-Collier, C., 284n56
Roylance, R., 292n26
Rubin, 291n14
Rubin, E. M., 100, 282n12
Rubin, K. H., 284n40
Ruble, D. N., 288n85
Rueda, M. R., 293n73
Ruff, H. A., 287n26
Ruffman, T., 288n63, 288n71, 288n77
Ruiz, A. M., 285n67
Ruiz Soler, M., 284n31
Ruparel, K., 126–28, 127f, 283n8, 283n11, 283n20
Rusch, B. D., 283n20, 284n22
Russell, M. A., 292n40, 292n42
Rutter, M., 279n25, 279n31
Ryskfna, V. L., 285n99

Sabbagh, M. A., 288n65
Sachser, N., 126–28, 127f, 283n8, 283n11
Sagi, A., 288n77
Salapatek, P., 287n26
Salisbury, A. L., 280n62
Sameroff, A. J., 287n22
Sander, D., 283n6
Sandman, C. A., 279n41
Santiago, C., 286n103
Santidrián Tomillo, P., 278n3

Santos, L. R., 285n67
Sanz, C., 290n130
Satto, Y., 277n16
Savage-Rumbaugh, Sue, 205–6, 281n32, 290n131
Sawin, D., 283n8
Sazthmáry, E., 285n86
Sbarra, David A., 237, 292n28
Scarf, D., 288n77, 290n138
Scarr, Sandra, 56–57, 279n38
Scelza, B. A., 290n157
Schapiro, S. J., 282n45
Scherer, K. R., 283n6
Schertz, K. E., 292n36
Schleihauf, H., 285n60, 289n113
Schlomer, G. L., 278n46, 279n43, 280n45
Schmalhausen, Ivanovich I., 77–78, 281n9
Schmidt, M. F., 289n95, 290n164
Schmidtling, E. Y., 290n130
Schmuckler, M., 286n123
Schneider, D., 288n71
Schneider, F. W., 290n150
Schneider, W., 285n69, 285n75
Schön, R. A., 291n3
Schore, A. N., 287n35
Schulz, L., 252–53, 293n86
Schuyler, Chelsea, 236f
Schwartz, J. H., 282n16
Schwartz, R., 286n104
Schwebel, D. C., 285n69
Sclafani, V., 289n106
Scott, John Paul, 74, 280n3
Scott, R., 288n69
Sedikides, C., 285n69
Seifer, R., 280n62
Seligman, Martin E. P., 145–46, 285n71, 285n73
Sellers, P. D., II, 284n59, 293n62
Semenov, A. D., 293n73, 293n76
Senese, V. P., 283n7
Senghas, Ann, 154, 285n92
Sercombe, Howard, 229, 283n62, 284n50, 291n12, 292n22
Setliff, Alissa E., 256–57, 294n104
Shablack, H., 292n46, 292n48
Shackelford, T. K., 277
Shafto, P., 252–53, 293n86
Shakespeare, William, 108
Shapiro, S. J., 290n161
Sharp, M. L., 294n107

Shaver, P. R., 287n39
Shea, B. T., 282n13, 282n25
Sheehy, Gail, 243
Shepeleva, D. V., 277n15
Sheridan, M. A., 280n57
Sherman, G. D., 284n21
Sherman, K., 256–57, 294n103
Sherman, P. W., 277n11
Sheskin, M., 290n139
Shin, H-E., 285n76
Shore, T. J., 279n14
Shulman, E. P., 231–32, 233f, 292n19
Sideris, J., 287n22
Siegler, R. S., 283n52
Siepel, A., 282n12
Silk, J. B., 278n47, 288n81, 290n157, 290n159, 290n161
Silver, L., 292n24
Silverstein, M., 294n106
Šimić, G., 282n44
Simion, F., 278n40, 287n23, 287n26
Simpson, A., 294n108
Simpson, E. A., 287n34
Simpson, J. A., 280n47
Singer, T., 288n72
Singh, Joseph A. L., 45–46, 279n15
Skenazy, Lenore, 220–21, 291n1
Skinner, A. T., 280n45
Skulachev, M. V., 105t
Skulachev, V. P., 105t
Slagboo, P. E., 281n21
Slagt, M., 280n55
Slatcher, R. B., 237, 292n28
Slater, A. M., 278n41, 287n27
Slaughter, V., 287n31, 288n64
Slieker, R. C., 281n21
Smilansky, S., 293n71
Smith, E. D., 286n125, 294n107
Smith, E. O., 282n47
Smith, I. M., 293n72
Smith, Peter K., 164, 285n69, 286n114, 286n116
Smuke, A. T., 279n25, 279n31
Smyth, G. K., 282n12
Snyder, A. Z., 282n44
Snyder, H. R., 293n73, 293n76
Society for Research in Child Development, 56–57, 279n34
Soderstrom, M., 286n101
Sol, D., 281n36

Somel, M., 282n44
Sommerville, J. A., 290n165
Sonuga-Barke, E. J., 279n25
Southgate, V., 288n86
Spear, L. P., 283n55
Spear, Norman E., 37–38, 278n8
Speed, T. P., 282n12
Speekenbrink, M., 231, 291n16
Spelke, Elizabeth S., 9, 252–53, 277n9, 290n153, 293n86
Spence, M. J., 286n100
Spinath, B., 285n69
Spinath, F. M., 285n69
Spotila, J. R., 278n3
Sprengelmeyer, A., 283n7, 283n12
Sprengelmeyer, R., 283n7, 283n12
Stamperdahl, J., 280n53
Stansfield, C., 292n38
Stark, E. A., 283n6
Stearns, S., 279n43
Steer, C. D., 278n12
Steers, Mai-Ly N., 241, 292n50
Stein, A., 283n6, 283n12
Stein, A. D., 281n21
Steinbeis, N., 288n72, 290n163
Steinberg, Laurence D., 60–61, 231–32, 233f, 279–80n45, 280n56, 291–92n20
Stengelin, R., 289n114
Stenhouse, D., 282n32
Stephens, B. R., 287n25
Stevens, E., 285n88
Stimpson, C. D., 282n45
Stipek, Deborah, 149, 285n70, 285n78
Stival, R., 283n10
Stotz, K., 280n4
Striano, T., 288n59, 288n62
Stright, A. D., 280n54
Stroud, L. R., 280n62
Strouse, G. A., 294n102
Suchiman, H. E. D., 281n21
Suddendorf, T., 278n44, 284n54, 287n31
Suderman, M., 280n61
Suderman, M. J., 280n64
Sugiyama, Y., 281n31, 289n127
Sumner, J. A., 280n57
Sung, S., 280n47
Suomi, S. J., 287n34, 289n106
Sutcliffe, K., 292n38
Sutter, M., 290n167
Svaren, J., 280n63

Svenning, J-C., 294n113
Svetlova, M., 290n158, 291n178
Symons, D., 287n42
Számadó, S., 285n86
Szepsenwol, O., 280n45
Szkrybalo, J., 288n85

Tajfel, H., 289n91
Tang, L., 282n44
Tankak, M., 288n62
Tanner, J. M., 282n40
Tardif, T., 288n65
Tarulli, D., 284n43
Tattersall, I., 277n17
Taylor, K., 292n24
Telzer, E. H., 291n4
Tenenbaum, H. R., 293n92
Tennie, C., 289n100, 289n129
Thapar, A., 279n42
Thomaes, S., 285n69
Thomas, J., 292n38, 293n79
Thomas, K. M., 279n14
Thomas de Benitez, S., 283n54
Thompson-Schill, S. L., 284n34
Thomsen, T., 167–68, 286n128
Thomson, K. W., 282n16
Thulborn, K. R., 283n55
Tinbergen, Nikolaas, 292n27
Tipper, S. P., 289n90
Tobi, E. W., 281n21
Tollrian, R., 281n14
Tomaselli, K., 289n114, 289n117
Tomasello, Michael, 150–51, 155, 176, 186–89, 189f, 196–97, 199, 204, 205–6, 208, 212–13, 215–16, 218–19, 249–50, 273, 281n32, 283n59, 285n60, 285n67, 285n85, 285n89, 285n93, 286n7, 287n48, 288n51, 288n56, 288n58, 288n62, 288n67, 288n73, 288n76, 288n81, 288n88, 289n93, 289n95, 289n98, 289n100, 289n102, 289n110, 289n126, 289n128, 290n131, 290n134, 290n144, 290n149, 290n152, 290n156, 290n159, 290n166, 290n170, 291n174, 291n183, 291n186
Tomonaga, M., 288n62
Tooby, J., 277n7
Toub, T. S., 293n90
Träuble, B., 288n64

Trevanthan, W. R., 282n41
Trevarthen, Colwyn, 182–83, 287n36
Trevathan, W. R., 282n38
Trivers, Robert L., 110, 173, 283n1, 286n5
Troller-Renferee, S., 279n25
Tromholt, M., 292n47
Tronick, E., 280n62
Tronick, E. Z., 184, 287n37, 287n43
Troseth, G. L., 256–57, 294n103
Trump, Donald, Jr., 226
Trut, Lyudimila N., 102–3, 104, 277n15, 282n21
Tsirogiannis, C., 294n113
Tucker-Drob, E. M., 280n2
Tulving, E., 284n54
Turati, C., 287n26
Turkewitz, G., 278n7, 294n111
Twenge, Jean M., 227–29, 234, 238–40, 244, 291n9, 292n25, 292n32, 292n41, 292n56
Tyler, S., 148, 285n77

Ulber, J., 290n149, 290n155
Uller, T., 278n3
Umbel, V., 289n105
Umiltà, C., 287n26
United Nations Treaty Collection, 284n53
Ursini, G., 278n11
Üstün, T. B., 292n54
Uttal, D. H., 293n88
Uylings, H. B. M., 282n44

Vaish, A., 288n59, 290n142, 290n152
Valdez, J. N., 283n20
Valenza, E., 287n25
Vallortigara, G., 287n23
van Aken, M. A. G., 280n55
van den Bree, M., 279n42
Vanderborght, M., 256–57, 294n103
Vanderhasselt, M. A., 283n19
van Duijvenvoorde, A. C. K., 291n4
van IJzendoorn, Marinus H., 68, 280n54, 280n57, 280n60, 287n41
van Loon, M., 285n75
Van Schuerbeek, P., 283n19
van Vugt, M., 277n21
van Zwet, E. W., 281n21
Vartanian, L. R., 284n47
Venuti, P., 284n22

Venutti, P., 283n7
Verduyn, P., 292n46, 292n48
Vernon, L., 292n32
Vickers, M. H., 279n40
Vladimirova, A. V., 277n15
Volk, Anthony A., 126, 130–31, 278n34, 283n2, 283n9, 284n25, 294n123
von Duhn, B., 288n71
Vonk, J., 288n81, 290n159
Vouloumanos, A., 286n100
Vygotsky, Lev S., 136–37, 160, 187–88, 247–48, 250, 284n42, 288n50, 293n63, 293n75
Vyssokikh, M. Y., 105*t*

Waddington, Conrad H., 23–24, 76*f*, 78, 278n31, 281n10, 281n12
Wagner, E., 288n78
Wakefield, J. C., 277
Wakeford, L., 287n22
Waldo, J., 293n62
Walker, C. M., 284n37, 293n67, 293n81
Wall, S., 183–84, 287n38
Wallace, C. S., 279n13
Walldorf, U., 282n8
Waller, K. L., 283n8
Walsh, D. A., 292n32
Walsh, K., 280n57
Wang, J., 294n121
Wang, M-T., 280n45
Wang, Y., 290n164
Want, S. C., 289n102
Wapstra, E., 278n3
Warneken, Felix L. U., 210, 212–13, 215–16, 288n61, 288n67, 288n89, 290n145, 290n147, 290n156, 290n163, 290n166, 291n176, 291n183
Warner, R. R., 278n2
Wartella, E., 294n103
Waters, E., 183–84, 287n38
Watson, J., 288n63
Watson, K. S., 284n40
Watson, L. R., 287n22
Watson-Jones, R. E., 289n119
Waxman, S., 286n100
Weisberg, Deena Skolnick, 253, 293n87, 293n90
Weismann, August, 74–75, 81, 95

Weissman, M. M., 292n54
Wellman, H. M., 288n63, 288n65
Werker, J. F., 287n29
Wesson, R., 282n16, 282n27
West-Eberhard, Mary Jane, 74, 280n5, 281n13, 281n15, 282n20
Wheeler, A., 278n41
Wheelwright, S., 278n39
While, G. M., 278n3
Whitaker, R. C., 292n33
White, D. A., 293n72
White, J. W., 278n2
White, K. P., 282n12
White, R. E., 293n74, 293n77, 293n81
White, S., 293n65
Whitehead, H., 289n127
Whitehouse, H., 218–19, 291n185
Whitelaw, E., 280n8, 281n20
Whiten, Andrew, 176–77, 203–4, 281n31, 285n60, 285n81, 287n13, 287n15, 287n45, 287n47, 289n108, 289n115, 289n117, 289n122, 289n128
Whitham, J. C., 286n103
Wickham, Robert E., 241, 292n50
Wiesel, T. N., 278n27
Wiesmann, C. G., 288n72
Wiessner, P. W., 287n21
Wigfield, A., 285n69
Wilkinson, G. W., 286n6
Williams, B., 278n12
Willoughby, T., 240, 292n45
Wilson, A. C., 89*t*, 281n35
Wilson, David Sloan, 174–75, 287n10, 293n62, 294n119
Wilson, E. O., 7, 174–75, 238, 286n7, 292n35
Wilson, M., 282n29, 283n3
Winick, M., 279n32
Winning, A., 290n150, 290n157
Winsler, A., 284n44
Witherington, D. C., 22, 277n23, 278n26
Wittig, M., 290n168
Wobber, V., 188–89, 189*f*, 288n55, 289n126
Wong, I., 130–31, 284n25
Wong, W. P. S., 279n40
Wood, L. A., 285n62, 293n64

Woolley, J. D., 284n32
Wordsworth, William, 266
Wörle, M., 289n94
Wrangham, Richard W., 110, 188–89, 189*f*, 282n28, 282n30, 287n19, 288n55, 289n126
Wray, G. A., 282n11
Wyles, Jeff S., 88–89, 89*t*, 281n35
Wynn, K., 208, 290n137, 290n139

Xiao, N. G., 288n84
Xu, F., 288n65
Xu, L., 283n19, 284n23

Yaeger, D. S., 294n123
Yaeger, J., 284n44
Yahr, J., 287n27
Yamaguchi, M. K., 278n41
Yamamoto, R., 283n12
Yan, Z., 282n44
Yang, F., 288n88
Yang, X., 288n88
Yanovitzky, I., 284n48
Ybarra, O., 292n46
Yeates, M., 294n107
Yoo, H., 287n36
Young, A. G., 285n60, 289n111
Young, E. S., 280n45, 280n47
Young, J., 240–41, 292n49
Young, J. F., 280n62
Young, K. S., 283n12, 292n37
Youngson, N. A., 280n8
Yun, J. E., 290n164

Zack, E., 294n102
Zahn-Waxler, C., 288n78
Zani, A., 284n28
Zeanah, C. H., 279n25, 279n31
Zeanah, Jr., C. H., 279n22
Zebrowitz, L. A., 284n26
Zelazo, P. D., 293n72, 293n74
Zephoria Digital Marketing, 292n23
Zhao, W., 283n19, 284n23
Zheng, X., 283n19, 284n23
Zijdenbos, A., 283n55
Zingg, R. M., 279n15
Zmyj, N., 288n86, 289n113
Zuckerman, B., 294n106

Subject Index

Page numbers followed by n indicate endnotes. Tables and figures are indicated by *t* and *f* following the page number.

For the benefit of digital users, indexed terms that span two pages (e.g., 52–53) may, on occasion, appear on only one of those pages.

A Capella Science, 95–96
acceleration, 101
acetylation, 67–68, 68*f*
adaptable ancestral children, 90–91
adaptation(s), 11–15
    conditional, 29, 58
    deferred, 27–28
    evolutionary, 15–19
    of infancy and childhood, 25–29
    intellectual, 187–88
    ontogenetic, 28–29, 124, 267
    value of immaturity for, 123
adaptive evolution, 74
adaptive lag, 222–23
ADHD (attention deficit hyperactivity disorder), 239–40
adolescence, 116, 119*f*, 121, 271
    biology of, 245
    evolution of, 118–19, 119*f*
adolescents, 123
    digital natives, 73
    drive for social interaction and belonging, 230–35
    early-life adversity and, 280n45
    egocentricity, 138–40
    mismatches with, 223, 235–42, 244–45
    social media and mental health, 238–39, 239*f*
adoption, 50
adrenarche, 121
adulthood, 116
    emerging, 245
    evolution of, 118–19, 119*f*
adulting, 244–45
adversity, early-life, 280n45

affordances, 164–65
age differences, 130–31
agency, 229
aggression
    proactive, 108
    reactive, 108, 270–71
Aka people, 202–3
alloparents, 179
altruism, 172
    benefits of, 174–75
    reciprocal, 173–74
Amala (feral child), 45–46, 46*f*
amnesia, infantile, 141
anatomical evolution, 88–89, 89*t*
ancestors
    adaptable, 71
    embryos and, 92
    Stone Age, 17–18
Android phones, 234
animals, domesticated, 103*f*, 103–4
Anirida gene, 99
anticipating the future, 57–58
anticipating harsh and unpredictable environments, 59–66
antisocial behavior, 39–40, 40*f*
anxiety, 238–39, 239*f*, 240–41
anxious relationships, 183–84
apoptosis, 43, 111
apprenticeships, 56
Archaea, 174
artifacts, cognitive, 187–88
artificial selection, 102–3
artificial stimuli, 235–36, 236*f*
assimilation, genetic, 78
assumption of relevance, 203–4

366 SUBJECT INDEX

attachment. *see also* belonging
  first relationships, 182–84
  forming, 179–85
  insecure-avoidant, 183–84
  insecure-resistant, 183–84
  reward and, 283n20
  secure, 183–84
  types of, 183–84
attention
  to biological motion, 180*f*, 180–81, 287n23
  to faces, 27
  shared (joint), 188–90, 217*t*, 273
attention deficit hyperactivity disorder (ADHD), 239–40
audience, imaginary, 138–39
auditory imprinting, 34–35, 35*f*
Australia, 243
Australopithecines, 88–89, 89*t*, 106–7
Australopithecus afarensis, 119*f*, 119
average expectable environment, 56–57
avoidant relationships, 183–84
axolotls, 102
axons, 111

babyness, 125–26, 130–31
baby schema *(Kindchenschema)*, 1, 2*f*, 102, 125–30, 127*f*, 133–34, 179–80, 272
baby talk, 158
Bach, Johann Sebastian, 87–88
Baka Pygmies, 191–92
Baldwin effect, 75–77, 76*f*
Beethoven, Ludwig von, 87–88
behavior
  antisocial, 39–40, 40*f*
  instinctive, 34–39, 35*f*, 37*f*, 270
behavioral epigenetics, 67, 69–70
behavioral neoteny, 108–10, 270–71
behavioral plasticity, 34–41, 268
behavior problems, 50–51
belief-desire reasoning, 194
belonging. *see also* attachment
  adolescents' drive for, 230–35
bias, 179–82
bidirectional interaction, 21
big brains, 177–78
biogenetic law, 101, 104–5
biologically primary abilities, 254–55

biologically secondary abilities, 254–55
biological motion
  infants' attention to, 180*f*, 180–81, 287n23
  self-propelled motion, 287n23
biology
  of adolescence, 245
  evolutionary developmental (Evo Devo), 94–104, 270
biophilia, 238
bistrategic controllers, 208
Blackberry, 234
Block Design, 71–73
bonobos *(Pan paniscus)*, 118
bottleneck effects, 15
brain
  baby schema and, 129–30
  social, 171, 272
brain development, 110–14, 177–78
  plasticity and, 42–45
  social brain, 171
brain size
  and evolution rate, 88–89, 89*t*
  social brain, 177–78
breeders, cooperative, 17–18
breeding, selective, 102–3
British Common Law, 117–18
bullying, 263–64
byproducts, 12–13

candle problem, 143*f*, 143–44
Canis familiaris (domesticated dogs), 103
Capra hircus (domesticated goats), 103*f*, 103
capuchin monkeys, 213–14
Catholic Church, 23, 117–18
cell death, selective, 43, 111
cell differentiation, 111
cell proliferation, 111
Center for Great Ape's sanctuary (Wauchula, Florida), 93*f*
change, evolutionary, 74–81. *see also* evolution
changeable children, 70
Chaoborus flavicans, 78–79
cheater detection, 197–98
child development

changes in performance with, 188–89, 189f
early-life adversity and, 280n45
exterior gestation or exterogestation, 113–14
extrauterine spring, 113–14, 119–20
fourth trimester, 113–14
individual, x
today, 220
child-directed speech, 158
childhood, 1, 116, 119f, 271
adaptations of, 25–29
evolution of, 118–19, 119f
extended, 29–30
middle, 116
childhood maltreatment, 39–40, 40f
children. *see also* infants
adopted, 50–52
ancestral, 90–91
benefits of language for, 155–56
biological preparation for language learning, 151–56
changeable, 70
deaf, 154–55, 155f
digital natives, 73–74
evolutionary perspective on, 1
feral, 45–47, 46f
institutionalized, 47–54
invention of humanity by, 266
mismatches with social media, 235–42
orchids and dandelions, 64–66, 280n58
preschool, 116–17, 136
promiscuous normativity, 199
recommended limits for digital-media time, 257–58, 258f
sensitivity to context, 280n57
short-term store, 157–58
social learning, 201–4
today's, 220
young, 245–59, 258f
chimpanzees *(Pan troglodytes)*, 1–2, 3f, 86–87
developmental changes in performance, 188–89, 189f
female/male survival rates and paternal care, 83–85, 84t
life history stages, 118–19, 119f
social cognition, 193, 194f, 206, 207f

social learning, 204–5
China, 243
close relationships, 183–84. *see also* attachment
cognition. *see also* reasoning
developmental changes, 188–89, 189f
developmental stages, 117
evolved probabilistic mechanisms, 25–28
face-processing mechanisms, 27
immature processing, 156–59
language development and, 156–59
metacognition, 146–48
physical, 188–89, 189f
self-centered, 136–37
social, 193, 194f
cognitive artifacts, 187–88
cognitive empathy, 195, 217t
cognitive neoteny, 122, 124, 134–50, 271
cognitive self-guidance, 136–37
collaboration, 214–18
collective intentionality, 188, 196–97, 208, 216, 217t, 273
collective monologues, 136
collectivism, 243
computer literacy, 260–61
conditional adaptations, 29, 58
contemporary educational practices, 249–51
context, 64, 274, 280n57
contingent life strategies, 57–59
Convention on the Rights of the Child (UN), 139–40
cooperation, 110, 174–75
cooperative breeders, 17–18
cooperative play, 162
cooperative problem solving, 217t
core knowledge, 9
counterfactual thinking, 120, 162, 167, 168f, 191–92, 217t, 271
cranial flexure, 107
creoles, 153–54, 271–72
Crick, Francis, 96
Cronkite, Walter, 137–38
cues
cuteness, 126 (*see also* baby schema *(Kindchenschema)*)
of immaturity, 131–34

cultural change, 223, 264–65
cultural differences, 120–21, 245
curricula
    Montessori, 254
    preschool, 251–55
cuteness, 126, 130–31. *see also* baby schema *(Kindchenschema)*

dandelions, 64–66, 280n58
Daphnia cucullate, 78–79
deaf children, 154–55, 155*f*
declarative memory, 140–41
deferred adaptations, 27–28
dendrites, 111
depression, 238–39, 239*f*, 241
deprivation, 48–49
design, 143–44
Despacito Biology Parody (Evo-Devo), 95–96
development, ix–x, 30–31
    adolescent, 280n45
    behavioral plasticity in, 34–41
    brain, 42–45, 110–14, 177–78
    canalized, 53, 217–18
    changes in task performance, 188–89, 189*f*
    child, 113–14, 188–89, 189*f*, 220, 280n45
    definition, 41–42
    early-life adversity and, 280n45
    evolution and, 122
    evolutionary developmental biology (Evo Devo), 94–104, 270
    evolutionary mismatches in, 273–74
    evolutionary perspective on, 1
    evolved social brain, 171
    extending, 115–22
    gene × environment × development interactions, 39–41
    importance of, 266–68
    individual, x
    language, 150–59
    life history stages, 118–19, 119*f*
    ontogeny, 4–5
    phylogeny, 4–5
    plasticity and, 41–45
    of play, 162–69
    postnatal, 116
    prenatal, 23, 24*f*, 58–59
    proximal, 247–48
    psychological abilities associated with, 119–22
    stages of, 116–22, 119*f*
    theory for evolutionary psychology, 21–25
    vision, 43–44
    zone of proximal development, 247–48
developmental plasticity, 5–6, 71
developmental psychopathology, 63
developmental systems, 21–22
Diagnostic and Statistical Manual of Mental Disorders (DSM-5), 238–39
Dictator Game, 210–11
didactic instruction, 253
differential sensitivity to context, 64
digital media, 257–58, 258*f*, 260
digital natives, 73–74, 123
discovery learning, 252–53, 262–63
distal explanations, 66–67
DNA (deoxyribonucleic acid), 96
DNA methylation, 67–69, 68*f*
domestication
    of animals, 103*f*, 103–4
    self-domestication, 108, 175–76, 270–71
Drosophila melanogaster (fruit flies), 78, 97–99

early-developing perceptual bias, 179–82
early experience, 34–39
education, 246–48
    contemporary practices, 249–51
    formal practices, 245–59
    mismatches with, 245–59
    modern schools, 274
    recommendations for educators, 261–64
egocentricity, 135–40
Einstein, Albert, 170, 177
embryology, 94–95, 104
emerging adulthood, 245
empathy, 194–96, 283n20
    cognitive, 195, 217*t*
emulation, 86
encephalization quotient, 110–11
enculturation, 86, 205–6
environment(s), 255
    average expectable, 56–57
    of evolutionary adaptedness, 15–19

gene × environment × development interactions, 39–41
  harsh and unpredictable, 59–66
epigenetics, 23–25, 66–70, 77–78, 269, 281n20
  behavioral, 67, 69–70
  theories of evolution, 77–81
epiphenomena, ix–x, 74–75, 269
Esposito (surname), 48
eukaryotic cells, 174
eusociality, 172, 174
Evo-Devo (Despacito Biology Parody), 95–96
Evo Devo (evolutionary developmental biology), 94–104, 270
evolution, 1, 70
  adaptive, 74
  anatomical, 88–89, 89t
  brain size and, 88–89, 89t
  byproducts of, 12–13
  developmental plasticity and, 71
  development and, 122
  epigenetic theories of, 77–81
  evolved probabilistic cognitive mechanisms, 25–28
  evolved psychological mechanisms, 9–11
  evolved social brain, 171
  hominin, 16, 17t
  of human life history stages, 118–19, 119f
  importance of, 30–31
  processes of, 12–15
  timeline of, 16, 17t
evolutionary adaptedness, 15–19
evolutionary developmental biology (Evo Devo), 94–104, 270
evolutionary developmental perspective, 5–6
evolutionary mismatches, x, 18–19, 220, 273–74
evolutionary perspective, 1
evolutionary psychology, 7, 8–25
execution hypothesis, 110
executive function, 249–50
experience, early, 34–39
experience-dependent processes, 44
experience-expectant processes, 43–44, 152

explicit memory, 140–41
exterior gestation (exterogestation), 113–14
extrauterine spring, 113–14, 119–20
eyeless gene, 99
eyes, 99

fables, personal, 138–39
Facebook, 230, 234, 240–41
faces and facial features, 4
  baby schema *(Kindchenschema)*, 1, 2f, 102, 125–30, 127f, 133–34, 179–80, 272
  human and great ape, 1–2, 3f
  infants' attention to, 27, 181
fairness, 212–14
false-belief tasks, 191f, 191–92, 217t
families, 61–62, 107–8
fantasy play, 160–61, 162, 163, 166–68
fast life history strategy, 60, 61f, 62–63
fathers, 82, 83–85, 84t
fear of missing out (FOMO), 240–41
feral children, 45–47, 46f
fetalization theory, 104–6
fitness, inclusive, 173
fixedness, functional, 143f, 143–44
Flynn effect, 71, 87–88
folk psychology, 9, 10f
fostering, 47–54
founder effects, 15
foundling homes, 47–54
fourth trimester, 113–14
free play, 253, 261
fruit flies *(Drosophila melanogaster)*, 78, 97–99
functional fixedness, 143f, 143–44

Galapagos turtles, 32–33, 33f
Galilei, Galileo, 87–88
Gapun people, 56
Generation X (GenX), 228
Generation Z (zoomers), 227
genes, 21–22, 39
  gene × environment × development interactions, 39–41
  Hox, 97–98
  regulatory, 96, 99–100
  and sensitivity to context, 280n57
  and sex determination, 33f, 33
  small-effect, 40–41

genetic assimilation, 78
genetic determinism, 19–20
genetic drift, 15
genetic mutations, 76–77
Genie (feral child), 47
gerontocracies, 54–57, 221–22
gestation, exterior (exterogestation), 113–14
gestures, 154–55
globally depriving institutions, 50–51
glucocorticoid receptor gene (NR3C1), 69
goat yoga, 103*f*, 103
goodness paradox, 110
Google, 230, 234
great apes, 1–2, 3*f*, 204–7
Great Britain, 243
group-minded "we," 188–89, 216, 217–18, 217*t*, 273
Grub (human-reared chimpanzee), 92, 93*f*
guided play, 253–54
gunshine state, 123

Haitian Creole, 153–54
Halloween, 226
handling, 79–80
harshness, 59–66
health, mental, 238–41, 239*f*
helping, 208–10
heterochrony, 100–4, 270
Hobbes, Thomas, 218
hominin evolution, 16, 17*t*
hominoids, 88–89, 89*t*
Homo erectus, 16, 17*t*
   brain size and anatomical evolution, 88–89, 89*t*
   life history stages, 118–19, 119*f*
Homo ergaster, 16, 17*t*
Homo habilis, 16, 17*t*
   brain size and anatomical evolution, 88–89, 89*t*
   life history stages, 118–19, 119*f*
Homo neanderthalensis, 16, 17*t*
Homo sapiens, 5–6, 16–18, 30–31, 168–69
   acquisition and transmission of cultural knowledge across generations, 120–21
   brain development, 114–15, 175–76
   brain size and anatomical evolution, 88–89, 89*t*
   cranial flexure, 107
   evolved characteristics, 268–70
   life history stages, 118–19, 119*f*, 271
   as moral species, 218–19
   as most educable, 246–48
   taming of, 108–10
   timeline, 16, 17*t*
   vaginal slope, 107–8
Hox genes, 97–98
human development. *see* development
human evolution, 1, 70. *see also* evolution
humanity, 5–7, 266
Hunger Winter, 80–81
hyper-individualism, 223, 242–45, 274
hypermorphosis, 101
hypersociality, 172, 185–218, 272–73

iGen'ers, 227–29, 238, 244, 273–74
imaginary audience, 138–39
imitation, 120–21, 200–1, 271
   meta-imitation, 146–48, 147*f*
   mutual, 201
   neonatal, 28–29, 181–82
   overimitation, 120–21, 142, 202–4, 217*t*, 248, 271
   rational, 201–2
immaturity
   adaptive value of, 123
   cues of, 126, 131–34 (*see also* baby schema (*Kindchenschema*))
   language development and, 156–59
implicit memory, 140–41
imprinting, 34–35, 35*f*
inclusive fitness, 173
individual development, x
individual differences, 57. *see also* hyper-individualism
infancy, 116, 121–22, 125
   adaptations of, 25–29
   evolution of, 118–19, 119*f*
   jealous protest in, 184–85, 185*f*
infant-directed speech, 158
infantile amnesia, 141
infants, 1–2, 2*f*, 3*f*, 125. *see also* children

attention to biological motion, 180f, 180–81, 287n23
attention to faces, 27
forming attachments, 179–85
as individuals, x
psychological weapons to compete with parents, 125, 133–34
recommended limits for digital-media time, 257–58, 258f
sensitivity to human speech, 181
visual media for, 255–59
young, 179–85
information-processing domains, 9, 10f
inheritance
of acquired characteristics, 74–75
hard, 76–77
soft, 76–77
inhibition, 109
innateness, 20
insecure-avoidant attachments, 183–84
insecure-resistant attachments, 183–84
Instagram, 230, 234, 240–41
instinctive behavior, 34–39, 35f, 37f
instincts, 11, 20, 270
institutions, 45–57
instructed learning, 200–1, 204, 217t
instruction, didactic, 253
intellectual adaptation, 187–88
intelligence, 176–78
intelligence quotient (IQ), 51–52, 52f, 71–73, 72f, 87–88
intentional agents, 190, 273
intentional beings, 189–94, 217t
intentionality
collective, 188, 196–97, 208, 216, 217t, 273
joint, 188
shared, 176, 186–89, 273
intentional stance, 190
Internet, 230, 238
intersubjective meaning, 188
in vitro fertilization (IVF), 59
iPhone, 234

Japan, 243
jealous protest, 184–85, 185f, 272
Jefferson, Thomas, 87–88
Johnny (foster child), 49

joint (shared) attention, 188–90, 217t, 273
juvenile period, 116, 118–19, 119f

Kalahari Bushmen, 202–3
Kamala (feral child), 45–46, 46f
kin, 8
Kindchenschema (baby schema), 1, 2f, 102, 125–30, 127f, 133–34, 179–80, 272
kin selection, 173–74
knowledge
acquisition and transmission across generations, 120–21
core, 9
cultural, 120–21

laboratory rats, 79–80
language, 150, 271
benefits for children, 155–56
child-directed speech, 158
infant-directed speech, 158
pidgins and creoles, 153–54, 271–72
protolanguages, 153–54
sign language, 154–55
language development, 150–59
learning, 41–42
discovery, 252–53, 262–63
imitative, 200–1
instructed, 200–1, 204, 217t
language, 151–56
social, 199–207, 249
through watching and playing, 248–55
young child, 245–59
less is more hypothesis, 157
life history strategies, 268–69
fast, 60, 61f, 62–63
slow, 60, 61f, 224–25
life history theory, 60–64, 61f
life strategies, contingent, 57–59
literacy, 246–47
local (stimulus) enhancement, 200–1
locomotor play, 162–64
Louisiana Creole, 153–54
Loulis (chimpanzee), 206
Lucy *(Australopithecine)*, 106–7

Machiavellian intelligence, 176–77
maltreatment, childhood, 39–40, 40f

mammals, 82–83, 116
Marjorie Stoneman Douglas High School (Parkland, Florida), 123–24
maternal deprivation, 48–49
maturation, 231–32, 233f
meaning, intersubjective, 188
Meaningful Roles Intervention, 263–64
memory, 140–43
   declarative, 140–41
   explicit, 140–41
   implicit, 140–41
   short-term store, 157–58
   working, 249–50
menarche, 121–22
Mendel, Gregor, 74–75
mental health, 238–41, 239f
mental models, 183–84
Messenger, 234
metacognition, 146–48
meta-imitation, 146–48, 147f
Mexican walking fish, 102
middle childhood, 116
Millennials, 228
mimicry, 200–1
minimal groups paradigm, 198
mismatches, x, 18–19, 220, 273–74
   adolescent, 244–45
   with educational practices, 245–59
   in maturation, 231–32, 233f
   recommendations for dealing with, 260–64
   between social media and children's and adolescents' lives, 235–42
   between visual media and how young children learn, 255–59
   youth, 264–65
mobile devices, 255–56
model organisms, 97
modernity, 222–23
modern synthesis, 74–75, 104
modules and modularity, 9, 10f, 97, 270
monoamine oxidase A gene *(MAOA)*, 39–40, 40f
monologues, collective, 136
Montessori curriculum, 254
morality, 218–19
morphology, 76–77
mothers, 82–87, 110

motor areas, 283n20
multilevel selection theory, 174–75, 272
mutual imitation, 201
myelin, 111
myelination, 114
MySpace, 234

National Rifle Association, 123
naturalistic fallacy, 63–64, 223
natural pedagogy, 203–4, 248
natural selection, 8, 15, 44
natural thinking, 132–33
nature-deficit disorder, 238
neo-Darwinism, 74–75
neonatal imitation, 28–29, 181–82
neontocracies, 54–57, 221
neoteny, 1–2, 3f, 101, 102
   behavioral, 108–10, 270–71
   cognitive, 122, 124, 134–50, 271
   effects on physical form, 106–8
   human, 104–15, 105t, 270–72
Netflix, 73–74
Netherlands, 80–81
neural adhesion, 100
neurogenesis, 111–12
neurons, 38, 111
neurotransmitters, 111
newborns. *see also* infants
   attention to faces, 181
   attention to self-propelled motion, 287n23
   sensitivity to human speech, 181
Nicaraguan Sign Language *(Idioma de Señas de Nicaragua)*, 154, 155f, 271–72
normative overimitation, 203
normativity, 142, 196–99
Northern elephant seals, 15
NR3C1 (glucocorticoid receptor gene), 69

object play, 162, 164–66
object substitution, 166–67
ontogenetic adaptations, 28–29, 124, 267
ontogeny, 4–5, 94–95, 102, 266–67, 274–75
optimism, protective, 148
orchids and dandelions, 64–66, 280n58
organic selection, 75–77

orphanages, 47–54
others
    as intentional beings, 189–94, 217*t*
    social, 179–85
overimitation, 120–21, 142, 202–4, 217*t*, 248, 271
Ovis aries (domesticated sheep), 103
ovists, 23

Pan paniscus (bonobos), 118
Pan troglodytes (chimpanzees), 1–2, 3*f*, 86–87
    developmental changes in performance, 188–89, 189*f*
    female/male survival rates and paternal care, 83–85, 84*t*
    life history stages, 118–19, 119*f*
    social cognition, 193, 194*f*, 206, 207*f*
    social learning, 204–5
parallel play, 136, 162
parents
    adoptive, 50
    alloparents, 179
    aversion to children's risky play, 292n36
    recommendations for, 260–61
    Western, 292n36
Parkland, Florida school shootings, 123–24
Pashtu people, 55
paternal care, 83–85, 84*t*
paternalism, 82
Pax-6 gene, 99
pedagogy, natural, 203–4, 248
perceptual bias, 179–82
personal fables, 138–39
perspective taking, 217*t*
phonology, 151–52
phylogenetic legacies, 58
phylogeny, 4–5, 94–95, 266–67, 274–75
physical cognition, 188–89, 189*f*
physical play, 163
pidgins, 153–54, 271–72
plasticity, 70, 266–67, 268–70
    behavioral, 34–41, 268
    developmental, 5–6, 41–45, 71
    neuronal, 38
play, 2–4, 159–69
    cooperative, 162

definition of, 161–62, 249
development of, 162–69
fantasy, 160–61, 162, 163, 166–68
free, 253
guided, 253–54
learning through, 248–55
locomotor, 162–64
object, 162, 164–66
parallel, 136, 162
physical, 163
in preschool curricula, 251–55
pretend, 162
risky, 292n36
rough-and-tumble, 162, 163
social, 162
sociodramatic, 120, 166–67, 168*f*
solitary, 162
styles of, 28
symbolic, 162
types of, 162–69
polygyny, 18
post-displacement, 101
predictability, 59–60
pre-displacement, 101
preferences, 179–80
preformationism, 23, 24*f*
pregnancy sickness, 11–12, 13*f*
prenatal development, 23, 24*f*, 58–59
preschool curricula, 251–55
preschoolers, 116–17, 136
pretend play, 162
primates, 83–85, 84*t*
private speech, 136–37
proactive aggression, 108
probabilistic cognitive mechanisms, 25–28
probabilistic epigenesis, 25
problem solving, cooperative, 217*t*
progenesis, 101
prokaryotic cells, 174
promiscuous normativity, 196–99
prosociality, 207–14, 217*t*
protective optimism, 148
protest, jealous, 184–85, 185*f*, 272
protoconversations, 182–83, 217*t*
protolanguages, 153–54
proximate explanations, 66–67

psychology
  of adaptedness, 15–19
  developmental psychopathology, 63
  developmental stages of, 119–22
  evolutionary, 7, 8–25
  evolved mechanisms, 9–11
  folk, 9, 10f
  research, 54–55

ratchet effects, 200
rational imitation, 201–2
Raven's Progressive Matrices, 72f
reactive aggression, 108, 270–71
reasoning
  belief-desire, 194
  counterfactual thinking, 120, 162, 167, 168f, 191–92, 217t, 271
  natural thinking, 132–33
  reflective thought, 109
  supernatural thinking, 132–33
  thinking you're better than you are, 145–50
recapitulation theory, 101
reciprocal altruism, 173–74
recovery, 45–57
red foxes *(Vulpes vulpes)*, 102–3
reflective thought, 109
Regents Academy (Binghamton, New York), 263
regulatory genes, 96, 99–100
relationships
  first, 182–84
  romantic, 183–84
relevance: assumption of, 203–4
representational insight, 167
reproduction, 8
research, psychological, 54–55
reward and attachment, 283n20
risky play, 292n36
rituals, 142
romantic relationships, 183–84
rough-and-tumble play, 162, 163
Russian orphanages, 50–51

safetyism, 223, 225–30, 273
salamander axolotl, 102
scaffolding, 247–48
school shootings, 123–24

school strikes, 123
screen time, 255–56
  recommended limits for infants and toddlers, 257–58, 258f, 260
secure relationships, 183–84
selection
  artificial, 102–3
  kin, 173–74
  multilevel, 174–75, 272
  natural, 8, 15, 44
  organic, 75–77
selective breeding, 102–3
selective cell death, 43, 111
self-centered cognition, 136–37
self-domestication, 108, 175–76, 270–71
self-efficacy, 145
self-guidance, cognitive, 136–37
selfies, 73
selfishness, 174–75
self-propelled motion, 287n23
self-referencing, 137–38
semantics, 151–52
sensitivity to context
  children's, 280n57
  differential, 64
sensorimotor development, 117
sex determination, 32–33, 33f
sex differences
  in baby schema effects, 128–29
  in object play, 165–66
  in play styles, 28
shared (joint) attention, 188–90, 217t, 273
shared intentionality, 176, 186–89, 273
sharing, 210–12
sign language, 154–55
Singapore, 243
skeletal competencies, 9, 165–66
slow life history strategy, 60, 61f, 224–25
small-effect genes, 40–41
Small eye mouse gene, 99
smartphones, 234, 292n24
snakes: adaptive response to, 26–27
Snapchat, 73–74, 230, 234, 240–41
social brain, 171, 230–35
social brain hypothesis, 29–30, 176–78, 272
social cognition, 193, 194f

developmental changes in task
 performance, 188–89, 189f
human-unique abilities, 217, 217t
social complexity, 177–78
sociality, 207–14, 217t
social learning, 199–207, 249
 in children, 201–4
 in great apes, 204–7
 types of, 200–1
social media, 223, 230–42
 and mental health, 238–41, 239f
 mismatches with children's and
  adolescents' lives, 235–42
 mismatches with social
  relations, 237–38
 as supernormal stimulus, 273–74
social norms, 197–99
social others, 179–85
social play, 162
social referencing, 190, 217t
social relations, 8
 adolescents' drive drive for, 230–35
 mismatches with social media, 237–38
 neontocracies vs gerontocracies, 54–57
 treating others as intentional beings,
  189–94, 217t
sociodramatic play, 120, 166–67, 168f
socioeconomic status (SES), 59–60
soft inheritance, 76–77
solitary play, 162
South Korea, 234
spandrels, 12–14, 14f
species differences, 188–89
speech. *see also* language
 child-directed, 158
 egocentric, 136–37
 infant-directed, 158
 newborns' sensitivity to, 181
 private, 136–37
 protoconversations, 182–83, 217t
 talking to yourself, 136–37
stimulus
 artificial, 235–36, 236f
 supernormal (superstimulus), 235–36,
  236f, 273–74
stimulus deprivation, 48–49
stimulus (local) enhancement, 200–1
Stone Age, 17–19

students, 123
Sudbury Valley School (Framingham,
 Massachusetts), 254, 263
supernatural thinking, 132–33
supernormal stimulus (superstimulus),
 235–36, 236f, 273–74
survival, 8
symbolic play, 162
synapses, 111
synaptogenesis, 111
syntax, 151–52

Taíno, 153–54
talking to yourself, 136–37
taming
 of domesticated animals, 103f, 103–4
 of *Homo sapiens*, 108–10
Tapajós villages, 56
teaching, 200–1, 204
teratogens, 11–12
thalidomide, 12, 13f
theft, tolerated, 211–12
theory of inheritance of acquired
 characteristics, 74–75
theory of mind, 14, 191–92
thinking. *see* reasoning
timing, 270
toddlers, 255–59
tolerated theft, 211–12
tools, 143–44, 187–88
traditions, 204–5
Tuomela, 215
Twitter, 230, 234
2D displays, 256–57
Type I and II families, 61–62

Ultimatum Game, 213
United Nations Convention on the Rights
 of the Child, 139–40
United Nations Summit on Climate
 Change, 123
United States, 243, 263–64
updating, 249–50

vaginal slope, 107–8
Victoria, 92–93
video deficits, 256, 274
videos, 256

visual attention, joint, 190
visual development, 43–44
visual media
    for infants and toddlers, 255–59
    recommended limits for exposure to, 257–58, 258f, 260
Vulpes vulpes (red foxes), 102–3

Wait Until 8th, 260–61, 294n112
Washoe (chimpanzee), 206
watching and playing: learning through, 248–55
water fleas, 78–79
Watson, James, 96
"we," group-minded, 188–89, 216, 217–18, 217t, 273
Wechsler Intelligence Scale for Children (WISC), 71, 72f
WEIRD (Western, educated, industrialized, rich, democratic) societies, 54–55, 58, 221–23, 224–25, 229–30, 244–45, 247, 263–64
Western parents, 292n36
WhatsApp, 234
WiFi service, 230

wildness, 108
working memory, 249–50
World Health Organization (WHO), 238–39, 292n54
World War II, 80–81

Xhosa people, 56

Yale University, 226
Yoruba people, 55
young children
    learning, 245–59
    recommended limits for digital-media time, 257–58, 258f
young infants
    forming attachments, 179–85
    orientation to social others, 179–85
youth
    benefits of, 169–70
    mismatched, 264–65
YouTube, 234

zone of proximal development, 247–48
zoomers, 227
Zulu people, 56